Dublin Castle
and the
Irish People

Also from Westphalia Press
westphaliapress.org

Dublin Castle and the Irish People

by R. Barry O'Brien

WESTPHALIA PRESS
An Imprint of Policy Studies Organization

Westphalia Press
An imprint of Policy Studies Organization
1527 New Hampshire Ave., NW
Washington, D.C. 20036
info@ipsonet.org

ISBN-13: 978-1-63391-659-3
ISBN-10: 1-63391-659-6

Cover design by Jeffrey Barnes:
jbarnesbook.design

Daniel Gutierrez-Sandoval, Executive Director
PSO and Westphalia Press

Updated material and comments on this edition
can be found at the Westphalia Press website:
www.westphaliapress.org

DUBLIN   CASTLE

AND

THE   IRISH   PEOPLE

DUBLIN CASTLE

AND

THE IRISH PEOPLE

BY

R. BARRY O'BRIEN

Author of "The Life of Charles Stewart Parnell"

DUBLIN AND WATERFORD

M. H. GILL & SON, LTD.

LONDON

KEGAN PAUL, TRENCH, TRÜBNER & CO., LTD.

DRYDEN HOUSE, GERRARD STREET, W.

1909

"Now what I have been telling you relates to Great Britain alone. There is, besides, Ireland. Well, I am not going to touch on Ireland. In the first place it is a different system of administration, and one with which I am not so conversant; and, in the second place, this is at present a harmonious meeting, and I have discovered that there is no topic so likely to terminate the harmony of a meeting as that of the administration or the government of Ireland."

—LORD ROSEBERY.

Address. to the Associated Societies of the University of Edinburgh.

CONTENTS

PART I

INTRODUCTORY

DUBLIN CASTLE AND THE IRISH PEOPLE

PART I

INTRODUCTORY

I

Who (or what) rules Ireland ?

It may be the English Cabinet ; it may be Dublin Castle ; it may be the " Irish " Boards ; it may be all three combined, but it is not the Irish people. *They*, to invert Mr. Birrell's happy phrase, are " switched off " from the Government of their own country. Let us look at the Cabinet, the Castle, and the Boards.

The English Cabinet consists of some sixteen gentlemen who divide the principal offices of State between them. John Bright once said in effect that what he saw chiefly in the English House of Commons was the struggle of sixteen gentlemen sitting on one bench to oust sixteen gentlemen sitting on another. Party Government is certainly a splendid game of political cricket in which sometimes, as Bright suggested, everything is lost sight of except the urgent necessity of bowling the man who is in, out. In England each department of Government has a separate Minister of the Crown at its head ; while the Prime Minister is responsible for the administration as a whole. For example :—

		Salary.
The First Lord of the Treasury ..	.. Prime Minister ..	*£5,000
Exchequer	.. Chancellor	£5,000
Board of Trade	.. President	£2,000
Local Government Board	President	£2,000
Board of Agriculture ..	President	£2,000
Home Office	.. Secretary	£5,000
Post Office	.. Postmaster-General	£2,500
Board of Education	.. President	£2,000
Foreign Office	.. Secretary	£5,000
War Office	.. Secretary	£5,000
India Office	.. Secretary	£5,000
Colonial Office	.. Secretary	£5,000
Works	.. First Commissioner	£2,000
Law ..	.. Lord Chancellor ..	£10,000

The Cabinet is formed by the most popular and influential man in the party which has won at the polls. Even the sovereign cannot stand between him and the Premiership. Queen Victoria tried to do it, after the General Election of 1880, but failed. Mr. Gladstone was then the idol of the people ; the *bête noir* of the sovereign. But the will of the people prevailed,† and he became Prime Minister. The sovereign cannot do violence to the popular will with impunity ; neither can the Cabinet. "In England," says Mr. Gladstone "when the nation can attend, it can prevail."‡ In England the will of the nation is the the law of the land. In Ireland all these things are

* The Treasury consists of several "Lords Commissioners," the principal ones being the first Lord (who is, *ipso facto*, Prime Minister), whose duties are mainly political, and the Chancellor of the Exchequer who is responsible for Finance.

† It is unnecessary to refer to the case of Lord Palmerston. Hated by the Sovereign, but popular with the nation ; he became Prime Minister in defiance of the wishes and the efforts of the Crown.

‡ "Gleanings," I., p. 223.

different. The sovereign may appoint a Prime Minister whose name is execrated by the Irish people. He may appoint a Lord Lieutenant who can only move through the streets of Dublin under the' protection of soldiers and police. He may send over a " Chief Secretary," who cannot walk in the Castle yard without having a brace of detectives at his heels. Public opinion in Ireland is of no account. The Cabinet, the Castle, the Boards may do violence and constantly have done violence to it with impunity. " It is idle and absurd to shut your eyes to the degrading fact. We have positively nothing to look to [in Ireland] but the army." So said Lord Anglesey in 1831 ; and, as I walked up Cork Hill, twelve months ago, and saw the red-coated sentry, who with fixed bayonet kept guard at the Castle gate, I could not help feeling that it was he who represented the foundation on which English rule in Ireland rests to-day.*

The English Minister in London is within an easy walk of his office, he goes there every day, and remains for several hours. He has an opportunity at all events (whether he takes advantage of it or not) of learning the business of his department. As he walks to his office he feels that he moves among a people with whom he is, in essentials, in complete sympathy. He breathes the same national atmosphere as they do, takes pride in the same historical associations, and like them, " glories " in the " British Empire." If the Minister happens to be the Liberal President of the Board of Education, and if, on his way to Whitehall, he meets a bishop in Trafalgar Square, there is no reason why both should not join hands in doing homage to the memory of Nelson. The party feeling is lost in the National sentiment.

In Ireland the English Minister is a foreigner who spends nearly all his time in London, and does not

---

* "The [English] system in Ireland is founded on the bayonets of 30,000 soldiers, encamped permanently as in a hostile country" (Mr. Chamberlain at Holloway, June 17th, 1885).

even get a chance of learning his business.* There is no common bond of union between him and the people. Nelson's pillar standing in the middle of O'Connell Street represents the dominion of England ; O'Connell's statue at the end typifies the Irish people.†

The symbols represent things apart. The Irish agitator who represents his people will not salute Nelson. The average English Minister who represents *his* people will not salute O'Connell. The channel of hostility which divides the nations has never been bridged. The differences between the bishop and the Liberal President of the Board of Education are party differences. The differences between the English Minister to Ireland, and the Irish people are international differences. Unless this fact is realised the essence of the " Irish difficulty " will never penetrate the English mind.

An English official in Ireland asked me :

> " What are the exact relations between the Prime Minister of England and the ministers at the head of the various departments ? Has he got a ' look in ' in the work of the departments ? Does he interfere ? Is he responsible for anything that goes wrong ? Or is the minister of the department practically independent and alone responsible for what happens in his office ? "

* At this moment : " An Irishman cannot move a 'step, he cannot lift a finger in any parochial, municipal or educational work, without being confronted with, interfered with, controlled by an English official, appointed by a *foreign* government, and without a shade or shadow of representative authority " (Mr. Chamberlain at Holloway, June 17th, 1885).

Mr. Bryce says : " The English Government of Ireland is still practically a foreign Government. It seems to them [the Irish] an external power, set in motion by forces they do not control, conducted on principles which may or may not be good, but which are not their principles " (Bryce, *Century Magazine*, June, 1883).

† When O'Connell's statue was unveiled a coal porter standing by said, as the veil dropped : " Now Nelson you've got your match,"—a rough and ready expression of the popular estimate of the relations between the monuments.

I replied :

"So far as I know the minister of the department is practically alone responsible. The Prime Minister does not really interfere with his work. If anything went wrong in the office the minister of the department would have to stand the racket in the Cabinet and in the House of Commons. Of course, the Prime Minister, as the head of the whole Administration might, constitutionally, look in everywhere, but in practice he does not look in anywhere, except perhaps at the Foreign Office. However, if the minister of any department fell under public odium the Prime Minister would have to remove him or the English people would know the reason why. 'The nicest of all the adjustments involved in the working of the British Government,' says Mr. Gladstone, 'is that which determines, without formally defining, the internal relations of the Cabinet. On the one hand, while each minister is an adviser of the Crown, the Cabinet is a unity, and none of its members can advise as an individual, without, or in opposition, actual or presumed, to his colleagues. On the other hand, the business of the State is an hundredfold too great in volume to allow of the actual passing of the whole under the view of the collected Ministry. It is therefore a prime office of discretion for each minister to settle what are the departmental acts in which he can presume the concurrence of his colleagues, and in what more delicate, or weighty, or peculiar cases, he must positively ascertain it.'"*

The official said :

"Of course, in a sense, it is different in Ireland. The Chief Secretary here holds a position analagous, to some extent, to that of the Prime Minister in

* Gladstone "Gleanings," I., p. 242.

England. The Chief Secretary is head of the whole administration. So far he is like the Prime Minister, but, unlike the Prime Minister, he is also the head of every department. He has a two-fold responsibility. He is responsible for the administration as a whole, and he is responsible for every department."

I said :

"Yes; he is a minister in compartments: it is a complicated position. But there is one important point in which he has an advantage over the Prime Minister. The Prime Minister would, as I say, be bound practically to remove any minister in England who fell under public odium. But in Ireland, if say the Vice-president of a particular department, who in my illustration holds an analagous position to the ministerial head of a department in England, were to fall under public odium, the Chief Secretary need not take the least notice of the fact. He could snap his fingers at Irish public opinion. Why ? Because he has got the public opinion of England at his back."

Look then at the Irish question from every point of view; discuss it from every point of view; and we shall always have to come back to this one vital fact, the Irish people are governed by the public opinion of another country.

II

THE Chief Secretary for Ireland in every new ministry is a special object of curiosity and speculation. Other ministers may excite a homely interest. Except the Minister for foreign affairs, every one of them moves in his orbit within the charmed circle of the British Empire. Officially, he lives in a loyal atmosphere— he feels at home. Even the Secretary of State for India, comparatively speaking, feels at home.* But the Chief Secretary for Ireland—well —he is another minister for foreign affairs ; or perhaps, more accurately, the satrap of a hostile country.

The choice of an " Irish " Secretary has, for a hundred years, helped to a great extent to perpetuate the sentiment of international hostility. As a rule, he came among the people—a stranger and an enemy. He was ignorant of Irish history, Irish character, and Irish wants. He was indifferent to Irish claims. He had not a thought in common with the nation which he was sent to rule. In race, in religion, in interest, in feeling, in point of view, political aims and national aspirations, he was anti-Irish. Looking from his window in Dublin Castle, he watched the main stream of Irish national life as it passed by, " with a curious expression of mingled cynicism and amusement, coupled also with a passionate

---

* Englishmen have told me that the people of India love England. I don't know, but no Englishman has ever told me that the people of Ireland love England. " Well," said an Irish member to a Secretary of State for India who had been in office in Ireland, " which do you prefer India or the County Clare ? " " Well," said the Secretary, " I think, upon the whole, India ; it is quieter." (India has developed since.)

tutorial desire to teach the wild Irish people how to behave themselves. Just and exactly so might a great Roman Provincial, A.D. 120, living in his delightful villa in York, or Colchester, or Bath, have regarded the vagaries of the then inhabitants of this island."*

A list of the Chief Secretaries since the Union will not fail to show how seldom the office was held by men in sympathy with the people.

			Out of sympathy with
1801	Lord Castlereagh	Irish Protestant	national feeling.
,,	Mr. Abbott (afterwards Lord Colchester)	English ,,	,,
1802	Mr. Wickham	,, ,,	,,
1804	Sir E. Nepean	,, ,,	,,
1805	Mr. Vansittart (afterwards Lord Bexley)	,, ,,	,,
1806	Mr. Elliot	,, ,,	,,
1807	Sir Arthur Wellesley	Irish ,,	,,
1809	Mr. Dundas (afterwards Lord Melville)	Scotch ,,	,,
,,	Mr. Wellesley Pole (afterwards Earl of Mornington)	Irish ,,	,,
1812	Sir R. Peel	English ,,	,,
1818	Mr. Grant (afterwards Lord Glenelg)	Scotch ,,	in sympathy.
1821	Mr. Goulburn	English ,,	out of sympathy.
1827	Mr. Lamb (afterwards Lord Melbourne)	,, ,,	in sympathy.
1828	Lord F. L. Gower	,, ,,	out of sympathy.
1830	Sir H. Hardinge	,, ,,	,,
1831	Mr. (afterwards Lord) Stanley	English ,,	,,
1833	Sir J. C. Hobhouse	,, ,,	,,
,,	Mr. Littleton (afterwards Lord Hatherton)	,, ,,	,,

* Mr. Birrell in the English House of Commons, May 8th, 1907.

1833	Sir H. Hardinge	English Protestant	out of sympathy.
1835	Viscount Morpeth	,, ,,	in sympathy.
1841	Lord Elliot	,, ,,	out of sympathy.
1845	Sir T. Freemantle	,, ,,	,,
1846	Earl of Lincoln	,, ,,	,,
,,	Mr. Labouchere	,, ,,	,,
1847	Sir William Somerville	Irish ,,	,,
1852	Lord Naas	,, ,,	,,
1853	Sir John Young	,, ,,	,,
1855	Mr. Horsman	English ,,	,,
1857	Mr. Herbert	Irish ,,	,,
1858	Lord Naas		,,
1859	Mr. Cardwell	English ,,	,,
1861	Sir R. Peel	,, ,,	,,
1865	Mr. Chichester Fortescue (Lord Carlingford)	Irish ,,	,,
1866	Lord Naas	,, ,,	,,
1868	Colonel John Wilson Patten	English ,,	,,
,,	Mr. Chichester Fortescue	Irish ,,	,,
1870	Marquis of Harting-ton	English ,,	,,
1874	Sir M. Hicks Beach	,, ,,	,,
1878	Mr. Lowther	,, ,,	,,
1880	Mr. Forster	,, ,,	,,
1882	Lord Frederick Cavendish	English ,,	——
,,	Mr. Trevelyan	,, ,,	out of sympathy.
1884	Mr. Campbell Bannerman	Scotch ,,	,,
1886	Sir W. Hart-Dyke	English ,,	,,
,,	Mr. John Morley	,, ,,	in sympathy.
,,	Sir Michael Hicks-Beach	English ,,	out of sympathy.
1887	Mr. Balfour	Scotch ,,	,,
,,	Mr. W. L. Jackson	English ,,	,,
1892-1895	Mr. John Morley	,, ,,	in sympathy.

1895-1900 Mr. Gerald Balfour*
                              Scotch Protestant out of sympathy.
1900-1904 Mr. Wyndham   English ,,   out of sympathy·
1904-1906 Mr. Walter Long   ,,   ,,   ,,
1905-1907 Mr. James Bryce   Irish   ,,   in sympathy.
(Dec.)
1907 Mr. Birrell   Scotch ,,   ,,
January)

With the same object I shall supplement this list with the names of the Under-Secretaries.

1801 Alexander Marsden   English Protestant out of sympathy.
1806 James Trail   ,,   ,,   ,,
1808 Sir Charles Saxton,
      Bart.   ,,   ,,   ,,
1812 William Gregory   Irish   ,,   ,,
1831 Lieutenant-Colonel Sir
      William Gorsett   English ,,   ,,
1835 Thomas Drummond   Scotch ,,   in sympathy.
1840 Norman H. Macdonald   ,,   ,,   out of sympathy·
1841 Edward Lucas   Irish   ,,   ,,

* Though opposed to the national demand, it is only fair to add that Mr. Gerald Balfour and Mr. Wyndham had popular leanings. When Mr. Balfour was in Ireland, an Irish landlord on one occasion denounced the Irish Parliamentary Party in unmeasured language to me.

"These fellows," he said, "would have been hung up in the last century, and they ought to be hung up now."

"What do you think of Mr. Gerald Balfour ? " I asked, trying a turning movement.

"Gerald Balfour," he exclaimed ; "why, damn him, he ought to be hung up too."

He then told me that a landlord had called at the Castle to to see Mr. Balfour. The landlord said, "If you persevere in your policy, Mr. Balfour, the landlords will leave Ireland." "And what do you think," asked my acquaintance, "did Balfour say ? "

I replied I had not the most remote idea.

"Why, damn him, he said, ' Let them go.' "

The *Times* said that Mr. Balfour's policy "had driven the loyal portion of the Irish to revolt." See Sir West Ridgway's article " Nineteenth Century," August, 1905, p. 188.

Mr. Balfour was responsible for the Land Act of 1896, and the Local Government Act of 1898.

1845 Richard Pennefather	Irish	Protestant	out of sympathy.
1846 Thomas N. Redington (afterwards Sir Thos.)	,,	Catholic	,,
1852 John Wynne	,,	Protestant	,,
1853 Major-General Sir Thomas Larcom	English	,,	,,
1858 Colonel Sir G. R. Wetherall	,,	,,	,,
1869 Thomas Henry Burke	Irish	Catholic	,,
1882 Robert George Crookshank Hamilton	Scotch	Protestant	in sympathy.
1886 Major-General Sir Redvers Henry Buller	English	,,	——
1887-1892 Colonel Sir Joseph West Ridgeway	,,	,,	out of sympathy.
1892-1900 Sir David Harrel*	Irish	,,	——
1900-1908 Sir Anthony McDonnell	,,	Catholic	in sympathy.
1908 Sir James Dougherty	,,	Protestant	,,

The Lord Chancellors have generally played an important part in the Administration. I give a list of them.

1802 Sir John Mitford (created Lord Redesdale)	English.	Protestant.	out of sympathy.
1806 Rt. Hon. George Ponsonby	Irish	,,	——
1807 Thomas Manners Sutton (a Baron of the Exchequer in England), created Lord Manners	English	,,	out of sympathy.

* One, speaking with authority said of Sir David Harrel : " I could never know whether Sir David Harrel was a Home Ruler or not. He did his duty as an official, and never attempted to interfere with policy." The saying has been ascribed to Sir D. Harrel " ; " I am a policeman [he had been Chief Commissioner of Police]. I do what I am told."

1820 Thomas, Lord Manners continued.	English	Protestant	out of sympathy.
1827 Sir Anthony Hart, Knt. (previously Vice-Chancellor of England), resigned November, 1830	,,	,,	,,
1830 William Conyngham Plunket (Lord Plunket — previously C.J.C.P.), surrendered Nov., 1834	Irish	,,	,,
1835 Sir Edward Burtenshaw Sugden, Knt.	English	,,	,,
1835 William Conyngham (Lord Plunket), appointed a second time	Irish	,,	in sympathy.
1841 Sir John Campbell, Knt. (previously Attorney-General in England ; created Lord Campbell)	Scotch	,,	out of sympathy.
1841 Sir Edward Burtenshaw Sugden (afterwards Lord St. Leonards)	English	,,	,,
1846 Maziere Brady (previously Chief Baron of the Exchequer)	Irish	,,	,,
1852 Francis Blackburne (resigned December, 1852)	,,	,,	,,
1853 Maziere Brady (resigned February, 1858)	,,	,,	,,
1858 Sir Joseph Napier (resigned June, 1859)	,,	,,	,,

1859	Maziere Brady (re-signed July, 1866)	Irish Protestant	out of sympathy.
1866	Francis Blackburne (resigned March, 1867)	,, ,,	,,
1867	Abraham Brewster (resigned December, 1868)	,, ,,	,,
1868	Thomas O'Hagan (created Lord O'Hagan 1870, re-signed February, 1874)	,, Catholic	in sympathy.
1874	Commissioners : Sir Joseph Napier,Bart.,	,, Protestant	out of sympathy.
	Mr. Justice Lawson,	,, ,,	,,
	William Brooke	,, ,,	,,
1875	John Thomas Ball, (resigned April,1880)	,, ,,	,,
1880	Lord O'Hagan (re-signed November, 1881)	,, Catholic	in sympathy.
1881	Hugh Law	,, Protestant	——
1883	Sir Edward Sullivan, Bart.	,, ,,	out of sympathy.
1885	John Naish	,, Catholic	in sympathy.
1885	Edward Gibson (created Lord Ash-bourne)	,, Protestant	out of sympathy.
1886	(to July) John Naish	,, Catholic	in sympathy.
1886	(from July) Lord Ashbourne	,, Protestant	out of sympathy.
1892	Samuel Walker	,, ,,	in sympathy.
1895	Lord Ashbourne	,, ,,	out of sympathy.
1900	Lord Ashbourne	,, ,,	,,
1906	Samuel Walker	,, ,,	in sympathy.

I shall conclude with the Lords Lieutenant who have been, generally, but not always ornamental functionaries.

1801	Earl Hardwicke	English	Protestant	out of sympathy.
1806	Duke of Bedford	,,	,,	,,
1807	Duke of Richmond	,,	,,	,,
1813	Earl Whitworth	,,	,,	,,
1817	Earl Talbot	,,	,,	,,
1821	Marquis of Wellesley	Irish	,,	in partial sympathy.
1828	Marquis of Anglesey	English	Protestant	,,
1829	Duke of Northumberland	,,	,,	out of sympathy.
1830	Marquis of Anglesey	,,	,,	,,
1833	Marquis of Wellesley	Irish	,,	,,
1834	Earl of Haddington	Scotch	,,	,,
1835	Earl of Mulgrave	English	,,	in sympathy.
1839	Lord Ebrington	,,	,,	,,
1841	Earl de Grey	,,	,,	out of sympathy.
1844	Lord Heytesbury	,,	,,	,,
1846	Earl of Bessborough	Irish	,,	,,
1847	Earl of Clarendon	English	,,	,,
1852	Earl of Eglinton	Scotch	,,	,,
1853	Earl of St. Germains	English	,,	,,
1855	Earl of Carlisle	,,	,,	,,
1858	Earl of Eglinton	Scotch	,,	,,
1859	Earl of Carlisle	English	,,	,,
1864	Earl of Kimberley	,,	,,	,,
1866	Duke of Abercorn	Irish	,,	,,
1868	Earl Spencer	English	,,	——
1874	Duke of Abercorn	Irish	,,	out of sympathy.
1876	Duke of Marlborough	English	,,	,,
1880	Earl Cowper	,,	,,	,,
1882	Earl Spencer *	,,	,,	,,
1885	Lord Carnarvon	,,	,,	——
1886	Lord Aberdeen	Scotch	,,	in sympathy.
,,	Marquis of Londonderry	Irish	,,	out of sympathy.

* Lord Spencer subsequently (1886) became a strong supporter of Irish national claims.

1892 Lord Houghton	English Protestant	in sympathy.
1895 Lord Cadogan	„ „	out of sympathy.
1900 Lord Dudley*	„ „	„
1906 Lord Aberdeen	Scotch Protestant	in sympathy.

Out of some 157 persons entrusted with the government of Ireland since the " Union," there have been about sixteen only in touch with Irish public opinion.

There have been five only professing the religion of the nation.

If the Spanish Armada had been successful 300 years ago, England might now be governed by Spaniards and Catholics in the interests of Spain. Assume the existence of a Spanish colony, or the descendants of Spanish colonists in Northumberland and Cumberland (receiving all the loaves and fishes, which the Spaniards at home could spare), while the rest of England consisted almost exclusively of Englishmen and Protestants (who were hewers of wood and drawers of water to the privileged classes)—assume, I say, this condition of things, and then you will have something like a parallel to the case of English rule in Ireland.

It is the foreign influence permeating the Administrative life of Ireland, and reminding the people that the stranger sits in judgment at their gates, which makes the Irish question of to-day. When, in the time of the Church agitation, John Bright was told that there was a State Church in England, and that many people objected to it, and that there was a State Church in Scotland, and that many people objected to it too, and that the State Church in Ireland ought not to be treated differently from the churches of England and Scotland, he replied :—

" But some others say that there is no ground of complaint because the laws and institutions of Ireland are, in the main, the same as the laws

* When Lord Dudley came he was out of sympathy with Irish national feeling ; but I shall not say that he is out of sympathy with Irish national feeling now.

and institutions of England and Scotland. They say, for example, that if there be an Established Church in Ireland, there is one in England and one in Scotland ; and that Nonconformists are very numerous both in England and in Scotland ; but they seem to forget the fact that the Church in England or the Church in Scotland is not in any sense a foreign church."

That is the kernel of the whole matter. The Protestant State Church in Ireland was a foreign institution. To-day there may be defects in the administrative system of England as there are defects in the administrative system of Ireland ; but the government of England is not in any sense a foreign government. "The government of any nation," said Mr. Carlisle, the first Resident Commissioner of the "National" Schools in Ireland, "must necessarily partake of the character, particularly the religious character, of the nation."

The Administration of England will stand this test. The Administration of Ireland will not.

III

The congratulations which a Chief Secretary for Ireland receives, on his appointment, from his friends in England, are mingled with expressions of sympathy, and perhaps sometimes even of regret. He is congratulated, as a man who is promoted to an office on the Gold Coast is congratulated : for Ireland is the grave of many English political reputations. Perhaps the Chief Secretary himself expects sympathy from the Irish people : but he does not get it. Why should he ? *They* do not want him. Of course, there are chief secretaries and chief secretaries. Some of them are less intolerable than others. There is the chief secretary who thinks that he has discovered Ireland, and comes to settle everything in a twelvemonth, and goes back at the end of the twelvemonth a sadder, though probably not a wiser, man. People say : " Serve him right " ; for what Irish people hate most is the patronising, cocksure Englishman. Then there is the chief secretary who says : " I am going to Ireland ; I don't know a damn about the country : the people know my ignorance, and there is that common bond of understanding between us." He will probably come to be called a good fellow, and when he goes away, people will say : " God speed you, and good luck to you." As a matter of fact, this man is not as ignorant as he pretends to be, and he may catch the spirit of the people more successfully than the philosopher or the doctrinaire. The Irish heart goes out to the man who is not a humbug.

The Chief Secretary may try to persuade himself that after all, Ireland is not so remote, that it is just the same as England, and that going to Dublin is like going to York. But he does not succeed in deceiving himself, though the Englishman's capacity for self-deception is infinite. When he takes his ticket at Euston for Westland Row, he feels a sense of remoteness which even the Governor-General for India probably does not experience when he books from Charing Cross to Bombay. " Ireland is so near, and yet so far," said an Englishman to me, walking up and down the pier at Calais, discussing the Irish question. That man was not a Cabinet minister —he was a statesman.

Arrived in Dublin, the Chief Secretary dines probably at the Vice-regal Lodge. That may be his first introduction to what he calls Ireland. But, of course, the Vice-regal Lodge is no more Ireland than Park Lane is Ireland. It has been said that the population of Ireland " consists of the Irish people and English officials." Some one has added, " And carrion crows."

At the Vice-regal Lodge the Chief Secretary meets the officials and the " crows." Next day he goes to the Castle, curious perhaps, to see that notorious institution of which he has heard so much. As he approaches the place he beholds, or may behold, a conspicuous building hard by, from which a green flag flies defiantly. " What the devil is that ? " he may ask ; for in his general ignorance he may take the building to be part of the Castle. However, he soon finds himself close to the Castle gates, and is consoled by seeing the Union Jack fluttering in the breeze.

" But," he asks, " what is this building which flies the emblem of Irish nationality at the very gates of the citadel ? " He is told that it is the city hall. If he is a typical Chief Secretary, he says, " Damned rebels," and takes shelter in the fortress. He is shown to his room in the Castle—a pleasant room in the upper yard facing south, and fronting the vice-regal state apartments. *Physically*, the outlook is cheerful.

Of course, the first official who comes to him is the Under-Secretary—his sheet anchor. It may be that he looks curiously at the Under-Secretary, for he has heard a great deal about Irish officials, and the Under-Secretary may look curiously at him ; for he has his own views of the men who are sent from England to rule Ireland.

How much the Chief Secretary learns of his duties depends in the first instance on the Under Secretary ; for the former cannot even ask the questions which would lead to knowledge.

I once went through the various departments ; an official said to me : " You are doing precisely what every Chief Secretary who comes to this country ought to do " ; then he added, after a pause, " Well, I don't know that it would do them much good. They would not know the questions to ask. After all, a man does not learn much, unless he knows something of the subject beforehand."

Before the Under-Secretary takes his Chief in hand, he may perhaps show him the offices of the most important officials—a good way to begin. Well, the Chief Secretary's room opens into the Under-Secretary's, and the Under-Secretary's into the Assist-ant Under-Secretary's. In the passage outside to the right is the Council Chamber, where the Privy Council assembles as occasion demands. At the other end of the passage to the right are the Law Officers' departments. The Attorney-General and Solicitor-General sit in one room, and this opens into the Lord Chancellor's room. A short stone staircase, outside the Chancellor's room, leads to the apartments (opening into each other) of the Inspector-General and Deputy-Inspector-General of the Constabulary. In the same block of buildings in which is the Chief Secretary's room, the Commissioners of Prisons are housed. In the lower Castle Yard are the offices of the Chief Commissioner and the Assistant Commissioner of the Metropolitan Police. Thus it will be seen that the forces of law and order are geographically concentrated in the Castle.

The Chief Secretary on the occasion of his first visit probably spends a week—it may be more, and it may be less—in Dublin, signing papers and eating dinners; and then he returns to London as wise as he came. But he does not lose touch with Ireland when he goes back to England. There is an " Irish " office in London, in Great Queen Street—a gloomy abode. It may be my imagination, but the place always seems to me to look like a haunted house—haunted by the spirits of departed reputations. Again, it may be my imagination, but it seems to me that the policeman at the Irish Office does not look like any other policeman : he is watchful and melancholy ; he stands generally at the top of a stone staircase leading downwards to St. James's Park. Overhead is the word " cockpit "—very suggestive, for Ireland has only too often been the cockpit of English parties.

At the " Irish " Office which he attends regularly, the Chief Secretary is kept in telegraphic communication with the Castle. His first acquaintance, however, with Ireland, is really made through the medium of the Irish Parliamentary Question.

The Irish Parliamentary Question is a tremendous instrument of torture. It is the first thing which takes the starch out of the Chief Secretary. It has long ago taken the starch out of the unfortunate officials in Ireland.

" Well, how are you to-day ? " I once said to an " Irish " official.

" Oh, very well," he replied, with a languid air. And then, holding up a large sheet of paper, added, " I have these questions to answer immediately." " If they were necessary questions," he said, " I would not mind. But the half of them are quite unnecessary."

" Ah, well," I said, " you can't complain. It is part of the war. If Irish members are obliged to go to the English Parliament when they want to sit in their own Parliament at home, you can't object if they harrass the Administration in every way open to them. It is, as I say, part of the war."

" I suppose so," said he, with resignation ; " but it is devilish hard lines for me."

Which I frankly admitted.

However, he was not the only victim of what Mr. Ritchie calls " The imbecility of English Rule in Ireland."

One day I was in a department, probably making myself as troublesome as any Irish member. An official said, " Here is a question just come in, bearing on your point."

I was delighted to be brought face to face with the Irish Parliamentary Question in its destructive flight through officialdom. It was a rare chance of good luck. " Ah," I said, " this is what I want to see. I want to know all about it, its whole course, the beginning, the end, and what becomes of it."

Its course is easily described. Notice is given of the question in the House of Commons ; the notice is sent to the " Irish " Office in London, where it is scanned with curiosity and even perhaps with anxiety ; it is then wired to Dublin Castle ; the Castle sends it to the department concerned ; the department works out the answer, and sends it to the Castle ; the Castle flashes back the answer to the " Irish " Office, where an official, who has nothing else to do but answer questions, throws the answer into Parliamentary shape, gives it to the Chief Secretary, who puts his personal impress on it, and fires it off in the House of Commons.

I asked the official to tell me how he went to work to answer the particular question in hand, and he told me.

I said : " It is a stiff job answering these questions ; this will take you the whole day."

" Oh," said he, with a smile, " it has to be answered in the House of Commons this afternoon. But I don't mind this question. It is quite fair, and it is right that the information should be given. But we get a lot of questions which are quite unnecessary and useless."

Different Chief Secretaries deal with questions in different ways. I knew a Chief Secretary who was an honest, conscientious, nervous man. When notice of a question was given he set all the wires in motion and taxed himself and the officials to the utmost in obtaining the reply. I saw him one day at the " Irish " Office—he was a wreck.

There was another Chief Secretary who took the business easily. One day his Secretary read an answer to a question to him, saying, " That is the best answer I can give."

" An answer good enough for the blackguards," said he.

I have come to the conclusion that the Irish Parliamentary Question is an infernal machine, the operations of which would almost satisfy a *Sinn Féiner* that an Irish representation at Westminster may after all be turned to some good account.*

When the recess gives him the opportunity, the Chief Secretary comes again to Ireland. Whatever awaits him here can scarcely be worse than the Parliamentary Question. On his second visit, it may be that he will learn something more—though the point is problematical—of the various departments for which he is responsible. Mr. Birrell once said in the House of Commons that as President of one department he was constantly in conflict with himself as President of another. One cannot help recalling the memory of Pooh-Bah, " Lord High-Everything-Else " of the Mikado of Japan. Who forgets the

---

* It is unnecessary to say that an Irish Parliamentry Party in the English House of Commons to be effective must be troublesome.

memorable scene between him and Ko-Ko, the Lord High Executioner, on an occasion of supreme importance ?

" *Ko-Ko.*—Pooh-Bah, it seems that the festivities in connection with my approaching marriage must last a week. I should like to do it handsomely, and I want to consult you as to the amount I ought to spend upon them.

" *Pooh-Bah.*—Certainly. In which of my capacities ? As First Lord of the Treasury, Lord Chamberlain, Attorney-General, Chancellor of the Exchequer, Privy Purse, or Private Secretary ?

" *Ko-Ko.*—Suppose we say as Private Secretary.

" *Pooh-Bah.*—Speaking as your Private Secretary, I should say that as the city will have to pay for it, don't stint yourself : do it well.

" *Ko-Ko.*—Exactly—as the city will have to pay for it. That is your advice ?

" *Pooh-Bah.*—As Private Secretary. Of course you will understand that, as Chancellor of the Exchequer I am bound to see that due economy is observed.

" *Ko-Ko.*—Oh, but you said just now ' Don't stint yourself ; do it well.'

" *Pooh-Bah.*—As Private Secretary.

" *Ko-Ko*—And now you say that due economy must be observed.

" *Pooh-Bah.* As Chancellor of the Exchequer.

" *Ko-Ko.*—I see. Come over here, where the Chancellor can't hear us. (They cross stage). Now, as my Solicitor, how do you advise me to deal with this difficulty?

" *Pooh-Bah.*—Oh, as your Solicitor, I should have no hesitation in saying Chance it——

" *Ko-Ko.*—Thank you (shaking his hand) ; I will.

" *Pooh-Bah.*—If it were not that, as Lord Chief Justice, I am bound to see that the law isn't violated.

" *Ko-Ko.*—I see. Come over here where the Chief Justice can't hear us. (They cross the stage). Now, then, as First Lord of the Treasury ?

" *Pooh-Bah.*—Of course, as First Lord of the Treasury, I could propose a special vote that would cover all expenses if it were not that, as leader of the Opposition, it would be my duty to resist it, tooth and nail. Or, as Paymaster-General I could so cook the accounts that as Lord High Auditor I should never discover the fraud. But then, as Archbishop of Jitipu, it would be my duty to denounce my dishonesty and give myself into my own custody as Commissioner of Police."

This play was, I understand, recently forbidden by the Lord High Chamberlain of England, because, as was said, it threw ridicule on the Administration of Japan. The prohibition was unnecessary, for the Mikado might easily have had his revenge. He could have sent some of the Gilberts and Sullivans of Japan to write a comic opera on the English Administration of Ireland.

I shall mention some of the Boards and Departments over which it is said the Chief Secretary either directly or indirectly exercises authority as " Lord High-Everything-Else."

The Local Government Board.
Department of Agriculture.
The Congested Districts Board.
The National Board of Education.
The Intermediate Education Board.
The Royal Irish Constabulary.
The Metropolitan Police.
The General Prisons Board.

Inspectors of Lunatics.
Land Commission.
Estates Commission.
Reformatory and Industrial Schools.
Treasury Remembrancer.
Law and Justice.
Magistracy.
Finance.
Board of Works.
Registrar General.
Commissioner of Valuation.
Registrar of Petty Sessions Clerks.

What are the duties of these various departments ? What are their relations to the Castle ? Are they independent of it ? What is the Castle ? Does it permeate the administrative life of the country ? These questions I shall now try to answer in detail. *Place au Château.*

PART II

THE CASTLE

PART II

THE CASTLE

I

" This is the most queerly governed country, the most expensively governed country, and the most inconsistently governed country in the world." So said an English official in Ireland to me some months ago.

" I suppose," I asked, " that you mean by inconsistently governed, that practically you have neither the Union nor the Repeal of the Union."

He laughed, and said, " Well, it is very like that. The Unionists called the Home Rule movement a Separatist movement, but is it clear that the Union itself was not a Separatist arrangement ? I am neither a Unionist, nor a Nationalist. I want good government and consistent government in Ireland, however it is to be brought about. We all know that the Union did not make the two countries one. There was a Legislative Union, but not an Administrative Union. That was the mistake. Before the Union, Ireland was like a colony. She had a Parliament and a Governor. The Union took away the Parliament, but left the Governorship—left the Vice-royalty and the Castle. That is the inconsistency. If they wanted to make the Union consistent, they ought to have swept away the Castle as well as the Parliament, and put Irish affairs in the hands of a Secretary of State in London. That was not done. The Castle was kept. You have now two Executives: an Executive in Dublin, and an Executive in London. That is separation."

Looked at from any point of view, this is intelligent comment. Mr. Birrell said some time ago, " It is not that Dublin Castle is a sink or seat of jobbery and corruption. It may have been so once ; it certainly is so no longer." This may or may not be true.

An ex-Chief Secretary said to me : " The Castle is not as black as it is painted." This also may or may not be true. But, in any event, the Castle can not be judged merely by what one may see, or may not see, to-day. We must go a little farther back. We must know something of its history. We must get the atmosphere. Sometimes the officials are praised, sometimes they are denounced. But praise or denunciation of officials does not touch the main issue. We are not dealing with persons, but with a system. Some Englishmen of the present day talk about the Castle as if it were an infernal Irish institution for which England had no responsibility ; they apparently regard the English Minister to Ireland as an angel of perfection, who would do everything that is right, were he not prevented by the imps on Cork Hill.

An Englishman once said to me, speaking of a particular Chief Secretary, " I think that So-and-So will do very well if he is only strong enough to resist the officials in Dublin Castle."

I told this to an official (I will not say whether he is in Dublin Castle or not). He said,

"Rubbish! Officials in Ireland are like officials everywhere else ; they carry out the instructions of the Government. I know that Irish officials are not popular in Ireland. But why ? Because successive English Governments have opposed popular movements in the country ; and the officials have naturally been on the side of

the Government, whose instructions they had to
carry out. If all these Governments had been on
the popular side, the officials would have been
on that side too, and the whole situation would
be different. But to say that a minister is sent
over from England to carry out a particular
policy, and that the officials obstruct and thwart
him—it is simply rubbish. Officials have to carry
out instructions, they have to obey their masters,
and pay-masters. To put the matter in a homely
way, men don't fight with their bread-and-butter.
We have to obey the people who employ us, not
to oppose them."

That is a statement of the case which must, at all
events, go to the jury.

But what is the Castle ? Well, *physically* it is not
a Castle at all. " When Americans come here," said
an official, " they expect to find bastions and moats, and
draw-bridges and dungeons ; and they are disappointed
when they see that there is really no Castle at all."
In fact, the thing is more like a barrack than a castle.
It stands on an elevated piece of ground called Cork
Hill. There are two large squares : in one—the upper
Castle Yard—you see the Vice-regal apartments,
and a number of offices ; in the other—the lower
Castle Yard—you see more offices. In this yard there
is a tower—the Bermingham tower—the only relic
of antiquity, and the only suggestion of a Castle.

Politically, the Castle is the Executive, and the
Executive consists of the Lord Lieutenant, the Chief
Secretary and the Under-Secretary. The Chief Secretary, who is generally in the English Cabinet, is really
the captain of the ship, as the late Sir William Harcourt,
who revelled in nautical phraseology, might have
said. The Lord Lieutenant, who, as a rule, is not
in the English Cabinet, wears the insignia of command,
but only signs the log. The Under-Secretary is the
man at the wheel.

But how has the Castle grown up *physically* and *politically?* Physically and politically the Castle began to grow about the time of the Norman invasion. It would indeed seem possible that the Danes had built a fort on the site where the Castle now stands; and a stronghold of some kind seems to have been in existence in the time of Henry II., for we learn that the Anglo-Norman king " summoned his principal adherents in Dublin, and committed that city with its Castle, to the custody of Hugues de Lasci," who became practically the first Viceroy of Ireland. This " Castle," however, did not satisfy King John, who (about 1204) authorised the Lord-Justice Fitz-Henri

> " to erect a Castle at Dublin, well fortified, with good fosses and thick walls, strong enough to defend or control the city, directing him to commence the works by the erection of a tower, and to leave the other buildings to be more leisurely constructed. Of the features or defects of the then existing Castle at Dublin, we find no details in accessible records, which are also silent on the progress which may have been made in the new fabric by Fitz-Henri."*

However, I am not writing a history of Dublin Castle, and need not therefore trace its growth, physically or politically, from infancy to old age. My object simply is to get the atmosphere of the place, and I shall accordingly only touch on such subjects as are necessary for this purpose.

In Norman days, as in our own, the titular head of the English Administration in Ireland was the Lord Lieutenant.† By his side were the Lord High

---

* Gilbert's " Viceroys " p. 64 ; see note on Dublin Castle in Appendix.

† He was called by various names : Constable, Justiciary, Lord Deputy, Lord Lieutenant. In his absence Lords Justices were appointed to take his place. (Rowley Lascelles " Establishments of Ireland." Part III., p. 52 W.)

Chancellor and the Lord High Treasurer.* The three may be said, in modern parlance, to have formed the Executive. Such was the beginning of what has come to be called the "Irish" Government, but which is no more Irish to-day than it was in the middle ages. The Lord Lieutenant took his commands from England then, and he takes his commands from England now. We read how, in the reign of Edward II., the Lord Lieutenant was bound to keep " a special body of fully equipped horse soldiers . . . always in readiness for military service, *on behalf of the Crown of England.*"† We are told that in the reign of Elizabeth

> " The Lord Deputy [was] assisted with a counsell of the most choyce and select men for their knowledge and experience in the affayres of that cuntrye. Eche of the presidents have also a particular counsell appointed unto them for the decydinge and determyning of matters in their chardge, and are chiefly dyrected from the lord Deputy and counsell at Dublin as they are *directed from tyme to tyme by her Maiestie and Counsell in Englande.*"‡

* The first Lord Lieutenant was apparently appointed in 1173; the first Lord Chancellor in 1186 ; and the first Lord Treasurer in 1217 (*Ibid.* Table, p. 523.)

† Gilbert, "Viceroys," p. 120.

‡ Dymmok, " A Treatise of Ireland," pp. 10 and 11. Dymmok was an Englishman, who visited Ireland about 1599. He gives the following account of the establishments of the country at the time :—

> " For the present gouerment of that country [Ireland], yt is devided into three partes, Ecclesiastical, Martiall and Cyvill or Justiciall.
> " The Ecclesiasticall estate is composed of fowre Archbushoppes and 29 Bushoppes, disposed into severall Cuntries in every province, besydes Deanes, Suffragans and Parsons.
> " The Martiall gouerment is distributed into thre partes of that cuntrye. The lo : Deputy is lieutenant generall over the whole, assisted by two presidents for his more ease, as well in the true Administration of Justice, as

So it has always been. Mr. Bright once said : that
when the Irish people prayed they looked to the West.
When the Lord Lieutenant prays he looks to the East.

The Lord Lieutenant of course had many Secretaries.
In time, one of them became a Chief Secretary ; and
the Chief Secretary—" the mayor of the Palace "—
finally usurped the functions of the viceroy.*

We find that the following offices had sprung up
in the time of Henry III., and that the King had
vested them all in one man, Pierre de Rivaulx.

> " The Treasury-ship of Ireland, the Chamberlain-
> ship of the Exchequer at Dublin ; the prisage
> of wines; the custody of the ports, navy, wards,
> and escheats ; the custody of the Castles of
> Athlone, Drogheda, and Randown, with the
> Crown's five Cantreds of land in Connaught ; the
> Custody of vacant sees, and of the Jews in
> Ireland ; the custody of the city of Cork, and
> of the city and Castle of Limerick."†

---

for the ready repressing of such disorders as might happen
in the upland Cuntry ; one of them placed in Munster,
the other in Connaught, and both corresponde with
the lo : Deputy, residing at Dublin for the moste parte.
" The Martiall gouerment is not of yt selfe alone, but mixed
with cyvill (vntill such tyme as the cuntrye may be
reduced vnto that obedience, as Justice may have course
of yt selfe with out forces to suport yt) and the lo :
Deputy assisted with a counsell, of the most choyce
and scelect men for their knowledge and experience in
the affayres of that cuntrye. Eche of the presidents
have also a particular counsell appointed unto them for
the decydinge and determyning of matters in their
chardge, and are chiefly dyrected from the lo : Deputy
and Counsell at Dublin as they are directed from tyme
to tyme by her Maiestie and Counsell in Englande."

* The Lord Lieutenant was commander-in-chief of the forces
in early days.   But we learn that these duties were discharged
by his Secretaries.   At one time there was an Under-Secretary
of State for Civil affairs, and one for Military affairs (Rowley
Lascelles).

† Gilbert " Viceroys," p. 94.

I need scarcely say that under the Normans, an Irishman in sympathy with his people had no more chance of being allowed to enter Dublin Castle as an " official," than the late Paul Kruger had of being made an English Privy Councillor ; and what Dublin Castle was under the Normans it remained under Tudor, Stuart and Guelph. The spirit of the Statute of Kilkenny * was the spirit of Dublin Castle. The suppression of the native race, and the government of the country in the English interest only, was its policy from the beginning to our own day.

In spite of the Castle, however, Norman and Irish might have come together, and combined to form a compact Irish nation ; but the incursion of English

---

* Sir John Gilbert summarised the statue of Kilkenny (passed in 1367) thus :

> " All Englishmen, or Irish living amongst them, were to use the English language, be called by English names, follow the English customs, and not ride otherwise than in saddles in the English manner. If ecclesiastics dwelling amongst the English did not use the English language, the profits of their benefices were to be seized by their superiors ; but, adds the Statute—which was written in French—the language of the upper classes of England, ' they shall have respite to learn the English tongue, and to provide saddles between this and the Feast of St. Michael next coming.'

> " That English should not be governed in the determination of their disputes by Brehon law, or the law used in the ' Marches ' or borders. That no Irishman should be admitted into any cathedral, collegiate church, or benefice, by promotion, collation or presentation ; and that religious houses should not receive Irishmen into their profession. That the English should neither admit nor make gifts to Irish musicians, story-tellers, or rimers, who might act as spies or agents. That dwellers on the borders should not, without legal permission, hold parleys or make treaties with any hostile Irish or English. That differences should not be made between English born in England and English born in Ireland, by calling the former ' English Hobbes,' or clowns, and the latter ' Irish dogs ' ; and that religious houses should receive Englishmen, without considering whether they were born in England or Ireland. That English subjects should not war upon each other, nor bring Irish to their assistance for such purpose."
> (Gilbert, pp. 224, 225.)

settlers during and after the Tudor Wars made this
chance of amalgamation impossible. Newman is
right when he says; [Up to the Tudor Period] The
settlers in the conquered soil became so attached and
united to it and its people, that, according to the
proverb, they were *Hibernis hiberniores.* "The
Tudor not the Plantagenet introduced the iron age of
Ireland."

Elizabeth, James, Charles, Cromwell, Anne, the
Georges—all these potentates represented the one
idea so admirably expressed (according to tradition)
by the Great Protector; "To hell or Connaught
with the Papists." What the sovereigns of England
and their Ministers wished, the Castle of Dublin did.
It was ever the instrument of foreign domination. Its
atmosphere was never Irish.

> " Turk, Jew or Atheist may enter here,
>   But not a Papist."*

These words, according to report, were once written
on the gates of Bandon. They might have been
written on the walls of Dublin Castle for nearly two
hundred years after the treaty of Limerick.

Lord Pembroke was Lord Lieutenant in 1707. We get
the character of the Administration from him. Writing
as the Governor General of the country, he referred
to the Catholics who constituted the vast mass of the
population as " domestic enemies." Lord Wharton
was Lord Lieutenant in 1709. He reminded the
House of Commons " of the great inequality between
Papists and Protestants in this Kingdom "; and
urged it " seriously to consider whether any new
bills are wanting to enforce and explain those good
laws [the penal code] which you have already passed
to prevent the growth of Popery."

* Everybody knows what Swift is said to have written under
these words.
    " Whoever wrote this, wrote it well.
    For the same is written on the gates of Hell."

Lord Carteret was Lord Lieutenant in 1724. He said :

> " All the Protestants of this Kingdom have but one common interest, and have too often fatally experienced that they have the same common enemy."

Archbishop Boulter several times, between 1726 and 1740, filled the position of a Commissioner, authorised in the absence of the Lord Lieutenant to discharge the duties of that functionary. We get atmosphere from Boulter. He wrote :

> " The only way to keep things quiet here, is by filling the great places with the natives of England,"

and again :

> " I must request your Grace, that you would use your influence to have none but Englishmen put into the great places here for the future."

The Duke of Dorset was Lord Lieutenant in 1735. He urged Parliament to secure

> " a firm union amongst all Protestants who have one common interest, and the same common enemy."

Lord Chesterfield was Lord Lieutenant in 1745. He wrote :

> " The Lords Massarene and Powerscourt are men of good sense, and good estates, and will be of use at the Board. They are both what we call *Castle-men*, that is to say, they meddle with no Cabals, nor parties, but they belong to the Lord Lieutenant."

Lord Chancellor Bowes was one of the Commissioners discharging the functions of the Lord Lieutenant in 1765. He said :

> " That Catholics were only known to the laws for the purposes of punishment."

Lord Westmoreland was Lord Lieutenant from 1790 to 1794. The English Cabinet was frightened into surrender on the question of the admission of the Catholics to the Elective Franchise by the revolutionary agitation of John Keogh and Wolfe Tone. But the Castle protested and urged the Cabinet not to give way. The Lord Lieutenant wrote :

> " I must tell you the inevitable results of communicating these statements of yours [that politico-religious distinctions should be done away with, and that the power of England would not be exercised to maintain them]. The fears and jealousies that universally affect the Protestant mind are not confined to Parliament, but affect almost every individual and every public body. The steadiest friends of British Government apprehend that indulgence will give the Catholics strength to press for admission to the state. In this they see the ruin of political power to the Protestants, and—trifling as you may consider the danger—a total change of the property of the country. . . . Why sacrifice our present strength ? Why sacrifice an old and established policy, which has for a century maintained the Government of Ireland ? "

In the end both Castle and Cabinet were forced to yield. The revolutionists triumphed. The Catholics were admitted to the Franchise in 1793.*

Every one has read the correspondence of Lord Cornwallis, who was Lord Lieutenant from 1798 1801 ; every one knows what the Castle was in those days—a den of jobbery and corruption used by the

---

* " Can we forget," wrote Peel, thirty-five years later, " in reviewing the history of Ireland, what happened in 1782 and 1793 [the establishment of the legislative independence of Ireland by force of arms]. It is easy to blame the concessions that were then made, but they were not made without an intimate conviction of their absolute necessity in order to prevent greater dangers."

English Cabinet to bring about the destruction of the Irish Parliament.

" By this time," says Mr. Birrell, putting the matter in a nutshell,

> " we know well enough how the Act of Union was carried : by bribery and corruption. Nobody has ever denied it for the past fifty years. It has been in the school text books for generations."

Swift, according to Cornwallis himself, anticipated the situation in well-known lines :

> " Thus to effect his monarch's ends,
> From hell a viceroy-devil ascends,
> His budget with corruption crammed,
> The contributions of the damned,
> Which with unsparing hand he strews
> Through courts and senates as he goes ;
> And then at Beelzebub's black hall
> Complains his budget is too small."

We get the atmosphere of the Castle at this time in the following extract from a letter of Lord Cornwallis :—

> " The conversation of the principal persons of the country all tend to encourage this system of blood, and the conversation even at my table, where you may suppose I do all I can to prevent it, always turns on hanging, shooting, burning, etc., etc., etc., and if a priest has been put to death, the greatest joy is expressed by the whole company. . . . Their conversation and conduct point to no other mode of concluding this unhappy business than that of extirpation."

We have another statement from the same authority :—

> " Those who are called principal persons here, are men who have been raised, in consequence only, by having the entire disposal of the patronage

of the Crown in return for their undertaking the management of the country, because the Lords Lieutenant were too idle, or too incapable, to manage it themselves. They are detested by everybody but their immediate followers, and have no influence but what is founded on the grossest corruption."

Lord Castlereagh was Chief Secretary from 1798 to 1801. His correspondence reeks with Castle atmosphere. When he died (by his own hand), Byron wrote :—

> " So *he* has cut his throat at last ! He ? Who ?
> The man who cut his country's long ago." *

Yet Castlereagh, wonderful as it may seem, was not the worst of the gang. He wished to keep faith with the Catholics (who were promised emancipation), but the English Cabinet was too strong for him ; and Castlereagh, who " cut his country's throat," was scandalised by Pitt, who besmirched his country's honour.†

* " It is a wonder," said O'Connell, with grim humour, " that they did not make us pay for the knife with which he cut his throat."

† In reference to the negotiations with the Catholics, at the time of the Union, Mr. Lecky says :—
" It was becoming evident how gravely the ministers had erred in failing to ascertain and modify the opinions of the King before they raised the question of the Union, and before they involved themselves in negotiations with the Catholics. As, however, the situation stood, it was, as it seems to me, the duty of Pitt at all hazards to persevere. It would be scarcely possible to exaggerate the political importance of his decision, for the success of the Union and the future loyalty of the Catholics of Ireland depended mainly upon his conduct ; and beside the question of policy, there was a plain question of honour. After the negotiations that had been entered into with the Catholics, after the services that had been asked and obtained from them, and the hopes which had been authoritatively held out to them in order to obtain those services, Pitt could not, without grave dishonour, suffer them to be in a worse, because a more powerless, position, than before the Union, or abandon their claims to a distant future, or support a ministry which

In 1798, Cornwallis wrote to Pitt :—

" I certainly wish that England could make a union with the Irish nation, instead of making it with a party in Ireland."

And again :—

" It has always appeared to me a desperate measure for the British Government to make an irrevocable alliance with a small party in Ireland (which party has derived all its consequence from, and is in fact entirely dependent upon the British Government), and to wage eternal war against the Papists" [who constituted the bulk of the Irish population].

But the " Union " condemned by Cornwallis, was the Union made by Pitt.

Lord Redesdale was sent as Lord Chancellor in 1802. He struck the keynote of the Union policy.

" The Catholics," he wrote, " must have no more political power."

And again :—

" I have said that this country must be kept for some time as a garrisoned country. I meant a Protestant garrison."

The Lord Lieutenant, Lord Hardwicke, acted as Mr. Lecky says, " In the same spirit, though with more discretion of language." But we get the " spirit " without the " discretion " from Lady Hardwicke.

---

was formed in hostility to them. . . Pitt sent a message to the King, promising that whether in or out of office, he would absolutely abandon the question during the whole of the reign, and he, at the same time, clearly intimated that he was ready, if Addington would resign power, to resume the helm, on the condition of not introducing Catholic Emancipation, and not suffering it to pass " ("History of Ireland," Vol. V., pp. 441-456).

Writing to her friend, Mrs. Abbot,* from Dublin,
on the 10th September, 1803, she says :—

> "By the way, my dear friend, what can you
> possibly mean by saying, 'I am so delighted
> to hear that old Dr. Troy [Catholic Archbishop
> of Dublin] begins to lose ground in your good
> opinion'? Dr. Troy never possessed it in
> any way. This same Dr. Troy, whom I never
> saw, and scarce ever thought about, has no
> footing whatever in the Castle Yard. Lord
> Hardwicke's is the only Administration that
> has never given the *Heads* of the Catholic Clergy
> an invitation to the Castle : he in no way recog-
> nises them further than the law admits them
> to be priests."

The "Union" had been made with a "party,"
and the "nation" was now to be governed through
that party in the interests of England alone. A hand-
ful of Protestant Episcopalians composed of the
descendants of English settlers, and forming the
"garrison," were to hold all positions of power and
emolument ; while the Catholics, representing the
old race and constituting four-fifths of the population,
were to be outlanders in their own country.

It had been the policy of Grattan to make the
"party" and the "nation" one. That policy had
borne fruit between 1777 and 1782.

> "As the English in Ireland," says Edmund
> Burke, "began to be domiciliated, they began
> also to recollect that they had a country. The
> *English interest*, at first by faint and almost
> insensible degrees, but at length openly and
> avowedly, became an *independent Irish interest*.
> . . . With their views, the *Anglo-Irish* changed

* Mr. Abbott was Chief Secretary from May 25th, 1801, to
February 13th, 1802. He was now Speaker of the English
House of Commons.

their maxims ; it was necessary to demonstrate to the whole people that there was something at least of a common interest combined with the independency, which was to become the object of common exertions. . . . The Irish Parliament and nation became independent."*

But the policy of assimilation preached by Grattan was defeated by the policy of " Union," carried out by Pitt. During the nineteenth century Protestant Ascendency, from its centre in Dublin Castle, radiated throughout the whole country, rekindling the fires of racial distrust, and international hatred.†

* There were the following relaxations of the Penal Code between 1778 and 1793 inclusive :
In 1778, Catholics were allowed to hold landed property on a lease for 999 years. Previously they were enabled to hold on lease not exceeding thirty-five years, at a rental of two-thirds of the full annual value. In 1782, they were allowed to keep a school on condition of obtaining the licence of the Protestant bishop of the diocese ; there was also the repeal of the Acts against hearing or celebrating Mass ; against Catholics having a horse above the value of £5, or dwelling in the cities of Limerick or Galway ; repeal also of Act empowering Grand Juries to levy on Catholics the amount of any losses sustained by privateers, robbers, and rebels. In 1792, Catholics were admitted to the bar but not to the rank of King's Counsel ; allowed to be attorneys, to keep a school without obtaining the licence of the Protestant bishop of the diocese, and to intermarry with Protestants, provided the service was performed by a clergyman of the Established Church, and they were empowered to hold land in the same way as Protestants. In 1793, Catholics were admitted to the elective franchise, to the magistracy, to the Grand Jury, to the Municipal Corporations, to the Dublin University, and allowed to hold commissions in the army, under the rank of General. They were also allowed to carry arms when possessed of certain property.

† The war between the masses of the Irish people, and the descendants of the English colonists was not a religious war. The Irish Protestant was distrusted, not on account of his religion, but on account of his English affinities. Lord Redesdale is worth quoting on the point :—
" ' If a revolution were to happen in Ireland, it would, in the end, be an Irish revolution, and no Catholic of English blood would fare better than a Protestant of English blood.' So said Lord Castlehaven, an Irish Catholic of English blood, one hundred and seventy years ago, and so said a Roman Catholic of Irish blood to me confidentially twenty

We get atmosphere from a paper prepared by Mr. Abbott (Chief Secretary 1801-1802), giving reasons why a measure should not be passed for the payment of Irish Catholic priests by the State.   He says :—

> "It would form a lasting and irrevocable bar to the long established policy of gradually Protestantising the country, and wearing out the attachment to the Catholic religion. It would establish a rival power in everlasting hostility to the Established Church, and might even tend to detach the Protestants of Ireland from their affection to the Parliament and Crown of the United Kingdom."

We get some atmosphere from the Duke of Wellington who was Chief Secretary in 1807.   Writing of these times thirty-seven years later, he says :—

> "When the Union was carried, many of the resident gentry were dissatisfied for years. I recollect that, when I was appointed Chief Secretary, Mr. Foster, who had been speaker of the Irish House of Commons, and his family and friends, were greatly dissatisfied, and this was the cause of great uneasiness to the Cabinet of the Duke of Portland.
> "Foster was appointed Chancellor of the Exchequer, and others promoted to other high office, and we heard no more of the dissatisfaction of the Protestants with the Union."

This was the Duke's delicate way of saying that as hostility to the Union in certain quarters had been disarmed before it was carried, by bribery and cor-

---

years ago. . . 'The question is not simply Protestant and Catholic, but English and Irish.' These words were written in 1824; nearly a century and a half before (1685), Lord Clarendon, then Lord Lieutenant of Ireland, wrote to Rochester : 'The contest here is not about religion, but between English and Irish, and that is the truth.'"

ruption, so dissatisfaction with it afterwards, in the same quarters, was disarmed by corruption, too.

Sir Robert Peel was Chief Secretary from 1812 to 1818. No one has played a more important part in the Administration of Ireland than this Tory statesman ; no one has done more, I will not say to form, but to thicken the atmosphere of Dublin Castle than he. What that atmosphere was, when Peel arrived, the editor of his private correspondence and papers tells us.

> " Patronage, in most times and in most countries an acknowledged source of influence, was in Peel's time and in Ireland an engine of government so necessary that it must be understood and used by one who meant to govern. The Chief Secretary being practically also Patronage Secretary, and the country being ruled largely by Ascendency of class and creed and methodised corruption, one of his first duties was to keep together the more venal adherents of the party in power, by promising from time to time, and as occasion offered, paying to each man his price. For this purpose, as regards the greater county potentates, Mr. Peel's chief guide at first appears to have been a confidential paper bequeathed to him by a predecessor. Sir Arthur Wellesley, in his own handwriting, had drawn up a list of counties, registering in each the families of greatest influence, their ' objects,' and the favours they had received, with occasional remarks when for the present they ought to be content. To a young administrative hand this was a useful manual, soon supplemented by his own experience."

Sir Robert Peel was twenty-four years of age when he became Chief Secretary. " Ireland was then," to use the words of the editor of his letters, " an almost unknown country to him."* He had indeed been an " Irish " member for three years, member for the pocket borough of Cashel, but he had never visited his constituency.

The Duke of Richmond was at the time Lord Lieutenant. We get a taste of his quality in the following extract from a letter which he wrote to Peel at a time when his Excellency feared that some concessions might be made to the Catholics.

> " Pray put ministers on their guard against reducing our force, especially cavalry, at present. Perhaps things may go quietly, but we ought to be prepared for the worst. Please God, if we are obliged to draw the sword, the [Catholic] Committee gentlemen shall have their full share of it, if I can catch them."

This Viceroy of a Catholic country thought that the demand of the Catholic population for civil and religious liberty should be resisted at the point of the sword.

Mr. Saxton was Civil Under-Secretary. He retired almost immediately on Peel's appointment, and was succeeded by Mr. Gregory, another Ascendency man. The Duke of Richmond left Ireland some eleven months after the arrival of Peel, to the immense joy of the people. Peel remained for six years the supreme Governor of the country ; and he governed, as everybody knows, on uncompromising Protestant Ascendency principles. In October, 1812, he wrote to the Attorney-General Saurin :—

> " I entirely agree with you in your opinion upon the service which the Protestant cause would derive from the active exertions of an Irishman in the House of Commons, who would share with Dr. Duigenan in zeal, but would temper it with a little more discretion. At the

* Parker, Sir Robert Peel.

same time I must own that I could never bring myself to propose to Dr. Duigenan to resign his seat in Parliament, after all his labours, and all his persecutions for righteousness' sake, and all the obloquy he has braved and will brave in the cause of the Protestant Ascendency."*

Some one seems to have suggested that Peel was not opposed to the " perpetual " exclusion of Catholics from positions of power and emolument in the State. Peel repelled the calumny thus :

" I see one of the papers reports me as having said I was not an advocate for perpetual exclusion. It might be inferred that I objected only to the time of discussing the question. That is not the case."

On March 16th, 1813, Saurin wrote to Peel anent a debate in the House of Commons on the Catholic claims.

* Duigenan had been born and brought up a Catholic. He became a Protestant, and developed into a furious and crazy bigot. Grattan's first speech in the English House of Commons was made in reply to one of Duigenan's periodical anti-Irish and anti-Catholic harangues :
" The speech of the honourable member," said Grattan, " consists of four parts. *First*—An invective against the religion of the Catholics. *Second*—An invective against the present generation. *Third*—An invective against the past ; and *Fourth*—An invective against the future. Here the limits of creation interposed, and stopped the number.
" It is to defend these different generations that I rise ; to rescue the Catholics from his attack and the Protestants from his defence."
Curran said that Duigenan's speeches were :
" like the unrolling of a mummy—nothing but old bones and rotten rags. . .
" The nation to whom he owed his birth he slandered ; the common people from whom he sprung, he vituperated ;
. . . he abused the people ; he abused the Catholics ; he abused his country ; and the more he caluminated his country the more he raised himself."
Duigenan became a Privy Councillor.

" Your defence of the Protestant cause was not only by far the ablest and best, but the only one which did not seem to strengthen the cause of the adversary by some concession of principle."

In 1814, Peel wrote to the Under-Secretary Gregory.

" I admire the principles that the Orangemen maintain and avow."

In the same year he wrote to Abbot, the speaker of the House of Commons.

" As for the Catholic question, your letter reminded me of it, for, strange to say, though in Ireland, I had almost forgotten it."

Though Peel admired the principles of Orangeism, he was " jealous " of the Orange Society. He writes :

" I must confess I cannot look [on the Orange Society] or any other political association in Ireland that is controlled by any other authority than that of the Government, without jealousy."

Peel seems to have been opposed to public liberty of any kind. He writes :—

" I believe an honest despotic Government would be by far the fittest Government for Ireland."

Peel's idea of " honesty " may be gathered from the following extracts in reference to the management of the Protestant Ascendency members in the House of Commons. He writes to the Lord Lieutenant :—

" Perhaps you will think me very insatiate in the demands which I prefer from our parliamentary friends. But you will recollect that I have the whole accumulated host upon my back, and you must make some allowance for the torments which they inflict upon me. They are apt to expect reward where they perform the service—upon the field of battle."

At the same time he wrote to Mr. Gregory :—

> " I do not write to Lord Whitworth on these matters. He will recollect that I am in the midst of all the vultures, and must throw a little food among them occasionally."

A despotism based on coercion and jobbery, and subject to no inquiry, was Peel's idea of the best government for Ireland. He writes :—

> " I have been trying to impress Lord Liverpool with the extreme danger of a political inquiry into the affairs of Ireland. The more I think of it the more I am inclined to deprecate it."

In February, 1816, he wrote to the Lord Lieutenant.

> " I told truth enough to alarm many an honest Englishman, and convince him that he knows about as much of the state of Ireland as he does of the state of Kamchatka."

Yet in October of the same year he wrote to the Prime Minister :—

> " If you can, send an Englishman to succeed me ; he may be inferior to Irish competitors in many respects, and still upon the whole better suited for this office, from the very circumstance of his not being an Irishman."

and again

> " I feel it of so much importance that the Lord Lieutenant and the Secretary should be unconnected with this country, that I doubt whether you have made a very good choice of a Lord Lieutenant in Lord Talbot."

Peel did not wholly trust even the Irish Protestant Ascendency party. An *English* despot—" who knew about as much of the state of Ireland as of the state of Kamchatka " was his panacea for Irish ills.

It is scarcely an exaggeration to say that at no time was the atmosphere of Dublin Castle more anti-Irish and Anti-Catholic than during the Administration of Sir Robert Peel.

A Scotchman, Charles Grant (afterwards Lord Glenelg), succeeded him. Grant was in favour of the Catholic claims ; but he was sandwiched between a no-popery Lord Lieutenant (Lord Talbot) and a no-popery Under-Secretary (Mr. Gregory). The wisdom of Downing Street called this " impartiality " —the wisdom of the Irishman in the street called it " Tomfoolery." The Irishman in the street was right. The Sandwich system made confusion worse confounded. With the Chief Secretary pulling one way, and the Lord Lieutenant and the Under-Secretary pulling the other, stable government became impossible. The Talbot Administration was grotesque.

Peel, as we have seen, did not approve of the appointment of Lord Talbot on account of his Irish connections. Yet Talbot had the true faith of the Ascendency.

> " We had a famous Protestant dinner yester-
> day," he writes. " The glorious, pious and im-
> mortal memory was drunk as it ought to be."

Assuredly this ought to have been a man after Peel's own heart.

Grant, whom O'Connell described as " the mildest, kindest and best mannered man Ireland has ever seen," believed that Irish Catholics ought to be " known to the law," for " other purposes " than those of punishment.* This was a startling innovation.

> " Galway," sneers Gregory, " is the most
> Catholic county in Ireland, and now is in a state
> of almost open rebellion, yet Grant wants to work
> through the Priesthood."

A few months after Grant's arrival, a great meeting was held at the Rotunda in support of Catholic Emanci-

* Ante, p. 39.

pation. The new Chief Secretary, with his known popish sympathies, was in a sense held responsible for this outrage on the city.

Gregory was scandalised. He wrote to Lord Whitworth (the ex-Viceroy) :—

" In proportion to the high station you filled here, so must be to you the satisfaction at having withdrawn from it without witnessing those disgusting scenes which have lately disgraced this heretofore Protestant city. The change appears to me as sudden as the shifting of the scenes in a harlequin farce, and when in a few months the glorious memory is banished from the Mayoralty house, and the Lord Mayor calls an aggregate meeting to support the Catholic claims, is it too much to expect the elevation of the host in the streets before the expiration of the year ? But I trust the day of triumph is far off."

At the same time Gregory wrote to Grant, gently hinting at the delinquencies of his chief, even in holding opinions favourable to the masses of the people who paid Gregory his salary.

" I did not think it possible that in a few short days such a change could be effected, but the Catholic question now engrosses the attention of all ranks."

Grant has been described as amiable, clever and irresolute. But he showed some strength about this time. The *Hibernian*,—one of the papers subsidised by Peel, for Peel did not hesitate to do what he could to nobble the Press in the Ascendency interest,— made a truculent attack upon the Catholics. Grant withdrew the subsidy on the instant, and the *Hibernian* came to an untimely end. In the absence of the Viceroy, Lords Justices were as usual appointed, to take his place. One of the first acts of their Lordships was ; (adopting the old Castle method of coercion) to proclaim certain baronies, without consulting Grant who happened to be in London at the time. Grant protested. First because he did not think the proclamations necessary, secondly, because he thought that he ought to have been consulted beforehand on the subject. He had to defend the policy of the " Irish " Executive in the House of Commons, and he therefore considered that he should have had a voice in the framing of that policy.

"That which I wish," he wrote to Gregory, " is to check the rage [of the Lords Justices] for proclaiming, and to give me in fact a veto on the proceedings before they are actually in progress."

The Lord Lieutenant, the Lords Justices and Gregory were indignant.

"I yesterday," wrote Talbot, from London, to Gregory, "saw Lord Sidmouth (the Home Secretary), to whom I spoke without reserve on the subject of our Chief Secretary. I told him that *we* felt he had no confidence in *us*," which was certainly true.

About the same time Gregory wrote :—

"Grant, though tired to death of his *unsuccessful* work, has not the least notion of resigning."

Later on we read that "Grant looks worn to death."
It is clear that a man cannot resist the Castle atmosphere with impunity. Still Grant lived on. And now an extraordinary thing happened. Of course Grant ought to have resigned, or died, or been dismissed, and a good and true Ascendency man sent in his place. That naturally was the view of every Loyalist in Ireland. It may well be conceived how often the Lord Lieutenant and Under-Secretary put their heads together to plan the removal of their objectionable colleague. Loyalty was entitled to its reward, and the reward of loyalty was the dismissal

of " popish Grant " (as the Chief Secretary was called by the Ascendency gang). But the ways of English rulers in Ireland are wonderful.

" One fine morning," as O'Connell would have said, Lord Talbot came down to breakfast. He opened a letter from the Prime Minister. Perhaps his Excellency breathed the hope that it might contain something about Grant. To his horror he read that his own services as Chief Governor of Ireland were no longer needed. Not a word of explanation was vouchsafed, not a single reason given for this astounding communication. He was dismissed without ceremony and almost with contempt.

> " I have been turned out of office," he subsequently said to Lord Sidmouth, " in less time than I should deem it right to turn a servant away, without having been told *why*—in other words I have been condemned unheard."

" Grant, worn to death," was also impartially recalled. He retired with honour, but left the Castle atmosphere unchanged. So ended the first Sandwich administration.

John Bull is slow in taking in a new idea. He is equally slow in letting it out when once he has taken it in. The Sandwich experiment proved a fiasco. Yet it was not to be given up. Two more Sandwich men were sent to rule Ireland. Lord Wellesley (a supporter of the Catholic claims), was appointed Lord Lieutenant. Mr. Goulburn " an Orangeman," was appointed Chief Secretary.* Gregory remained at his old post.

The second Sandwich Administration was as unsatisfactory as the first. The fears of the Ascendency were

---

* " Mr. Goulburn had unfortunately the reputation of being a member of the Orange Society ; and though he probably withdrew from it after the law denounced Orange lodges as illegal bodies, the mass of the people regarded this important public functionary as one of their *sworn* enemies " (Pearce, " Memoir of the Marquis Wellesley," Vol. III., p. 333).

raised, and the hopes of the people disappointed.
The tug of war, between the Lord Lieutenant on one
hand, and the Chief Secretary and Under-Secretary
on the other, served only to distract and scandalise.*
The younger Grattan said that Wellesley

> " Showed himself a friend of liberty, but was
> thwarted by subordinates."

Grant had said that in his absence Gregory was
" the master of the whole machine of government."
Gregory was more master now than ever.

> " The petitioner at the Castle," says Mr. Wyse,
> " did not ask what the Lord Lieutenant thought,
> but what the Lord Lieutenant's Secretary thought,
> or rather what his Secretary's Secretary thought.
> It was not Lord Wellesley, nor even Mr. Goulburn,
> but it was Mr. Gregory who held in his hand the
> destinies of Ireland."

In fact Mr. Gregory was the government, and to
Mr. Gregory, government and Protestant Ascendency
were convertible terms.

He had been nine years at the wheel. He steered the
ship and sometimes gave the course. Lord Wellesley
came to emancipate, but remained to coerce.†

Well might O'Connell have spoken of

> " the tantalizing and bitter repetition of expecta-
> tions raised only to be blasted, and prospects of
> success opened to close upon them in ten-fold
> darkness."

* Lord Grenville said of this Sandwich system of Government :
" What can exceed the ridicule of thus systematically
coupling together a friend and an enemy to toleration, like
fat and lean rabbits, or the man and his wife in a Dutch toy,
or like fifty other absurdities made to be laughed at, but
certainly never before introduced into politics as a fixed and
fundamental system for the conduct of the most difficult
and dangerous crisis of a country."

† During his Administration the Insurrection Act was passed,
the Habeas Corpus Act was suspended, and a measure for the
suppression of the Catholic Association became law.

Early in 1827, the great Liverpool Ministry ended, and Canning became Premier. William Lamb (afterwards Lord Melbourne), a supporter of the Catholic claims, became Chief Secretary.

Canning sent for him on the eve of his departure for Ireland. The Prime Minister said in effect that though justice demanded the emancipation of the Catholics yet he feared that a bill for the purpose could not be carried through Parliament immediately. He seems to have thought that relief would have to come through administrative reform. He apparently believed that if the barriers raised to prevent the appointment of Catholics to office in Ireland were thrown down " so far as a bigoted code [of laws] allowed," and if the public mind of England became accustomed to see Catholics engaged in the public service, the objections to their claims would gradually fade away and reform in law would follow reform in administration. Lamb was therefore practically sent to Ireland to destroy the system by which Catholics were excluded from posts under the Government and generally to popularise the Executive. His presence in Dublin Castle was unwelcome. We learn that Gregory " groaned."* Gregory had once written to Lord Talbot saying :—

> " Your account of the fixed determination to maintain the Protestant religion is very consoling."

But he found no consolation in the presence of William Lamb. It has been hinted that on Lamb's arrival the Under-Secretary kept away from the Castle for a time in chagrin.† But Lamb, to adopt his invariable phraseology, did not care " a damn." He did not send for Gregory. He worked away on his own account, and got the strings of Administration into his own hands. He saw everybody, did every-

* Torrens, "Life of Lord Melbourne."
† Torrens, "Life of Shiel."

thing, dined even with agitators and astonished the Attorney-General by proposing that the subsidies to the press, on which Peel had so much relied, should be stopped. Had Lamb remained long enough at Dublin Castle he might have purified the atmosphere. But Canning died in August, 1827 ; and Lord Goderich became Prime Minister. The Goderich ministry, distracted by differences, went to pieces in five months ; and in January, 1828, the famous Wellington-Peel ministry was formed. Ministerial changes in England produced changes in the administration of Ireland. Lord Wellesley had left in December, 1827, and was succeeded by the Marquis of Anglesey. Lamb left in June, 1828, and was succeeded by Lord Francis Leveson-Gower.

After the alarms—false alarms of the Sandwich Administrations,—after the accession to office of a Minister practically pledged to Emancipation, after the disturbing appearance of Lamb at Dublin Castle, the Protestant Ascendency breathed freely once more. Wellington had refused to serve under Canning, because Canning was favourable to Catholic Emancipation. Peel had refused for the same reason, and now the Duke of Wellington was Prime Minister and Peel was his first lieutenant in the Commons. What could be more consoling, as Gregory might have said. In March, 1827, Peel had declared in the House of Commons that :—

> " To admit Catholics within the walls of the House of Commons would be dangerous to the Constitution, would lead to interference in every election between landlord and tenant, and would increase discord and dissension."

In May, 1828, he said :—

> " I am persuaded that the removal of their [the Catholic] disabilities would be attended with danger to the Protestant religion against

which it would be impossible to find any security equal to that of our present Protestant Constitution."

In June, the Duke of Wellington said :—

" The securities which we now enjoy, and which for a length of time we have enjoyed, are indispensable to the safety of Church and State."

What better guarantee could be given against the inroads of popery, and for the perpetual maintenance of the Protestant Ascendency, than a Government with Wellington at its head and Peel at its tail ? But alas, for the uncertainty of all human expectations. I have said that Wellesley came to emancipate, but remained to coerce. The Wellington-Peel Ministry came to coerce, but remained to emancipate.

Daniel O'Connell had lashed the people into fury. The tide of rebellion was surging round the gates of Dublin Castle itself. And, in the midst of the tumult and " treason " of the hour, the Iron Duke and " orange " Peel lowered their flag, and granted the Catholic demands, avowedly because less was to be feared from surrender than from resistance. In February, 1829, Peel introduced a Bill for emancipation, and in April it became law. The Ascendency were betrayed by their avowed friends.

Well, indeed, might Lord Talbot have written in distress, as he did to his old friend and colleague Gregory :—

" Little did I ever expect to have seen our friend [Peel] at the bar of our house upon such an occasion. Had I been told of such a circumstance two years, nay one year, ago, I should have scouted it as impossible. . . . I hope I shall not be reproached if I say that in future I *cannot confide* in his stability. *Expediency* is a sorry word. I say, give me *principle* as my watchword."*

People naturally thought that the result of Catholic Emancipation would be to clear the atmosphere of Dublin Castle. But they were disappointed. The atmosphere remained as foul as ever. Mr. Lecky describes the character of the Irish Administration four years after the passing of the Catholic Relief Act. He says :—

> " In 1833—four years after Catholic Emancipation—there was not in Ireland a single Catholic judge or stipendiary magistrate. All the high sheriffs with one exception, the overwhelming majority of the unpaid magistrates and of the grand jurors, the five inspectors-general, and the thirty-two sub-inspectors of police, were Pro-

---

* Peel's reasons for surrendering are interesting. He wrote, on February 8th, 1829 :

> " In the course of the last six months, England being at peace with the whole world, has had five-sixths of the infantry force of the United Kingdom occupied in maintaining the peace, and in police duties in Ireland. I consider the state of things which requires such an application of military force much worse than open rebellion. . . ."

Subsequently he wrote :

> " In the year 1829 we passed the Act for the relief of the Roman Catholics. I never took any credit for the part I had in passing that measure, because I own it was forced upon me."

The Duke of Wellington's reasons are equally interesting. On May 4th, 1829, he wrote :

> " If you glance at the history of Ireland during the last ten years you will find that agitation really means something short of rebellion ; that and no other is the exact meaning of the word. It is to place the country in that state in which its Government is utterly impracticable, except by means of an overawing military force."

And again he said :

> " If we cannot get rid of the Catholic Association, we must look to civil war in Ireland. It is quite clear that the organisation of the disaffected in Ireland is more perfect than ever. If they can raise money they will have good arms and ammunition, and then the contest may for a moment be serious."

testant. The chief towns were in the hands of narrow, corrupt, and, for the most part, intensely bigoted corporations. Even in a Whig Government, not a single Irishman had a seat in the Cabinet, and the Irish Secretary was Mr. Stanley, whose imperious manners and unbridled temper had made him intensely hated. For many years promotion had been steadily withheld from those who advocated Catholic Emancipation, and the majority of the people thus found their bitterest enemies in the foremost places."

As might be expected from the Anti-Irish character of the Administration, the whole strength of the Executive was used to crush every popular movement. Tithe reformers, church reformers, land reformers, were all the enemies of the Castle because the Castle was the enemy of Ireland. The forces of the English Crown were employed to shoot down Irish Catholic peasants because they refused to pay tithes to the parsons of an English Protestant Church, and to evict at the point of the bayonet starving tenants because they could not pay impossible rents to unconscionable landlords.

At length, in 1835, there was a change. Melbourne was Prime Minister. Lord Mulgrave became Lord Lieutenant, and Lord Morpeth Chief Secretary. Gregory had been dismissed from the office of Under-Secretary in 1831,* with the view of liberalising the Administration. But the Administration was not liberalised. Gossett, who succeeded him, was another Ascendency man. On Mulgrave's appointment, Perrin, the Irish Attorney-General, said to the new Viceroy :—

" My Lord, [the Under-Secretary] will be your right eye, and if we have to spend our time plucking old beams out of it, your Government will not go straight."

* See Mr. Gregory's interesting correspondence in Lady Gregory's valuable book, " Mr. Gregory's Letter Box."

Gossett was accordingly removed, and Thomas Drummond took his place.

The new Under-Secretary was the real ruler of the country. The Lord Lieutenant and the Chief Secretary, in truth, played subordinate parts. Drummond was the virtual head of the Administration. His record is unique. He was a success. Why? The answer lies on the surface. He knew Ireland. He loved the people, he had a policy, and he stood to his guns. What was his policy? Lord Cornwallis had said that he would rather make a union with the " nation " than with a party. That was the policy of Drummond. He flung to the winds the party which represented injustice and tyranny, and he stretched out his hand to the nation who demanded the redress of material wrongs, and the removal of the civil and religious inequalities, which, in spite of Catholic Emancipation, were still maintained. He conferred constantly with O'Connell, and, through the leader of the people, kept in touch with the people themselves. He broke with the traditions of the past ; and attempted the extraordinary feat of trying to make Dublin Castle an Irish institution. A single Act will sometimes reveal the whole man ; and in Drummond's famous letter to the Tipperary magistrates we discover the key to his character. He believed that true statesmanship consisted in seeking for causes as well as in dealing with effects. The eternal land war was raging. Tenants were ground to powder. Landlords were shot. The Tipperary magistrates cried out for coercion ; because the landlord's idea of justice and statesmanship was associated only with martial law and the gallows.

Lord Chesterfield is reported to have said, when he was in Ireland :—

" If the military force had killed half as many landlords as it had Whiteboys, it would have contributed more effectually to restore quiet."

Drummond did not say this to the Tipperary magistrates ; but he wrote a letter which fluttered the dovecots of landlordism in every part of Ireland.

He said :—

" When the character of the great majority of serious outrages occurring in many parts of Ireland, though unhappily most frequent in Tipperary, is considered, it is impossible to doubt that the causes from which they mainly spring are connected with the tenure and occupation of land."

He added :—

" Property has its duties as well as its rights ; to the neglect of those duties in times past is mainly to be ascribed that diseased state of society in which such crimes take their rise, and it is not in the enactment or enforcement of statutes of extraordinary severity, but chiefly in the better and more faithful performance of those duties, and the more enlightened and humane exercise of those rights, that a permanent remedy for such disorders is to be sought."

Lord Donoughmore, who received this letter, was horrified. He suppressed it. Subsequently he told a Committee of the House of Lords why—

" I considered the reply of such a nature [that] I was very unwilling to make it public."

Committee : " Your Lordship considered it a dangerous thing with regard to the landowners of the country ? "

Lord Donoughmore : " I considered it of that nature."

Committee : " Will your Lordship have the goodness to point out the passages which appear to you to have that tendency ? "

Lord Donoughmore : " The part of this answer to which I particularly objected was this : ' Property has its duties as well as its rights ; to the neglect of those duties in times past is mainly to be ascribed that diseased state of society in which such crimes take their rise.' "

Lord Donoughmore wished to see the Whiteboys hanged, but was aghast at any reference to the diseased state of society which made Whiteboyism not only possible but inevitable. His Lordship looked only at the fruit. Drummond struck at the root of the tree that produced it.

Poor Charles Grant tried to clear the atmosphere of Dublin Castle, and was " worn out " in the effort. Drummond did clear it, and then he died. He was scarcely in his grave when it became as thick as ever.

Residents in the English capital sometimes see how a sudden outburst of sunshine will disperse the vapours of a London fog ; and then the sun disappears and the fog gathers again, and everything is wrapped in darkness. So it was with the moral atmosphere of Dublin Castle in Drummond's day. The light which he shed on the Administraton went out with him.

O'Connell had supported the Melbourne Ministry, in order, as he said, to see if it were possible for an English Parliament to do justice to Ireland. The experiment, in his opinion, had failed, and he at once unfurled the banner of repeal. The Castle, opposed once more to the National movement, put forth its strength to destroy the National leader.

Sir Robert Peel himself tells us what was the character of the " Irish " Executive during this time.

> " The Executive," he says, " as at present constituted, is of a very exclusive character. The Lord Lieutenant, the Chief Secretary, the Lord Chancellor, the Law officers, the Judges whom we have appointed, all without exception are Protestants."*

* Peel to Lord Heytesbury, July 18th, 1845.

In 1843 a great constitutional repeal meeting was summoned by O'Connell : it was to be held at Clontarf. The meeting was proclaimed and the guns of the Pigeon-house Fort were trained on the spot. In 1844, O'Connell was arraigned for seditious conspiracy, because he had tried by open agitation to obtain the repeal of the Union. The Bench was packed, the jury was packed, and the vast resources of the Crown were used with unscrupulous dexterity to secure a conviction.

> " Next morning," says Sir Gavan Duffy, writing of the way in which the trial had been arranged, " it was known throughout the United Kingdom, and speedily known over Europe and America, that the most eminent Catholic in the Empire —a man whose name was familiar to every educated Catholic in the world—was about to be placed upon his trial in the Catholic metropolis of a Catholic country, before four judges and twelve jurors, among whom there was not a single Catholic."*

O'Connell was, of course, convicted. But even the House of Lords was staggered by the infamy of the proceedings, and quashed the conviction.

Some years later still, the story of James Birch exposed the folly and corruption of the Executive. Birch was a scoundrel. He owned a paper called *The World ;* it lived by blackmail. Birch himself

---

* Duffy's own trial, in 1848, was a public scandal. He was arraigned five times for treason. Owing to the zeal with which the Crown sought to pack the juries which tried him, he was never convicted (See *Irish Memories*). On the second trial the jury disagreed ; eleven were for conviction, one for an acquittal. The obstinate juryman was Martin Burke, then the proprietor of the historic Shelbourne Hotel, which may fairly be described as one of the Institutions of Dublin. There is a good story told of Burke. One day he was standing at the door of his hotel, and a company of soldiers passed by. The sergeant stepped out of the ranks, to ask for some information. Going up to Burke, he said, " I say, sir, do you belong to this 'ere hotel ? " " No, sir," said Burke, " but this 'ere hotel belongs to me."

had been imprisoned for attempting to obtain hush-money. His character was well known to the citizens of Dublin, and no human being could by any possibility be made a penny the worse or the better for anything that appeared, or did not appear, in the wretched publication for which he was responsible. But the wisdom of our English rulers is sometimes like the innocence of doves. The Peel traditions lingered in the Castle ; and the Lord Lieutenant (Lord Clarendon, 1847-1852) and his advisers, determined to subsidise *The World* in the interests of law and order.

Mr. James Birch defending Dublin Castle and traducing the Irish national party of the day, was as fine a spectacle as Mr. Richard Pigott, in later times, lending the weight of his reputation to sustain the tottering fabric of falsehood and calumny raised by the enemies of the Irish people. Lord Clarendon sent for Mr. Birch. The Editor of *The World* and the Viceroy of the English Sovereign took counsel together ; and Mr. Birch was sent forth to do battle for the Constitution. As time went on, Mr. Birch came to place a very high price on his services. Those who served the Castle, he knew, were often jobbed into important positions. Mr. Birch wanted high office. A colonial governorship probably would not have been below his ambition. Lord Clarendon, however, though willing to give Birch money in secret, was not prepared to make him a public servant. Birch was disgusted and indignant, and threatened to make terrible disclosures if his talents and his loyalty were not properly rewarded. He had received £1,000, but that was mere dross. He wanted public recognition and no doubt an invitation to the soirées at the Castle as well as any other man who was doing the Castle's work. Lord Clarendon gave him £2,000 to hold his tongue. He took the £2,000, but did not hold his tongue. When the money was gone, he brought an action against the Chief Secretary on a count for "work and labour done." The Castle then discovered that he was "a hangdog looking wretch," an "assassin of character, and one of the basest of mankind." Nevertheless, he got a verdict, though only for a nominal sum. But in the course of the trial everything was disclosed; and all Dublin laughed at the sages on Cork Hill.*

I have already quoted some extracts from Peel's correspondence when he was Chief Secretary. I shall now quote some extracts from his correspondence when he was Prime Minister in 1841-46. I commend these extracts—indeed I commend the whole career of Peel—to the careful study of Irish Protestants.

Peel was an English statesman *par excellence*. How did he treat the Protestants of Ireland? In 1812, he went to Ireland to uphold the Protestant ascendency. In 1829, he betrayed it, because it would have cost more to defend the Protestants than to desert them. Nevertheless, despite this betrayal, he remained a bitter enemy of Catholic liberty between 1829 and 1841. Indeed, it was not likely that he could be true to the Catholic cause in which he did not believe, when he had been false to the cause of Protestant ascendency, in which he did believe.

> "Gentlemen," Wellington is reported to have said to his staff at Waterloo, "very fine pounding this; but the question is, Who can pound the hardest?"

The question with Peel always was, "Who can pound the hardest?" He surrendered to the pounding of the Catholics in 1829, but he was not converted, because as I have said between 1829 and 1841 he still remained the bitter opponent of the Catholic claims. Between 1841-46 there was a change. Ireland then rang with the cry of repeal; and it seems to have suddenly dawned upon Peel that the promotion of

* See Sir Gavan Duffy's "Four Years of Irish History," and the contemporary press.

Catholics to office might be a wise policy. It was certainly one way of trying to sap their integrity, and to demoralise the national forces. O'Connell was to be crushed, but the alluring bait of office was to be held out to Catholics, who, if untempted, might have remained faithful to the Irish cause.

Peel had once said :—

> " I cannot consent to widen the doors to the Roman Catholics. I cannot consent to give them civil rights and privileges equal to those possessed by their Protestant fellow countrymen."

But put not your trust in English statesmen, Protestants of Ireland. They will betray you, as readily as they have wronged the Catholics, if it suits their purpose ; and the memory of the Boyne will not save you. In 1843, Peel wrote :—

> " We must look out for respectable Roman Catholics for office."

When he was Chief Secretary, he had divided the Catholic population of Ireland into four classes :

> " the clergy, the lower orders of the people, the moderate and respectable part of the Catholics, and the violent party, with O'Connell and Scully at their head."

We may take it then that in Peel's judgment a " respectable Catholic " meant a " moderate man," who might be drawn away from O'Connell and his " tail." In 1843, he again wrote :—

> " I wish we could take this opportunity of selecting some Roman Catholic barrister of high character and moderate opinions for the office of Third Sergeant."

In the following sentence the cloven foot appears :—

> " I have a very strong impression that occasional *favour* shown to a Roman Catholic will

be very advantageous, and diminish the influence
and power of those who are hostile to British
connection.' "

Peel italicised the word " favour," which is significant. In plain language Roman Catholics were to
be bribed to desert the cause of repeal which, in Peel's
opinion, was " hostile to the British connection."

In fact, the principle of his administration at this
time was, in his own words :—

> " To give satisfaction to a great body of moder-
> ate men and withdraw them from the ranks of
> our opponents."

This has been called " administrative reform " :
I call it administrative corruption.*

Let Irish Protestants who believe in the " loyalty "
of English statesmen read the next sentence, written
by a man who was one of their greatest champions.

> " Depend upon it, we must discard that favourite
> doctrine of Dublin Castle : ' You cannot conciliate
> your enemies ; therefore give everything to the
> most zealous of your friends.' "

Peel was now clearly of opinion that a tame Catholic
was as good any day as a zealous Protestant. Perhaps
he was right.†

The Lord Lieutenant, Lord de Grey, did not approve
of Peel's tactics. He wrote :—

> " I am as willing as any man to act towards
> the Roman Catholics with the utmost impar-
> tiality, but I do not feel that it is either wise

---

* The word is no doubt offensive to the delicate English
palate. An Englishman never calls a spade a spade. An
American once asked an English friend the meaning of the word
perquisites. The English friend told him. " Well," said the
Yankee, " in our country we call that ' thievings.' "

† I heard a Protestant official in Ireland say, " The worst of
Catholic appointments is that a Catholic in office tries so damned
hard to be like a Protestant."

or expedient to appoint an unfit man to an office
merely because he is a Catholic. Conciliation
is a chimera. I would not be deterred from doing
what I thought right by any fear of their anger,
nor would I do what I did not honestly believe
to be right with any hopes of obtaining their
praise."

Peel's reply was characteristic. He wrote :—

" What motive can we hold out to the well-
affected Roman Catholic to abjure agitation,
and the notoriety and fame which are its rewards,
if the avenue to lucrative appointments and
to legitimate distinction be in point of fact closed
to him."

In 1845 Mr. Lucas retired from the office of Under-
Secretary at Dublin Castle. Peel suggested that he
might be succeeded by a Catholic. He wrote to Lord
Heytesbury, who had now succeeded Earl de Grey as
Viceroy :—

" The selection of a successor to Mr. Lucas
will be no easy matter. Will you turn in your
mind whether it would be practicable to nominate
a Roman Catholic gentleman to this office.*
I confess I think it would be of immense importance to establish a closer connection between
the Executive Government and the Roman
Catholic body to facilitate the means of friendly
communication."

The reply of Lord Heytesbury is in every way a remarkable document, not only in reference to its bearing
on Peel's policy, but on account of the light which
it throws generally on the Castle system. He wrote :—

* Curiously enough on the retirement of Lucas he wrote,
" We shall miss him most as the medium of communication with
the heads of the Orange party. They had the greatest confidence
in him." Clearly Peel did not altogether wish to be off with the
old love, though he was certainly anxious to be on with the new.

" I enter fully into all your views of policy
with regard to this country. I am as desirous
as yourself that Roman Catholics should be
placed, as soon as may be, in offices of honour
and emolument, and gradually in those of trust
and confidence. But I cannot think that the
time is yet come for making a Roman Catholic,
untried and unknown, the mainspring of your
Government in Ireland ; the channel of confidential communication with all your authorities,
—military, civil, and ecclesiastical ; the depository not only of all the secrets of Government,
but of those of everybody connected with it ;
the man, in short, upon whom must rest, during
at least eight months of the year, the details
of administration. Recollect, I entreat you,
what the position of the individual himself would
be in a government, and in an office, manned,
unfortunately, upon the most rigid exclusive
principle. No confidential communication would
ever be made to him from the provinces. Mr.
Pennefather, to whom more than hopes of the
succession were held out last year by Lord Eliot,
would, I doubt not, immediately resign. There
would be nobody left to counsel or direct a Roman
Catholic successor. On the contrary, a sort of
passive resistance would spring up, which would
meet him everywhere, but which he would find
it almost impossible to grapple with or overcome.

" Under such circumstances, the machinery,
which ought to be entirely under his control,
would be made to work with the greatest difficulty, and the whole action of the Government
would be paralysed.

" I think, however, I could suggest a way
in which your principal object might be effected,
without stirring up all those evil passions which
would be put in motion by the appointment of
a Roman Catholic, at one bound, to so immensely

important a post in the administration of the Government. The course which I would recommend is the following :—

" Promote Mr. Pennefather to the office vacated by Mr. Lucas, and select some Roman Catholic, well connected and of fair acquirements, to be Mr. Pennefather's successor in the second place. There he would be trained to habits of business, get accustomed to office and office get accustomed to him, and thus be rendered fit and eligible for higher employment whenever it could safely be entrusted to him. This concession to the Catholic party, who expect nothing of the sort, would be considered as flattering to them as if he were placed in the most responsible office ; and we should avoid the angry rupture with the Protestant party which would be the inevitable consequence of his appointment to the delicate trust which has ever required so much management and tact."

Peel accepted Heytesbury's suggestion that a Protestant should be appointed to the office of Under-Secretary and a Catholic to that of Chief Clerk, and he proposed that the title of Chief Clerk should be changed to that of Assistant Under-Secretary with an increase of salary.

Finally Mr. Pennefather (Protestant) was promoted from the office of Chief Clerk to the office of Under-Secretary, and Mr. McKenna (Catholic) was made Chief Clerk or Assistant Under-Secretary, which was the new title given to the office.* It is unnecessary to say

---

* Mr. McKenna would seem to have been the first official who received the title of Assistant Under-Secretary. But in 1852, a Treasury Committee of Inquiry recommended a return to the old title of Chief Clerk. This recommendation was for a time accepted. But finally, in 1876, the title of Assistant Under-Secretary was adopted. The Assistant Under-Secretaries since 1845 have been : Mr. McKenna (Catholic), Mr. Henry Robinson (Protestant), Mr. Kaye (Protestant), Sir James Dougherty (Protestant), Mr. Ennis (Catholic), whose tragic and untimely death was a shock to all who knew that kindest and most unselfish of men, and Edward O'Farrell (Catholic).

that the appointment of Mr. McKenna did not help in any way to liberalise the administration of Dublin Castle. He went around with the wheel, like everybody else.

It was also a part of Peel's policy to make " allies " of the Catholic bishops, and to draw them from the national movement. The establishment of the new Board for Charitable Trusts* might, it was hoped, have a beneficial effect in Anglicising the Hierarchy.

In 1844, Heytesbury wrote to Peel :—

" The *Gazette* containing a list of the New Board appeared last night. It has given great satisfaction to all the most respectable part of the Roman Catholic community, and if the prelates remain firm, we shall have achieved a victory and secured the due enforcement of a law which was meant to be, and is, one of the greatest boons ever tendered to the Roman Catholics of this country."

In the same year Eliot, the Chief Secretary, wrote to Heytesbury :—

" Of those with whom I had an opportunity of conversing not one failed to consider the conduct of the Roman Catholic bishops who have joined the Board, as likely to produce results of the greatest importance. To bring the Roman Catholic hierarchy into connection with the State, they said, was in itself a great step towards an alliance between the Roman Catholic Church and the Government.

" To do this in spite of O'Connell and McHale, (the Archbishop of Tuam) was to dissolve existing party bonds, and to make the distinction between parties in Ireland, as in England, political and not religious. The Roman Catholic party, as such, has ceased to exist. O'Connell can no longer rely on the support of the Church. He has

* *Post.*

coaxed and he has menaced the most esteemed prelates, and his threats and his cajolements have proved equally unavailing. Dr. Crolly and Dr. Murray have withstood both.''

In the same year Heytesbury wrote to Peel :—

" We have erected a barrier—a line of Churchmen—behind which the well-thinking part of the Roman Catholic laity will conscientiously rally, and aid us in carrying out those measures of conciliation and peace which Her Majesty's Government have so deeply at heart.''

Whatever other bishops may have done, John, Archbishop of Tuam,—the " Lion of the Fold of Judah "—(" well paired with O'Connell," says Mr. Parker), remained true to the cause of Irish Nationality. His memory is to-day green in the hearts of the Irish people.* Peel's policy of " administrative reform " —of sops and doles—and " *favours* "—came to nothing. Ireland was not pacified by charitable trusts, Maynooth grants, or Catholic appointments. Famine, insurrection, wholesale clearances and emigration on a gigantic scale, followed the downfall of his ministry; and between 1850 and 1886, despite his policy of " administrative reform," there has not been a single Administration in Ireland which possessed the confidence of the Irish people.

" The Castle," said an Irish member, in the House of Commons in 1850, " is anti-Irish in everything."

Indeed, to this hour the name of the castle is associated with coercion, and only with coercion. Is it to be wondered at ? What is the record between 1800 and 1835 ?

* Mr. Parker ascribes what he considers Peel's success in dealing with the Catholic bishops to "the resolution of Peel, the diplomacy of Heytesbury and Graham, and the aid of the Court of Rome " (See Parker, " Sir Robert Peel").

1800-1801. Insurrection Act, Habeas Corpus Suspension Act, and Martial Law.

1803. Insurrection Act.

1804. Habeas Corpus Suspension Act.

1807-1810. Insurrection Act, Martial Law and Habeas Corpus Suspension Act.

1814. Habeas Corpus Suspension Act.

1814-1818. Insurrection Act.

1822-1824. Habeas Corpus Suspension Act.

1822-1824.* Insurrection Act.

1825-1828. Act for Suppression of Catholic Association.

1830. Arms Act.

1831-1832. Stanley's Arms Act.

1833-1834. Grey's Coercion Act.

1834-1835. Grey's Coercion (continuance) Act amended.

What is the record between 1835 and 1906 ? From 1835 to 1840 Ireland was governed by the ordinary law, under the Administration of Drummond, who did not enforce the Coercion Acts on the Statute Book.

(Aug.) 1843-1845. Arms Act.

(Dec.) 1847. Crime and Outrage Act.

1848-1849. Habeas Corpus Suspension Act, Crime and Outrage Act, Removal of Aliens Act.

1850-1855. Crime and Outrage (continuance) Act.

1856, 1857. Peace Preservation Act.

1858-1864. Peace Preservation (continuance) Act.

1865. Peace Preservation (Continuance) Act.

1866-1869 (off and on). Habeas Corpus Suspension Act.

1870, 1871. Peace Preservation Act.

1873-1880. Peace Preservation Act, or Protection of Life and Property Act.

* Lecky, " Leaders of Public Opinion," p. 261.

1881-1882.   Mr. Foster's Coercion Act.

1883-1886.   The Crimes Act.

1887-1906.   Mr. Arthur Balfour's "Perpetual" Crimes Act.*

Let these Acts be explained as they may, they prove one fact beyond all question, namely, that throughout almost the whole period of Mr. Pitt's Union the Executive of Ireland has been out of touch with the people of Ireland. The country has been governed in a state of siege.

Concessions followed coercion, but concessions were only made under the pressure of fear. The late Lord Derby has stated the case. He says :—

" .   .   .   In the history of English relations with Ireland it has always been the same. By an unfortunate fatality every concession made to the weaker State has been under pressure. Take as a sample the creation of the almost wholly independent Irish Parliament in 1780-1782. Was that a spontaneous gift ? Notoriously it was the reverse. English resources were exhausted by the unsuccessful war with America ; the Irish volunteers mustered stronger than any force which could have been brought together at short notice to oppose them ; the alternative was to yield to the Irish demands or to engage in a sanguinary civil war, exactly resembling that which had ended so disastrously on the other side of the Atlantic ; and the decision taken, probably a wise one, was to let Ireland have her

* This Act is unique in the sense that it has been made permanent ; other coercion Acts were passed for a limited time only. The essential principle of the Act is that persons may be examined as witnesses before a secret tribunal in Dublin Castle, even where no one is in custody ; and if the persons refuse to answer the questions asked, they may be sent to prison for an indefinite time.

Trial by two magistrates has been substituted for Trial by Jury, and the venue may be laid wherever the Executive pleases. Mr. Birrell has refused to put this Act in force.

own way. Not very dissimilar was the history
of Catholic Emancipation, except that at that
date it was a humane and rational aversion to
civil war, not an actual disability to carry it on,
which determined the issue. Sir R. Peel and
the Duke of Wellington did not rest their cause
on the alleged justice of the Catholic claims ;
they could not well do so, having for many years
opposed these claims as unfounded. But they
could and did say that the mischief of yielding
to them was less than the mischief of having
to put down an Irish insurrection. The same
argument that had prevailed in 1782 prevailed
in 1828-1829. A third example of the same
mode of procedure is in the memory of everybody.
The Fenian movement agitated Ireland from
1864 to 1867, producing among other results the
Clerkenwell explosion. Mr. Gladstone's statement
as to the effect of this and similar attempts on
the public mind of England, though too significant to be ignored, is too familiar to be repeated.
I have too often heard that speech censured as
unwise ; to me it has always seemed a gain that
the exact and naked truth should be spoken,
though at the cost of some unpleasant criticism.
A few desperate men, applauded by the whole
body of the Irish people for their daring, showed
England what Irish feeling really was ; made
plain to us the depth of a discontent whose existence we had scarcely suspected ; and the rest
followed of course. Few persons will now regret
the Disendowment of the Irish Church or the
passing of the Land Act of 1870 ; but it is regret-
able that, for the third time in less than a century,
agitation, accompanied with violence, should
have been shown to be the most effective instrument for redressing whatever Irishmen may
be pleased to consider their wrongs. . . .
Fixity of tenure has been the direct result of

two causes—Irish outrage and Parliamentary obstruction. The Irish know it as well as we. Not all the influence and eloquence of Mr. Gladstone would have prevailed on the English House of Commons to do what has been done in the matter of Irish tenant-right if the answer to all objections had not been ready, ' How else are we to govern Ireland ? ' " *

Between 1886 and 1906 there were two administrations which possessed the popular confidence more or less ; the Home Rule Administration of Lord Aberdeen and Mr. Morley in 1886, and the Home Rule Administration of Lord Crewe and Mr. Morley in 1892-1895.

It may be added that the Administration of Lord Aberdeen and Mr. Birrell to-day enjoys the popular toleration as much as any English Administration can or ought to enjoy it. Mr. Birrell, governing in the spirit of his fellow countryman Drummond, has refused to adopt a policy of coercion in obedience to the persistent demands of an Anti-Irish faction, and has shown his determination to identify himself with the popular claims. But peace and contentment will not reign in Ireland while an English Parliament usurps the rights of an Irish National Assembly.

I have already quoted the statement of Mr. Carlisle that the government of a country should partake of the character, especially the religious character, of the people. How does the " Irish " executive stand this test. Four-fifths of the population are Catholics. Since the English revolution of 1688 there has not been a Catholic Viceroy.† There never was a Catholic Chief Secretary. There have been 3 Catholic Under Secretaries. There have been 2 Catholic Chancellors.‡ In the High Court of Justice

* *Nineteenth Century*, October, 1881.

† To this day the Viceroy cannot by law be a Catholic.

‡ It was only in 1867 that the legal disabilities preventing Catholics holding the office of Chancellor were removed.

there are 17 Judges ; 3 of them are Catholics. There are 21 County Court Judges* and Recorders ; 8 of them are Catholics. There are 37 County Inspectors of Police ; 5 of them are Catholics. There are 202 District Inspectors of Police ; 62 of them are Catholics. There are 5,518 ordinary Justices of the Peace ; 1,805 of them are believed to be Catholics.† There are 68 Privy Councillors ; 8 of them are Catholics.

One day, in the spring of 1907, I happened to be present at a meeting of the Privy Council—assembled to hear certain legal causes which came up for consideration and judgment. There were six members in attendance. Five of them were Protestants. The able and courteous Clerk of the Council was a Protestant. The advocates and the parties in the cases were Catholics. I was struck by this anomalous condition of things. What would the intelligent foreigner have said to it ? What would the intelligent foreigner say, if on entering a court of justice in India, he saw upon the judgment seat, five " whites," and one " black "—a " tame " black—while the advocates and suitors, and spectators were, to a man, " black "—what, I repeat, would the intelligent foreigner, who witnessed this scene, say ? Assuredly, the idea, at least, would strike him,—that the blacks were not masters in their own land.

* There are sixteen County Court Judges and five Recorders. It should be noted that the Recorders (except Dublin) are the County Court Judges of the counties in which the Boroughs of which they are Recorders are situated. The Recorder of Cork is County Court Judge for East Cork ; the Recorder of Belfast is County Court Judge for Antrim, and the Recorders of Derry and Galway are County Court Judges for the counties of Londonderry and Galway respectively.

† There are seventy-five Justices of the Peace whose religious persuasion, I learn, has not yet been ascertained. There are 200 ex-officio Justices of the Peace whose religion has not been ascertained either. In reference to ex-officio Justices, the Chairman of a County Council is a magistrate for the county, the Chairman of a District Council, with a population of over 5,000, is a magistrate for his district. (See post Local Government Act of 1898). Of 885 magistrates appointed between 26th April, 1906, and the 20th May, 1908, 536 were Catholics.

However, in mentioning the number of Catholic officials let it not be supposed that I suggest that they are necessarily more in touch with public opinion than their Protestant colleagues. Indeed, the " Papist rat," who has often earned promotion by detaching himself from his own people, is a greater object of popular aversion than any Anglo-Ascendency Protestant who ever thought that his natural position was a safe seat on the neck of the Irish Popish multitude.*

The Castle officials, who are merely the instruments of the Executive, have often been attacked. I cast no stone at any official in Ireland. It is a poor business to attack the individual where the system is to blame. I have found officials in Ireland frank, able, courteous gentlemen, and I am satisfied that if we had a national Government to-morrow they would serve Ireland as faithfully and as ably as they now serve England. But—and this is the only word of adverse criticism I shall utter on the *personnel* of the " Irish" Administration—they live, move, and have their being in an atmosphere which is not Irish.

---

* " Catholic Appointments," said a Catholic official, " cloud the issue." The Irish question is not a question of " Catholic " or " Protestant " appointments by a foreign Government. Ireland wants *Irish* appointments (Catholic and Protestant) by a National Government.

II

WORK

WE have passed through the atmosphere of the Castle. Let us turn to its work. The original Anglo-Norman Executive, as I have said, consisted practically of the Lord Lieutenant, the Lord High Chancellor, and the Lord High Treasurer. The first task to which every Government applies itself, is to maintain law and order, and to get money. Hence, the sword, the purse, and the ermine are the emblems of the State.

The chief business of the Castle for the first 300 years after the Norman Settlement consisted in fighting and plundering ; extending its pilfered territory, and defending captured lands. Nevertheless the upshot of the struggle of 300 years was that when the Tudors came to the English throne, the Norman settlement was confined to Dublin, and a fortified ring around it. This, as we all know, was called the Pale.* Then came the wars of the Tudors, and the subjugation of the country (so far as it has been subdued)† and the extension of the jurisdiction of the Castle. In Norman times certain offices sprang up, and we read of Privy Councillors, Lord High Constables, Lord High Marshalls, Lord High Butlers, Lord High Stewards ; Sheriffs, Escheators, and Seneschals. But the Castle had not much opportunity for the creation of offices, as its time was consumed in defending its existence. Between the accession of the Tudors, and the beginning

* The Pale included the County Louth, half the County Dublin, half the County Meath and half the County Kildare.

† A child was asked in a London school what was the date of the Conquest of Ireland ? She answered : " It began in 1169, and it is going on still."

of the nineteenth century, other offices sprang up ;
Magistrates, Grand Juries, Surveyors-General, Auditors-
General, Interpreters of the Irish tongue, Chief Remem-
brancers, Treasury Remembrancers, Accountants
General, Auditors-General, Principal Secretary of
State, Revenue Commissioners, Commissioners of
Customs and Excise, Board of Works, Post Office,
Keepers of the Records ; Ulster King at Arms,
Commissioners of Stamps, Keeper of the State
Papers in the Bermingham Tower, Clerk of Requests,
Swordbearer to the Lord Deputy, Wardrobe-Keeper
at Kilmainham, Athlone Pursuivant, Registrar of
Forfeitures, Customer and Comptroller of the Wine
Impost only, Commissioners for reducing the National
Debt, Commissioners of Hearth Money, Commissioners
of Inland Navigation, Commissioners of Stamps,
Board of Fruits, Revenue Board, Paving Board,
Medical Board, Linen Board, Navigation Board*
and so forth.

When the office of Chief Secretary was created I
cannot say. It has been suggested that some Lord
Lieutenant wished to get his private Secretary into
Parliament, and that out of this arrangement the office
came into existence. We do, however, know that
Addison was Chief Secretary to Wharton as early as
1709,† and that there is an official list of Chief Secretaries, from the appointment of Mr. Rigby in 1760,

---

* The springing up of the various important departments may
perhaps be said to have dated mainly from the reign of Charles II.

† " Besides the Chief Secretaryship, which was then worth
about two thousand pounds a year, he obtained a patent,
appointing him keeper of the Irish Records for life, with a salary
of three or four hundred a year. Budgell accompanied his cousin
in the capacity of private secretary.
" Wharton and Addison had nothing in common but Whiggism.
The Lord Lieutenant was not only licentious and corrupt, but
was distinguished from other libertines and jobbers by a callous
impudence which presented the strongest contrast to the
Secretary's gentleness and delicacy." (Macaulay " Essays.")
Addison was member for the borough of Cavan in the Irish
Parliament.

to the present time. In 1801, Lord Pelham, writing about the office said :—

" In settling what should be the character and situation of the Lord Lieutenant now that the Union has taken place, some assistance may be collected from the experience of His Majesty's reign, during which period Ireland has been at one time governed by British laws ; at another it has been governed by its own Parliament alone ; and now it is subject to an United and Imperial Parliament. During the first period the Lord Lieutenant did not always reside. The sessions of Parliament were only once in two years, and his Secretary was not always a member of it. The Chancellor and many of the Judges were Englishmen ; the concerns of Ireland were frequently discussed in the British Parliament, and the minister of the day took the lead in those questions.

" During the second period, when the independence of the Irish Parliament was admitted, annual sessions were the inevitable consequence, and the political importance of the Lord Lieutenant and his Secretary was materially affected. The former became constantly resident, and the latter gradually acquired the power and influence of a minister entrusted with the management of an independent Parliament."

In 1850, Sir Robert Peel said :—

" When there was a local Parliament in Ireland, the relation of the Chief Secretary to the Lord Lieutenant was a national and constitutional relation. The Chief Secretary was then in immediate connection with the Lord Lieutenant. He stood in a subordinate capacity ; all he did emanated from the authority of the Lord Lieutenant, and his relation to him corresponded in all material respects to the relation in which a Minister of State ordinarily stands with reference to the Crown. When you abolished the local legislature, and transferred the Secretary's Parliamentary functions to this side of the water, you altered materially the relations between the two parties. You put the office of Secretary aside from that of the Lord Lieutenant ; you made him a Minister responsible for the Administration of Justice in Ireland. A Minister necessarily possessing great power, and exercising that power sometimes without communication with his Chief, however desirous he might be of doing so. You thus placed him in a position in which it was very difficult for any man with the very best intentions to carry on the public business without the risk of occasional embarrassment."*

During the eighteenth century there were two Under-Secretaries at the Castle—an Under-Secretary for Military affairs, and an Under-Secretary for Civil affairs. After the Union a second Civil Secretary, who had his office in London, was appointed. Thus at the beginning of the nineteenth century, there were three Under-Secretaries, as well as a Chief Secretary. The official list of Chief Secretaries, as we have seen, begins with Mr. Rigby in 1760 ; the official list of Civil Under-Secretaries begins with Sackville Hamilton in 1730. In 1887, the office (temporary) of Parliamentary Under-Secretary was created, and Col. King-Harman was appointed (unpaid) to it. In 1888, a Bill was introduced to make the office permanent, with a salary attached. In the same year Col. King-Harman died ; the vacancy was not filled up, the Bill was dropped, and the office disappeared.

After the Union the question of the Administration of Ireland, under the new régime seems to have been raised. Ought the Lord Lieutenancy be abolished ?

* Hansard, June 17th, 1850.

If not, what were to be the duties of the Viceroy in future ? What were to be the relations of the Irish Government to the Home Office, and generally ? What changes, if any, should be made in the management of Irish affairs ? George III. was opposed to the immediate abolition of the Viceroyalty. He wrote to the Prime Minister, Addington :—

> " Mr. Addington must not think that the King will unnecessarily take up his time with letters ; but, at the outset of our business, it would be highly wrong to have anything omitted that occurs. The more the King reflects on the conversation of last night and the proposed arrangements, the more he approves of them. But he blames himself in having omitted to mention the natural, nay, necessary, return of the Marquess Cornwallis from Ireland. He well knows many have thought the office of Lord Lieutenant should altogether cease on such an event. The King's opinion is, clearly, that perhaps hereafter that may be proper, but that at present it is necessary to fill up that office with a person that shall clearly understand that the Union has closed the reign of Irish jobs ; that he is a kind of President of the Council there ; and that the civil patronage may be open to his recommendation, but must entirely be decided in England."

It is amusing to turn from this reference to "jobs" to the following entry in Lord Colchester's diary.*

> " The whole patronage of the army in Ireland will be here under the Duke of York "

—the son of the King, the enemy of Catholic Emancipation, and a man whose jobs at one time caused so much scandal that in 1809 he was forced to resign his

* Lord Colchester, as Mr. Abbot, was, it will be remembered, Chief Secretary for Ireland in 1801.

position as commander-in-chief of the forces in England.*

Lord Colchester proceeds :—

> " There is to be no Secretary of State for Ireland : the Secretary of State for the Home Department will do the State business for Ireland since the Union. The signet now held by Lord Castlereagh is to be separated from the office of Chief Secretary ; and perhaps (if the King will consent) it will be given to Lord Castlereagh as a sinecure for his life ; but he will have no concern in the office of Chief Secretary, which will be the efficient office, and is intended for me with the rank of Privy Councillor, at the fixed salary of £4,000 a year, and £500 more for travelling expenses, making the whole (as I was told originally) between £4,000 and £5,000 a year. The office of Chief Secretary will not vacate my seat, as it is supposed to be in the ostensible gift of the Lord Lieutenant."

When it was decided to retain the Lord Lieutenancy, the English Minister seems to have suggested that the powers of the office ought to be abridged. A correspondence passed on this subject between the Castle and Downing Street. Lord Hardwicke, the first Union Viceroy, was not opposed to a certain abridgment of his powers ; but he was strongly of opinion that the office of Viceroy should be something more than a pageant and a name. He wrote to the Cabinet :—

> " Lord Hardwicke has endeavoured to consider the extent of authority proposed to be assigned to the office of Lord Lieutenant, and the line

* The Duke of York made promotions in the army under the influence of Mrs. Clarke, a lady to whom he was attached. The Duke was subsequently restored to the office of Commander-in-Chief. See account of the transaction in Mr. Percy Fitzgerald's " Royal Dukes and Princesses of the family of George III," Vol. 2, p. 117, *et seq.*

most expedient to be taken in any reduction of it which may be necessary. In regard to the limits of patronage, Lord Hardwicke feels it his duty to pay the greatest deference to the opinion which seems to be entertained of the impossibility of defining with precision the extent of the patronage proper to be vested in a Lord Lieutenant ; but he is unable to satisfy himself upon that point, inasmuch as in the patent delivered to him, and to every preceding Lord Lieutenant, a clear and distinct line is drawn, by reserving to the Crown certain enumerated honours and offices, and leaving all others to the absolute disposal of the Lord Lieutenant. Lord Hardwicke however has always been perfectly disposed to admit the necessity, upon true Union principles, of abridging in some degree the patronage which has hitherto been annexed to the office. The following are the offices which the Crown, by the terms of the patent, has hitherto thought fit to reserve to its own immediate disposal :—

" 1.—Chancellor.
" 2.—Treasurer and Under-Treasurer : two Lords Commissioners of the Treasury.
" 3.—Judges.
" 4.—Attorney and
" 5.—Solicitor-General.
" 6.—Military Governors.
" 7.—Archbishops.
" 8.—Bishops.
" 9.—Deans.

" In addition to these, Lord Hardwicke conceives, and submits it to the consideration of His Majesty's ministers, that it may be very proper and expedient to enlarge this enumeration in the patent and to leave in the hands of His Majesty's ministers the following honours and offices, divesting the Lord Lieutenant of the power which he has hitherto been permitted to exercise in regard to any of them :—

" 1.—All honours exclusively (excepting the discretionary and occasional use of ordinary knighthood).

" 2.—Privy Councillors.

" 3.—Privy Seal.

" 4.—Chancellor of the Exchequer.*

" 5.—Clerks of the Pells.

" 6.—Auditor.

" 7.—Teller.

" 8.—Postmaster-General.

" 9.—Provost of Trinity College.

" If his Majesty's ministers should think it advisable to leave the remaining patronage in the hands of the Lord Lieutenant, upon public grounds and for public uses, Lord Hardwicke will endeavour to the best of his ability to conduct the King's Government in Ireland ; and desires it may be explicitly understood, that it will be his invariable object to employ these means for the advancement of His Majesty's interests, and the support of the measures of His Administration. If any other line be taken, he cannot forbear expressing his strong apprehension that a greater reduction of the patronage hitherto entrusted to the Lord Lieutenant may prove materially injurious to the general influence of Government by lessening the respect due to the office of Lord Lieutenant, and by depriving him of the means of conciliating and attaching the supporters of the King's Government, and of rewarding the meritorious services of persons unconnected with Parliamentary interest.

* From the Union up till 1817, Ireland had a separate Exchequer. In 1817, the Exchequers were united, and the English Chancellor of the Exchequer henceforth represented both countries.

" It is proper to be observed that the description of patronage which, upon this view of the subject, will remain with him, is the more necessary to be left in the hands of the Lord Lieutenant, as, since the Union of the two countries, and the consolidation of the army, the whole of the military patronage has been taken from him. Lord Hardwicke perfectly concurs in the opinion that the Lord Lieutenant must be the only acknowledged channel of communication between Ireland and the Government of the Empire. He also agrees to the propriety of leaving to the Lord Lieutenant a power of ordering the movement of troops for the purpose of preserving the peace.

" With regard to the patent and instructions to the Lord Lieutenant, which it is proposed to alter ' in every point which gives a separate and independent authority,' Lord Hardwicke thinks it necessary now to state that the following powers, as given by the patent and instructions, are, in his opinion, essential to the authority of a Lord Lieutenant, and necessary to be recognised and continued :—

" 1.—The power of pardoning crimes (except treason against the King's life), of remitting fines, and issuing proclamations for regulating the police.

" 2.—Of ordering issues of money from the Treasury, and

" 3.—Compelling accountable officers to account to the Exchequer.

" He is equally of opinion, and submits it accordingly, that the following powers and directions contained in the instructions (which appear to have been originally drawn with great equity and wisdom) are also necessary to be retained.

" *Article* 1.—Inquiry into the state of the Kingdom.

" *2nd.*—Settling Church matters, and bestowing Crown livings upon proper persons.

" *4th.*—Calling upon the Commissioners of the Revenue to give an account of their proceedings in the management of their Commission, and the execution of their trust.

" *20th Article.*—' Offices reserved to the Crown not to be filled up without communication with the Lord Lieutenant.'

" Having specified these articles of the patent and instructions as necessary to be retained, Lord Hardwicke is equally impressed with the propriety of communicating with His Majesty's ministers upon any of the points herein contained of public and general importance previously to his making any definite arrangement concerning them. Lord Hardwicke understands, with much satisfaction, that it is the intention of His Majesty's confidential servants, that the grace of communicating the grant of favours from the Crown, in regard to all civil appointments in Ireland, shall be vested exclusively in the Lord Lieutenant ; and to this circumstance Lord Hardwicke attaches considerable importance, as it will clearly manifest to His Majesty's subjects in Ireland a system of cordial and entire co-operation in all the acts and intentions of His Majesty's Ministers, in respect to this part of the United Kingdom.

" Upon these principles, therefore, Lord Hardwicke feels fully disposed to concede and relinquish all the remaining powers in the patent and instructions, with which his sovereign was graciously pleased to invest him."*

The Home Secretary, Lord Pelham, wished to clip the wings of the Viceroy, but the Prime Minister,

---

* Lord Colchester's " Diary." In reference to Lord Hardwicke's Administration generally, see Mr. MacDonagh's excellent book " A Viceroy's Post Bag."

Mr. Addington, was apparently in favour of maintaining the *status quo*. Colonel Littlehales, the Under-Secretary for Civil affairs, reports a conversation with him thus :—

> " He appeared to think that any alteration in the present form of Government in that country [Ireland] was entirely, at this period, out of the question ; and, on my observing that it seemed requisite not to diminish the due and proper weight, influence, and dignity, which ought necessarily to attach to the Viceroy, as any degradation of actual authority would tend to lessen the King's interests in Ireland, he stated generally, that his opinions went to strengthen, as far as was consistent and right, the consequence of the Lord Lieutenant, to enable him to administer impartially, and with temperance, energy, and decision, the public concerns of that country."

Generally the views of Lord Hardwicke (which prevailed), were these ; that large discretionary powers should be given to the Lord Lieutenant, but that on all important questions he should consult the Cabinet by direct communication with the Prime Minister. Nevertheless the Castle was not to be in any sense an adjunct of the English Home Office, or of any other English Department.

" It is much too soon," his Excellency says, with delightful naïveté,

> " to consider Ireland on the footing of an English county." *

---

* Pelham, in his paper to Lord Hardwicke, says that the Irish Executive must direct its chief attention to the " police of the country, but acting in immediate subordination to the General Executive Government of the Empire."

He also says :

> " All reports touching the internal state of the country from the judges and other officers, as well military as civil,

No doubt, considering that the English army of occupation at the time numbered over 50,000 men, his Excellency had not much difficulty in satisfying the Prime Minister that Ireland was not yet reduced to the condition of an English county—that Cork was not York.

The following important extract from the diary of the Chief Secretary of the day will give a fair idea of the extent of the power and the work of the Castle :—

" In consequence of general conversations with Mr. Addington, and also upon this point with Mr. Pelham before I left England, I issued circular orders in the month of August, calling upon all the departments of Government, civil and military, in the Lord Lieutenant's name, to make returns of their establishments, duties, salaries, etc., in the same manner I had practised in the British Parliament when Chairman of the Finance Committee. Several returns to these orders were made during the time of my continuance in Ireland, but very reluctantly, and sometimes evasively. Those from the Customs and Excise were very imperfectly delivered, within a few days only of my departure from Dublin.

" Some Boards, however, underwent revision, and were considerably reformed. The Revenue Board was divided into Customs and Excise, according to a plan long ago proposed under successive Lords Lieutenant, but never till now executed. The two senior Commissioners were superannuated, and others appointed to the head

---

whose duty it is to furnish them, should be made to the Lord Lieutenant and the substance of them, when deemed of importance sufficient to merit the attention of the Imperial Government, should be conveyed by him to the Secretary of State for the Home Department."

"Lord Colchester's Diary."

It would, however, seem that in cases of emergency the Lord Lieutenant could act on his own responsibility.

of each separate Board, with the addition of two new Surveyors-General. By an examination of the different Reports formerly made by Commissioner Beresford (who stayed in the North of Ireland during all this autumn), and by further inquiries through Mr. Croker, the Acting Surveyor-General of the Port of Dublin, the frauds long extensively practised upon the Quay of Dublin were greatly checked, and a stricter discipline established throughout this department, where, by the confession of all principal Commissioners, taken down by myself in writing, it had been shamefully and corruptly relaxed.

" The Board of Accounts was instructed in making up its annual account of defaulters according to the modes used in England.

" The Stamp Office was new modelled throughout, and the consignments to distributors, as well as their form of appropriation in their returns, were settled in a way to be practically correct and useful. This office (like the English Stamp Office), having the management of a revenue which had risen gradually from small beginnings to a considerable degree of importance, had been wholly neglected and produced little.

" The Board of Works, whose accounts had not been settled for many years, and whose conduct, under Lord Tyrawley, was demonstrated to be criminally negligent, if not corrupt, was made the subject of a special inquiry by three Commissioners, viz., the Right Hon. Sackville Hamilton, the Right Hon. Richard Annesley, and the Hon. Colonel Napier, Comptrollers of Army Accounts ; and upon their report the office was new-modelled, and directed to act according to a new set of instructions framed under the Lord Lieutenant's particular direction.

" The Military Finance was, by a long negotiation between the War Offices of England

and Ireland, assimilated in many important points.

" Several other matters were brought under the consideration of Government during the same period. The distilleries, fisheries, mines, canals and harbours, and the state of the public charities and hospitals in Dublin, and the condition of the poor throughout Ireland.

" The question of opening the distilleries after the dearth of grain in the preceding years, produced a long and detailed despatch from the Lord-Lieutenant to Lord Pelham, in which, by the aid of Mr. Corry, the general taxes were fully discussed, and the particular circumstances of the crisis minutely detailed. This despatch was received with approbation in England, and the distilleries were afterwards opened in both countries.

" The consideration of the state of the Fisheries led to a strong opinion that the Nymph Bank was the only part of the Irish Seas deserving attention, and an experimental survey of the bank was projected for the ensuing season.

" Upon the mines, Mr. Kirman was prevailed upon to draw up the heads of a Bill for establishing a Mining Board, which should bring over from England and the Continent persons sufficiently skilled to work the known mines, and explore others, particularly of coal, which are supposed to abound in different parts of Ireland.

" The Navigation Board, having received various plans for extending the canals and improving the navigation of the Shannon and the Dublin Harbour, new surveys of the Shannon were ordered, and Mr. Rennie was brought over to survey and report upon Dublin Harbour ; which he did accordingly, with remarks upon the plans of Sir Thomas Page and others, who had been antecedently employed for the same object.

" The public charities and hospitals of Dublin were recommended to Parliament for an augmentation of their annual support ; and Lord Hardwicke gave £300, and I gave £200, towards the establishment of a Fever Hospital in Dublin. Lord Hardwicke gave audience in Dublin Castle two days in every week till my arrival. His Excellency then limited his audience days to Tuesday, which was the regular day for holding a Privy Council ; and I gave audience twice a week ; besides attending in Dublin Castle every day in the week, from eleven till five o'clock.

" The Lord Lieutenant attended divine service, with his family, at the Castle Chapel, till it was shut up to be repaired or rebuilt ; and then he went regularly from the Park to St. Werburgh's, the parish church of the Castle. He gave public entertainments in St. Patrick's Hall, and in the state apartments in the Castle ; and kept up a splendid table at the Park, to which all persons of distinction belonging to the different branches of Government in Dublin, and those who passed through it to or from England, were constantly invited. In the Castle a library was formed of books upon Irish affairs and British history and politics, into which the collection formerly belonging to the Irish House of Lords was brought, and many parliamentary reports and papers were added to it from England.

" The Parliament House was sold during this period to the Governors and Company of the Bank of Ireland, for £40,000 ; with a private agreement that the two Chambers of Parliament should be accommodated to the uses of the Bank in some such manner as should completely alter their former size and appearance.

" The invalids of the Royal Hospital at Kilmainham were placed upon a more liberal allowance of clothing and diet, with the intention of giving them advantages equal to those of Chelsea Hospital.

"A complete survey of the City of Dublin was made out by the Commissioners, of wide streets, under my directions ; making out all the actual and intended improvements under their management. And I brought this Board and the Ballast Office to act in conjunction for widening and extending the quays along both sides of the Liffey up to the Barracks and the Royal Hospital."*

The Peel correspondence throws more light on the work of the Castle.

Mr. Parker, says :—

"The ordinary Administration of the Irish Government, at the time when Mr. Peel undertook it [1812], fell into four departments,—civil, military, legal and financial. For civil and for military affairs there were separate Under-Secretaries in Dublin, besides the Under-Secretary in London. Legal business was conducted by the Attorney-General and the Solicitor-General, neither of whom was in Parliament. Finance was in the hands of an Irish Chancellor of the Exchequer, sitting in the House of Commons, but all communications between the Irish and the Imperial Treasuries (as yet separate) passed through the Chief Secretary. He, in short, as the Viceroy's principal adviser, was responsible to the Cabinet and to Parliament for whatever was done or left undone in Ireland."

Peel gives his opinion on what he conceives should be the duties and powers of the Castle, in no uncertain manner. He says :—

"All the experience I have had since I came into office confirms the opinion—which, even

* Colchester "Diary."

without that experience, might, I think, have
been very naturally formed—that in a country
situated and governed as this is, there ought
to be a paramount authority somewhere, an
authority not merely superior to all others, but
one upon which all others are dependent."

That paramount authority was vested in the Lord
Lieutenant and Chief Secretary. Lord Liverpool,
the Prime Minister, clinched the question. He wrote
to Peel :—

> " The Unity of the Government in Ireland under
> the Lord Lieutenant must be preserved ; the
> Chief Secretary is the channel through which the
> power and patronage in Ireland must flow. They
> ought to be exercised, undoubtedly, with every
> attention to those who are at the head of other
> departments ; and with mutual good under-
> standing, there need never be any material diffi-
> culty. Without it, there must always be a ques-
> tion of authority or conflict."

The Irish Chancellor of the Exchequer wished to
cut his department adrift from the Castle, and to
communicate directly with the Cabinet. But Peel
would not have it, neither would the Prime Minister.
Peel wrote to Liverpool :—

> " And why should not other departments,
> as well as the Treasury, seek for the transfer
> to themselves exclusively of that authority which
> is held by the Lord Lieutenant ? I think that
> the Commander of the Forces might with equal
> reason protest against all interference with the
> military under his command, and against the
> correspondence which the Chief Secretary carries
> on with the Generals in command of districts,
> and might require that all applications for de-
> tachments and military assistance in aid of the
> civil power should be made to him."

Peel was determined to hold all the strings of Government in his own hands.   He interfered in all departments.   He writes to Sir Edward Littlehales, the Military Under-Secretary :—

> " The more my attention is turned to the barrack department the more I am satisfied that a radical reform is necessary."

Indeed he tells us himself that :—

> " We do exercise a much greater control over the military than is exercised by any civil authority in Great Britain."

He writes in reference to the Stamps Department :—

> " I think Mr. O. should be dismissed, the appointment of his successor offered to Lord E., and the stamps informed that the ground of their recommendation was not satisfactory."

He discovers frauds in the Customs, and reprimands the Grand Canal Company, because they

> " have descended to unworthy and ungrateful artifices."

He condemns the Teller of the Exchequer who was in receipt of £2,000 a year, for discharging his duties by deputy, and he finds fault with malversation in the yeomanry corps.   He criticises the Pension List, and has a fling at the Public Works and Grand Jury.

> " I return those ponderous and lengthy documents which accompany the Skibbereen Report. I have toiled through them, and the chief impression which they have left on my mind is one of surprise at the zeal and devotion with which a respectable body of men [the Grand Jury of the County of Cork] have laboured in defence of as notorious a job as ever graced the annals of Irish history.   As they are a party to it, however, there is perhaps no great cause for surprise.

" I think we have done our duty in pressing
for an inquiry, and I have no doubt the publicity
which has been given to this case, the suspension of advances, the charge of the judges, etc.,
will do some good. The more I see of the
system, the more I am convinced of its radical
defects."

At this time and afterwards the Castle was everything. Indeed no one did more than Peel to consoli-
date its strength, and to intensify its unpopularity.
But it must not be supposed that the Castle has always
done everything on its own initiative. One now-a-days
often meets Englishmen—converted Englishmen—
who speak as if the Castle were always pulling one
way—a malevolent way—and the Cabinet pulling
another, and, of course, a benevolent way. These
persons would fain persuade one that the Cabinet had
so to say come *down* to govern Ireland ; while the
Castle had come up. But there has always been as
much brimstone stored in Downing Street as on Cork
Hill. I, for one, shall not paint the officials in the
Castle all black, and the Ministers in England all white.
Castle and Cabinet are *particeps criminis* in the Administration of Ireland, with the difference that the
Cabinet is the predominant partner.

At the " Union " the principle was laid down that
the " Executive " in Ireland should be " subordinate,"
to the " Central Executive of the Empire," and this
principle has always been acted on. The Cabinet has
been advised of all that is done, and of all that is going
to be done at the Castle, and this practice has been
observed not only upon questions of the first importance, but in reference to matters which, one would
suppose, might very well be left to the discretion of the
Lord Lieutenant alone. I shall give an illustration.
Lord Mulgrave was sent to Ireland as Lord Lieutenant,
in 1835, with a message of peace. He formed the
tremendous project of asking Daniel O'Connell to dine

at the Vice-Regal lodge. *The Times* was scandalised and wrote :—

> " It has been proved beyond a doubt that Lord Mulgrave has actually invited to dinner that rancorous and foul-mouthed ruffian O'Connell."

King William IV. was indignant, and apparently asked the Prime Minister, Lord Melbourne, whether the Lord Lieutenant intended to make the Irish Leader a Privy Councillor. Melbourne replied :—

> " Viscount Melbourne feels certain that the Lord Lieutenant of Ireland entertains no intention of advancing Mr. O'Connell to the dignity of a Privy Councillor."

He added " That the burden of blame, if blame be justly due," for inviting O'Connell to dinner at the Vice-Regal lodge, should be divided between himself and Lord Mulgrave ; and goes on :—

> " Upon the termination of the Session of Parliament, the Lord Lieutenant of Ireland, being at a distance and perceiving the very effectual support which your Majesty's Government had received from Mr. O'Connell in the House of Commons, very naturally wrote a confidential letter to Viscount Melbourne to inquire what was to be the conduct of the Irish Government towards that individual upon his arrival in Ireland. To this letter Viscount Melbourne immediately replied that there was to be no approach towards him whatever, no correspondence with him, no communication of a political character. The Lord Lieutenant then desired to be informed what he should do with respect to the ordinary intercourse of life, stating that it had been his rule and practice, since he had been in Ireland, to invite to his table every member of Parliament

who passed through Dublin, whatever had been their political opinions, and whatever had been their public conduct. Viscount Melbourne at once and unhesitatingly replied that it was better, in his opinion, not to make Mr. O'Connell an exception from the general rule which had been laid down. Your Majesty will therefore perceive that whether the steps were culpable or not, the Lord Lieutenant of Ireland did not take it without a full sense of its importance, without previously consulting Viscount Melbourne upon the subject, and without receiving Viscount Melbourne's sanction and approbation. Your Majesty will also perceive that this is not a marked attention paid to Mr. O'Connell, inasmuch as he receives it in common with all other members of Parliament."*

The King in his reply said :—

" There may be and are exceptions to all rules ; and His Majesty cannot help considering Mr. O'Connell an exception on the present occasion, inasmuch as he was taught to do so by the government of which Viscount Melbourne and others of his present colleagues were members, when they advised him to denounce Mr. O'Connell in a speech from the throne as a disturber of the public peace."

Though the closeness of the relations between the Castle and the Cabinet, at any given period, depended on special circumstances, and to some extent on the *personnel* of the " Irish " Executive for the time being, yet it may be taken as a rule that constant communciations were kept up between the Executive in Ireland, and the Executive in England, and that there was united action in everything. Let Englishmen of the present day, who are disposed in their

* Sanders, "Lord Melbourne's Papers."

moments of penitence to shift all the blame of Irish misgovernment from the English to the Irish side of the Channel, remember this fact. Lord Beaconsfield once said that the key of India was in London. The key of the " Irish Government " is in Downing Street, and not at the Vice-regal Lodge.

Having so far dealt with the state of affairs at the Castle during the early part of the nineteenth century, we shall now consider the question, how far have the powers of that ancient institution been diminished between the time of Lord Melbourne and the present day. For this purpose I shall now take up the " lengthening chain " of Irish Administration link by link.

I have already said that the " Irish " Executive (Dublin Castle) consists of the Lord Lieutenant, the Chief Secretary and the Under-Secretary.* This

---

* The question is sometimes raised as to the relation of the English Home Secretary to the Irish Executive. I take the following note from Todd's " Parliamentary Government " :

" The Secretary of State for the Home Department has direct supervision over all matters relating to the internal affairs of Great Britain and Ireland ; but England is such a self-governing country that a large proportion of admintrative business is transacted without the necessity of his immediate control. His duties and responsibilities are principally confined to the maintenance of the internal peace of the United Kingdom, the security of the laws, and the general oversight in the administration of criminal justice . . . His authority extends over England, Wales and Scotland, the Channel Islands and the Isle of Man, and he is the organ of communication between the Cabinet and the vice-regal government of Ireland, for which he is deemed personally responsible ; and though he does not interfere actively in lesser matters, he is informed of and advises upon all the more important measures adopted in that country. . . The following political officers, all of whom are usually in Parliament, are subordinate to the Home Secretary ; *i.e,*. the parliamentary Under-Secretary for the Home Department, the two law officers of the Crown, the President and Secretary of the Poor Law Board, the Chief Secretary for Ireland, and the Attorney-General for Ireland and the Lord Advocate for Scotland.

" There are two Under-Secretaries—one permanent and the other parliamentary. The former has charge of law

is speaking by the card. But for practical purposes
I must expand the definition : I must add the Assistant
Under-Secretary. Nobody will object to that. But
I must also add two other personages ; the Lord
Chancellor and the Attorney-General.

"Oh," it will be asked, "assuredly *they* do not
form part of the Executive ? "

Unquestionably they do ; and not infrequently
exercise a preponderating influence in the Administration.

In 1834, O'Connell wrote to Lord Duncannon, then
Home Secretary :—

> " [The office of Attorney-General] is, you well
> know the most important office in the Admin-
> tration of the Government of Ireland—consulted
> upon everything—advising, guiding, directing
> everything. The Irish Government is identified
> with the Attorney-General."

Mr. Ewald, the biographer of Sir Joseph Napier,
who filled the offices of Attorney-General and Lord
Chancellor of Ireland, says :—

> " In Ireland the influence of the law advisers
> of the Crown is exercised after a more close
> and direct fashion than in England. There the
> Attorney-General is not only the first law officer,
> and as such bound in conjunction with the
> Solicitor-General to advise on all legal matters
> submitted for his opinion, but he is also, unlike
> his brother in England, always a member of the
> Privy Council, and consequently frequently

---

and criminal business, and the general domestic correspondence ; the latter conducts the correspondence with Ireland,
Scotland, and the Channel Islands together with the Parliamentary business and the correspondence connected
therewith" (Vol. II., pp. 499, 504, see also Civil Service
Estimates for the year ending March 31st, 1869, Class II.,
No. 3).

consulted by the Lord Lieutenant on the general policy of the Administration. An Irish Attorney-General, and especially when he has enjoyed . . . much parliamentary experience, is therefore both a law adviser and a general adviser of the Viceroy or Chief Secretary."*

We have an illustration in the life of Blackburne, of how a strong Attorney-General may carry his point with the Executive. In 1841, Blackburne being then Attorney-General, advised that Mr. Brewster should be made law adviser to the Castle. O'Connell strongly objected to the appointment, and raised a storm of criticism. The Government were in consequence shaken in their resolve to follow Blackburne's lead and appoint Brewster.

"The Government," says Mr. Blackburne in the life of his father,

> "continued in a state of great perturbation, and seriously doubted whether they would ratify Mr. Brewster's appointment."

But Blackburne remained firm,

> "and intimated to the Lord Chancellor that he would not tolerate the refusal to ratify his selection."

Ultimately the Lord Lieutenant, the Chief Secretary, the Home Secretary, and even the Prime Minister gave way, and Brewster was appointed. Mr. Blackburne says :—

> "[It is clear] that the minds of the members of the Government were by no means set at rest, and that they questioned very much the wisdom or prudence of the step which they had taken ; and it is plain that, but for the determined attitude

* Ewald, "Life of Sir Joseph Napier," pp. 101 and 102.

of the Attorney-General and the intimation which he gave that his resignation would be the certain result of the refusal of the Government to confirm the appointment, it would have been cancelled with but little hesitation."

Stanley, writing to Blackburne in May, 1832,* says :—

" With regard to the management of Ireland (the only point in which you are *politically* concerned), I cannot anticipate that there will be much change of system, if any."

Melbourne, on another occasion, in his shrewd way, wrote :—

" [The Attorney-General's opinion] is very loose, and, as you will find in all Irish opinions, a great mixture of law and of general political reasoning."†

Finally Sir West Ridgway (formerly Under-Secretary), writing in the *Nineteenth Century* of August, 1905, says :—

" Sir Anthony MacDonnell refused to be guided, except in legal matters, by the law officers. ' These two officers of the King's Government' pathetically, and, of course unselfishly, complained Mr. W. Moore, K.C., ' were shut up in their law rooms in a position very little better than that of Law clerks '—just as if they were mere law officers, like the Attorney-General and Solicitor-General for England ! . . . In my opinion it is very desirable to go still further than Sir Anthony MacDonnell when an oppor-

* Blackburn was first appointed Attorney-General in 1830 ; and re-appointed in 1841.

† Melbourne "Papers."

tunity occurs. Instead of being shut up in their rooms at the Castle, the law officers in question should be domiciled in their law rooms at the Law Courts. Castle lawyers are able and honourable men, but they are saturated with the traditions and steeped in all the prejudices of the *ancien régime*, and the influence which they exercise in political matters upon the Chief Secretary or Under-Secretary fresh from England is not always elevating."*

Let the fact be borne in mind that from time to time the " Irish " Government has so to say been " run " by a single man. Sometimes it has been run by the Lord Chancellor, sometimes by the Attorney-General, sometimes by the Chief Secretary, sometimes by the Under-Secretary. At other times honours have been more equally divided, and every man has taken a turn at the wheel.

Saurin (Attorney-General) ran the Government in the time of the Duke of Richmond. Peel came in 1812. He ran the Government himself plus Saurin. Peel left in 1818. Gregory (Under-Secretary) then ran the Government, again plus Saurin. Saurin was dismissed in 1822 ; then Gregory, though " thwarted " by Wellesley and Grant, ran it single-handed until 1831, when he too was dismissed. Stanley became Chief Secretary in 1830, and Colonel Gossett succeeded Gregory in 1831. Stanley, Gossett and the Attorney-General (Blackburne) ran the Government between them until 1833, when Stanley gave way to Hobhouse. Gossett *plus* Blackburne then ran the Government until 1835, when Blackburne went out with the Tories, and Gossett was dismissed. Thomas Drummond succeeded Gossett, and remained the real ruler of the country until 1840, when he died.

From 1841 to 1846 Peel, the Prime Minister, practically dominated the Amdinistration. These were

*Page 190.

the repeal years, and the country was in a state of crisis all the time. Peel took the wheel himself, and Sir James Graham, the Home Secretary, " stood by." Lord Clarendon (1847-1852) was one of the few Viceroys who was a real force in the Government. He was, in fact as well as in name, the head of the Administration.* The next strong man was General Sir Thomas Larcom, who was Under-Secretary between 1853 and 1868. In his day the Government was compendiously described as Larcom and the police. It was said

" Ireland is governed by a Colonel of Engineers. In the departments, Carlisle [Lord Lieutenant] does the dancing, Horsman [Chief Secretary] the hunting, and Larcom the work."

Mr Burke was Under-Secretary between 1869-1882, and naturally during so long a period of service exercised a commanding influence in the Administration. Lord Spencer was also a real Governor. Sir Edward Sullivan was Solicitor-General (1865-1866), Attorney-General (1866-1869), Master of the Rolls (1869-1883), and Lord Chancellor (1883-1885). I have been informed by one who knew what he was talking about, that no person exercised more authority in the Administration of Ireland, in his day, than this able lawyer. I must add the names of Lord Ashbourne, Lord O'Brien of Kilfinora, and Lord Atkinson, to the list of working Governors and Governors-General of their unfortunate country.

How often has the Attorney-General of the day, on his way to the Courts, dropped in to the Castle, to see if all is going well. How often, too, does the Lord Chancellor on his way back call to discuss high politics with the Under-Secretary or Assistant Under-Secretary.

* Sir William Somerville was Chief Secretary, and Mr. Redding-ton Under Secretary.

" Do you mean to say," I asked one whose evidence
on the point cannot be disregarded, " that the Lord
Chancellor and the Law Officers go to the Castle, as
part of their daily business, to discuss questions of
Administration ? "

" Unquestionably," he answered. " In fact these
things are common knowledge."

" I want to see Lord Ashbourne's room," said
a shrewd Scotchman who visited Dublin Castle when
Lord Ashbourne was on the woolsack. The Scotch
are a very intelligent people.

" Who ran Long ? " I heard one Dublin citizen
ask another.

" John Atkinson, of course," was the answer.

" As for Peter O'Brien," quoted another citizen,
" he ran everything."

" Who ran Gerald Balfour ? " asked a collector
of information.

" He ran himself," was the flattering reply.

" Who runs Birrell ? " " Himself." In fact, there
is nothing so interesting about the Irish Administration as to find out the man who from time to time
runs the show.

I now come to the question, Who practically appoints
the Irish Executive ? The answer is—The Prime
Minister of England, who, as I have before said, may defy,
and often does defy the public opinion of Ireland.
He appoints the Lord Lieutenant. He appoints the
Chief Secretary. He appoints the Lord Chancellor,
the Attorney-General and the Solicitor-General. The
Chief Secretary appoints the Under-Secretary and
the Assistant Under-Secretary, but will scarcely act
in this matter without consultation with the Prime
Minister and the Home Secretary.*

* On the retirement of Saxton from the office of Under-Secretary, Peel wrote to his friend Beckett :

" Now my dear Beckett, let me know what you think of
this. Nothing would give me more real pleasure than if
you could be induced to come here. Remember that I

At p. 349 I state with whom *technically* these appointments rest. Here I state who, in the main, has the actual power. Thus let it be taken at once, that the Irish Executive is appointed by what Mr. Chamberlain would call :—" a foreign government." I wish people, who blame Dublin Castle for everything, would remember this fact.

I now turn to the departments over which the Castle exercises direct control and to the special business which is wholly transacted within its walls. Let me begin with a quotation from O'Connell.

> " [The Castle," he says " is the] centre towards which all persons who have any business to transact with the Government naturally and necessarily turn themselves. The clerks of the Castle, high and low, form the political medium through which all the affairs of the internal regulation of Ireland must pass."

Quite true ; but the shadow of Downing Street overhangs the Castle all the time. The Castle is the

---

want you, as far as I am concerned, to act with, not under, me. The Duke knows nothing of this application, and I only wish to be prepared in case he should consult me."

Peel again writes to Beckett :

" Lord Sidmouth himself apprised me that he was favourably disposed to Mr. Hawthorne. I do not know him ; indeed, I have not seen him ; but should any objections occur to me to his appointment, or should I feel a decided preference in favour of any other individual on public grounds, I should have no difficulty, of course, in stating this to Lord Sidmouth. Whoever is appointed, I must have confidence in him. There is but one alternative, and I should adopt it without a moment's hesitation."—*Parker*.

Of course the Lord Lieutenant nominally appoints the Chief Secretary, but if a particular Lord Lieutenant objected to a particular Chief Secretary, and if the Prime Minister wanted him, the Lord Lieutenant would have to retire or accept. I have heard the case of a Chief Secretary who insisted on a Lord Lieutenant of his own choice, and got his way. Of course the whole question of authority turns upon the man who is in the Cabinet, and the Chief Secretary is, as a rule, in the Cabinet.

centre of the "Irish" Administration ; the Chief Secretary is the centre of the Castle. Let me take him—Pooh-Bah—in compartments.

I. *As Prime Minister.*

In his capacity of Prime Minister, he has practically all the patronage in his hansd.

" Whatever jobs are done in Ireland," once said a Chief Secretary, with a lively appreciation of what was expected of him, " are done by me."

Officialdom hangs on his breath. Every Irishman who hopes to become a servant of the English Crown in any capacity whatever looks to him as an Englishman of the same expectations looks to the Prime Minister of his country. A characteristic story often throws more light on a situation than volumes of narrative. Some twelve months ago I was interested in collecting money to erect a monument to the memory of the Irish Brigade, on the field of Fontenoy. One day I went to the Four Courts. I asked a barrister if he thought I would be likely to get any subscriptions from the bar for the Fontenoy Monument. He smiled, shook his head, and said " I am afraid not."

> I said " Suppose I were to tell the bar that the Fontenoy Monument is just the one thing in which Mr. Birrell takes a real interest."
>
> " Ah," said the barrister, with a twinkle in his eye, " if you tell them that, you will get more money in a day than you will know what to do with."

Well, then, to descend to details. The Chief Secretary practically appoints the Privy Councillors* and exercises the prerogative of mercy. He appoints

---

* Of course technically the Privy Councillors are appointed by the Crown. In England the Crown means the Prime Minister. In Ireland the Crown means the Chief Secretary, the Irish Prime Minister.

the Lord Lieutenant of the county, the High Sheriff of the county,* the Deputy Lieutenants of the county,† the County Court Judge, the resident magistrate, the Clerks of the Crown, the Crown Solicitor, the Clerk of the Peace, and the Clerks of the Petty Sessions,‡ the High Sheriff of the boroughs.§ He appoints the Commissioners of all the principal Boards, the Land Commissioners, the Estates Commissioners, the Inspector-General of Constabulary, the Chief Commissioner of the Dublin Metropolitan Police, the Assistant-Inspector of the Dublin Metropolitan Police, the Keeper of the Records and the Ulster King at Arms.‖

II. *As Home Secretary.*

As Home Secretary it is the duty of his office to receive and answer a variety of communications

---

* Three names are sent to the Lord Lieutenant by the going Judges of Assize for the county and he, advised by the Chief Secretary, selects one.

† The Deputy Lieutenants of the county are selected by the Lord Lieutenant of the county, subject to the approval of the Viceroy.

‡ Technically the Clerk is appointed by the magistrates, subject to the approval of the Lord Lieutenant.

§ The Municipal Council sends up three names to the Lord Lieutenant, who selects one.

‖ The following appointments are made by King's letter alone, but, in effect, on the recommendation of the Chief Secretary:
Vice-President Local Government Board.
Commissioners Local Government Board.
Clerk of the Crown and Hanaper.
The Presidents, Professors and Deans of Residences of the Queen's Colleges.
Commissioner of Charitable Donations and Bequests.
Senators of the Royal University.
Congested Districts Board.
Land Commissioners.
Estates Commissioners.
Officers of the Order of St. Patrick (other than Ulster).

—*Post*, p. 349.

similar to those made to the Home Department
in England, and, in addition to them, reports
from the Constabulary, and a large daily correspondence with the local and stipendiary magistrates as well as all applications addressed to the
Government on the state of the country. It
is also the duty of the office to bring under the
notice of the Lord Lieutenant all correspondence
of an important nature which requires his personal
attention, and also to communicate regularly
with several public departments of the Government both in Dublin and London.

" Every man with a grievance," it has been
said, " writes to the Lord Lieutenant."

The Chief Secretary as Home Secretary ought to
deal with these " grievances " by letter, or interview,
or by both.
" But," asks the intelligent foreigner, " does the
Chief Secretary do all these things ? "
Not quite, considering that he spends only about
three months of the year in the country. These things
are in fact chiefly done by the Under-Secretary* and
the Assistant Under-Secretary, the permanent officials
who are always on the spot.
" What," again asks the intelligent foreigner, " are
the relations between the Castle as Home Office ? or
Home Department, with say the magistracy unpaid and
paid ? "
Ordinarily speaking, the unpaid magistrates in
Ireland act, in the discharge of their duties, independently of the Castle, as magistrates in England
act in the discharge of their duties, independently
of the Home Office ; that is to say, a magistrate will
not communicate with the Castle before fining a man
for being drunk and disorderly. But, suppose the

* See M'Lennan, "Memoirs of Thomas Drummond," p. 250.

man, while drunk and disorderly had said, " To hell with the Pope," or " To hell with the King," then I know not what might happen.* The question might perhaps be raised to the dignity of a political issue ; and the introduction of politics in any degree into the administration of affairs in Ireland makes all the difference.

At one time there was an official at the Castle called the Law Adviser who used to advise the magistracy on all knotty questions. Speaking of him, Lord Russell of Killowen said :—

> " There was another official at the Castle, one occupying so anomalous a position that I will just refer to him.   This is the Law Adviser, a member of the bar, who is in direct communication with the whole of the magistrates throughout Ireland, who write to him for advice on all matters in which there is anything doubtful, and on that advice they shaped their course ; and I contend that this connection between the magistrates and the Executive is prejudicial in principle, and highly to be condemned in practice."†

It must not be forgotten in considering political issues, that owing to historical causes, which have been at work for centuries, the course of " law and order " is intercepted by political currents, which are unknown on the English side of St. George's Channel.

That is the whole question.

" What were those boys doing ? " I heard a solicitor ask a policeman before a bench of magistrates, in a

---

* A witty barrister once said that there were only two parties in Ireland worth considering : the party of " To hell with the Pope," and the party of " To hell with the King."

† The last Law Adviser was Mr. Naish, in 1886. On the abolition of the office a Crown Solicitor (who also has his office in the Castle), was appointed instead, as Chief Crown Solicitor for Ireland.

case where a number of youths were charged with treasonable practices.

" They were marching," said the policeman.

" Were they doing anything else," asked the lawyer.

" They were cheering," was the reply.

" For whom were they cheering ? " pressed the lawyer.

" For Brian Boru," was the answer.

One is reminded of Lord Rosebery's saying :—

> " The Irish question has never passed into history, for it has never passed out of politics."

The matter might be put in another way ; in Ireland historical issues are living issues. Lord Rosebery could unveil a statue of William Wallace ; could Mr. Asquith unveil a statue of Wolfe Tone ?

But to return to the concrete question of the Castle and the Magistracy.

The Castle may on occasion interfere, and interfere sharply, with the magistracy. I shall give an illustration. In 1837, Colonel Verner, Deputy Lieutenant of the County Tyrone, gave the toast of the battle of the Diamond* at a public dinner, where the company included many magistrates. Drummond, who was then Under-Secretary, sent a circular letter to Colonel Verner and the other magistrates, asking if the newspaper report was true, and

> " whether it could be possible that you were thus a party to the commemoration of a lawless and most disgraceful conflict."

The other magistrates replied that they were not present when the toast was proposed. Verner " parried the question," refusing to say yes or no. Then Drummond, the Chief Secretary (Morpeth), and the Attorney-General (Woulfe), took counsel together,

* At a place called the Diamond in the County Armagh, there was a conflict between Protestants and Catholics in the year 1795.

and despatched a joint letter (signed by Morpeth), to the recalcitrant magistrate, containing this passage :—

" It is the invariable practice when any representation is made to Government affecting the character and usefulness of a magistrate or other public officer, for whose appointment or continuance the Executive Government is responsible, to communicate such representation to him before any proceedings are taken thereon, that he may have an opportunity of explaining or disavowing the statements made to his prejudice. That course was followed in the present instance, and his Excellency conceives that he had a right to expect a distinct and unequivocal avowal or disavowal of your having been a party to the proceedings in question, or a satisfactory explanation that the nature and tendency of the proceedings did not deserve the character imputed to it. His Excellency deems the public considerations dependent upon this transaction to be of such importance, that he is less inclined to remark upon the extraordinary tone in which your whole letter is written, considering that it is an answer to an official communication, addressed by direction of Her Majesty's representative, to a gentleman holding a commission of the peace, and requiring an explanation of his conduct. Upon a full consideration of the case, his Excellency will deem it expedient to recommend to the Lord Chancellor that you should not be included in the new commission of the peace about to be issued, and will also direct your name to be omitted from the revised list of Deputy Lieutenants for the county of Tyrone.

" MORPETH."

In 1843, the Lord Chancellor dismissed Lord French from the Commission of the Peace, for "connecting himself with a political movement [the Repeal Movement] respecting which the Executive Government had so recently declared the hostility of the Crown, and which collected bodies of the people so multitudinous that they had an inevitable tendency to a breach of the peace."*

Some ten other magistrates were dismissed at the same time for the same reason.

Drummond may or may not have been right, in removing Verner from the commission of the peace, the Lord Chancellor may or may not have been right in removing Lord French and his colleagues ; but right or wrong the essential fact is that the English ruler of Ireland for the time being can decide in a given case whether the conduct of a magistrate is or is not open to censure, and can deal with the " offender " accordingly without the slightest reference to Irish public opinion. The Castle, backed by the Cabinet, dominated by English public opinion, is omnipotent. Ireland does not count. No doubt in the case of Verner, Drummond acted in accordance with Irish opinion. But Drummond was an exceptional man. He flung English public opinion to the winds ; was just and feared not. Of course, he would have been powerless had he not been supported by the Cabinet ; which, be it remembered, owed its existence to the Irish vote. Since the Union, however, there have been only three such Cabinets : (1) The Melbourne Ministry, 1835, 1841 ; (2) The Gladstone Ministry, 1886 ; (3) Gladstone Ministry, 1892-5.

In Drummond's time (as before and afterwards) the unpaid magistrates were landlords and Protestants almost to a man. They were partizans, they were corrupt, they were the enemies of the people. They could not be trusted to dispense even-handed justice. Accordingly, Drummond sent out stipendiaries (who

* Gavan Duffy, "Young Ireland."

were appointed, and removable by the Castle), to keep the local magnates in check. Those stipendiaries knew what was expected of them. They were aware that there was a strong resolute man in the Castle, who was determined that justice should be done. The stipendiaries did it, and, for the time, gave the people confidence in the law.

"Grossly," says Drummond, "have the local magistrates abused their power in many—in very many—instances; but their wings are clipped, and I hope and believe that there is some chance of justice being better administered soon, and ultimately being well administered. The confidence of the people will be regained; though given to the Government [of Lord Melbourne] now, it is withheld from their local courts, and no wonder."

After Drummond's death the old order of things was revived, the Castle resumed its original position as the executive of a foreign state established to check popular movements and to hold the nation down. The stipendiaries did what was expected of them under Drummond; and they continued to do what was expected of them under his successors. Drummond, so to say, pressed a spring in Dublin Castle and the whole administration responded to his touch. His successors pressed the same spring, and the administration once more responded to the touch, but with different results. In the one case the rights of an oppressed people were guarded; in the other the interests of a corrupt and tyrannical oligarchy were upheld. The popular confidence which the stipendiaries had for a time inspired was soon lost, and in our own day—under the *régime* of Mr. Forster and of Mr. Arthur Balfour—these officials became the most detested class in the community.

Poor Forster, it is impossible not to feel sympathy for him. Never did a man mean better, never did a man fail more deplorably. In O'Connell's time the Executive and the people stood face to face. In Forster's time the situation was the same. The Habeas Corpus Act was suspended. Forster was enthroned as an autocrat, with unbridled powers.

" The Irish Executive," he said, " must have power to shut up any person they consider dangerous."

That power was given to him.

" They talk," he said, " of the Czar of Russia, but the Czar was not more of a personal and absolute ruler than I was."

Like Drummond he brought the stipendiaries into action, but unlike Drummond, he placed them in antagonism to the people. He wrote to the Prime Minister :—

> " I am planning also another step, which I hope to carry out this week, which is to divide the district counties into, say, six districts, and to appoint in each district a temporary commissioner who shall be responsible to me."

Thus the " special magistrates," as they were called, came into existence. We have a picture of the Irish Executive of those days from the pen of one who seems to have had special knowledge on the subject :—

> " A long mahogany table," says *Veritas*, " with writing materials, and about a dozen dismal chairs, upholstered in black-hair cloth, are the only articles of furniture visible. Here have I seen assembled the great ones of the Irish Executive. The Lord Lieutenant himself, the Chief and Under-Secretaries, the Attorney and Solicitor-General, the Law Adviser, and Castle Attorney. Somehow, I thought that the majority of them were not much at ease, and did not take kindly to the Star Chamber business. Mr. Forster

was the leading spirit. The proceedings were of a very brief and simple character. No oath was administered. The Sub-Inspector told his story, which went to show that A. B. was suspected to be the perpetrator of some outrage ; the Resident Magistrate was then asked his opinion, and, if he concurred, Mr. Forster simply pronounced the words :—

" ' Let a warrant issue,' and next day the gates of Kilmainham closed upon another suspect. Such was government as practised by Forster and Co. ; such was their coercion."

And what did it all end in—Habeas Corpus Suspension Act, Arms Act, Special Magistrates, solemn conclaves in the Castle, *Lettres de Cachet* consigning hundreds of suspected persons (whom Mr. Forster thought " dangerous.") to Kilmainham and other gaols, the imprisonment of the Irish leader himself— What did it all end in ? Simply this : After twelve months of " Czardom," the English Prime Minister practically dismissed Mr. Forster, and made a " Treaty " with the " arch Irish rebel Parnell," whom Forster had vainly tried to crush.* In its most tragic efforts there is almost always a touch of comedy in the operations of the English *Raj* in Ireland. After all Mr. Ritchie perhaps is right.

" Imbecility " is the dominant characteristic of English rule in what with unconscious irony is so often called the " sister isle."

The stipendiary magistrate is not naturally a vicious person. His sins are the sins of the system which he is called upon to administer. He obeys orders.

* The Treaty—the Treaty of Kilmainham, as it was called —came to this ; the Government agreed to bring in a Bill to wipe away the arrears of rent due by the tenant to the landlord, and Mr. Parnell agreed to use his influence to keep the country quiet. He was released in April, 1882. Mr. Forster did not approve of the Kilmainham Treaty. The Kilmainham Treaty —made over his head by the Prime Minister—practically meant his dismissal.

Sometimes he receives precise instructions from the Castle, sometimes he is left a free hand.

" I may here notice," wrote Lord Cowper to the Cabinet, when he was Lord Lieutenant,

> " that complaint has been made of the troops being exposed to stoning without being allowed to act in return. A certain amount of this may be unavoidable, but troops, in my opinion, should never be brought face to face with the mob unless they are intended to act. It is not fair for the troops, and it diminishes the moral effect upon the people. The police should, if possible, be employed in preference, as they can use their batons, which they are not afraid to use, and which inflict just the right sort of chastisement.
>
> " *These are the general principles which are impressed upon each Resident Magistrate, but as to details he must, of course, in each individual instance use his own discretion.*"*

The " discretion," which the stipendiary exercises, depends upon what he knows the Castle expects from him ; and the Castle expects what the English Cabinet desires. The chain of causation runs thus : the stipendiary looks to the Castle, the Castle looks to the Cabinet, the Cabinet looks to English public opinion. To-day the order may go forth : " Do not let the police baton the peasants," ; to-morrow it may be : " Do not hesitate to shoot."† But whether the peasants break the heads of the police, or the police break the heads of the peasants, Irish public opinion is not considered one way or another in the matter. Police or peasants are made the victims of the hour as it best suits the exigencies of party warfare in England.

* The italics are mine.

† A message reported to have been once sent to the Police by a Divisional Commissioner.

When there is a truce in the struggle between the Irish people and the English Government—a struggle which sometimes assumes one form and sometimes another, but which in one form or another is almost incessantly going on—the stipendiary is allowed a freer hand. But the chain of the Castle —be it a lengthening chain, or a shortening chain, is always round his neck. I had a conversation on this subject with an intelligent "loyal" Dublin citizen, and I think his views whether right or wrong should be set forth.

I said, " Drummond (so to say) pressed a spring at Dublin Castle, and the whole Administration responded to the touch. Is the spring still in Dublin Castle ? '

He said, " Yes, certainly."

I said, " The spring is there whether it is touched or not ? "

He said, " Certainly."

I asked, " Is it touched as much as it probably was in Drummond's time ? "

He said, " No ; for instance, take the case of the magistracy in Drummond's time. The magistracy were constantly in touch with the Castle and at a later period even, it was the case. At one time there was a Law Adviser in the Castle, and the magistrates used frequently to seek advice in the administration of their work from him, so that it was part of his duty to advise the magistrates, but that is not so now, and the magistrates are left completely free—the Castle does not interfere with them. The Law Adviser-ship was abolished in 1886, and the practice has been changed since. The magistrates, stipendiary magistrates, make a report to the Castle once a month. These reports are nothing in particular. They are signed by————and they are initialled by the Under-Secretary, or in his absence by the Assistant Under-Secretary, to show that the matter has come under their observation."

I asked, " With reference to the action of magistrates in the country, are they not likely to be influenced in what they do by the policy which they think may prevail at the Castle ? "

He said, " Yes, that is quite true. There is no doubt that the opinion of the Castle is reflected in their action in the country."

I said, " In other words, they are influenced by the opinion of the Castle, magistrates and police ? "

He said, " Yes ; that is so."

I said, " That is not the case in England."

" Ah, yes ! " he said ; that, of course is true, because in England you have Local Government, and police and magistrates act in their particular district without reference to the central authority."

" In Ireland," I said, " the case is different. The central authority has clearly a constant pull."

I also had a conversation with an ex-R.M., and it is right that his statement should be set forth, too.

" The Castle does not now exercise control over the R.M's. Previously it did. In the troubled times Forster appointed six Special Commissioners, those Special Commissioners controlled the R.M's. I, myself, was an R.M. I was under the control of a Special Commissioner ; the Commissioner received instructions from the Castle and conveyed the instructions to me. I had to carry out what the Special Commissioner directed. The Castle instructed the Special Commissioner, and the Special Commissioner instructed me : that was the procedure. I condemned the procedure and submitted a paper on the subject to the Chief Secretary of the day, and on his representation the practice was abolished. Now the Resident Magistrates are perfectly free, they have to report themselves, sometimes they are directed by the Castle to attend a particular Petty Sessions, but when they get there, they do whatever they think right without any reference to the Castle.

" Suppose a transaction takes place under the Statute of Edward III. this would be the procedure as a rule ; the Sergeant would report any matter which he thought deserving of attention to the District Inspector ; the District Inspector would report it to the County Inspector, the County Inspector would report it to the Inspector General, the Inspector General would send it to the Under-Secretary, the Under-Secretary if he thought it necessary would consult the Law Officers, and then the Inspector-General would communicate the decision to the local authorities."

The whole matter comes to this. The Castle is master of the situation. To-day the Resident Magistrate may have a free hand ; to-morrow he may be instructed in almost every detail of his work. The Castle has the power, whether the power be exercised or held in abeyance. One Chief Secretary appointed the Special Commissioners ; another abolished them, a third may re-appoint them to-morrow. But let the Castle act as it may, Irish public opinion has nothing to do in the business. That is the main point, to which, at every turn in the winding course of Irish Administration, we inevitably come back. To sum up : the Resident Magistrate is the servant of the Crown ; and in Ireland the servant of the Crown is never the servant of the people. In England the case is different. There the servant of the Crown and the servant of the people are convertible terms.

I now pass to the *Royal Irish Constabulary.*

The *Royal* Irish Constabulary is directly under the control of the Castle.

" The Police Force," said Sir Thomas Larcom. " became (under Drummond's hands), an almost perfect machine, which, like a delicate musical instrument, responded at once from the remotest part of Ireland to his touch in Dublin Castle."

What the police force was in Drummond's time, it is still—*facile princeps*, a Castle organisation. The Chief Secretary is practically supreme. The Inspector-General could not so much as dismiss a man in the ranks without the authority of the Castle. Of course there may be cases in which the police would act on their own responsibility ; but the political rocks which are always ahead have to be avoided. What is a political rock ? I wonder that the Irish Executive have never issued an official catechism to the police (perhaps they have, I don't know), defining what are politics, and what are not. It would be interesting to see a policeman in an Irish village in some given case pulling out his catechism to see whether he could act, or not act off his own bat. It has been wisely said when in doubt " ask a policeman." The policeman in Ireland when in doubt asks the Castle. A humorous illustration—not the less apt, because humorous, has been given to me of cases which the police might consider political and which they might not.

" Suppose," it has been said, " a man were drunk in the street and causing a disturbance of a minor kind. They would arrest him without any consultation with the Castle ; but if the same man were to say : ' down with land grabbers ' they would probably not arrest him without communication with the Castle because that might involve political consequences."

Assuredly the humour of the English Administration in Ireland is its most salient feature. However, all things are subject more or less to explanation ; and the explanation of the difference in the conduct of the police dealing with a man who was simply drunk and in dealing with a man whose intoxication was complicated by views on the land question is this ; the latter case might lead to a question in the House of Commons, the former, humanly speaking, could not.

Thus without a catechism the police have apparently settled the problem themselves. The Parliamentary question is the test.

The police, I have been told, are very timid about acting without the instructions of the Castle.

> " They wish," said my informant, " to be covered by the authority of the Castle for whatever they do. I think the local police keep constantly in touch with the Castle and reports are, I believe, sent in frequently."
>
> I asked another authority : " Are the police timid to act on their own responsibility ? "
>
> He said : " Yes, that is so."
>
> " Is the timidity caused by the fear that they may get into trouble ? "
>
> He said : " Yes."
>
> I asked again : " I suppose that the questions asked by Irish members in Parliament have a great deal to do with this timidity ? "
>
> He said : " Yes, they have."
>
> I said : " Then these questions have a good effect."
>
> He said : " That depends on the point of view. If you think it a good thing to make the police timid, they have. But I think it is unfortunate, the police ought to act more on their own responsibility, at times, than they do."

I asked three persons in authority (X. Y. Z.) whether the reports of the police were coloured by the policy which prevailed at the Castle for the time being.

X. " Yes." Y. " I am afraid they are." Z.
" I think that when a Liberal Government is in office
they report less outrages."

The following secret circular issued by the Castle, in
1886, has the inevitable touch of humour and the
humorous element is considerably enhanced by the
fact that it appeared almost as soon as it was issued
from the Castle, in the National organ *United
Ireland*.

" Circular issued to the different Police Stations
in Ireland."

" Secret.   County of——

9th November, 1886.

" Furnish without delay a list of persons in
your sub-district now alive, who for the last five
years have taken a prominent part in the Irish
National movement either as Fenians or Nation-
alists.   The list is to include :

1.—All Fenians or members of the I.R.B. to
rank of county centre or whose influence
is worth noting.

2.—Prominent secret society men of considerable
local influence, who have taken, *or are
likely to take, a leading part in the commission
of outrages.*

3.—Active influential Fenians who travel about
the country organising and promoting the
interests of secret organisations.

4.—*Roman Catholic clergymen*, and other persons
of note, who take a leading part in the
National movement, and from their position
and status have influence over the people.

5.—Persons of prominence who move about
between Ireland and Great Britain, or who
are in the habit of visiting Ireland from
America ; also persons of note, who have

recently returned from America to settle in Ireland. In the list, opposite each man's name, his antecedents, character, *opinions* (whether extreme or moderate), in fact, every-thing known about him in connection with Fenian or National movements should be given. The list to be in following form. . . ."

A British newspaper—*The Dundee Advertizer*—was much scandalised by this circular. It wrote :—

" No readier means could be found to provoke needless irritation in Ireland. The people of Scotland or of England would not tolerate such a system of inquisition as the police circulars suggest, for one hour. Why should they claim the power to appoint policemen to pry into the opinions and character of individual Irishmen ? It is a tyrannical claim such as was wont to be made by the servants of arbitrary sovereigns ; but it is the logical outcome of the idea that the Irish are a race of ' Hottentots ' that can be treated at discretion."

United Ireland published two more documents from the Castle, which, with its comments, I shall give.

" We have had the felicity of perusing the police report from the County Waterford, in reference to a suggested prosecution of one of the Special Commissioners of *United Ireland*, with the observations of Sir M. H. Beach and of Attorney-General Holmes thereupon ; and we think that upon perusing their minutes in the calm light of print, these high officials will see reason to regret their imprudence, if not to repent their vindictiveness. It is no part of the mission of our Special Commissioners to do anything except inquire into facts and relate the results in these columns. One of them was, however, in the course of his peregrinations induced to make some short observations at a meeting of the Kilmacthomas (County Waterford) Branch of the National League, on 8th August last. Accordingly, under date Kilmacthomas, 9th August, the local police spy ' forwarded for the information of the Government ' a report of the speech, which we have enabled the gentleman in question to read, and which he pronounces to be a misleading and grotesque travesty of what he said. It is not with the report (which set forth prominently the speaker's connection with *United Ireland*) we are concerned, however, but with the minutes of the Chief Secretary and Attorney-General in reference thereto. They are as follows :—

" ' Although the speech is bad, there is no attack upon specific individuals, and I doubt much whether it could be made the foundation of a successful prosecution. The future movements and speeches of this person ought to be watched and noted.

" ' (signed) H. Holmes, 16 8 '86.'

" ' I agree. If this man attacks individuals, or in any other way lays himself open to prosecution, he should not be spared.

" ' (signed) Michael Hicks-Beach, 18 8 '86.' "

I shall give another confidential police circular which appeared in *United Ireland*.

" Confidential.

" Let me have as soon as possible a full report regarding your sub-district on the following points :—

" 1.—Is there any combination against the payment of rents ?

" 2.—Ability of tenants to pay rents ?

' 3.—Are there many cases where tenants are able to pay and refuse to do so, and for what reason ?

" 4.—Are the landlords inclined to be lenient and to give time ?

" 5.—*Names of landlords inclined to enforce the law to extremity of eviction.*

" 6.—Approximate number of ejectment processes entered, and decrees obtained at October Quarter Sessions.

" 7.—Interference of the National League with payment of rent.

" 8.—Any illustration of answers to the foregoing.
" 6th November, 1886."

Mr. Clancy, M.P., explains how it came to pass that this circular was issued. He says :—

" [The policy of the Unionist Government in 1886 was to show] that the peace of Ireland could be preserved and coercion avoided without granting Home Rule, and, as it knew that this end could not be achieved without putting a stop to evictions, it proceeded immediately after the autumn session of 1886 to put secret pressure on the landlords to induce them to give large abatements of rent and forego the luxury of eviction. This startling fact was admitted by the Chief Secretary himself, in his speech at Bristol on the 14th November, and has since been abundantly proved by the publication of documentary evidence which, of course, the Government never expected to see brought into the light of day."*

All appointments in the Constabulary are made by the Lord Lieutenant. The recruiting is carried on in the following way. A man who wishes to join

* Clancy. " Six Months of Unionist Rule."

the force presents himself at the local police barracks, he is sent to the Castle, examined there, and if approved of sent to the depôt in the Phœnix Park. It takes six months to make a policeman. With respect to officers in the Constabulary, a man is noimnated for a Cadetship* by the Chief Secretary ; then there is a competitive examination by the Civil Service Commissioners, and if he passes he is sent to the depôt at Phœnix Park, and is promoted to the rank of District Inspector, when a vacancy occurs. The Castle overshadows the Force all the time.

The Police are timid because the Executive is weak ; and the Executive is weak because Irish public opinion is not at its back, and the public opinion of England on which it relies varies from Parliament to Parliament, and indeed sometimes almost from session to session. In the perplexity of councils—the ever changing councils —which afflicts and confounds the Castle, the unfortunate policeman often does not know where he is, but, amid the general insecurity, he has, with creditable intelligence, marked out a path of safety for himself. What is it ? Any path that does not bring him within the fire of the Irish members.

I now pass from the Constabulary to the Dublin Metropolitan Police. The Metropolitan Police, like the Constabulary, are under the direct control of the Castle. The Chief Commissioner is appointed by the Lord Lieutenant, and as I have said, he has his office in the Lower Castle Yard. However, it is possible that this force is allowed a freer hand than the Constabulary. The Chief Commissioner, for instance, unlike the Inspector-General of Constabulary, could dismiss a man in the ranks without the *fiat* of the Lord Lieutenant. Nevertheless, it is doubtful if the Chief Commissioner would, any more than the Inspector-General, act in any important

---

* By 46 and 47 Vic, Cap 14 Sec. 12 the designation of Sub-inspectors, Constables, Acting Constables of the R.I.C. was from 1st October, 1883, changed to District Inspectors, Sergeants, Acting Sergeants, and Constables respectively.

matter without consulting the Chief Secretary or Under-Secretary. Yet the following case has been put to me :—

> " For instance, if there were a meeting to be held in Merrion Square, the Chief Commissioner would interfere to prevent it, if in his discretion he thought it unlawful. But, in similar circumstances, the Inspector-General of Constabulary would not interfere with a meeting in Tipperary without communicating with the Executive."

It is right that I should give this illustration as it has been given to me. At the same time the balance of probability is in favour of the view that in such a case the Chief Commissioner would confer with the Chief Secretary or Under-Secretary, or that the Chief Secretary or Under-Secretary would drop in to see the Chief Commissioner before anything was done.

The Metropolitan Police are, perhaps, on the whole allowed a freer hand than the Constabulary because their path is not so much beset by political entanglements, and they are therefore more out of range of the disconcerting fire of the Parliamentary questions.

The office of the Prisons Board is, as I have said, also in the Castle.

> " This Board," said one of my informants on the subject, " is certainly under the control of the Chief Secretary. The Chief Secretary appoints the Board and regulates the Board. It is subject to him. The Commissioners do not take a free hand. They will do nothing of importance without consulting the Chief Secretary. There is certain ordinary work that they will do without consulting him, but practically they are under his control. Of course, in the absence of the Chief Secretary they will keep in touch with the Under-Secretary or Assistant Under-Secretary."

Then there is the Convict Department,—that is also under the Chief Secretary. Questions relating to the reduction of punishment would come before the Chief Secretary who would advise the Lord Lieutenant.

As I write, the following newspaper cutting has been brought under my notice. It may to some extent illustrate the relations between the Castle, the Prisons Board, and the Visiting Justices.

From the *"Freeman's Journal,"* December 28th, 1907.

"A strange development has taken place in the case of Mrs. Bridget Murphy, Ardpatrick, who was brought to the Cork Female Prison on Sunday night to undergo a sentence of one month's imprisonment, in default of giving bail on a charge understood to be one of cattle-driving, though the fact that the Press representatives were refused permission to be present when the sentence was imposed makes the details in this direction impossible correctly to convey. Mr. A. Roche, M.P., in his capacity as Visiting Justice, attended at the City Jail on Tuesday morning, and was astonished to find Mrs. Murphy attired in ordinary prison costume, having regard to the fact that she was a bail prisoner. He immediately sent the following telegram to the Chief Secretary :—

"'Bail female prisoner Bridget Murphy is being treated as ordinary criminal; new departure; will cause intense indignation; please make inquiries.

"'Augustine Roche.'

"In the course of the afternoon he received the following reply :—

"'Your telegram *re* Bridget Murphy received. General Prisons Board has already issued instructions that this woman was to be treated as a bail prisoner."

"'Assistant Under-Secretary.'

"Mrs. Murphy was released last week. Mr. Roche subsequently saw her, and was told that the officials informed her that they had received an order for her release. Mrs. Murphy expressed a desire to see Mr. Roche, but was informed she had no option but to leave immediately. She was provided with a third-class ticket to Kilmallock by the 9.30 a.m. train, but did not avail herself of it.

"It is understood Mrs. Murphy contemplates other steps in connection with the matter."

The Inspectors of Lunatic Asylums naturally have their office close to the Castle. They are appointed by the Lord Lieutenant, and they enforce the regulations drawn up by him for the Administration of the Asylums.

"What then is the special work of the Castle?" I asked one in authority who was describing the intricacies of the "Irish" Administration to me.

He answered: "Police, Prisons, and Lunatic Asylums." A delightful commentary upon the English administration of the country.

Swift once quoted the words :

"Oppression maketh a wise man mad,"

and he added that one reason why the Irish were not mad was because they were not wise. They have become wise since, with terrible results. The Inspectors of Lunatic Asylums are doubtless allowed a free hand in dealing with all lunatics—who are not politicians.

The Ulster King at Arms and the Registrar of Petty Sessions Clerks are housed in the Castle. The insignificance of these offices gives their holders comparative independence ; but of course they are subject to the control of the Chief Secretary, should the occasion for exercising it arise.*

The Registrar-General may be said to come under the jurisdiction of the Chief Secretary as Home Secretary; but the nature of his duties makes him comparatively independent. The office is geographically at all events, separated from the centre of Government. It is at *Charlemont House*, Rutland Square— let us hope that the name is not without its inspiration even in an English Government establishment in Ireland.†

Previous to the Local Government Act of 1898 the High Sheriff was one of the most important functionaries in the country, and he is an important functionary still. Writing in 1808, Sydney Smith said :—

" One of the greatest practical evils which the Catholics suffer in Ireland is their exclusion from the offices of Sheriff and Deputy Sheriff. Nobody who is unacquainted with Ireland can conceive the obstacles which this opposes to the fair administration of justice. The formation of juries is now entirely in the hands of the Protestants ; the lives, liberties, and properties of the Catholics in the hands of the juries. And this is the arrangement for the administration of justice in a country where religious prejudices are inflamed to the greatest degree of animosity."

The Lord Lieutenant appoints the Sheriff and may dismiss him. Mr. Clancy, M.P., writing before 1898 says :—

" To sum up the facts on this head. The British Cabinet appoints the Lord Lieutenant ;

* This was recently shown when the Chief Secretary appointed a Commission to consider whether the late Ulster King at Arms was in any way to blame by negligence in the discharge of his duty, for the loss of the Crown jewels left in his custody in the Upper Castle Yard.

† Charlemont House was the residence of Lord Charlemont, the head of the Irish Volunteers of 1782.

the Lord Lieutenant appoints the Sheriffs ; the Sheriffs appoint the Grand Juries ; and the Grand Juries practically constitute the County-at-large and Baronial Sessions Courts and the Inland Navigation Boards. The tax payers, as such, have no power in the matter at all ! "

We learn from an incident in the life of Drummond how the Castle may deal with an objectionable Sheriff. Sir Charles Gavan Duffy, a contemporary authority— tells the story.

" The High Sheriff of Monaghan appointed as his Sub-Sheriff, on whom the business of selecting juries principally fell, Sam Gray, a notorious Orange leader, who had been tried for murdering a Catholic in broad day, and only escaped by the favour of his brethren in the jury box. Any time between the Union and the Irish Administration of Mulgrave and Drummond such an appointment might have been made with perfect impunity. It was said, indeed, that if Judas Iscariot was selected for such an office the remonstrance of Catholics would be treated as an impertinence. But there was at length a strong, just man in authority, and when O'Hagan brought the facts under his notice immediate action was taken. Mr. Drummond wrote to the High Sheriff, pointing out the impropriety of the appointment which he had made, and requesting that he would substitute some unobjectionable person for Mr. Gray. There was wrath and indignation among Northern squires, and consultations with the Tory leaders in Dublin. The High Sheriff, duly advised from headquarters, at length replied that it was his undoubted right to select his deputy ; neither law nor usage entitled the Executive to interfere with his choice, and by his choice he was determined to abide. Drummond, in rejoinder, promptly admitted the right of the Sheriff to select his deputy, but he pointed out that the right of the Lord Lieutenant to appoint and remove the Sheriff himself was equally beyond controversy. That right, he informed the arrogant Shirereeve, his Excellency had thought proper to exercise by superseding him in office. The Northern gentry were frantic with amazement and indignation, and, under the advice of party leaders who had grown grey in office before the coming of the Whigs, they resolved to checkmate the administration—to boycott it, as we would say just now. An agreement was come to that no gentleman of the county would consent to hold the office from which the patron of Sam Gray had been removed. It was like a cordial to the heart of Ulster Catholics, who had never before had a taste of fair play in such contests, to see how Drummond and his colleagues dealt with this impediment. A Catholic gentleman of insignificant estate, but of good sense and good education, was immediately appointed High Sheriff, and for the first time since a M'Mahon held the office under James II., a Catholic framed grand an petty panels, controlled prisons, and received the circuit judges in the ' gap of the North.' "*

As in the case of Colonel Verner, so in the case of Sam Gray, Drummond might have been right, or might have been wrong, but both cases illustrate the omnipotence of the Castle.

III. *As President of the Local Government Board.*

In considering the position of the Chief Secretary as President of the Local Government Board—indeed, in considering his position in every capacity—we must bear in mind not only what he *does* but what

* " My Life in Two Hemispheres," Vol. I., p. 39.

he *can* do. He may do little, he may do much, he may do nothing, but he is master of the situation all the time. He has the authority whether he exercises it or not.

" I am the Board," a Chief Secretary once said. He was right ; that is to say, so far strictly speaking as there is a " Board." But in point of fact there is practically no " Board." It is a Department; and the permanent head is the Vice-President with whom are associated two Commissioners ; the Under-Secretary is also a member of the " Board." The Vice-President and the Commissioners are appointed, and may be dismissed by the Castle.*

By a Board, we mean ordinarily a body which passes resolutions and decides things. The " Local Government Board " passes no resolutions and decides nothing. The Vice-President takes a particular line on a given issue ; he may communicate his views to the two Commissioners. But whether they agree with him or not, he sends a statement to the Chief Secretary directly, or (according to the wishes of the Chief Secretary), through the Under-Secretary. The final course is determined by the Chief Secretary and the Vice-President, and in case of a difference of opinion between them, by the Chief Secretary. The Chief Secretary as President may, of course (if his other duties permit), preside at the " Board." He may dominate the " Board." He may order the " Board " to meet at his room in the Castle. It must also be borne in mind that in his absence the Under-Secretary, who is always on the spot, has opportunities for attending the Board regularly and representing him. In fact, constitu-

---

* Of course an objectionable official may be got rid of without being technically dismissed. He may be " promoted." He may for instance be made Governor of the Windward Islands.

Sir Robert Hamilton, an excellent official, was not " dismissed " from the office of Under-Secretary on account of his Home Rule opinions, but he was made Governor of Queensland on general principles. As the saying is : " There are many ways of killing a sheep, besides cutting its throat."

tionally, the Chief Secretary, as President, is supreme. In reference to appointments under the " Board," out-door officials (Inspectors and Auditors) are appointed by the President (Chief Secretary) and the instrument of appointment under Seal is signed by the Vice-President. As regards indoor officials, practically the whole staff is comprised of civil servants sent by the Civil Service Commissioners. These officials are divided into various grades. Promotions are made from one grade to another by the Vice-President. The Secretary and Assistant Secretaries and the Staff Officers are promoted from the staff of clerks. Of course, in all these appointments the Chief Secretary, as President, has a voice if he wishes to use it. Having so far considered the constitutional position of the Chief Secretary, let us now see what, in practice, may occur.

In 1872, " the Board " was established. From the outset it, necessarily, kept in touch with the Chief Secretary. Sometimes, the papers were sent to him, through the Under-Secretary (in which case they would pass through the usual Castle " mill,") sometimes they were sent to him direct (in which case they would presumably be opened by his private secretaries only).

At one period the Castle exercised control either through the Under-Secretary, or the Chief Secretary ; at another the " Board " was given, comparatively, a free hand. Between 1872 and 1882, the papers, so far as I can gather, were sent, sometimes, through the Under-Secretary. But the Under-Secretary of that period, it is said, concentrated himself on Police and Prisons, and left the Local Government Board alone. Nevertheless, within that period we find a Chief Secretary doing a high-handed act as President of the " Board." In 1881-2, Mr. Forster, in the double capacity of " Prime Minister " and " Home Secretary," imprisoned Dr. Kenny, a Nationalist member of Parliament under the Habeas Corpus Suspension Act. Then in his capacity as President of the Local

Government Board he dismissed Dr. Kenny from his post of medical adviser to the North Dublin Union. Mr. Gladstone spoke to me some years later on this subject. He said :—

> " Forster did not understand the nature of the Habeas Corpus Act. I will give you an example of what I mean. There was a doctor in Dublin. He was Medical Adviser to the Local Government Board. He afterwards became a member of Parliament. I think his name was Kenny. Forster put him in gaol under the Habeas Corpus Suspension Act, and he then dismissed him from his office under the Local Government Board. He never told me a word about it. Of course it was monstrous. He could put a man in gaol on suspicion, but he could not dismiss him from his post on suspicion. The first thing I heard of the matter was when an Irish member asked a question about it in the House of Commons. I was sitting next to Forster at the time. I turned round and said to him : ' Why, you can't do this. It is quite unwarrantable.' He said : ' Well, I suppose you will get up and say so.' I said : ' Indeed I will.' And I did."

Again Mr. Forster used to send an Inspector of the Local Government Board to attend evictions, and to report thereon to him. Here we have Mr. Forster once more acting in a double capacity. As "Home Secretary" he sends the police to assist at evictions, and as President of the Local Government Board he sends an inspector to attend also, and to write to him on the subject. Between 1882 and 1887 the Board, I learn, continued upon the whole to enjoy comparative freedom from direct Castle control. But, in 1887, a change was made. At that time it would seem that the practice was to send the papers direct to the Chief Secretary. The Chief Secretary of the day, however, ordered that in future they should be sent to the Under-

Secretary. The result was that between 1887 and 1892 the Under-Secretary, as I am informed, dominated the Board.

In 1892, there was another change. The Chief Secretary of that day asked how it was that he did not see the papers of the Local Government Board. He was informed that they were sent to the Under Secretary. He said in effect : " Let that practice cease ; send the papers direct to me in future."*

From 1892 to the present day the papers have been sent to the Chief Secretary direct. When he is in Dublin they are sent to him at the Castle, when he is in London they are sent to the " Irish Office." In each case, they are opened by his private secretaries. They do not fall into the hands of the Under-Secretary at all. An attempt was made recently to revert to the practice of sending papers through the Under-Secretary † ; but it was not persevered in.

Whatever may have been the practice in sending papers between 1872 and 1908, the Chief Secretary was, at all times, to quote a statement made to me :—

> " consulted on every important matter ; and for the simple reason that he had to defend the policy of the ' Board ' in the House of Commons. No question which was likely to come before the House of Commons, and no question involving a new departure could be taken without his advice. There was telephonic communication (in later years) between the Chief Secretary's room at

* There was at the time a change of Under-Secretaries as well as of Chief Secretaries.

† The story is told—of course I do not vouch for its accuracy— that the Under-Secretary, in this particular case, requested the papers to be sent to him. The Vice-President obeyed orders. One morning the Under-Secretary came to his office in the Castle. Looking through the window he saw the Castle yard filled with heavily laden carts. He asked : " What is all this about ? " pointing to the carts. " These, Sir," said the attendant, " are the papers from the Local Government Board."

the Castle and the Vice-President's room at the
Custom House. Sometimes the Chief Secretary
would ring up the Vice-President to come to him.
Sometimes he would call on the Vice-President.
There were occasions on which the Chief Secretary
attended the Board, and there were occasions when
he summoned the Board to meet at his room in
the Castle." He, as I have said, was supreme.

I shall now consider the functions of the Chief
Secretary as Minister of Education.

IV. *As " Minister of Education."*

The Castle appoints, and may dismiss, the " National "
Board of Education. The resident Commissioner
holds his place at the pleasure of the Lord Lieutenant.
No change can be made in the fundamental rules
without the consent of the Lord Lieutenant. Mr.
Starkie, the Resident Commissioner, writing recently
anent a particular book (of which more anon) says:—

> " *By a fundamental rule of the Code,* which
> cannot be altered without the consent of the Lord
> Lieutenant, no books can be used in any National
> school to which a reasonable objection can be
> made on religious or political grounds."

and again

> " As to the proposal that the book should be
> used solely in Catholic schools, *I may point out that
> this could not be done without the consent of the Lord
> Lieutenant; and, as is well known, the Lord Lieu-
> tenant refused his consent to such a proposal under
> two successive Governments about fifteen years ago.*"

On questions of finance and all that hinges on
finance the Castle is supreme. For the rest, the

Board is left comparatively free; though, it must not be forgotten that, by virtue of its creation, it is a Castle " Board." And is it too much to suppose that the shadow of the Castle hangs over the deliberations of the Commissioners when they sit in solemn conclave to consider any question—it may be the question of the admission of Irish history into the schools, or the teaching of the Irish language—which might, by any chance, come within the terrible circle of politics and nationality? It has been said that " finance is everything." It will certainly be allowed that the man who holds the purse is an important, if not the predominant partner in any business. I shall give a concrete case to show how far the Board is independent of the Chief Secretary as " Minister of Education," and how far dependent on him as " Chancellor of the Exchequer." The Board once decided to erect certain buildings. The Chief Secretary could not interfere with this decision as " Minister of Education," but as " Chancellor of the Exchequer " he would not find the money, and, accordingly, the work was not executed. I shall give two other cases to illustrate the real power of the Chief Secretary. The annual report of the Board has to be laid on the table of the House of Commons. It is sent to the Castle for that purpose. But the Chief Secretary may or may not, as he chooses, lay the report on the table. On one occasion the Chief Secretary objected to some paragraphs in the report, and requested the Commissioners to withdraw them ; the Commissioners refused ; whereupon the Chief Secretary cushioned the report, which remained suppressed for six months. On another occasion, the " Board " voted fees for the teaching of Irish, and the Chief Secretary of the day agreed, and found the money. Then another Chief Secretary appeared, he objected to the fees, and withdrew the grant. A third Chief Secretary came on the scene, he approved of the fees, and obtained a new grant. I shall give another case. A Chief Secretary expressed the opinion that the teachers ought to be allowed to be members of the County Councils. The Board objected, and its decision was final.

The Castle appoints, and may dismiss, the Intermediate Board of Education. It is said that the Board, subject to this important reservation, is independent of the Castle. This statement, however, must be taken with some qualification. For instance, a copy of the Rules of 1908 lies before me. I read :

" The Intermediate Education Board for Ireland in pursuance and by virtue of the Intermediate Education (Ireland) Act, 1878 to 1900, do hereby, with the approval of His Excellency, John Campbell, Earl of Aberdeen, Lord Lieutenant General and General Governor of Ireland, make the following rules for the purpose of the said Acts."

I also read Section I. of Act of 1900.

" I. (1) Notwithstanding anything in the Intermediate Education (Ireland) Act, 1878, or the Local Taxation Customs and Excise Act, 1890, the funds placed at the disposal of the Intermediate Education Board for Ireland in this Act referred to as ' the Board ') may subject to the proviso in sub-section (4) of section five and to section seven of the said Act of 1878, be applied by them in the manner provided by rules to be made by the Board, with the approval of the Lord Lieutenant, for the purpose of carrying out the recommendations contained in the General Summary of the Report of the Commissioners, appointed by the Lord Lieutenant to report upon the system of intermediate education in Ireland, dated the eleventh day of August one thousand eight hundred and ninety-nine, and presented to both Houses of Parliament by command of Her Majesty."

Section 6 of the Act of 1878 provides that :

> " The Board shall, from time to time, with the approval of the Lord Lieutenant, make rules for the purposes of this Act."

Namely (interalia) :—

> " (1) For prescribing the duties and powers of the assistant commissioners and other officers."

It must also be borne in mind that with respect to appointments under the Board, the procedure is : the Board nominates, then the names are forwarded to the Castle for the approval of the Lord Lieutenant and the consent of the Treasury. In reference to the rules, the Lord Lieutenant has a veto on them. If he condemns them, they are quashed ; but he cannot frame rules of his own. *Apropos* of the rules I shall tell a story, which is not without the touch of humour that occasionally illustrates and even illuminates, the English administration of our country. It must be understood that the rules, having received the sanction of the Lord Lieutenant, are laid on the table of the House of Commons for forty days. One year— I shall not state the year—the Board sent the draft rules, as usual, to the Castle for approval. The rules were approved. The Chief Secretary, accordingly, moved to have them laid on the table of the House. An Irish member objected to something in them (something I think, relating to the Irish language), whereupon the Chief Secretary threw over the Board, threw over the Lord Lieutenant, and withdrew the rules, which were disallowed by the House and quashed. We have seen how a Chief Secretary suppressed the annual report of the National Board because he did not like it, and now we have an example of another Chief Secretary abandoning the rules of the Intermediate Board, because someone else did not like them. In each case, the Chief Secretary proved himself to be the man of authority.

On the subject of the disallowance of the Intermediate Education rules by the House of Commons,
a correspondence passed between the Castle and the
Board, from which I shall take a couple of extracts
to illustrate the authority of the Executive. The
Board, while, of course, recognising the right of the
House of Commons to veto the rules, declined, in the
first instance, to amend them in accordance with the
vote of the House. The Castle, on the other hand,
wished to have the rules altered in accordance with the
wishes of the House. In the course of the correspondence the Under-Secretary fired off the following
significant sentence :

> " The Board must remember, that under the
> statute establishing them the Lord Lieutenant,
> in whom the power of appointment and removal
> is vested, is constitutionally responsible for the
> efficient working of the system created by the
> statute, and that he cannot divest himself of
> that responsibility. For these, among other
> reasons, His Excellency trusts that the Board
> will recognise the plain duty which the law casts
> upon them of preparing rules conformable with
> the views and wishes of the House."

This was plain writing. The Under-Secretary said,
in effect, to the Board :

> " I wish to remind you, gentlemen, that we
> can dismiss you, and we shall do it, if you fail
> to carry out our instructions."

The Board felt this too, as the following extract
from their reply shows :—

> " In conclusion, they venture to add that the
> tone of the letters addressed to them by the
> Under-Secretary reveals a conception of their
> relation to the Executive which they cannot

accept. The Board are now practically ordered to make certain changes in their rules before a certain date, under the thinly-veiled threat of removal from the position, the duties of which they were invited to undertake. If this represents the deliberate opinion of the Irish Government as to the relations of the Board with the Executive, it is difficult to see how men of any standing and self-respect can continue to hold a position which will be rendered not only irksome, but humiliating. The Board cannot think that His Excellency intends this to be the effect of the peremptory tone of the Under-Secretary's letters. The Board are ready to perform zealously their statutory duties as they have done heretofore. But if they are to be in future treated as a department, receiving peremptory instructions from the Executive Government, it will become a serious question how long they can be responsible for the charge committed to them, with any respect to themselves or advantage to the interests of education."

Nevertheless, the Board hold their position at the mercy of the Lord Lieutenant as another extract from the letter of the Commissioners shows :—

" They believe it, however, to be their duty to exercise, in respect of changes, that independent judgment which the Act requires them to use, and which they consider it inconsistent with their duty to abandon. Although they do not anticipate that, upon His Excellency's consideration of the Draft Rules in the autumn, his views will be so divergent from those of the Board as to render agreement impossible, they suggest that, if such disagreement should, unhappily, arise, the constitutional method of determining it will be the dismissal by His Excellency of those members of the Board whose opinions are not in harmony with his own."

Rules were ultimately framed which were satisfactory to his " Excellency," as the following letter shows.

" Dublin Castle,

. . .

" GENTLEMEN,

" I am directed by the Lord Lieutenant to acknowledge the receipt of your letter of the 27th ultimo, transmitting for His Excellency's approval, the Draft Rules and Programme of Intermediate Examinations for the year 1908, and to return the same with His Excellency's approval duly noted thereon.

" I am, Gentlemen,
" Your obedient Servant,
" J. B. DOUGHERTY.
" The Assistant Commissioners of
Intermediate Education.
" 1, Hume Street, Dublin."

I shall give another illustration of what the Castle may do. The Intermediate Board is merely an examining body ; it gives results fees to schools and colleges, whose pupils pass the examinations. It has no official cognisance of the working system in the schools or colleges, and the success of the pupils may be, and no doubt often is, the result of mere cramming. The Board recently proposed that the schools themselves should be inspected with a view to good management and efficient teaching ; and asked that some of the funds should be allocated for this purpose. The Castle refused to have the funds so allocated, on the ground, apparently, that such an allocation would be an infraction of the Act of Parliament. For, it is contended by the Executive, that the Act provides for the payment of results fees only, and that the inspection of the schools is a purpose altogether different from the one contemplated by the Legislature.*

Whether the contention of the Castle is right or not, I shall not venture to say ; but the effect of its action is that the proposal of the Board, with reference to the Inspection of Schools, has not been carried out.†

* So the matter has been stated to me by an important official, but I quote Mr. Long (Chief Secretary) on the subject.

"Chief Secretary's Office,
"Dublin Castle.
"11th November, 1905.

"My Lords and Gentlemen,—

"I have taken the opportunity afforded by the Parliamentary Recess of reviewing the correspondence that has passed between the Board of Intermediate Education and the Irish Government relative to the question of the introduction, as part of the system of Intermediate Education in Ireland, of a scheme providing for the inspection of Intermediate Schools by a staff of permanent Inspectors.

"That Scheme was the direct outcome of the Rules made by the Board, with the approval of the Lord Lieutenant, under the authorty of the Intermediate Education Act of 1900 ; but the Government have, so far, felt themselves unable to recommend the adoption of the Scheme to the Treasury. It appears to me, however, that the question might now be usefully reconsidered in the light of, and in conjunction with, the suggestions made by Messrs. Dale and Stephens in their recently published Report on Intermediate Education.

"The more important of these suggestions is, perhaps, that dealing with the co-ordination of the systems of Primary and Intermediate Education. Legislation would be necessary to secure co-ordination of the character contemplated in the Report of Messrs. Dale and Stephens, and, without expressing an opinion on the desirability of such legislation, I cannot avoid the conclusion that much can be done in this direction by Administrative action within the powers already possessed by the two Boards concerned, and that many educational advantages might be attained by the extended adaptation of existing machinery."

I understand that in the years 1902-3 an inspection was held by Inspectors who were appointed merely for the occasion ; with this exception the sole function of the Board has been to examine pupils sent up for that purpose. Recently the English Treasury have consented to the appointment of six Inspectors, but at wholly inadequate salaries, according to the view of the Board.

† It is I understand, the contention of the Castle that an act of Parliament would be necessary to carry out the recommendations of the Board.

I shall tell another story of Castle interference, which will, perhaps, be a surprise to many persons. In the rules sent up on one occasion to the Castle for approval, the list of subjects for a pass, in all grades, included the following :—

The ancient language, literature, and history of Greece ;
The ancient language, literature, and history of Rome ;
The language, literature, and history of Great Britain and Ireland ;
The language, literature, and history of France ;
The language, literature, and history of Germany ;
The language, literature, and history of Italy ;
The language, literature, and history of Spain ;
History and Geography ;
Mathematics, Arithmetic and Algebra, Geometry ;
Experimental Science ;
Music.

A correspondence on the subject, from which I take the following extracts, passed between the Castle and the Board.

Extract from letter of Sir James Dougherty, Assistant Under-Secretary :—

> " Dublin Castle,
> " *22nd October*, 1906.
>
> " Gentlemen,
> " I am directed by the Lords Justices to acknowledge the receipt of your letter of the 17th instant, forwarding, for submission to Their Excellencies, the Draft Rules and Schedule containing the Programme of the Examinations for the year 1908, under the Commissioners of Intermediate Education.
>
> " Their Excellencies desire me to express their thanks to the Commissioners for the very full explanations of the alterations, as set forth in the Schedule, which the Commissioners have introduced into the Draft Rules and Programme now under consideration.

" Their Excellencies observe that, under Rule
No. 7, the Commissioners have omitted ' History '
from that part of the Rule referring to the Honour
subjects in the Language and Literature of
Ireland, although the programme of examination
in Irish, in the Senior Grade, prescribes an examination in the outline of the Literary History
of Ireland for a definite period, as in the cases of
the Honour Examinations in the same Grade
for French and other Modern Languages.

" Their Excellencies feel that the omission of
' History ' in Rule No. 7, as regards Ireland, will
lead to misapprehension, and provoke criticism.
They, therefore, desire me to request that the
Commissioners will be so good as to consider
the propriety of inserting History in the part
of Rule No. 7 referring to Ireland.

" Extract from reply of Commissioners.

" Sir,   " *24th October*, 1906.

" The Intermediate Education Board for Ireland
at their meeting this day, had under consideration
your letter of the 22nd instant, and we are directed
to inform you, for the information of Their Excellencies, the Lords Justices, that they have
decided to amend Rules 6 and 7 of the Draft Rules
for the year 1908, by inserting ' History ' after
the word ' Literature ' in the lines ' Language
and Literature of Ireland ' in each Rule, so that
these lines may now read, ' Language, Literature
and History of Ireland.' "

Let this item be set down to the credit of the Castle,
so that it may be remembered when the day of judgment comes.

V. *As " Minister of Lands."*

The Castle appoints the Judges of the Land Commission and some other important functionaries;

but in its work (apart from the duties of the Estates Commissioners) the department is independent of the Castle. It has been said that the Estates Commissioners are independent. But this statement must be taken with some reservation. It would seem that the Castle exercises control in four things. It makes the appointments ; it makes regulations, which the Commissioners are bound to obey; it approves the instructions under which the Inspectors do their duties, and, in connection with the English Treasury, it exercises control in matters of finance.

Section 23, Sub-Section 8 of the Act of 1903, gives the Castle its authority ; it provides :—

"The Estate Commissioners, in carrying the foregoing provisions of this Act into effect, shall be under the general control of the Lord Lieutenant, and shall act in accordance with such regulations as may be made by him from time to time."

It is notorious that there was friction in 1904 between the Commissioners and the Castle on the interpretation of the word "control." It is also notorious that the Castle, which at that particular day meant the Attorney-General, forced a set of regulations on the Commissioners which they resented, and held to be *ultra vires*. It is well known in fact, that a deliberate attempt was made by the Castle to dominate the Commissioners. The change of Government in December, 1905, ended the dispute.

The Congested Districts Board is supposed to be independent of the Castle, but it must be borne in mind that both the Chief Secretary and the Under-Secretary are members of it. It must further be borne in mind that, by a resolution of the Board, the Chief Secretary is its chairman. When he is in Dublin, he presides at the meetings ; when he is absent the Under-Secretary presides. Considering the position of the men in the general administration of the country, it is idle to suppose that their position on the Board does not give them a preponderating power. It should also be noted that the Vice-President of the Department of Agriculture and the Inspector of Fisheries are *ex-officio* members of the Board.

An ex-Lord Lieutenant said to me :—

> " Certainly, the Castle interferes with the Congested Districts Board ; —— tried to make out that we did not interfere with the Board, but the Under-Secretary made it clear that we did."

VI. *As " Minister of Agriculture."*

I have been told that the Department of Agriculture and Technical Education is quite free from the control of the Castle. In fact, it has been said that the Castle dominates all the boards and departments, except the Department of Agriculture. An amusing aspect of this subject of " Irish " Administration is the readiness with which any one connected with any department is disposed to say that his department alone is free from the Castle.* But it does seem to me that in some shape or form, and to a greater or lesser extent, the Castle can get its hand in everywhere.

Though the Department of Agriculture has peculiarities of its own distinguishing it from other departments, nevertheless the ubiquitous Chief Secretary is

---

* The holder of a particular office said to me, " This is the only Home Rule department under Government."
I asked :—
Q.—" Who appoints you ? "
A.—" The Lord Lieutenant."
Q.—" Can he dismiss you ? "
A.—" I suppose so, practically."
Q.—" Who prepares the regulations for the management of the business of your office ? "
A.—" The Lord Lieutenant."
Q.—" Who can dismiss your principal subordinates ? "
A.—" The Lord Lieutenant."
Q.—" Does any popular body exercise control over you ? "
A.—" No."
Q.—" Where is your office ? "
A.—" In the Castle Yard."

its President; and I think I may say that, practically, though not technically, he appoints the Vice-
President. The position of the Vice-President as a
subordinate official in an Irish Department is peculiar,
for he goes in and out with the Government like any
other Minister. He is independent of the Chief
Secretary in the sense that he is not appointed *technically* by the Castle (technically he is appointed by one
of the principal Secretaries of State), but I think I
may say that he is dependent on the Chief Secretary
in the sense that no one would be appointed to, or
retained in, the post, who was obnoxious to the
Minister responsible for the Administration of Ireland
as a whole.

"Could any of the Principal Secretaries of
State," I asked one in authority, "appoint the
Vice-President of the Irish Board of Agriculture ? "

"Yes," was the reply.

"The Secretary of State for India for
instance ? "

"Certainly."

I said: "That seems a strange arrangement.
Would it not have been more natural to have the
appointment made by the Lord Lieutenant of
Ireland ? "

"Well, the reason that this was not done was
because Mr. —— considered it advisable to keep
the department clear from the odium of the Castle."

A significant reply. One could not help thinking
that the Department might have been kept still more
free from the odium of the Castle by keeping the Chief
Secretary out of it altogether.

The position of the Vice-President is peculiar in
another respect, viz., that when he is in Parliament
he represents his department in the House of
Commons, and is, I suppose, responsible for it;
though I do not know what would happen if the Chief
Secretary decided on assuming the responsibility

himself. I suppose that the Vice-Presiednt would have to submit, and take a back seat. Then the Vice-President might not be in Parliament, as happened in the case of Sir Horace Plunkett.* In this case, the Chief Secretary would represent the department in the House of Commons. Again it should be noted that the Chief Secretary could preside at the deliberations of the Department,—in fact, the President and Vice-President are the Department,— and overshadow the Vice-President. On the other hand the Under-Secretary has no constitutional connection with the Board. Nevertheless, I understand that, at one time, he interfered much; that, in fact, there was telephonic communication between his room at the Castle, and the Vice-President's room in Merrion Street, and that the telephone was kept going constantly. Recently the present Vice-President (Mr. T. W. Russell) took occasion in speaking at Belfast, to refer to what he considered the independence of his Department. The Chief Secretary (Mr. Birrell) who followed, said :—

> " It is all very well for Mr. Russell. He represents—as he most truthfully said in his most powerful speech—his department, and he represents Ireland ; but whenever there is any difficulty of a character which requires surmounting, difficulties particularly with reference to finance, why, then, he says, ' That is a matter for Dublin Castle (laughter) ; go to Dublin Castle and there you will find the Chief Secretary, whose duty it is to extract from the British Exchequer the money necessary to run any department.' "† (laughter.)

---

* It need not be said that the Chief Secretary must have a seat in Parliament. It is the necessary condition of his appointment. Hamlet must be in the Bill.

† Of course, this would apply to moneys outside the endowment of the department.

I shall state a concrete case which has been put to me to illustrate, in some respect, the relations between the Chief Secretary and the Vice-President.

A particular Lord Lieutenant and Chief Secretary wished the Vice-President of the day to do something. He refused. The Lord Lieutenant and the Chief Secretary pressed the point, but the Vice-President held his ground, and his colleagues gave way. I said to my informant :—

" But assuredly, if the Lord Lieutenant and Chief Secretary persevered they must have succeeded. The one was governor of the country; and the other President of the department?"

My informant said :—

" No, the Vice-President would have succeeded; because, in order to do the particular thing, money was necessary, and money could not be got without the consent of 'the Board. The Vice-President knew his Board and they would have been sure to have voted with him."*

This case is interesting as showing one of the distinguishing characteristics of the Department; but, on the other hand, the issue was not fought out. In this particular instance the Board might have gone with the Vice-President. But it is conceivable that in other circumstances the Board might have gone with the President. In any case the President could have intervened, which is the point I wish to emphasise.

Another case has been put to me. The Vice-President increased the salary of an official, without consulting the President. But then there are Presidents and Presidents. One President might take the matter easily, another might not; and if a President insisted on being consulted, his wishes would have to be complied with.

* The constitution of the Department is explained in Part III.

The Vice-President is not the Department. The President and Vice-President are as I have said the Department; and how far the Vice-President shall practically have a free hand or not depends on the particular President, *i.e.*, the Chief Secretary.

To sum up; the Agricultural Department, by virtue of the fact that it has or may have a Minister of its own in the House of Commons, and that it has a Consultative Council, enjoys a distinction which no other Irish Department possesses. Nevertheless, as Mr. Birrell shows, the shadow of the Castle covers it too.

I now turn to the Chief Secretary

VII. *As " Chancellor of the Exchequer."*

Mr. Birrell has dealt with the subject compendiously. He says :—

> " Every day I receive deputations from important interests in Ireland, and I am much struck by their honesty and their ability. They have pleaded the several causes before me ; they have asked for this, and asked for that ; they have to a very considerable extent, in most cases, made good their claims for consideration, and then they go away, having done their duty, after having put before the Chief Secretary not the task of one man, but the task of twenty, and then they leave him to cross your stormy channel, to go and see my friend, Mr. Asquith, in the Treasury Office, and make demands which, if they be put into cash, would amount to millions (laughter and applause). Gentlemen, I say that is a task beyond the capacity of mortal man. Then everything else is expected from him."*

" All finance passes through the Castle," so it has been said. What is the procedure ? Some particular

* *Freeman's Journal*, November 25th, 1907.

department wants a grant. The Secretary writes to the Castle. The letter in the ordinary routine of business comes into the hands of the gentleman who is head of the Finance Department. It is then sent on by him with a covering letter to the English Treasury. The covering letter is signed by the Under-Secretary, and initialled by the Head of the Finance Department. The Castle may recommend the Treasury to make the grant or express an adverse opinion, or give no view upon the subject one way or the other. The Treasury sends back the communications to the Treasury Remembrancer, who may be described as the financial agent of the English Treasury in, Ireland. The Treasury Remembrancer then communicates with the department which wants the money, and inquires into the subject in every detail. Finally he makes his report to the Treasury, probably giving his advice on the question, and the Treasury then decides, and the decision is conveyed through the Castle to the Department in question. In certain cases the matter would be brought under the notice of the Chief Secretary, and it may be that he would approach the Chancellor of the Exchequer directly. So that really though all Finance passes through the Castle, the decision rests with the English Treasury in all cases. No doubt if the Chief Secretary put pressure on the Chancellor of the Exchequer there might be a favourable response. But it does not follow. Indeed I have been told of a case where much pressure was put on the Treasury to obtain a grant for a certain amount to be spent on the reorganisation of the Castle itself, but the Treasury refused the money, and the projected scheme of reorganisation was not carried out. Of course 1 think we may assume that if the Chief Secretary were to oppose a grant, his opposition would be decisive. The Treasury would readily follow the lead of a Chief Secretary who would refuse to spend money on any-thing—would, indeed look upon him as a " Daniel come to judgment." On the other hand they would

not be equally willing to follow the lead of a Chief
Secretary who advised expenditure.

VIII. *As " Minister of Works."*

The Castle appoints the Commissioners of Works ;
but the Board itself is really a branch of the English
Treasury.   However it is not wholly disassociated
from the Castle.   The procedure seems to be
this :   A locality wants something to be done—
say, the inhabitants wish a pier to be built—
a letter is written to the Castle formulating the local
demand. (The letter might even be written to the
Board of Works direct ; but in that case it would be
forwarded to the Castle.)   The Castle then takes the
first step.   An inspector is sent down to advise upon the
general utility of the scheme.   If the report is favourable, the Castle then communicates with the Board of
Works, who send down an inspector to consider
the feasibility of the proposed construction from an
engineering and financial point of view.   If this
inspector should advise in favour of the work the Board
will find the money and carry it out.*

The Board never takes the initiative.   The Castle
does this.   If the Castle objects there is an end of the
matter ; but if it is in favour of the local demand
then the matter may have to be fought out with
the Board of Works, that is to say, with the English
Treasury.   If the Board of Works were for any reason
—engineering or financial—against the project,
the probabilities are that it would not be carried
out ; though, of course, much might depend upon the
individual character of the Chief Secretary.   There

* I was informed that sometimes when the Castle asks the
Board to send down an inspector, the Board might reply :
" Yes, if you will pay the expenses."   And if the latter declined
to pay the expenses, the project would fall through.   On the
other hand, I have been told that this state of things is not
possible, and that the Board of Works will always pay the expenses
of their own inspector.

might be a Chief Secretary who would force the Board
of Works and the Treasury into action ; and there
might be a Chief Secretary who would succumb to the
opposition of those mighty obstructives.*

IX. As "*Minister of Justice.*"

The relations between the Executive and the
Judiciary are peculiar. There is nothing like it
in England. The Irish Judge is *par excellence* a
politician. He is a politician before he gets on
the Bench, and he remains a politician when he is
on the Bench. I once heard a story of a witty barrister
who asked for the adjournment of his case in order that
certain witnesses might be present. The case was
adjourned till next day. When the hour arrived for
the resumption of the trial, the judge said :—

" Well, Mr. ——, are you ready to go on ? "

" No, my Lord," was the reply, " the train in which
my witnesses are coming has not yet arrived."

The Judge said :—" What kind of a train is it—is
it an express train or a parliamentary train ? "

" It is a parliamentary train, my Lord, but it isn't
as fast a parliamentary train as the one by which your
Lordship travelled to the Bench."

As a rule the judges in Ireland travel to the Bench
by parliamentary trains. In England—a country
governed by national opinion—a young barrister
first thinks of getting on by *bona fide* professional
means. In Ireland—a country governed by foreign
opinion—a young barrister first thinks of getting on
by attaching himself to one of the foreign political
parties.

" What is Dorothy's religion ? " a German princess
was asked by a friend, who was interested in the welfare
of the daughter of the house.

---

* There is a *mot* of Mr. Gerald Balfour's, anent the Board of
Works, which is worth preserving. " It is a good thing," he
is reported to have said, " that the Board of Works are not tried
by their Peers (Piers)."

" Well, we really don't know,"was the reply, " until
we see whom she is going to marry." The place-
hunting young Irish barrister chooses his politics
when he selects his party. The late Lord Russell of
Killowen wrote a remarkable letter on this subject,
when he decided to practise in England, instead of in
Ireland.

I take this extract from it :—

> " My change of profession having been once
> made, the question next presented itself—where
> was it to be practised ? It may be that you
> looked upon it as a matter of course that I
> should practise in Ireland without, in fact,
> considering the question. The matter is
> not to be determined in this way; it is
> one of very serious import, not hastily to be
> resolved upon, and requiring mature consideration
> and attentive observation. Let us calmly talk
> it over, and let me have the benefit of your calm
> judgment and advice. I begin by saying that
> I think I have in Ulster a considerable professional
> connection, and some name which would probably
> be of material service to me as a barrister, but I
> rejoice that   .   .   .

[A page is here lost.]

serve their country best who shut their eyes to
anything of politics or public affairs, and upon
their business concentrate their energies. But
you will say, very naturally, Why cannot you
do *this* then which you point out ? In answering
the query you will allow me to say that if this
could be in the case of a *barrister* ; if, without com-
promising any opinions I hold sacred, I could
remain in Ireland, endeavouring successfully to
practise my profession—even though the business
might be less—even though the emoluments
might be smaller—I would gladly, so gladly, say

to myself, ' I'll remain in Ireland to do or die ! '
It *can't* be so. I'm not romantic in these notions,
but because of no risk whatever would I (now
that we are speaking out our minds on this
subject) withhold the expression of *all* the *views*
I have in the matter, and the reasons on which
those *views* rest, and therefore I say plainly
it's impossible to strive for success at the Irish
Bar, standing on neutral ground—you must either
go with the tide or oppose it—the first with my
ideas brings no honour, the latter is impracticable.
Who are the men who have of late years risen,
especially amongst the Catholics, to places that
are reputed stations of honour and dignity ?   Men
who   rose   because   they   forgot   their   early
instincts which shot right up like the young
sapling unbent by the gardener's ligature, or who,
if they didn't forget, then acted as if they did ;
men who did dirty business (excuse the speech)
for the people in high places, and so got their
wages ;   men who, amongst their brethren, were
not pre-eminent for learning and genius, but
only remarkable for the yieldingness of their
opinions, and so a profession which once reckoned
great men in its ranks and stood marked for its
independence would now be more fitly characterised for its servility and its absence of public
virtue.   But you say, ' you speak of those who
have attained judgeships and such-like ;   but
these are not aimed at by you, and, not being
aimed at, you can't suffer the inconveniences you
point out.'   Again you are right ; it is so—my
ambition extends to a decent competence honour-
ably obtained ; *but* unhappily, the same cancer
is widespread, and though many, many honourable
men are in its ranks, yet as a *whole* the profession
in Ireland is tainted with the servility spoken of—
and can it be otherwise ?   If there be poison in
the spring, you must expect it in the stream."

Russell subsequently developed these views in conversation.

> "Incomes at the Irish Bar," he would say, "are comparatively small; hence the inducements to take office, to accept judicial appointments, are proportionately large. Irish Barristers, therefore, run after office to an extent unknown in England, where the professional incomes are comparatively large, and where in point of fact, a man in first-rate practice would lose financially by becoming a judge."

In Ireland we know that things are different. There, a judgeship is financial salvation. It is something more and something worse. It is too often the reward of political partizanship. Russell did not go to the Irish Bar, because he knew that success meant the surrender of one's soul to the English Minister.

The road to fame and fortune opens for the average place-hunting young Irish barrister when he gets a brief in a Crown Prosecution. He wins his spurs at Green Street—the Irish Old Bailey.

"What have you been doing all the morning?" one Irish barrister asked another.

"Packing juries at Green Street," was the frank reply.

A Crown Prosecution in Ireland, like everything else connected with the English administration of the country is unique. In England, where the shadow of public opinion hangs over everything, counsel for the Crown conducts the case against the prisoner with judicial fairness. His purpose is not merely to get a verdict, but in truth to see that justice is done between the sovereign and the prisoner at the bar. He does not press the case unduly against the prisoner; on the contrary he gives him every fair play. Why? Because he recognises that he is something more than counsel for the Crown; he is the servant of the public, he

prosecutes for the public, and the public want not a
conviction in any event, but justice in every event.
In Ireland, owing to the historical causes, which affect
every incident of public life in the country, the case
is different. There the counsel for the Crown is not
the servant of the public, quite the contrary, because
the Crown and the people represent opposing forces.
In a political prosecution counsel for the Crown will
try to snatch a verdict *coûte qui coûte.*

> " We cannot get a verdict in Ireland, in political
> or agrarian cases," a minister of the Crown
> once said to me, " without packing juries."
> " I do not," he added, " go into the causes
> of this unfortunate state of things—the mis-
> government, the mal-administration, the loss of
> all confidence between the people, and those who
> are responsible for the law—but I simply state
> the fact."*

In political and agrarian causes, I say, counsel for
the Crown will fight for a verdict *fas aut nefas ;* and
he knows very well that owing to the popular distrust
of the law, which centuries of misgovernment have
associated in the popular mind with injustice and
wrong, he has to depend more on a " well and truly "
packed jury, than on his own forensic talents ! Mr.
Clancy, M.P., tells a delightful story of jury packing
and the Crown. He says :—

> " The state of things existing before Lord
> O'Hagan's Jury Act, which was passed about
> 1872, may be illustrated by an incident related

* Lord Houghton, father of the present Lord Crewe, once
said :—
> " The penal laws in Ireland have defiled the very fountain
> of justice in the popular imagination, and rendered the
> government of that docile and honest nation the most
> difficult problem of your legislation, because confidence
> between the lawmakers and the people is weak and un-
> certain " (" Essays on Reform ").

in the report of the evidence taken by the West-meath Committee of the House of Commons, in April, 1871. Mr. Stephen Seed, Crown Solicitor for the counties of Meath and Kildare, was under examination, and was telling how he had manipulated a Meath jury panel in the June of the previous year.

" ' I had a consultation,' he said, ' at the Castle with the Attorney-General, and the Attorney-General was quite shocked, as well he might be, when I handed him the panel for the special Commission of Meath. He said to me : ''What do you say to this?'' I said, " *Leave the matter to me, I will select a jury !* " '

" The matter was left to Mr. Seed, and he, in conjunction with some local officials, did ' select a jury,' which worked to his satisfaction. The impropriety of the prosecutor selecting his tribunal does not seem to have struck Mr. Seed at all."*

The following description, from the *Pall Mall Gazette*, of jury packing in Sligo in 1886, may be taken as a fair specimen of the system. *Ex uno disce omnes :—*

" The resistance to the Woodford evictions, or rather the protest against the confiscation of £800 worth of property to recover £128 of rent, took place in August, in Galway. The prisoners were committed on a charge of felony, and bail was refused them on that account, it is said, by the special instructions of the Attorney-General. As a consequence, seventy-five honest, decent-living peasants lay for four long weary months in Galway gaol waiting for the Winter assizes. When the assizes came round, it was decided to try them, not at Galway, but at Sligo. When the time of their trial approached it was reported that the jury panel, *which was prepared by a Tory*

* Castle System.

landlord high sheriff, a Tory land agent sub-sheriff, and a Tory Clerk of the Crown, all active partisans of the Tory landlords, had been packed. In Sligo there are nine Catholics to one Protestant ; but on the jury panel there were 128 Protestants to 122 Catholics.* When the assizes were opened the panel was impeached. It was, of course, defended by the Crown, but the Lord Chief Baron declared that it was improperly constituted. *'It was impossible to say,'* the judge remarked, *'that any man in the panel had any legal right to be there.'* Even after the judge had expressed himself strongly in this sense, the Crown objected to the quashing of the panel, but at last, the judge being resolute, it gave way, *the panel was quashed,* and the assizes stood adjourned for eight days to permit of the constitution of a new panel.

" The old panel was quashed. A new panel was constituted, and although there were some doubts as to its legality, the objections were not sustained, and the trial proceeded. . . *The government withdrew the charge of felony, on the strength of which they had secured the refusal of bail, and proceeded on other counts of a less serious nature, which deprived the prisoner of the right of challenging more than six jurors, while the Crown had the right to order any number to stand aside. Had the men been tried for felony they would have had a right of challenge almost equal to that of the Crown.* . . On the first panel from which the jury was drawn there were only twenty-nine Catholics and forty-eight Protestants. Even this proportion, however, was not maintained in the jury box. The prisoners challenged six names before half the jury were sworn ; their right was then exhausted. The Crown challenged no fewer than seventeen names,

---

* These figures are not quite correct. The Protestant majority on the panel was forty-five. In the population of Sligo county, we may add, there are nine Catholics to every Protestant (Clancy).

twelve of whom were Catholics and five Protestants.* The net result was, that when the jury got itself constituted at last there were *ten Protestants to two Catholics, and of these Catholics one was a landlord who has evictions pending against some of his own tenants, and the other was a bailiff.* The next day a second jury was empanelled, and this time the Crown was more successful. It only challenged twelve names, and succeeded in getting into the jury box *an exclusively Protestant jury—twelve men all Protestants to try twelve prisoners all Catholics*, and that in a county where the Catholics outnumber the Protestants by nine to one ! The third jury was got together with more difficulty. The prisoners objected to six, while the Crown challenged no fewer than thirty—twenty-five Catholics and five Protestants. As the net result, the jury ultimately contained only *one Catholic to eleven Protestants*. This was so flagrant that the counsel for the defence withdrew from the case, declaring that it was a humiliation to be compelled to take part in a trial in which their co-religionists were systematically and insultingly excluded from the jury box by the Crown, as if Papist were only another word for perjurer. This action on their part scared the prosecution, and when the next jury came to be empanelled, only nine Catholics were challenged, and a jury was ultimately got together of *nine Protestants and three Catholics*. The next juries were empanelled on December 30th. On the first panel twelve jurors were challenged by the Crown, and the jury ultimately was constituted of *twelve Protestants and no Catholics*. On the second panel sixteen Catholic jurors were ordered to stand aside,

---

* Amongst the Catholics ordered to " stand aside " by the Crown were an ex-mayor of Sligo and several magistrates, and among the Protestants similarly treated were some magistrates of Liberal tendencies in politics (*Ibid*).

and the jury ultimately consisted of six of each religion. This, therefore, is how the automatic action of the officials under Lord O'Hagan's Jury Act resulted in Sligo, in which there are nine Catholics to one Protestant, and two hundred and ninety-six Catholics eligible for jurors to two hundred and seventy-four Protestants :—

Jury.		Challenged by Crown.		By Prisoner.	Jury constituted.	
		C.	P.		P.	C.
1	..	12	5	.. 6	10	2
2	..	12	—	.. 6	12	—
3	..	25	5	.. 6	11	1
4	..	9	—	.. 6	9	3
5	..	9	3	.. 6	12	—
6	..	16	—	.. 6	6	6
Total		83	13	.. 36 ..	60	12

" So that the Crown objected to ninety-six jurors, as against the maximum of thirty-six objections allowed to the other side, and the net result was that with a Catholic majority on the jury list, only twelve Catholics were enrolled as jurors, to sixty Protestants.

" The Crown pressed to have jurors who had already returned a verdict of guilty against one lot of the accused empanelled to try other batches of the Woodford men. The Chief Baron said that he should make an order that such jurors should be excused. ' If I were to be tried myself,' he said, ' I should prefer to be tried by a jury which had not an opinion on the case before.' Notwithstanding this emphatic declaration, here is a list of some of the jurors who sat in judgment on more than one batch of rioters.

Alexander Sleator, Castle St., Sligo 1st and 3rd.
William Sleator, Market St., Sligo 2nd, 3rd, and 5th.
Gerald Graham, Ballenbeg 2nd, 3rd, and 4th.
Sam Lythe, Munena .. 2nd and 4th.
James Slush, Caltragh .. 1st, 2nd and 3rd.

" Either the judge ought not to have ordered these jurors to be excused, or he ought not to have allowed them to sit in judgment twice on what was practically the same case.

" The juries, even when thus empanelled, were by no means easy to convince. The first jury, after four hours' deliberation, declared that they could not agree ; they agreed the men were guilty, but they said they were justified, and they would not find them guilty. After much browbeating they returned a verdict ' that they had a right to defend the home of their neighbour, and that they acted through ignorance.' The foreman, being cross-examined by the judge, said, ' Some of the jurors are of opinion that the prisoners knew it was the sheriff, but that they acted in ignorance of the law.' On this the Lord Chief Baron directed a verdict of guilty on the count of wilful obstruction to the sheriff. The foreman thereupon wrote down a verdict of guilty of wilful obstruction to the sheriff, and a transaction which recalls the methods of Jeffries and Scroggs came to an end. Assuming that the case is correctly reported, the verdict was never found by the jury. The foreman was coerced by the judge into writing down a verdict in which the jurors did not concur."*

* Clancy, " Six Months of Unionist Rule."
Mc Lennan, in his life of Drummond, p. 282, says :—

" Prior to 1835 it had been the practice of the Crown to set aside, from the list of persons appointed by the Sheriff to try causes, all who were Roman Catholics, or of ' Liberal opinions.' They were challenged or ' put by,' according to legal phraseology, and not allowed to sit as jurors when called. This was done in virtue of an assumed right of peremptory challenge in the Crown, which however, it appears, did not belong to it otherwise than through usage. The effects of the practice, whether it was legal or not, were highly prejudicial. The people were never satisfied of the impartiality of the tribunals. It enabled the friends of a convict to excite a sympathy in his favour, no matter how properly he might have been convicted ; for they would point to some gentleman who had been challenged by the Crown, and prevented serving on the jury, and say that if it had been a fair case such a gentleman would not have been put off the jury.

The present Lord Chancellor of England (Lord Loreburn) said, in the House of Lords on February 3rd, 1908 :—

> " Packing juries was one of the methods by which alone a government determined to depart from the ordinary law and determined to govern against the sympathies of the people, could govern Ireland. Packing juries was sure to bring about injustice. Some three or four years ago, when Mr. Wyndham was Chief Secretary, he stated there were three or four innocent people who had been convicted and severely punished, and to whom he had to give monetary compensation. These men had been convicted by juries selected by the methods known as packing, while one man was so utterly persuaded he had no prospect of a fair trial that, although innocent, he pleaded guilty in the hope of getting a lighter sentence."

In political cases the Counsel for the Crown is a zealous, vehement, furious advocate, and what he is in these cases, he becomes by sheer force of habit, in all cases. His aim is to run the prisoner down, and to prove himself an able and successful, as well as a willing henchman of the party which employs him. The difference between a Crown prosecution in England and in Ireland, strikes everyone who has an opportunity of forming an opinion on the subject.

" I cannot," said Lord Russell of Killowen, " but recall an incident which happened during

---

The abandonment of this practice was one, and not the least, of the good consequences of the new *régime*. It was initiated in 1835 by Mr. Perrin, who had previously for years discountenanced the practice, it was carried on and completed by O'Loghlen and his successors in the Attorney-Generalship—no doubt in consultation with, if not under the directions of, the Government"

(Maclennan's " Life of Drummond)."

Like most of Drummond's reforms this one died with him.

the time when my learned friend near me was Attorney-General. A clergyman from the North of Ireland, a Presbyterian Minister, during the trial of some dynamitards, was in London, and was anxious to see the trial then proceeding at the Old Bailey. He went and heard it. He is a well-known person in the North of Ireland— Professor Dougherty [now Sir James Dougherty, Under-Secretary at the Castle]. When he returned he said he never was more amazed in his life. He said, if criminal trials in Ireland were only conducted as that criminal trial was conducted, then, indeed, the law would be respected as a different thing ; and he gave to my learned friend that praise which he so fully deserves ; but which, of course, was merely for conduct which we all knew he would pursue, of extreme fairness towards the prisoners and extreme desire that nothing should come out that was not strictly relevant to the issue and strictly evidence in the case."

Sir Henry James, now Lord James of Hereford, once used these words in the House of Commons :—

" I do not think it possible to assert that the conduct of criminal cases in Ireland is the same as in England. Anyone who watches the conduct of criminal cases in England knows that no prosecuting counsel ever thinks of exercising any ingenuity to secure a conviction. The Judge is always careful that no prosecuting counsel should for a moment exceed his duty. I hope and believe that is the state of things in Ireland ; but I am not quite sure, that, in some class of cases, there would not be an acuter phase of forensic rivalry than would be displayed in this country, so that the efficacious principle might not be the same in Ireland as in England."

I myself remember the case of a man who was tried at the Old Bailey as a dynamitard. The Attorney-General prosecuted. An Irishman who was a member both of the Irish and English Bars defended the prisoner. On the second day of the trial, the Attorney-General said to the prisoner's advocate, while they were robing :—

> " I have made up my mind not to go on with the case, the evidence is too weak, and I do not think that I shall be justified in pressing for a conviction. I am now going down to say this to the Judge."

He did say it, and the prisoner left the dock a free man.

> " Just imagine," the prisoner's advocate subsequently said to me, " Just imagine, an Irish Attorney-General doing this kind of thing."

An Irish Attorney-General indeed, having first secured his jury, would have fought the case out to the bitter end.

From the position of Crown prosecutor at Green Street to the rank of Attorney-General the ascent is gradual and safe. The Attorney-General may get into Parliament or he may not ; but in Parliament or out of it, he is an intense political partizan—the servile servant—of whichever English party butters his bread. As Attorney-General he is a Privy Councillor, and one of the most important members of the Executive. By the traditions of his office he is the enemy of popular movements, the prosecutor of popular leaders. There is a list of these Attorneys-General before me. They have all practically been the same. From the trial of O'Connell to the trial of Parnell, they were all naturally for the Crown against the people ; which is only to say, that they, too, are professionally and politically the product of those historical causes in which is to be found the

explanation of all that is vicious in the " Irish "
administrative system.   In time the Attorney-General
passes to the Bench, and the goal of his ambition is
reached.   At the Bar he was a political gladiator ;
and on the Bench his " gladiathoring " does not
cease.*

I once heard a story of a place-hunting judge.   He
had a little property in the West, and his tenants used
sometimes to come to Dublin to see him.   On those
occasions, he would give them an order of admission
to the Court.   One day there was a political trial.
Two of the tenants were present.   The psychological
moment arrived.   His Lordship summed up.   He
delivered a Balaclava charge against the defendants ;
thumped the desk, gesticulated furiously, thundered
at the jury, acted in fact as if his very life depended
on the verdict.

" Well, Tim," said one of the tenants to the other,
" Faith, I think the master will *win* " ; and he did
win.

Blackburne was Attorney-General in O'Connell's
time.   I do not wish to say a word against Blackburne
personally.   I do not wish to say a word against anyone engaged in any way in the Administration of Ireland
personally.   I cite cases to illustrate the system, that
is all.   Blackburne belonged to the Orange Ascendancy
faction.   To do him justice he had convictions, and
he had the courage of his convictions.   But they were
not the convictions of the Irish nation.   He was the
enemy of the nation.   In those days O'Connell stood
for Ireland.   Blackburne was the personal, as well as
the political foe of the popular leader.   O'Connell
says of him :—

" [The Whigs] selected for their Attorney-
General, Francis Blackburne.   You know him

* " What did you see the prisoner doing ? " a policeman was
asked, at the trial of a man charged with causing a public disturbance.
" He was ' gladiathoring ' about, my Lord," was the answer.

well. I appeal with confidence to the opinion which you must give your colleagues in the confidence of official intercourse. I appeal to your opinion as I would to your oath in a Court of Justice, for the truth of this assertion, that so unhappy and fatal a selection was never yet made. Of all the members of the Irish Bar, the very worst choice that could have been made by the Whigs was that of Blackburne. I care not what other barrister you name—I defy you to name one whose appointment could be more unfortunate for the Whigs, that is if their object was to conciliate the people of Ireland. If, indeed, their object was to exasperate the people, then, indeed they did right to select Mr. Blackburne. They could not possibly have devised any measure more calculated to excite popular resentment against them. They could not, in short, have better proclaimed hostility to the people of this country.

" Why was Mr. Blackburne chosen to be the principal instrument of the Whig Government ? The history of his life seemed to forbid such a choice. It is quite true that he had been successful in his profession ; his reputation as a lawyer was considerable ; an over-rated man certainly ; but a man of high standing in his profession ; but, then, he was the most constant and decided enemy of both the Whigs and the people. . . Yet it was this man, fresh from the oratory of bigotry, and from signing the last and worst petition against Emancipation, that Lord Anglesey appointed Attorney-General ! ! !

" Yes, my Lord, it is this very man, the Anti-Whig, the No Popery orator, the determined enemy of Emancipation, that you, Secretary as you are for the Home Department—this is the man that you and your colleagues continue in the office of Attorney-General."

In 1846, Blackburne was made Lord Chief Justice
of the Queen's Bench, and the people saw one of their
bitterest enemies in one of the foremost places. In
1848, William Smith O'Brien, a popular idol, was
arrested for high treason, and the Lord Lieutenant
of the day, Lord Clarendon, himself a political partisan,
and, as Viceroy, a party in the cause, wrote to the
Lord Chief Justice, who had, at all events, been a
political partisan, and was still tinged by political
predelictions, asking him—perhaps I ought to say
commanding him—to try the prisoner.

I quote the letter :—

> " Viceregal Lodge,
> " *August 24th*, 1848.
>
> " MY DEAR LORD CHIEF JUSTICE,
>
> " I am reluctant to encroach upon your vaca-
> tion or to propose to you a renewal of the arduous
> labour you undertook at the beginning of the year ;
> but I feel at the same time that I should fail
> in my duty to the public if I did not request you
> to preside over the special commission that must
> shortly issue for the trial of Smith O'Brien, and
> those of his associates who can be made amenable
> in Tipperary.
>
> " As high treason is fortunately rare in Ireland
> and trials for it may present complications and
> difficulties, I should deeply regret if on such an
> occasion, the country did not have the benefit
> of your invaluable services. . . I fear that
> this letter will be very unwelcome, but I am sure
> you will admit that I could not take upon myself
> the responsibility of not asking you to render
> an important service to your country.
>
> " Believe me, my dear Lord,
> " Truly yours,
> " CLARENDON."

It is needless to say that, in a case of this kind,
Blackburne could not possess the popular confidence.

Why ? because throughout his life he stood on one side of the line, backed by a despicable anti-Irish faction, while on the other were marshalled the masses of the people for whom O'Brien had now risked liberty and life. I need scarcely refer to the well-known career of Mr. William Keogh. He began public life as a violent political agitator. Bribed by the government he deserted the people and was made Attorney-General and finally a judge. He was afterwards appointed to try Fenian political prisoners—a selection which threw odium on the whole proceedings.

Irish Law Officers and Irish Judges in cases where public feeling is strongly moved, must necessarily be against the people, because the law is against the people, and they are the instruments of the law. O'Connell broke the law and was prosecuted. Parnell broke it, and was prosecuted. Crown lawyers and judges in Ireland cannot be expected, officially at all events, to appreciate the words of the distinguished English writer, who said :—

" From the impeachment of Strafford to Farmer Lynch's short ways with the scamps of Virginia, there have been triumphs of justice, which are mockeries of law."

I shall cite a recent case, to show that " gladiathoring " on the Bench has not yet ceased.

In 1907 the Attorney-General applied to the King's Bench for an order to change the venue of the trial of a number of persons, who were charged with cattle driving in the County Roscommon, from that county to the County of the City of Dublin. The application was made on the ground that a prejudiced and excited state of feeling existed in the county of Roscommon, in reference to the grazing system, and that feeling was shared by the class of persons who were summoned as jurors at assizes, in consequence of which a fair trial of the accused could not be had in the county.

To one accustomed to the humdrum proceedings of a court of law in a settled country, it would seem that this application was a very commonplace affair. But the one thing which is really charming about the administration of Justice under the majesty of English law in Ireland, is the unexpected turn which events may take at any moment, and the suddenness of the surprises which may be in store for the parties and the public. The present Lord Chief Justice of Ireland is Lord O'Brien of Kilfinora. In 1887, he became Solicitor-General. He was then simple Mr. Peter O'Brien, familiarly called " Peter " (which is to his credit) by the Bar. In 1888, he became Attorney-General. I have been told that he ruled Ireland during his term of office, but I say nothing on that point now; however, it will be allowed on all sides that, as law officer, he was as doughty a political gladiator as ever faced the Irish people in the interests of the English in Ireland. In time, he was dubbed Sir Peter by the English King (a reward for " good " and " loyal " service), and " Peter the Packer " by the Irish people (a compliment to the forensic skill with which he secured verdicts for the Crown).

In 1889, he was made Lord Chief Justice. The appointment filled Mr. Gladstone with wrath. He said :—

" The Attorney-General has been rewarded for his jury-packing in Ireland, and for his mode of conducting public business by being appointed Lord Chief Justice in Ireland. When these proceedings go on, do you think it odd that the Irish have not the same affection as you have, and do not place the same confidence as you are happily enabled to place in the judges of the land. . . Conduct of that sort indicates and illustrates the broad, vital, fundamental difference between the whole tone and spirit of the administration of the law in Ireland and the administration of the law in England."*

Lord O'Brien presided in the King's Bench Division on the occasion of the application in question. A case connected in any shape or form with the land movement could not fail to revive old memories in the mind of his lordship. He thought of the days when he put forth his whole strength to crush the popular leaders and to maintain " law and order," and he clearly was of opinion that the Attorney-General, Mr. Cherry, was not doing his duty. The dialogue which passed between the Lord Chief Justice and the Attorney-General is what they call in England " very Irish." But Englishmen forget that these " Irish " things are the product of the mischievous and demoralising system of administration established by England in our country. Lord O'Brien is not as a judge an Irish product, he is an English product ; he has, if I may say so, even an English accent, or as near an approach to an English accent as is possible for a man born in the County Clare. I have sat in his Lordship's Court, and have been both interested and perplexed in studying his lordship's accent. An Englishman would probably say that it was not English ; it certainly is not Irish. What is it ? I must confess to a feeling of relief when I passed from his lordship's court to the court of Chief Baron Palles, and listened to the Chief Baron's splendid Dublin brogue, and watched the operations of that extraordinary intellect, keen as a razor's edge. He is, if you like, an Irish product, even as a judge ! Lamentable it is that he is not in touch with the national sentiment of his country ; for, in any case, Ireland must be proud of him. He is the soul of honour, and the most brilliant lawyer, either at the Bar or on the Bench, in either island. But I must return to Lord O'Brien of Kilfinora.

* Quoted by Mr. John Redmond, in " Some Arguments for Home Rule," p. 57.

What " rats " was to the terrier in the famous picture, what " atrocities " was to Mr. Gladstone in *Punch*, cattle-driving was to Lord O'Brien in the present case.

> " Who are the defendants ? " quoth his Lord-ship—[a very proper question for a Judge].
> *The Attorney-General* : " One of them is a member of the County Council ; and as many as the police could identify have been prosecuted."
> *Lord Chief Justice* : " Have you got the men who incited them to do this thing ? "

Between the first and the second question his Lord-ship had, at a bound, passed from the position of Judge to the position of a member of the Executive.

As Peter O'Brien, Attorney-General, sitting in his room in Dublin Castle, it would have been very proper for him to consider the class of persons whom, in certain circumstances, he ought, or ought not, to prosecute. But as a judge called upon to decide whether, on the strength of certain affidavits placed before him, there ought, or ought not, to be a change of venue in a particular case, the question, with every possible respect to his lordship, was none of his business. The Attorney-General could not very well have said, What the devil has that to do with the case ? But these are the words which will rise to the lips of every man who has the slightest experience of the proceedings in Courts of Law in a settled country. As a matter of fact the Attorney-General answered with great ami-ability, " I think so."

His Lordship was now in full career, and he pro-ceeded to lecture the Attorney-General, as the head of the Administration might lecture a subordinate. He said :—

> " The reason I ask is this. I see in the news-papers that there are people going about the country inciting other people to do these things.

I don't know whether or not these inciters are prosecuted. A lot of poor boys are brought up from time to time before me for doing some of these things, but I think it would be more to the point to bring up those who incited them."

What on earth had his Lordship to do with the newspapers ? They were not judicially before him. All that was judicially before him was a pair of affidavits, within the corners of which he ought to have confined his remarks. Again, what business was it of his to say who ought to be prosecuted, whether poor boys or poor girls, the breakers of the law, or the inciters to the breaking of the law ? Is it Lord O'Brien's notion of the administration of Justice, that the Lord Chief Justice having read the newspapers, and having formed his opinion of the people who ought to be prosecuted should then communicate with the Attorney-General and say :—

" Let Brown, Jones and Robinson be arrested, and brought before me for incitement to a breach of the peace. I'll deal with them."

The Attorney-General again replied with great amiability ; he simply said, with perfect accuracy of course, but with excessive self-restraint :—

" That is rather a political issue."

The Lord Chief Justice then broke forth, with increasing irrelevance and vehemence :—

" A political issue ! Is it a political issue that you should indict those persons who incite others to commit offences ? "

The Attorney-General, if I may venture to say so, should have replied :—

" My Lord, I am not here to discuss what is or what is not a political issue with your Lordship.

I am here on a point of law, and I shall confine myself to it. It is not for your Lordship to instruct me in my duties. I am Attorney-General, your Lordship is Lord Chief Justice. I shall not exceed my duties, and I must ask your Lordship not to exceed yours."

The Attorney-General, however, said, encouraging the Lord Chief Justice in his irrelevance :—

" I think it is. It has been discussed on public platforms in England and in Ireland, in Parliament and in Press, as to whether persons should be prosecuted for making inflammatory speeches."

An English barrister, who read these proceedings, said to me, that he was as much surprised at the action of the Attorney-General as at the action of the Lord Chief Justice. A discussion in open court, between the Lord Chief Justice and the Attorney-General, in reference to a question which should occupy the attention of the Executive alone, seemed to him extraordinary. The English administration of Ireland only could produce such an incongruous scene. The Lord Chief Justice said :—

" That is a wholly different thing."

The Attorney-General, at length, beginning to realise his position, rejoined :—

" It is not a question that I am prepared to discuss here with your lordship."

The Lord Chief Justice parried this very proper remark by the wholly irregular question :—

" My question is, whether you have the inciters ? "

Again I venture to suggest that the Attorney-General should have replied :—

" The question, my Lord, is not whether I
have the inciters or not, but whether the men
I have are to be tried in Dublin or Roscommon."

But the Attorney-General, instead of keeping the
Chief Justice to the issue, wandered from it himself.
He replied :—

" A great deal depends on what incitement
means. I have myself been charged with having
incited others ; and the Chief Secretary had
been charged with doing it, by members standing
in their places in Parliament. We have here
the persons who were caught in the act of cattle-
driving—not the persons who made speeches.
In every case in which they have been identified
they have been prosecuted, whether that policy
is right or wrong——"

This amusing interchange of views between a present
Attorney-General and an ex-Attorney-General, as
to what the Executive ought to do, went on, with
ridiculous irregularity :—

The Lord Chief Justice :—" It is not a matter
of policy at all. It is a matter of justice which
the law recognises—incitement to offence."
The Attorney-General :—" Incitement is a vague
word."
The Lord Chief Justice :—" It is a word well
known to the law, and one of an elementary
character."
The Attorney-General :—" It has been employed
on platforms against members of the Government."
The Lord Chief Justice :—" You think that is
an answer to my question."
The Attorney-General :—" I would much prefer
to deal with the matter from the legal aspect than
from the political aspect."

The Lord Chief Justice now stood higher than ever on his hind feet, and broke forth with sonorous bray :—

> " Yes, and prosecute boys, and so on. Go on. I may tell you, Attorney-General, that when I was an Attorney-General there was a question as to whether Mr. John Dillon—who has the courage of his convictions—should be prosecuted for his part in promoting the Plan of Campaign. The case was submitted to me, and I gave as my opinion that it would be a disgrace to the administration of the law to prosecute the mere tools in these matters, and not to prosecute the father and the inciter to the Plan of Campaign. Mr. Dillon was prosecuted and convicted, and he took his punishment like a man."*
>
> *The Attorney-General* :—" As your lordship has mentioned that matter, I may say that a member of Parliament is being prosecuted by me, and that he will take his trial at the Winter Assizes on a charge of cattle-driving. I don't think that any-one can say that I shirk my duty."

Assuredly this was exactly the thing not to have said; the question was not whether the Attorney-General had shirked his duty (that was no affair of the Lord Chief Justice), but whether the Lord Chief Justice had exceeded his.

The next remark of the Lord Chief Justice is full of unconscious humour.

---

* O'Connell, upon one occasion tried to protect a young barrister who was browbeaten by the Bench. " Have you a brief in this case Mr. O'Connell ? " asked their Lordships.

" No, my Lord," said O'Connell, " but when it goes down for trial at the Assizes I shall have a brief in it."

" When I was at the Bar, Mr. O'Connell," sneered one of the Judges, " I did not anticipate briefs."

" My Lord," replied O'Connell, " when you were at the Bar, I did not follow your example, and now that you are on the Bench, I shall not submit to your insolent dictation."

The Lord Chief Justice :—" For the sake of the dignity and administration of the law I am glad to hear you say that."

Upon the whole I think that this is about the best specimen of " gladiathoring " that has ever been seen either on the Bench or off it.

" May I ask," I said, to one who spoke with knowledge on the subject, " is the Judiciary influenced by political feeling ? "

He answered :—" Yes, the charges delivered by the Judges on circuit are coloured by political feeling."

I put the same question to another authority.

He replied : " You can answer that question as well as I. Read the newspapers, read the addresses of the Judges to the Grand Juries. See for yourself how much they are coloured by politics. See what the Judges did when Lord Crewe was here ; see how they refused to adjourn the Courts at luncheon time, and to attend the Levée. Almost all the Judges are Unionists ; almost all the officials are Unionists."

That is the kernel of the whole matter. The Judges are political partisans, and they use their power as Judges, whenever they can, to promote political ends. It so happens that, at the present moment, they almost all belong to one English party ; and they carry their partisan feelings so far (as Judges, mark) that they will actually boycott the Viceroy of the other party, should he be sent to carry out a policy favourable in any degree to the demands of the masses of the Irish people. It is important in the first degree, that the community at large should be able to regard the addresses of the Judges on circuit as a fair, impartial and accurate representation of the state of the country. But in Ireland, the masses of the people have no more faith in the charges of the Judges than in the *pronunciamentoes* of the Orange Society. In England, Judges deliver charges to the Grand Juries, which mean a calm, impartial survey of the general situation. In Ireland they make speeches which mean political harangues.

I write of things which are notorious. Irish Judges are forced to be politicians, because the English Government makes judicial promotion in Ireland the reward of political services. This is one of the scandals of the Administration. The Chief Secretary practically appoints the Judges, and each Chief Secretary takes every opportunity offered to him of packing the Bench with the supporters of his party.

In England when an advocate reaches the Bench he ceases to be a politician. In Ireland he is always a politician. It has been said that the charges of the Irish Judges to the Grand Juries are coloured by the policy of the Castle for the time being. That might have been the case in the past. It is not the case at the present moment. The charges of the Judges now are coloured by the policy, for the time being, of the Unionist party. Until the Irish people are satisfied that there is no political connection between the Judiciary and the Executive, and that the Judges in the discharge of their duties are never influenced by political considerations, there never will be and there never ought to be public confidence in the administration of the law in the country.

I shall mention other offices which come under the jurisdiction of the Chief Secretary as Lord High Everything-Else, but which do not fill an equally important part in the Administration.

Reformatory and Industrial Schools.

Public Loan Fund Board.

Office of Public Trustee.

National Gallery.

Registry of Deeds.

Charitable Donations and Bequests.
Endowed School Commissioners.
Public Record Office.

The following offices stand apart; they are really branches of similar departments in England, and do not come within the jurisdiction of the Chief Secretary even as Lord High Everything-Else. They may be described as in a special sense English departments, as they are directly managed from the English side of the Channel.

Inland Revenue
   (*a*) Stamp.
   (*b*) Excise.
   (*c*) Estate.
Joint Stock Companies Registry.
The Customs.
Civil Service Commission.
The Board of Trade.
The Post Office.
Registry of Friendly Societies.
The War Office (Auditors' Office).
The Royal Navy Reserve Office.
The Inspectors of Factories.
Woods and Forests.
Ordnance Survey.
General Valuation and Boundary Survey.*
Stationery Office.
Irish Lights.
National School Teachers' Superannuation Office.

I shall add a brief note of a conversation : (1) with an ex-Chief Secretary ; (2) with an ex-Viceroy. The ex-Chief Secretary said :—

" The Chief Secretary is responsible for the Government of Ireland. He is responsible for

* The Commissioner of Valuation is appointed by the Treasury but he also holds the Office of Boundary Surveyor, and in that capacity he is appointed by the Lord Lieutenant.

all the Boards. He has to defend them in the House of Commons. He has to answer questions in relation to every one of them, except the Board of Agriculture, and may even have to answer questions for that (in the event of the Vice-President not being in Parliament). Now that may be a good system or a bad one. But it exists. And we have to work under it. I say, that when the Chief Secretary is responsible for every department he ought to take pains to know to some extent, at all events, what is going on in every department. I think that he ought to hold the strings of the whole Administration in his hands. Holding this view, I was of opinion that everything should come to Dublin Castle, that it should be the centre of the Administration and that the Chief Secretary should know everything. It might be a matter relating to police to-day, to education to-morrow, to local government the day after, to public works another time, then to finance. I felt that the Chief Secretary should know all these things."

I said :—" As regards the question whether the Castle dominates the administrative life of the country or not, it depends upon the individual Chief Secretary ? "

" Yes."

I said, " If an individual Chief Secretary wishes to get the whole administration under his thumb, he can do it."

" Yes ; and probably kill himself in the operation."

The ex-Viceroy said :—" Another point is the peculiar position of the Chief Secretary. He is the virtual Governor of the country. The Lord Lieutenant is a figure-head. He is chosen not for his brains but for his dollars. That is one side of the case. Then the Lord Lieutenant, who is nobody, lives in the country and has his opportunities of seeing the people and learning something about them. On the other hand the Chief Secretary, who is everybody, does not live in the country. He is almost always away; and has few opportunities of meeting the people or learning his business. He has to depend on Secretaries. The position is incongruous. Putting aside Home Rule and Unionism, taking the system as it is, the Lord Lieutenant ought to be made the real Governor of the country with a proper salary. The present salary is not enough for the position. It simply means that a man must get into debt. A Governor with brains should be sent to Ireland, he should be paid a proper salary, and the Chief Secretary should be his subordinate. The present practice of putting the Chief Secretary into the Cabinet, keeping him out of the country, while he is the real Governor of it, and leaving the Lord Lieutenant, who is merely a figurehead in the country and out of the Cabinet, is absurd."

I shall conclude with two sentences from a letter written by the well-known Resident Magistrate, Mr. Clifford Lloyd, to the *Times*, March 18th, 1889 :

" ' As to Dublin Castle it represents a system impossible to please even the best disposed. Unsympathetic and irritating in times of peace, it is inefficient in the hours of trouble.' "

PART III

BOARDS, OFFICES AND DEPARTMENTS

PART III

I SHALL now deal as briefly as possible with the growth of the various boards, offices, and departments which have sprung up since 1800, describing their functions apart altogether from the question of their relations with the Castle.

The Royal Irish Constabulary.

Practically the first Irish Police Act was passed in 1787. It empowered the Lord Lieutenant to appoint a Chief Constable for each barony ; sub-constables were appointed by the Grand Juries. No Catholic could enter this force.

In 1792, another Act was passed, enabling Grand Juries to increase the number of sub-constables fixed by the first Act. The next Act was passed in 1814. It empowered the Lord Lieutenant to appoint a Resident Magistrate, a Chief Constable, and fifty sub-constables in any disturbed district. The Lord Lieutenant decided (by proclamation) what was a disturbed district. This force was wholly independent of the local authorities. It was under the control of the Resident Magistrates, who acted on instructions from Dublin Castle.

In 1822, a fourth Act was passed. This was practically an amendment of the Act of 1787. Leaving to the Lord Lieutenant the power to appoint Chief Constables, it transferred the power of appointing sub-constables from Grand Juries to local magistrates. But its most important feature was the appointment (by the Lord Lieutenant) of four Inspectors-General— an inspector for each province.

In Drummond's time the Bill creating the present force was passed.* This measure deprived the local magistrates of the power to appoint constables, and placed the whole force under the control of an Inspector-General at Dublin Castle.   The Lord Lieutenant appointed the Inspector-General, and all the officers and men.   Under the Inspector-General were two deputy inspectors-general, four county inspectors, thirty-two sub-inspectors, chief constables and head constables.† At the present day the force consists of an Inspector-General, a deputy Inspector-General, three assistant Inspectors-General, thirty-seven County Inspectors, 202 District-Inspectors, 241 Head Constables, and 10,195 Sergeants and Constables.

Belfast and Londonderry, be it observed, are policed by extra forces of the constabulary, under special Act of Parliament.   The constabulary may, with truth, be described as a semi-military force, armed on occasion with rifle and bayonet.   On ordinary duty, however, the men only carry truncheons.   The constabulary, then, maintain "law and order," all over Ireland, except Dublin.

Dublin Metropolitan Police Force.

The Dublin Metropolitan Police were established about the same time as the constabulary.   Drummond tells the story :—

> "The condition of the Dublin police in 1835 was most wretched.   It consisted of a small number of day police, having an establishment

---

* The Bill had been drafted before Drummond came, but was not introduced until 1835.

† 6 Wm. IV., cap. 13.   The force numbered 13,500 men in 1882.

of peace officers somewhat similar to the old establishment of the metropolitan police officers, and a considerable number of watchmen—decrepit, worn-out, old men. For the purpose of a day police the watchmen were absolutely inefficient ; in fact, it was impossible to produce them. In the month of August, 1835, there was a large public meeting to be held in the Coburg Gardens, and it became my duty to consult with Alderman Daley as to the means of preserving the peace. He mentioned the small body of day police he had as being totally inadequate to the occasion. I suggested that he should bring out his watchmen. He said : ' Oh ! it will not do to call out the watchmen ; they will excite the ridicule of the people so much, that there would be a risk of their very appearance creating a disturbance. It will not do to show them in daylight.' [Immediate action was taken to remedy this state of matters.] A Bill was introduced in the Session of 1835 ; it passed the Commons, but it did not pass the Lords. It was reintroduced in 1836, and passed ; but considerable difficulty arose in providing sufficient funds, and before these could be removed and the necessary preparations made, a considerable time elapsed, and an amendment to the Act became necessary, so that it was not until January, 1838, that the [Dublin] Police Act was in operation. The effect of the change was to give 1,000 able and effective men for Dublin, and a certain district round it. The former force numbered between 400 and 500 men, underpaid, miserably clothed, old, and inefficient."

The Force now numbers 1,282 men, including Superintendents, Inspectors, Sergeants and Constables The commanding officers are, as has already been said, a Chief Commissioner, and an Assistant Commissioner.

It is a police force proper, corresponding practically to the Metropolitan Police Force in London, the Chief Secretary holding the same relation to it as the Home Secretary holds to the London Police.

With reference to the question of cost, I have had some difficulty in ascertaining precisely the exact details connected with the method by which the money necessary for the maintenance of the force is obtained. I have had conversations with several persons possessing knowledge on the subject. I shall give a note of one of these conversations.

I asked :—" A rate is struck for the payment of the Dublin Police ? "

Answer :—" I think that it is wrong to call it a rate ; it is a tax."

I said :—" Tax or rate. Who strikes it ? "

Answer :—" Nobody strikes it. It is struck in the Act of Parliament."*

Question :—" What is the practice ? Who first moves in the matter ? "

Answer :—" The Chief Commissioner prepares a requisition, setting out the amount which is necessary for the year."

Question :—" To whom is the requisition sent ? "

Answer :—" To the Corporation and County Council."

Question :—" Then what do they do ? "

Answer :—" The Corporation collects the rate, and is paid for collecting it."

Question :—" But how is the rate originally struck ? I am told that the Chief Commissioner strikes it, and then I am told that the Treasury strikes it, and then I look at the Act of Parliament, and I can't make out, from the Act of Parliament, how it is precisely struck. What is the machinery ? "

---

* 1 Vic., cap; 25. sec. 4 or 24.

Answer :—" It is struck by the Act of Parliament, and then it works automatically. The Chief Commissioner sends in an estimate to the Corporation, say for £150,000; the cost of the police for a year. The Treasury pays half that sum, and the Corporation pays the other half, always provided that the rate or the tax shall not exceed 8d. in the £."

[In accordance with the 1 Vic., cap. 25, sec. 4 it would seem that the Justices (now the Commissioner) were authorised to raise a rate, not exceeding 8d. in the £.]

Question :—" It looks from this Act, as if the Justice or Commissioner is authorised to raise the rate. Now, where does the Treasury come in? The Treasury is not named in the Act."

Answer :—" No, that is so, but I believe there was an understanding at the beginning that the Treasury would pay half the cost, and the citizens the other. Of course the Treasury might withdraw from that at any time."

Question :—" It comes to this, the Commissioner prepares an estimate for £150,000. Under the Act of Parliament the citizens are bound to contribute to that amount up to the rate of 8d. But suppose the contributions are not enough, and the Treasury refuse to pay their share?"

Answer :—" Exactly. The old practice was clearly this. The Justice, or Chief Commissioner as he is now called, originally raised the rate; then a collector of taxes was appointed to collect it, and finally by the Local Government Act of 1898 (61 and 62 Vict., cap. 37, sect. 66, sub-sec. 4; sect. 80, sub-sec. 2) the Corporation or County Council are bound to collect them. At the present moment, the Corporation has collected the rate at 8d. in the £, but they refuse to hand the money over to the Chief Commissioner."

Question :—" Can they be compelled to hand the money over ? "

Answer :—" No."

Question :—" Has the Commissioner no remedy against them ? "

Answer :—" Yes, the Imperial Treasury contributes a certain sum for the purposes of local taxation. But when the Corporation refuses to pay the police rate, the Treasury refuses to pay the grant in aid of local taxation."

With reference to the regulations for the management of the traffic, my informant said that the Chief Commissioner sent these regulations to the Town Clerk, and they were submitted to the Corporation, and when they were passed by the Corporation, they were submitted to the Recorder in Open Court, and were there subject to criticism, and if the Recorder did not accept them, they could not be put in force. The Recorder had a veto on them. The citizens of Dublin complain that they are unduly taxed or rated for the maintenance of the Police Force. And the Finance Committee of the Dublin Corporation have published the following table (see p. 197), showing the comparative cost of the police in Dublin and in various towns in Great Britain.

In May, 1907, the Lord Mayor of Dublin said in the House of Commons :—

" Frequent appeals had been made against the oppressive character of this tax, but all that was procured in reply were honeyed words. Mr. Wyndham, when Chief Secretary for Ireland, admitted it was a heavy tax, and expressed sympathy with the complaints put forward by the deputation that waited on him in reference to the subject, but no practical steps were taken. The citizens of Dublin could not afford to stand idly by and see this tax continue year after year.

of Streets Roads [clean]ed by the [Po]lice.		Area (in acres).	Population last Census.	Strength of Force.	Gross Cost.	Net Cost.	Valuation.	Police Rate.	Proportion of Population to each Policeman.	Cost per head of Population.		Observations.
					£	£	£			s.	d.	
0*	Dublin	20,585	390,187	1,172	160,183 (1901)	41,002	1,230,231	8d.	333 to 1	8	2¼	Police act as Fire Brigade.
2	Sheffield	23,654	408,994	515	51,354	25,545	1,453,274	4¼d.	794 ,, 1	2	6	
0	Bradford	22,843	279,767	396	38,890	21,883	1,421,200	3·63d.	713 ,, 1	2	9	
8	Glasgow	12,688	760,423	1,379	134,192	63,020	4,745,156	3·9 on Rents £10 & over 1¾ ,, under £10	551 ,, 1	3	5½	
75	Manchester	12,935	543,872	1,009	116,880	64,969	3,464,400 (1901)	5d.	539 ,, 1	4	3½	61 Members of the force are employed permanently on Fire Brigade duty, and 300 Constables in addition are trained in the use of fire appliances.
30	Liverpool	15,252	684,947	1,421	193,273	88,174	4,042,524 (1901)	5½d.	503 ,, 1	5	7½	
0	Bristol	11,607	334,632	499	53,906	31,118	1,596,213	5¾d.	659 ,, 1	3	3	Police act as Fire Brigade and Inspectors under Explosives and Petroleum Acts.
0	Nottingham	10,935	239,753	290	31,102	16,890	1,110,599	4⅘d.	826 ,, 1	2	7	25 Constables act as Auxiliary Firemen.
8	Bolton	15,270	168,205	167	16,566	8,661	737,251	2·93d.	1,007 ,, 1	1	11½	22 Constables engaged on Fire Brigade duties.
33	Huddersfield	11,854	95,008	120	12,074	7,526	459,404	4·62d.	792 ,, 1	2	6	
0	Leeds	21,572	428,968	572	53,332	27,836	1,741,373	3·84d.	749 ,, 1	2	6	Police act as Fire Brigade.
7	Hull	9,202	240,739	362	34,071	17,972	1,004,702	4·293d.	665 ,, 1	2	9½	Police act as Fire Brigade.
0	Belfast	16,745	348,955	937 (1901) 100 additional (1902)		16,925 (1901)	1,185,342 (1901)	3·43d.	372 ,, 1			
1½	Birmingham	12,705	522,182	820	82,055	45,686	2,759,032	4d.	636 ,, 1	3	1½	

* In Dublin the area taken is the Metropolitan Police Area, Oct., 1902.

Note.—The London County Council levy a 5d. Police Rate, and the London City Council about 5¾d. Police Rate.

In 1856, the valuation of Dublin was £510,559, and upon that valuation 8d. in the £ was levied for the upkeep of the force.   In 1892, the valuation was over £800,000, but still the 8d. was levied upon the increased valuation, though the police force numerically was the same.   When the tax was first imposed, it was understood that the maximum was 8d. but no matter how the valuation had since varied the 8d. was still maintained. The strength of the Dublin police was 1,172, or one policeman to every 333 of the population ; while in Glasgow, the strength of the police force was 1,379, or one policeman to 551 of the population.   In Birmingham the strength of the police was one to 636 of the population.   Surely it was unnecessary to argue the question further.   It was a crime to levy the charge of the upkeep of a force which was not required upon the people of a poor country like Ireland."

The Magistracy.

The unpaid Justices are, as a rule, appointed by the Lord Chancellor on the recommendation of the Lord Lieutenant of the County.   The Lord Chancellor, however, may, himself, appoint without any recommendation, or decline to appoint anyone recommended. Originally a property qualification was prescribed by the 18 Henry VI., cap. 11., viz. :—

"No Justice shall be assigned in any county if he have not land to the value of £20 by the year."

This provision has now been repealed.*

It would seem that stipendiary magistrates were first appointed in 1814 by 54 George III., cap. 131, entitled :—

* "Local Government and Taxation [Ireland] Inquiry." Special Report from Mr. W. P. O'Brien, p. 50.

" An Act to provide for the better execution of the laws in Ireland by appointing superintending magistrates and additional constables in certain cases."*

By the 6 William IV., c. 13, sect. 31, the Lord Lieutenant is empowered :—

" To appoint by warrant under his hand and seal stipendiary magistrates, and to dismiss them at his will and pleasure."†

Mr. O'Brien, in his report, says :—

" There were seventy-four resident magistrates employed in Ireland at the end of the year 1889, with salaries ranging from £424 to £675 (37 and 38 Vic., c. 23), and six Divisional Commissioners.

" By section 31 of 6 and 7 William IV., c. 13, a Resident Magistrate is constituted a Justice of the Peace, not only in and for the county or counties, or city or town, in and for which he shall be appointed magistrate, but also for ' Each and every county at large, or county of a city, or county of a town and liberties, or city or county adjoining to, or locally situate within such his proper county, city or town.' "

The number of stipendiary magistrates at present in Ireland is 66, of whom 20 are Catholics. There are 4 Divisional magistrates in Dublin, 2 of whom are Catholics. The office was created in 1842 (5 Vic. c. 24, sec 46). The appointment is made by the Lord Lieutenant, and the candidate must be a Barrister of six years standing.

In 1887, the number of unpaid magistrates in Ireland was 5,055 ; Catholics 1,229 ; Protestants, 3,826.‡

* For list of " Stipendiary Magistrates in Ireland between 1817 and 1831," see " Parliamentary Papers," Vol. xiii., for 1831-32.

† Mr. O'Brien's Report.

‡ Clancy, " Six Months of Unionist Rule," p. 425.

The number of stipendiary magistrates, at the same time, was 80; Catholics, 25; Protestants, 55. Dividing the magistrates by occupation in 1886 we find:—

Landlords	2,737
Land Agents	448
Farmers	354
Queen's Counsel	73
Barristers	41
Judges	15
Clergymen	13
Solicitors	26
Coroners	39
Military and Naval Officers	226
Constabulary Officers	3
Civil Servants	17
Doctors of Medicine	138
Bankers	40
Merchants	631
Other Occupations	157
Occupations unknown	75

Mr. Clancy says :—

"The Protestant landlord class and their hangers-on and sympathisers—amongst whom are to be counted land agents, Queen's counsel, many of the barristers, the military and the naval officers and others—thus practically monopolise the magisterial bench, in a country, the population of which is four-fifths Catholic, and in which there is a bitter antagonism between the small landlord class and the masses of the people. To put it otherwise ; in most districts in Ireland, the chief representatives of English rule with whom the people are familiar are the magistrate and the policeman ; and in nine cases out of ten the ordinary Irishman sees in the former his deadly enemy, socially and politically. Under the circumstances, is it very surprising that he should be disaffected with such a rule ? "

Veritas writes :—

" In this unfortunate country we are ' coloneled, majored and captained,' *usque ad nauseam ;* the holder of every second appointment in it is some retired warrior, about whose martial deeds existing chronicles are unaccountably silent, but who persists in styling himself Major or Captain, and insists upon others addressing him as such, even although at best, the title is but an honorary thing, acquired by service in the volunteers or militia.

" The sons of Mars particularly abound in the Resident Magistrate class, although there would not be any affinity between slaughtering the enemies of one's country, and dispensing petty sessions law, in a mudwall temple of justice. In the discharge of my duties, I am constantly brought in contact with these military magistrates, who play such an important part in the government of this country, and I have been always puzzled to find out why, if they were really capable men, they did not remain in the Army, or, having left it, upon what principles they were selected, armed with the commission of the peace, and scattered broadcast throughout the country, to distribute justice among a highly sensitive people, with whom they have no sympathy, and no ideas in common."

Coroners.

" This is the only class of magistrates appointed in Ireland by popular suffrage."* He was up to the passing of the Local Government Act, 1898,

---

* Mr. O'Brien's Report, 44 and 45 Vic. cap. 35, sec 1. Previously a Coroner was obliged to have an estate of inheritance of the value of £50 or a freehold estate of £100 a year. (9 and 10 Vic. cap. 37, sec 16.) Coroners are mentioned in a Charter, 925. Coroners were appointed in every county in England in the reign of Edward I.

elected by persons in the district possessing the Parliamentary franchise, and had to be a Medical Doctor, a Barrister, a Solicitor, or a Justice of the Peace of five years' standing. He is now elected by the County Council.*

Clerk of Petty Sessions.

" This office, though a subordinate one, is of considerable importance, as affecting the administration of justice to the humbler classes of the community. The appointment is vested in the justices of the district but is subject to the approval of the Lord Lieutenant, at whose pleasure the holder is at any time removable."†

Grand Jury.

Prior to 1898 the Grand Jury had the chief direction and management of the fiscal affairs of the county at large, as well as the discharge of those criminal functions involved in finding or not finding a bill of indictment, submitted for their adjudication at the assizes. The fiscal authority of the Grand Jury was based on a plan formed by Sir John Davies in the reign of James I., by which Judges on circuit were used as a species of Crown Administrators.‡

In the reign of Charles I. an Act was passed by the Irish Parliament (10 Car. I. c. 26, s. 2) by which :

" Justices of assize and of the peace were directed to inquire what bridges in the county were broken down or out of repair, and to award process or presentment against such persons as were chargeable with the repairs ; if the persons liable were unknown, the expense was to be borne by the

* *Post.*

† O'Brien.

‡ Hancock, on Local Government of Ireland in Cobden Club Essays, p. 194.

inhabitants of the county or barony where the bridge was situated, and the justices were directed to tax the inhabitants reasonably for that purpose, with the assent of the Grand Jury.*"

The next important Act was passed two hundred years afterwards (6 and 7 William IV., c. 116). I quote the preamble :—

" Whereas the laws heretofore made and in force in Ireland for the purpose of regulating the fiscal powers of Grand Juries have become obscure and complicated from their multiplicity, and their provisions have been found in many respects insufficient, and it is expedient, with a view to secure the better execution of public works, and facilitate the transaction of local business, that the said laws should be consolidated and amended, and that a uniform system of raising money by presentment of Grand Juries should be established in all counties in Ireland, whether counties at large, counties of cities, or counties of towns. Be it therefore enacted by the King's most Excellent Majesty, by and with the advice and consent of the Lords spiritual and temporal, and Commons, in this present Parliament assembled, and by the authority of the same, that from and after the commencement of this Act it shall not be lawful for any Grand Jury of any county, county of a city, or county of a town, except the county and city of Dublin, at any assizes to make any pre-

* This sanction by the Grand Jury to the taxation of the justices of assize is peculiar to Ireland. The earlier corresponding English Act of Henry VIII. requires the consent of the constables or the inhabitants of the city, town, or parish. The presentment for bridges was followed at the commencement of George III.'s reign by a series of enactments, originating with a Mr. Arthur French, member for Roscommon, enabling the Grand Juries to make presentments first on the county and afterwards on the barony rates for roads."—Hancock, " Local Government and Taxation," Ireland, p. 190.

sentment (save and except in the cases hereinafter specially reserved and excepted) for the execution of any public work whatsoever, or for raising any money, unless under the authority and by virtue of the provisions of this Act."*

The matters administered by the Grand Jury under this Act, and subsequent Acts, included, *inter-alia*, the construction and repair of roads, footways, bridges, gulleys, quay walls, the erection and repair of court or session houses, gaols† or bridewells, the maintenance of county prisons, the support of district lunatic asylums, reformatory and industrial schools, and the award of compensation for malicious injuries to person and property, and the levying of rates when necessary for extra police. After this reference to Acts of Parliament, Sidney Smith will be a relief.

" The Grand Juries in Ireland are the great scene of jobbing. They have a power of making a county rate to a considerable extent for roads, bridges, and other objects of general accommodation. ' You suffer the road to be brought through my park, and I will have the bridge constructed in a situation where it will make a beautiful object to your house. You do my job, and I will do yours.' These are the sweet and interesting subjects which occasionally occupy Milesian gentlemen, while they are attendant upon this grand inquest of justice. But there is a religion, it seems, seen in jobs ; and it will be highly gratifying to Mr. Perceval [the English Prime Minister] to learn that no man in Ireland who believes in seven sacraments can carry a public road or bridge, one yard out of the direction most beneficial to the public, and that nobody can cheat that public who does not

---

* O'Brien, p. 57.
† Prisons were referred to the Prisons Board, 1877, *post.*

expound the scriptures in the purest and most orthodox manner.''

Seventy years later the official Veritas says :—

" Descending from Castle to County Govern-ment, as at present practised through the medium of the several Grand Juries in Ireland, we find the same want of representation and power on the part of the people. They have nothing what-ever to do with the appointment of the High Sheriff, or the selection of the several Grand Jurors ; the High Sheriff nominates the latter.

" . . . As Grand Jurors, they possess the privilege of voting away the public moneys of the county, without, in the slightest degree, concerning themselves about the wishes, feelings, or inclinations of the cess-payers who have contributed to it ; they decide upon the necessity of all public county work, such as roads and bridges ; they are responsible for the maintenance and preservation of the county buildings, court-houses, gaols, bridewells, lunatic asylums, fever hospitals and infirmaries ; they enter into large contracts, and appoint, pay, and superannuate numerous county officials ; and all this they can do, perfectly irrespective and independent of the voice of the people who pay the cess which enables these multitudinous works and appoint-ments to be carried out and made.''

The writer of the article in the *Fortnightly Review* on " Local Government in Ireland,'' for July, 1885, says :—

" The Grand Jury, a body of which it has been truly said that ' instead of being selected for business capacity, it is a barometer for the measurement of social claims,' meets twice a year for one or two days at a time, votes taxes to

the amount of about a million and a quarter
sterling, and exercises out of public rates a patronage representing over one hundred thousand
pounds per annum."

This oligarchical system of county government
remained in existence up to the passing of the Local
Government Act of 1898. It was then swept away,
the fiscal functions of the Grand Jury being transferred
by that measure to the County and District Councils.
The functions of the Grand Jury are now confined to
adjudication on Bills of Indictment, sent up to them
at the Assizes.

The Presentment Sessions.

The Presentment Sessions for each barony and the
county* at large, was, so to say, a corrollary to the
Grand Jury.

> * " The baronies correspond to the ancient Irish terri-
> tories or sub-kingdoms, inhabited by distinct tribes or
> families. They represent consequently very ancient boun-
> daries, not coinciding with the modern distribution of
> population, The counties represent boundaries introduced
> by successive English monarchs from King John to King
> James I " (Cobden Club Essays, Hancock " Local Govern-
> ment and Taxation in Ireland," p. 186).
>
> Mr. O'Brien says :—
> " For the purposes of the Grand Jury system, the units
> of Local Government and, in general, the units of taxation
> are the county and barony.
> " The latter, which grew as a subdivision out of the larger
> county division, though bearing a title of English origin and
> introduction here, was in fact but the adoption for the
> purposes of county formation and government, of the
> ancient Irish territories as occupied by the native *Septs* or
> *Tribes* before the period of the Anglo-Norman invasion.
> " Sometimes the baronies as formed were exactly coter-
> minous with a single such ancient Irish territory, and some-
> times with a group of two or more, when the territories
> concerned were small, and sometimes, when very large,
> containing only a half, or even a quarter of one territory.
> "The present barony of Condons and Clongibbons, in the
> county of Cork, may be referred to as an instance of the

This Tribunal consisted of the unpaid magistrates of the county, and a certain number of cess-payers† " chosen by ballot out of a list fixed by the Grand Jury. Before these Presentment Sessions nearly all the presentments as to which the Grand Jury have any discretion are required to be first passed."

I believe that it was originally intended that the Presentment Sessions should be partly a representative body, and so far a check on the Grand Juries. But the intention was not carried out. The supposed representative element in the body—the associated cess-payers—were practically fixed by the Grand Jury.

" In the case of baronial presentment sessions, it is the Grand Jury of each county which fixes the number of rate-payers (called cess-payers from the name of the Irish county rates) to be associated with the Justices at the baronial presentment sessions.

" They must not be less than five, nor more than twelve ; the selection of these is by a complicated system. The Grand Jury prepare for each barony a list of double the number of associated rate-payers fixed to serve, out of a return

---

former, and the baronies of Oneilland East and Oneilland West, in the county of Armagh, of the latter. Many of the original baronies were subsequently divided, (see 6 and 7 Wm. IV., c. 116, s. 175), for the greater convenience of adminstration, into ' half baronies,' which are now treated for all purposes as distinct baronies, and a provision is made by the Grand Jury Amendment Act, 1856 (19-20 Vic. c. 63, s.8), for the subdivision by presentment of existing baronies for the purpose of the collection of the county cess." Local Government and Taxation Inquiry, pp. 42, 43).

† So called from the name of the Irish County rates.
" The Grand Jury Cess is a tax peculiar to Ireland. The purposes for which it is raised are chiefly those provided in England and Wales by the highway rate, turnpike tolls, county rate, rates for bridges, and police rate. The kinds of property assessable in Ireland correspond very closely to that rateable to the poor rate in England and Wales." Thom's Directory, 1887, p. 667.

made to them of 100 of the highest rate-payers in each barony (exclusive of persons in holy orders, ministers of religion, and justices of the peace). In making the list they must strike off all those who have served at the preceding baronial sessions, and if the prescribed number did not attend and serve, others must be struck off till half the previous list has been struck off.

" From the list so prepared by the Grand Jury, the rate-payers to serve are chosen by ballot, and if all attend only one half can serve.

" From this constitution it appears that the associated rate-payers are greatly weakened as an element of control. In the first place, no rate-payer, however efficient, can serve at any two baronial sessions for his barony in succession ; again, by the effect of the ballot, no matter how attentive he may be in attending when summoned, he may be thrown out from serving from session to session ; but lastly, he is not selected by the rate-payers, but chosen from a list of the highest rate-payers by the Grand Jury.

" Whilst the rate-payers element of the baronial sessions is thus weakened, the ex-officio or property element, is under no limitation, as justices of the county, whether connected with the barony by residence or property, or not so connected, may attend. The baronial sessions are, again, only the preliminary stage of the proceedings ; all they do has to come before the Grand Jury at the assizes for ratification, a body practically composed almost exclusively of proprietors or other representatives."*

The practice was that the Presentment Sessions should first consider the proposed works or malicious injury applications as the case might be, and the

* Cobden Club Essays. Hancock, Local Government and Taxation (Ireland), pp. 187, 188.

expenses to be incurred or the amount of damages to be awarded. Then they were to report to the Grand Jury with whom alone the final decision rested.* The Presentment Sessions was, in fact nothing more or less than a sort of Committee of the Grand Jury, appointed to consider and report to that body. The Presentment Sessions also remained in existence until 1898 and then disappeared with the fiscal authority of the Grand Jury.†

Lord Lieutenants of Counties and Custos Rotulorum.

These offices, though at one time separate, are now invariably held by the same person. The Custos

* " The baronial sessions are, again, only the preliminary stage of the proceedings, all they do has to come before the grand jury at the Assizes for ratification. . . .
" If the baronial sessions should, on two occasions, refuse an application, there is an appeal to the Judge of Assize and a common jury to try whether the work is proper to be executed. If the common jury find that it is so, and the judge, upon that finding, directs the grand jury to consider the application, then only have they the power to consider and present either the sum stated by the common jury to be sufficient for the execution of the work, or such lesser sum as they think proper, or to refuse altogether to make the presentment " (Hancock, pp. 188, 189).

† " The Grand Jury officers were : the Treasurer (appointed by the Grand Jury) ; the Secretary (appointed by the Grand Jury) ; the County Surveyor (appointed by the Lord Lieutenant, subject to a competitive examination, and paid by the Grand Jury) ; and the High Constables or baronial collectors, appointed by the Grand Jury " (O'Brien, " Special Report," p. 55).
Presentment Sessions are of two kinds :—
Baronial Sessions dealing with expenditure for the benefit of the Barony and
County at Large Sessions, dealing with the expenditure for works chargeable on the entire county (Bailey, " Local and Centralised Government in Ireland," p. 15).
" Next in order after the Grand Juries the Chief County Authorities for fiscal affairs are the magistrates and associated cess-payers assembled at Presentment Sessions, held for each barony separately, and for the county at large before every assizes."
" For the Baronial Sessions the Grand Jury fix the number of cess-payers resident in the barony, who are to be associated with the justices, subject to the limit that it is not to be more than twelve nor less than five " (O'Brien Report, p. 53).

Rotulorum was supposed to be the Chief Civil, the
Lord Lieutenant the Chief Military, authority, in the
county. The former had the custody of the county
records, and administered the oath of office to Under-
Sheriffs ; the latter had, at one time, large control over
the Militia and appointments to it, though his powers
in these respects are now circumscribed. His chief
duties, at present, are the appointment of such deputy-
lieutenants as the Viceroy may approve of, and the
recommendation to the Lord Chancellor of persons
entitled to become Justices of the Peace.

The Lord Lieutenant of the county is appointed by
the Crown (or subject to the direction of the sovereign,
by the Viceroy) ; the Custos Rotulorum is appointed
by the Viceroy, by letters patent under the Great Seal
of Ireland.*

The High Sheriff.

The High Sheriff, as we have already seen, is appointed by the Lord Lieutenant, from a list of three
names, submitted to him by the judge going assize.
The rule is that the Crown Judge going assize in each
county returns to the Lord Chief Justice the names of
three persons whom he considers fit to discharge the
duties of the office in that county and these names are
subsequently submitted by the Lord Chief Justice
to the Lord Lieutenant. The property qualification
for the office is specified in the Statute of Sheriffs,
9th Edward II. (1313) :—

> " None shall be Sheriff except he shall have
> sufficient land within the same shire where he

* O'Brien. Custos Rotulorum, keeper of the rolls or records of
the Sessions of the Peace, previously nominated by the Lord Chancellor, was, in 1545, directed to be appointed by a bill signed by
the King. The Act was confirmed in 1689 (Haydn's Dictionary
of Dates).
The office of Lord Lieutenant for counties was instituted in
England in the reign of Edward VI., and in Ireland in 1831 ;
their military jurisdiction abolished by Army Regulation Act,
1871 (Haydn's Dictionary of Dates).

shall be Sheriff, to answer the King and his people."*

The duties of the Sheriff, as is well known, include the conduct of elections for Parliamentary representatives, the election of coroner, the service of writs for both the superior and the County Courts, the selection of the Grand Jury, and so forth. He has the power of appointing a sub-Sheriff by whom practically the duties of the office are done.

Deputy Lieutenants.

This is an office which confers social rank and nothing more. The appointment rests with the Lord Lieutenant of the county, subject to the sanction of the Viceroy.

County Court Judge.

" This is an office of high rank and responsibility, it is in the gift of the Lord Lieutenant of Ireland, and can only be filled by a practising barrister of at least ten years' standing.†

" The holder of the office is Chairman of the Justices Quarter Sessions, and sole Judge of the Civil Bill Court of his county‡ (O'Brien, p. 50).

* This Act has been repealed as regards England by 50 and 51 Vic. cap. 55. (O'Brien, p. 48).

† O'Brien, p. 49.

‡ The Jurisdiction of the Court of Quarter Sessions comprehends nearly the whole range of the Criminal Code—except capital offences—and also certain statutory offences, as treason, felony, etc., but as a matter of practice the crimes of the graver type are usually sent for trial by the Crown authorities to the Court of Assize. The justices associated with the judge of quarter sessions exercise a co-ordinate jurisdiction and authority. The Court is assisted by a Grand Jury to find Bills of indictment and petty juries to try the prisoners (O'Brien, p. 64).

The Civil Bill Court has a jurisdiction up to £50 (O'Brien, p. 65).

Inland Navigation.

There are nine Chief Inland Navigation districts in Ireland. (*a*) Four (*viz.*, Ballinamore and Ballyconnell between Connaught and Ulster, Lough Corrib in Galway, and, in Ulster, the Upper and the Lower Bann) were under the management of trustees, originally appointed by Act of Parliament (5 and 6 Vic., c. 89), new appointments being made as vacancies occurred by the Grand Jury, with whom the right of removal also rested. The Trustees are now appointed by the County Councils. It may be said that at the present moment there is practically no navigation traffic in the Lower Bann, and its abolition was impliedly recommended by Sir Alexander Binnie, in a Report of 16th January, 1906. Neither is there navigation on the Ballinamore Canal, but the Upper Bann and Lough Corrib navigations are still used. (*b*) Five (*viz.*, The Upper and Lower Boyne, the Maigue, the Shannon, Tyrone and the Ulster Canal) were all formerly under the Board of Works.* But in 1889, the Ulster and the Tyrone† Canals were transferred to the Lagan Company (51 and 52 Vic., cap. 137), and in 1896, the Upper and Lower Boyne were transferred to the Boyne Navigation Company (59 and 60 Vic., cap. 96.) The Maigue (a negligable quantity) and the Shannon still belonged to the Board of Works.

The four canals under trustees were constructed ¡n the time of the famine of 1847, out of " Imperial "

---

* O 'Brien, p. 115.

† The Tyrone Canal is now, I believe, called the Coal Island Canal. It is, I understand, a paying concern. The Board of Works have no longer anything to do with it. By the 25 Geo II., c. 10 and 29 Geo. III., c. 31 the Commissioners for Promoting Inland Navigation in Ireland were formed into one company or corporation and empowered to make, among others, the Coal Island Canal, which is the same as the Tyrone Navigation. The 40 Geo. III., c. 51 transferred all Canals made with public funds, including Tyrone Navigation, to a newly created Board of Directors of Inland Navigation and on the creation of the Board of Works by the 1-2 Wm. IV., c. 33, they took over the powers of the Directors of Inland Navigation.

funds, and partly out of the rates. The Ulster Canal fell into the hands of the Board of Works, because the company were unable to repay the Government advances for its construction.

The following six canals are under private companies ; The Lagan, the Newry, Loch Erne, the Royal Canal (which is now owned by the Midland and Great Western Railway, who work the Canal subject to the supervision of a Board of Control on which the Board of Works is represented, 40 and 41 Vic., c. 139) the Grand Canal, and the Barrow.*

I am told that the flourishing Companies are the Grand Canal, the Newry, the Lagan and the Shannon. It may be added that in theory there is water communication from Limerick to Belfast; thus, the Shannon, Ballinamore Canal, Ulster Canal, Upper Bann, into Lough Neagh, and so into Belfast by the Lagan Canal, or to Newry by the Newry Canal, or to Coleraine by the Lower Bann; but the chain is broken at the Ballinamore and Ballyconnell link. There is, however, constant communication between Limerick and Dublin *via* the Grand Canal.

* " The Inland Navigations in Ireland are said to afford about 750 miles of water communication ; and they have absorbed a total capital expenditure, estimated to have been not far short of £5,000,000. Towards this sum public moneys have contributed about two-fifths, the rest having been provided for out of county and other funds. The execution of many of the works was commenced and assisted in the last century by the Commissioners of Works, afterwards the Directors General of Inland Navigation. These persons, originally called "Undertakers," were composed of members of Parliament and justices, who owed their first exis- tence to the Act 2 Geo. I., c. 12 ; who were by successive statutes from time to time charged with the promotion and maintenance of navigations in Ireland, and entrusted by the Irish and Imperial Parliaments with public grants ; and whose powers and author- ities were finally transferred to the Board of Public Works, on its constitution in 1831, by the Act 1 and 2 Wm. IV., c. 33. It was in this way or in their capacity as mortgagees in possession, that the Government came to acquire over most of the navigations a direct or indirect control)" (Report of Committee on Board of Works, Ireland, 1878, p. 36). There are three tidal navigations, *viz.*, the Blackwater (Co. Waterford) Slaney, and Suir.

Lunatic Asylums.

The first Act passed in connection with this subject, was in 1806 (46 George III., c. 95), when Grand Juries were enabled to make provision for lunatics by adding wards to the Houses of Industry and presenting sums not exceeding £100 a year, for each county, county of a city, or county of a town, or making up a possible expenditure of £4,000 a year for all Ireland.

The arrangements made under this measure were a failure, and, in 1817 another Act was passed (57 George III., c. 106), which placed the care of lunatics in the hands of the Lord Lieutenant. Under this measure and amending Acts, district lunatic asylums were established, under the control of Boards of Governors, appointed by the Castle. By an Act passed in 1821 (1 and 2 George IV., c. 33), commissioners of control were appointed, not exceeding eight in number. In 1855 (18 and 19 Vic., c. 109, sec. 5), the Chairman of the Board of Works for the time being was made an *ex-officio* member of the Board of Control. I gather that, in practice, the Board of control, up to 1890, consisted of four members. The Chairman of the Board of Works, another member of the Board of Works, and two inspectors of lunatic asylums. But by an order in council of the 18th March, 1890, the Chairman and the two Commissioners of the Board of Works, and the two Inspectors of Lunatic Asylums were constituted the Board of Commissioners for General Control of Asylums for the Lunatic Poor in Ireland.*

In 1867, the Lord Lieutenant in Council was empowered to determine from time to time the staff of officers, male and female, to be appointed for each asylum, and to regulate their salaries, and to define their duties etc., and the same Act enabled him to appoint the " resident medical superintendent," who was the principal executive officer connected with each

* O'Brien, pp. 102, 106.

asylum—all other appointments being made by the Board of Governors, subject to approval and confirmation however, in each case, by the Lord Lieutenant.

" Provisions were made by an Act passed in 1875 whereby upon voluntary agreement entered into between Boards of Guardians and Boards of Governors, respectively, chronic cases of lunacy, not being dangerous, might be transferred from the asylums to the workhouses, and paid for therein, subject to the approval of the Local Government Board and the Inspectors of Lunatics."*

" The Administration of the several boards of Governors," says Mr. O'Brien, " of lunatic asylums is necessarily limited to the purpose of superintending the management of these institutions, providing for the various wants of the inmates, making contracts for the various supplies incidental thereto, and the appointment and control of the several officers employed by them."

At present the District Asylums are managed in each case by a Committee of the County Council and by a Joint Committee in cases where the Asylum serves more than one County or County Borough.

The Inspectors are appointed by the Lord Lieutenant.

The Regulations are prepared by the local authorities (the Asylum Committees) but must receive the approval of the Lord Lieutenant before they become operative. The Inspectors, who are the advisers of the Lord Lieutenant in the matter, examine the Regulations, and see that certain essentials are embodied in them, and that none of them are *ultra vires*.

The duty of managing the Asylums being cast on the Committees, the giving of permission to visitors

* Mr. O'Brien's able Report was made in 1877, and brought up to the date 1890.

to enter them is vested in the Committees, but in practice, the Resident Medical Superintendents, who are the Chief Executive Officers of the Committee, admit *visitors* at their discretion.

In reference to the authority for sanctioning the admission of persons as *patients* there are various ways of securing admission, the principal of which are the ordinary admission form which is prescribed by the Regulations, and the Warrant of Committal under the 10th Section of the Act 30 and 31 Vic., cap. 118. The authorities who can authorise admission, are the Lord Lieutenant, the Lord Chancellor, the Inspectors of Lunatics, the Committee of Management and, in urgent cases, the Resident Medical Superintendent or any Medical Officer acting in his absence.

The Order of Committal under the Act 30 and 31 Vic., cap. 118, Sec. 10, is made by two magistrates.

The Medical Officers are appointed by the Committees of Management, but the appointment of every Medical Officer and the amount of his salary must receive the concurrence of the Lord Lieutenant.

The above statement relates to the public Asylums, and does not deal with Private Asylums and Endowed Institutions for the Insane, nor with the Central Criminal Lunatic Asylum at Dundrum which is a State Institution.*

Arterial Drainage.

" Arterial drainage has been carried out in Ireland under two systems.—1. Under the Drainage Act of 1842 (5 and 6 Vic., c. 89), and Amending Acts. In this case the Board of Works executed the drainage work themselves, having previously obtained the assent of the proprietors in value of two-thirds (afterwards one-half) of the value of the lands. On the undertaking being complete the expense was apportioned on

* See *post* L. G. Act, 1898.

the lands drained and the works handed over to a local body of trustees.

" 2. Under the Drainage and Improvement of Land Act, 1863 (26 and 27 Vic., cap. 88), [and amending Acts.] The works are in this case carried out, not by the Government, but by a Drainage Board constituted by a provisional order made by the Board of Works, and confirmed by Parliament, the assent of the proprietors of one-half in value of the lands having been first obtained to the scheme, [provided the owners of one-third in value do not dissent (41-42 Vic., cap. 59, s. 4.]. On the completion of the scheme the Board of Works make an award fixing the charge upon the [improved lands,] and the amount payable by each proprietor in repayment of instalments of loan and [his proportionate liability for the] cost of maintenance [thereafter.]

" By 29 and 30 Vic., cap. 49, the Board of Works may, in certain cases, execute necessary works [of maintenance] in a drainage district where the Drainage Board or Trustees fail to do so ; 121 districts were constituted under the Drainage Act, of 1842, and 59 were formed up to 31st March, 1887, under the Act of 1863—180 in all.

" Up to the 31st March, 1889, the number of districts formed under the Act of 1863 was sixty-two ; the number now is sixty-three. There are in all [147] arterial Drainage Districts in Ireland for the superintendence and management of which Local Boards are elected by the rate-payers liable to pay the drainage rate in each district."*

The Harbour.

Two harbours, Kingstown and Howth, are under the control of the Board of Works ; which body is also constituted (39 and 40 Vic., cap. 236) (local) the Harbour

* O'Brien, p. 117.

Board for a third harbour—Ardglass County Down. Dublin is governed by the Dublin Port and Dock's Board created in 1867 (30 Vic., cap. 81). The Board consists of twenty-five members : the Lord Mayor for the time being, three citizens appointed by the Muncipal Council, seven commissioners of Irish lights, chosen by that body, fourteen elective members— seven elected by the traders and manufacturers, and seven by the owners of shipping, registered in the Custom House Books or trading to the Port. Belfast is managed by twenty-one Elective Commissioners (46 and 47 Vic., cap. lix.) Cork and Londonderry, Waterford, Limerick, Dundalk, Drogheda, Sligo, Wexford, and Galway, and other harbours of less importance are all regulated by their own respective administrative authorities.*

Board of Works.

The Board of Works was established in 1831 (1 and 2 William IV. cap. 33). It consisted originally of three members, the number was afterwards raised to five, but subsequently reduced again to three, at which it stands to-day. The Commissioners are appointed technically by the English Treasury.† I have already said how its relations to the English Treasury have been compared to the relations of the branch of a big bank to the head office. As a " branch bank," it lends money at interest. It advises the " head office " on the subject of loans and receives instructions from the central authority.

With reference to the functions of the Board, in carrying out drainage works and lending money in private cases, the following concrete case has been stated to me :—

* O'Brien, p. 111.

† I think it may fairly be said that the Treasury would not appoint anyone of whom the Chief Secretary did not approve. In fact it is well known that the Commissioners are practically appointed by the Castle.

" Suppose a farmer wishes to have a system of drainage carried out ; he applies to the Board for a loan. An Inspector is sent down to consider the matter, to see if a system of drainage is necessary ; and if so, to decide on the best mode of doing it. The work is done by the farmer under the direction of the Inspector. Money is lent to the farmer, say £100 at 3½ per cent. to be paid back in twenty years. Of course the Board will see, like a bank, that the security is good."*

Besides its banking functions, it " carries on " " works," is responsible for the upkeep of public buildings, attends, as we have seen, to Shannon navigation and arterial drainage, and looks after " royal harbours " and, to a limited extent, the preservation of ancient monuments. It is also given certain powers under the Fisheries Piers Acts, Marine Works Act, 1902, and the Light Railways Acts. In fact, the Commissioners conduct the business which is delegated to two separate Boards in London, viz. : *The Commissioners of Works and Public Buildings*, and the *Public Loans Commissioners*, and part of that which is entrusted to the *Enclosures Commissioners*.

Some reports of the Commissioners lie before me, and I do not think I can give a better idea of the scope of their duties than by taking some items at random from them. Thus I read :—

A.—(WORKS) VOTED SERVICES.

NAVAL AND MILITARY BUILDINGS.

" Royal Hospital, Kilmainham, repairs."
" Royal Hibernian Military School, water supply."
" Ordnance Survey Depôt Phœnix Park, fitting up galvanised iron shed."

* I understand that the rates of interest on local loans (fixed by the Treasury) at present are 3½ per cent. for periods not exceeding thirty, and 3¾ per cent for periods not exceeding fifty years. The average rate of interest received in the year ended 31st March, 1905, was £3 9s. 5d. per cent. (" *Irish Executive*," p. 28).

Coastguard Stations.

" Building new Stations, repairing old."

State and Official Residences.

" Viceregal Lodge, improvements."

" Chief Secretary's Lodge, removing vineries."

" Dublin Castle, reflooring throne room, etc."

Legal Departments.

" Registry of Deeds, improvements."

" Four Courts, redecorating hall."

" Irish Land Commission, a series of important additions to the Land Commission buildings. etc."

Metropolitan Police Barracks.

" Chapelizod, new barracks."

Royal Irish Constabulary Barracks.

" Various repairs."

District and Minor Model Schools.

" General repairs."

Post Office Buildings.

" Repairs in capital and provinces."

Customs Buildings.

" Improvements, repairs."

Inland Revenue Buildings.

" Repairs."

District or Probate Registry Offices.

" Improvements, repairs."

Public Gardens.

" Phœnix Park and St. Stephen's Green, Dublin, and the Curragh of Kildare, usual works of maintenance and repair."

Royal Harbours.

" Kingstown, Howth, Dunmore East, Donaghadee and Ardglass, repairs, etc."

SHANNON DRAINAGE.

" Maintenance in good order."

RIVER MAIGUE NAVIGATION.

" Maintenance."

ANCIENT MONUMENTS.

" Protection."

B.—NON-VOTED SERVICES

" Arterial Drainage and Improvement of Lands. Drainage maintenance."

" Fishery, piers and harbours maintenance."

LOANS.

" Labouring classes dwellings, works carried out by Grand Juries."

" Loans for Public Libraries."

" Loans for Lunatic Asylum Buildings."

" Loans under the Public Health Acts."

" Loans under Labourer's Acts."

" Loans for Arterial Drainage."

" Loans for Land Improvement."

" Railway Loans."*

The Local Government Board.

The Local Government Board was created in 1872. (Act 35 and 36 Vic., cap. 69). It was preceded by the Poor Law Board, which it absorbed. The story of the introduction of the English poor law into Ireland— so characteristic of English operations in the country— must be told.

In 1833, a royal commission was appointed to consider the subject of Irish destitution in reference to the advisability of establishing "work-houses" to alleviate Irish distress. The commission consisted chiefly of Irishmen, though the Chairman, Archbishop Whately, was an Englishman. The commissioners

---

* The powers of the Board of Works are exercised under various Acts of Parliament passed between 1831 and the present time ; which it is not necessary for my purpose to enumerate.

took three years to consider the subject submitted to them ; and, at the end of that time, made a report which, in the light of subsequent events, must be pronounced a statesmanlike document. They said, in effect, that the cure for Irish distress was work not workhouses. The labouring poor were able-bodied men who only needed employment, and scope for their energies ; and should be provided with work which would develop the resources of the country, and remove the causes of poverty. A Viceregal poor law reform commission, which reported in 1906, refers to the report of the Commissioners in 1833, in the following language :—

" It will probably surprise most of those who study the condition of Ireland, and who have considered how to improve it, to find that a commission that sat seventy years ago recommended land drainage and reclamation on modern lines, the provision of labourer's cottages and allotments, the bringing of agricultural instruction to the doors of the peasant, the improvement of land tenure, the transfer of fiscal powers from Grand Juries to County Boards, the employment of direct labour on roads by such County Boards, the sending of vagrants to colonies to be employed there or to penitentiaries in this country ; the closing of public-houses on Sundays, and the prevention of the sale of groceries and intoxicating drink in the same house for consumption on the premises. Such were the recommendations of the Royal Commission of Inquiry into the condition of the poorer classes.*"

For the sick and impotent poor the Royal Commissioners reported practically that relief ought to be afforded by voluntary associations, controlled by State Commissioners, and whose revenues might be

* Poor Law Commission (Ireland) Report, 1903-6, p. 12.

strengthened by the imposition of a contributory parochial rate. Emigration, as a temporary expedient, was also recommended in certain cases.

The report of the Royal Commissioners was laid before Lord John Russell.

Lord John Russell, with that far-sighted wisdom and deep-seated knowledge which distinguish English statesmanship in Ireland, flung the report into the ministerial waste paper basket, and despatched a young Englishman named Nicholls, a member of the English Poor Law Commission, to report afresh on the subject. Mr. Nicholls paid a roving visit to Ireland. The Royal Commission had taken three years to consider the question, but they were Irishmen plus a few English colleagues. Mr. Nicholls disposed of the question in six weeks, but he was an English official, drawing his inspiration from an English minister, who was as competent to deal with the subject as himself.

Mr. Nicholls, of course, made the report that was expected of him. He recommended the establishment of workhouses. The government brought in a Workhouse Bill, which was opposed by the Irish members in committee and on the third reading, but it was carried, nevertheless, by overwhelming majorities.

This Bill (introduced by way of resolution on the 13th of February, 1837), proposed the erection in Ireland of 100 workhouses, where relief and employment should be afforded to the poor—infirm and able-bodied. The whole country was to be divided into unions, the landlords and tenants or occupiers of each union to be rated in equal shares for the support of the poor within the Union. The system was to be administered by local boards of guardians, consisting of *ex-officio* and elected members, the former not to exceed one-third of all the guardians chosen, and not to comprise clergymen of any denomination. There was to be no law of settlement,* and the local boards of guardians

---

* In England the law of settlement rendered a residence of three years in the district necessary to entitle a person to relief.

were to be placed under the control of a central authority in Dublin, to consist of commissioners chosen from the Poor Law Commissioners of England.

The reception given to some of the Irish Amendments in Committee is worth noting :—

> *O'Connell :*—" That the Act should be administered by an Irish Poor Law Board, not by the English Commissioners, as proposed in the Bill."

The amendment was rejected by 117 to 23 votes.

> *O'Connell :*—" That unions should not be divided into electoral districts for the election of Guardians unless with the consent of a majority of the Guardians."

The amendment was negatived by 84 to 47 votes.

> *O'Connell :*—" That clergymen should be eligible to be elected as Poor Law Guardians."

The amendment was negatived by 107 to 30 votes.

> *O'Connell :*—" That there should be no *ex-officio* Guardians."

The amendment was defeated by 124 to 44 votes.

> *Shaw :*—" That workhouses should only be built for the lame, impotent, old and blind."

The amendment was defeated by 134 to 75 votes.

> *Smith O'Brien :*—" That out-door relief should be given."

Defeated by 99 to 32 votes.

> *O'Connell :*—" That poor rate should be paid by the landlords alone."

Defeated by 71 to 22 votes.

> *Smith O'Brien :*—" That two-thirds of the rates should be paid by the landlords."

Defeated by 46 to 31 votes.

O'Connell :—" That the voting at the election of Poor Law Guardians should be by ballot." Defeated by 54 to 27 votes.*

Thus the English workhouse system was set up in Ireland by English authority, in defiance of Irish wishes.

Between 1838 and 1847 it was administered by the English Poor Law Board. In 1847 an Irish Poor Law Board, of which the Chief Secretary and Under-Secretary at the Castle were *ex-officio* members, replaced the English Commission as the central authority.† This Board remained in existence until 1872, when, as I have already said, it was absorbed by the newly created Local Government Board, of which the Chief Secretary became *ex-officio* President, and the Under-Secretary remained an *ex-officio* member.

In closing the story of the introduction of the English workhouse system in Ireland, I may give another short extract from the report of the Poor Law Reform Commission, 1903-6 :—

"The Irish Royal Commission (1836) recommended the development of the resources of the country, in order that undertakings might be started, which would, in due course, give employment to those able and willing to work ; and the opinion of the Commissioners was that, in this way, the widespread and exceptional poverty of Ireland ought to be relieved. This is our opinion also ; and we can point to the excellent results, as far as a merely experimental income permits, of the work of the congested Districts Board in the establishment of industries and fisheries leading to an ordinary commercial trade. Good

* Well might the late Sir Spencer Walpole have written : " [The treatment of Ireland] made representative government in Ireland a fraud. It is absurd to say that a country enjoys representative institutions if its delegates are uniformly out-voted by men of another race " (History of England, Vol. IV., p. 207).

† Hancock, p. 117.

results also can be traced to the improvements of traffic facilities, especially by water, for the carriage of cattle and goods."*

In passing to the operations of the Poor Law system, I may quote the following extract from Mr. Hancock :—

"The Poor Law arrangements," he says, "being modern and convenient, under active local bodies meeting frequently, and under active central control, have been adopted on nearly all occasions where a new local function was created, or an old one modified."

Thus we find that on the dissolution of many municipal corporations in Ireland, by what has been facetiously called the Municipal Reform Act of 1840, the properties of these defunct bodies (in towns where there were no town commissioners, or town councils) were vested in the Guardians for the benefit of the inhabitants.†

In 1844, Poor Law Unions were taken as the marriage registration districts, under the Registration of Marriages Act. They were also availed of in the administration of the Vagrant Act of 1847.

In 1848-49, the Guardians appear as concurrent health authorities under the Nuisance Removal and Diseases Prevention Acts.

In 1850, the Clerks of the Union and the Poor Rates collectors were selected to prepare the Parliamentary Voters Lists, under the Parliamentary Voters' Act of that year.

In 1851, the Guardians took part in the new system of Medical Relief, under the Medical Charities Act of that year.

The Guardians became one of the local authorities under the Common Lodging Houses Acts of 1851-60.

* Poor Law Commission, p. 15

† In 1840, there were sixty-eight corporations in Ireland. Of these fifty-eight were disfranchised, and a restricted franchise was given to the remaining ten. This was called "Municipal Reform."

By the Acts of 1851 and 1854, respectively, duties relating to the apprenticing of workhouse boys to the navy and the mercantile marine services were imposed on the Guardians.

In 1855, the Guardians were constituted the Burial Board in certain cases.

In 1861, the machinery of the Poor Law was used for defraying the expenses of the Cattle Disease Act for Ireland.

In 1863, the Guardians became one of the local authorities under the Bakehouses Regulation Act.

In 1865, they were constituted the sewer authorities under the Sewage Utilisation Act.

In 1866, they became the sole authorities for nuisances and sewers in all rural districts.

The Guardians became one of the local authorities under the Workshops Regulation Act in 1867.

By the Church Act of 1869, burial grounds not attached to existing places of worship were transferred from the Church authorities, and vested in the Guardians of the Poor alone.

In 1871 the Poor Law system of audit was generally adopted.

In 1874 the Guardians became rural sanitary authorities and in certain cases urban sanitary authorities.*

* A. In 1851 there was transferred to the Poor Law Union organisation, by the Medical Charities Act, the system of medical relief afforded through dispensaries, and which had been up to that time supplied by means of private subscriptions, aided by grants of similar amount from the county rates, made to local committees appointed by the subscribers, and subject to no official control (O Brien, p. 24).

B. The Sanitary Act of 1866, the Nuisance Removal Acts of 1855 and 1860, and the Public Health Act of 1874 have been repealed by the Public Health (Ireland) Act, 1878, and the several powers relating to the Sanitary Committees above referred to are no longer in force (O'Brien, p. 19).

C. Under an Amendment Act of 1843, a power was given to Boards of Guardians to send any "destitute poor," deaf and dumb, or blind children, under the age of eighteen, to any asylums approved of for the purpose by the Commissioners, and to pay for their maintenance therein (O'Brien, p. 21.)

I do not pretend to describe all the functions which
devolved on the Poor Law organisation between 1838
and 1898. I give a sample of them :—

> " The general tendency," says Mr. O'Brien,
> " of modern legislation, has been to take advan-
> tage, more and more each year, for divers purposes
> of local government, of this particular organisation,
> which has thus come, in course of time, to assume
> dimensions greatly exceeding those which were
> either contemplated or belonged to it at the time
> of its original institution."*

In the discharge of the duties so thrown upon them,
the Guardians acted under the superintendence, first
of the Poor Law Commissioners, and afterwards of
the Local Government Board which, as I have said,
was established in 1872. The Act of 1872 provided
that the Local Government Board should consist of
a President—who should be the Chief Secretary for
the time being—the Under-Secretary, a Vice-President
and two Commissioners. Lord Hartington, the Chief
Secretary, in moving the committal of the Bill, said
that the principal object was to " constitute a department, in which the public should have confidence,"
and which should superintend the administration of
the Poor Law, of the Local Government Acts, and of
the Sanitary Acts.

---

* " To discharge various functions," says Mr. Bailey, in
his admirable little pamphlet, published in 1888, entitled
" Local and Centralised Government in Ireland," " thrown
upon the Board of Guardians, committees are formed
consisting partly of guardians and partly of co-opted
ratepayers. The most important of these committees are
those constituted under the Medical Charities Act of 1851
for the management of the affairs of the district dispensaries
established by that Act. Similar committees are constituted
under the various Sanitary Acts. Each Union has a staff
of paid officers elected by the Board of Guardians, but subject
to the veto of, and liable to removal by, the Local Government
Board " (p. 30).

" The reason," he added, " why the Chief Secretary was made President was, in order to make his responsibility to the House complete."*

The superintending powers of the central authority, in reference to Boards of Guardians, were extensive :—

1. It decided upon the number of Guardians to be elected for each Union.

2. It also decided the qualification for candidates.

3. It regulated the mode of election, and appointed the returning officer.†

4. It had power to dissolve the Board of Guardians, in case of default in discharge of their duties, and to appoint paid Guardians instead.

5. The duties of the paid staff of the Guardians were carefully defined by the general orders of the Local Government Board, in whom also was vested a veto in every instance upon the appointments made, as well as an absolute power of removal in case of misconduct, unfitness or other sufficient cause.‡ In reference to the powers of the Local Government Board, in other respects, I shall quote Mr. Bailey :—

" Under the new system, the Local Government Board was empowered, in answer to a petition from the local body, to make all necessary inquiries, and, if there was no reason to the contrary, by provisional order give the desired privilege.

" These provisional orders could be confirmed by Parliament without expense or delay.

" The following powers might be thus obtained :—

* House of Commons, July 22nd, 1872. See also Mr. Bailey, p. 39.

† The elected Guardians are chosen annually on the 25th March, or within fourteen days of that date. The elections are conducted not by ballot, but by means of voting papers left and collected at the voter's residence, usually by members of the Royal Irish Constabulary especially engaged for the purpose (O'Brien, p. 14).

‡ O'Brien, p. 19.

"1. To purchase land for certain defined purposes of public utility.

"2. To incorporate adjoining districts with a town.

"3. To separate any part of a town from the jurisdiction of the governing body.

"4. To transfer to the governing body of a town, from the grand jury of the county, all authority with regard to roads, bridges, foot paths, and public works within the town, and all taxation for such purposes, and to make the necessary provisions in relation to such transfer.

"5. To authorise the making of rates in addition to the existing maximum.

"6. To provide for the future execution of, or alteration or repeal of, any local Act affecting the town, or any part thereof.

"7. To extend the borrowing powers in certain cases.

"Certain provisions were also made with regard to markets and fairs, the auditing of accounts, and the borrowing of money."

The Local Government Act of 1898 made a revolution in the Local Government of Ireland. It swept away the fiscal and administrative powers of the Grand Jury and appointed popular bodies elected on a democratic franchise to take the place of the old oligarchical system. These bodies were County Councils, Rural District Councils, Urban District Councils and Boards of Guardians.*

1. *County Councils.* The Local Government Board fixes the boundaries and number of members. The

---

* "The main object of the Local Government [Ireland] Act of 1898 was to transfer to popularly elected local bodies the powers and duties of the grand juries and of the county-at-large presentment sessions. . . .

"Additional duties were at the same time either imposed upon these councils or transferred to them from other local authorities" (Local Government Board Memorandum, 1899, *re* the effect of the Local Government [Ireland] Act, 1898, on Local Taxation).

qualifications of members and the franchise are the Parliamentary qualification and franchise with this difference : peers and women can vote and the former are eligible for membership* ; Ministers of religion cannot be members of the County Council. The elections are triennial and the voting is by ballot.

Every Chairman of a Rural District Council is a member of the County Council, and may be a Justice of the Peace.

All the functions of the Grand Juries have been transferred to the County Councils except two.

(*a*) The Grand Jury still retains the privilege of finding true bills at the assizes ; while (*b*) the County Court Judge now exercises the power of making presentments for malicious injuries, subject to appeal to Judges of Assize.

The County Councils alone collect the poor rates, and some other matters, formerly attended to by the Poor Law Guardians, have also been transferred to them. The lunatic asylums are managed by Committees of the County Councils. All the asylum officers are appointed by the County Councils, the Lord Lieutenant having a veto on the appointment of the medical attendant and assistant medical attendant.

The County Council appoints the Coroner, whose salary is fixed, with the approval of the Local Government Board. The Secretary of the Council, the County Surveyor, and the Assistant County Surveyor are

* Sec. 104 of the Local Government Ireland Act, 1898, gives power to the Lord Lieutenant in Council to make orders about various matters connected with the Act, *inter alia.*

(*a*) " disqualifications of persons for being members of a County Council, or District Council, or Board of Guardians."

By Order in Council (Local Government Application of Enactments Order 1898,) dated 22nd December, 1898,

(1) "No woman shall be eligible for election or being chosen as a COUNTY COUNCILLOR. (2) No person shall be disqualified by sex or marriage for being elected or chosen, or being a Guardian or Councillor of a Rural or Urban District other than a borough, or a Town Commissioner."

only removable with the consent of the Local Government Board.

The County Councils cannot engage surveyors and other officers without the sanction of the Local Government Board, which has also control over salaries.

In fine, the Lord Lieutenant by Order in Council regulates the procedure of County and District Councils under the Act. (Sec. 106).*

On the question of expenses, one of my informants said :—

> " The Councils are free to spend money, subject to the audit of the Local Government Board. In England, auditors are appointed by the Municipalities, but in Ireland the Local Government Board appoints auditors everywhere. In reference to the County Councils the auditors might disallow expenditure on the ground that it was illegal. Sometimes, however, the expenditure might be illegal, but it might, nevertheless, be allowed on the merits. I shall give you a case. A surveyor had built a shed to protect machinery. He had no authority for doing this, and the auditor disallowed the charge ; but the Local Government Board, on appeal, allowed it on the ground that it was a proper thing to erect a shed for such a purpose."†

* See Statutory Rules and Orders, 1899.

† Under Part V. of the Public Health Acts Amendment Act, 1890, as applied to Ireland, an urban sanitary authority, and under the Local Government (Ireland) Acts, 1898 to 1902, a county council, may, with the consent of the Board, exercise borrowing power by the creation of stock to be created, issued, transferred, dealt with, and redeemed in such a manner and in accordance with such regulations as the Board may prescribe, and the Board have made regulations for the purpose. Such regulations must be laid before each House of Paliament for thirty days, and, if no Resolution that they be no further proceeded with is passed by either House, they are to be confirmed by the Lord Lieutenant in Council.

The Board has this power by the Act of 1898. There is an appeal from the Board to the King's Bench, but only on a question of law.

It has been said that the ways of auditors are capricious ; and the following examples have been given to illustrate the fact.

> " On the occasion of the assassination of President McKinley, the Cork Corporation sent a cablegram of sympathy to Vice-President Roosevelt. They were surcharged for it."

On another occasion a sum of £20 was spent by the Council at Bandon, in presenting and preparing an address to the King of England (£6 6s. being paid for a special suit of clothes for the clerk). There was no surcharge, not even for the clerk's apparel.

On the other hand, the cost of preparing an address to the English King at Kingstown in 1905, was disallowed, though allowed on a previous occasion.*

In reference to the borrowing powers of the Council, another of my informants said :—

> " No local authority can borrow a penny without the consent of the Local Government Board. Suppose a local authority wanted money, they would communicate with the Local Government Board. They might ask the Board to get the money from the Board of Works, or the Local Government Board might issue a Stock order, which would appear in the daily newspapers, and all details would be fixed by the Local Government Board."

> " How have the County Councils done their work ? " I asked one, who was in a position to speak with knowledge on the subject.

> He answered : " Splendidly."

I quote some extracts from the annual reports of the Local Government Board for the years 1900, 1901 and 1902 concerning the manner in which the County Councils have done their work.

* C. Lehane's " Ireland's Burden under British Boards."

Extract from Annual Report of the Local Government Board for Ireland, year ended March, 1900.

General.

" 1900.

" Before concluding our references to the Local Government Act, we may be permitted to observe that the predictions of those who affirmed that the new local bodies entrusted with the administration of a complex system of County Government would inevitably break down have certainly not been verified. On the contrary, the County and District Councils have, with few exceptions, properly discharged the statutory duties devolving upon them. Instances have, no doubt, occurred, in which these bodies have, owing to inexperience and to an inadequate staff, found themselves in difficulties, and have had to receive some special assistance from us in regulating their affairs ; but this has been of rare occurrence, and we are confident that before the term of office of the first Councils elected under the Act expires, the new machinery will be working very smoothly throughout Ireland."

" 1901.

" Our further experience enables us to confirm the statement in our last Report, as to the satisfactory manner in which the duties of the County Councils and Rural District Councils have been discharged. No doubt, in some instances, there has been action, or sometimes inaction, which did not seem to accord with the intentions of the Legislature, but, apart from such exceptional instances, their duties have been satisfactorily and creditably discharged by the Councils and their officials throughout Ireland ; and the Councils, we are glad to observe, appear to recognise the zeal and ability with which they are served by their official staff."

" 1902.

" The term of office of the first County Councils and Rural District Councils on whom, with their officers, rests the credit of having successfully assisted in carrying the Local Government Act into operation, expired in June ; and the new Councils, with the experience of the past three years will, no doubt, endeavour to bring the system into a state of even greater efficiency. Attention has been directed to certain political differences which have been introduced by some of the smaller bodies into their ordinary business transactions with reference to the appointment of officers and the giving of contracts ; but it is only fair to state that these cases have been quite the exception, and not the rule ; they have been promptly dealt with, and we feel confident that the conduct of their affairs by the various local authorities and their officials will continue to justify the delegation to them of the large powers transferred to their control by the Local Government Acts."

Rural District Councils. The qualifications, franchise and election procedure are the same as the County Councils ; and, *inter alia* they exercise the powers hitherto possessed by rural sanitary authorities. But generally the duties of the Rural District Council, and its relation to the County Council have been tersely described by Mr. Gerald Balfour in the remarkably lucid speech in which he introduced the Bill of 1898. He said :—

" Speaking generally, County Councils will take over the powers and the duties of Grand Juries and Presentment Sessions of Counties at large, and the Rural District Councils will take over the powers of the Baronial Presentment Sessions. The effect of this will be that any expenditure on roads and other public works, payable by the Rural District Council will be proposed and presented by that Council to the County Council ; and the County Council may approve of them or disapprove. If it approve, if will be for the County Council to carry out the work through the County Surveyor."*

In order to have a link between the County Council and the Rural District Council every chairman of the latter is, *ipso facto*, a member of the former.

Urban District Councils. I shall again quote from Mr. Gerald Balfour's admirable speech :—

" I turn now to urban districts. Six cities and towns will, under the Bill, be constituted county boroughs, namely, Dublin, Belfast, Cork, Limerick, Londonderry and Waterford. The government of county boroughs will go on much the same as before, save that their councils will be elected upon the wider franchise already described, and they will obtain such powers and duties of County Councils generally as are provided, and which they do not possess already. In the case of other towns and boroughs, every place which is now, or becomes an urban sanitary district, will be an urban district under the Bill, and its affairs will be administered by an Urban District Council. Here, again, we do not propose to interfere with the existing constitution of the local governing bodies, either as to number, duration of office, or time of election—the franchise, of course, will be the Parliamentary franchise. The style or title of the Corporation or Council of a borough will remain unchanged. We propose further that,

* Hansard, February 21st, 1898.

in future, all Urban District Councils should be the road authority for their district, and that for this purpose there should be transferred to them, where they do not already conduct it, the business so far as respects their district of Baronial Presentment Sessions, and also the duties of the Grand Juries in relation to public works, except such public works as are in part or in whole chargeable on the county at large. Urban District Councils will also have the duty of levying and collecting all rates within their district."*

The Urban District Councils being more independent of the County Councils than the Rural District Councils, have not the privilege accorded to the latter of sending their chairman to represent them on the County Councils.

4. *Poor Law Guardians.* In rural districts the Boards of Guardians are constituted by the Rural District Councils ; that is to say every Rural District Councillor is, *ipso facto* a Poor Law Guardian.

In Urban areas the Guardians are elected triennially at the time of election of the County and Rural District Councils. There are no longer *ex-officio* Guardians.

The duties previously allotted to the Guardians as rural sanitary authorities are transferred to the District Councillors, and in fact, Boards of Guardians are confined to their original functions as the local administrators of the Poor Law, the area of administration being the Poor Law Union as before. However, the Committees of Management of Dispensary Districts have been abolished and their duties transferred to the Guardians.

I need scarcely say that it is impossible in a book of this nature to give an account of all the duties of the Local Government Board. In addition to what I have already said, I shall jot down two or three items which may give some idea of their scope.

* House of Commons, February 21st, 1898.

With respect to poor relief the Board make regulations for the guidance of guardians and their officers, and for the administration of relief.

They exercise supervision over the administration of the poor laws generally, examining every week the minutes of the Guardians' proceedings and they provide through their Inspectors, for the systematic inspection of Workhouses. They sanction the appointment of all poor law officers, regulate their salaries, inquire into complaints made against them, and exercise the power of dismissal over them. They ascertain the progress and condition of the children in the Workhouse schools.

The Board make regulations for the government of Dispensary Districts under the Medical Charities Act, for the administration of medical relief under that Act, and as to the qualification, appointment, and salaries of the Dispensary Medical Officers, whose removal they may order if necessary. They also exercise a general supervision over the administration of medical relief, and provide through their Inspectors for the inspection of dispensary buildings.

The Board approve market tolls, and revise and confirm the bye-laws of sanitary authorities for the regulation of common lodging-houses, markets and slaughter-houses, management of mortuaries, cleansing of streets, prevention of nuisances, construction of new streets and buildings, supply of water, and other purposes too numerous to be recited, under the Public Health (Ireland) Acts, 1878 to 1896, the Housing of the Working Classes Acts, the Local Government (Ireland) Acts, the Towns Improvement (Ireland) Act, 1854, and local Acts.

I have not, of course, attempted to give a full account of the changes made by the Local Government Act of 1898. My object has been to make such a statement within the limits, which I have mapped out for myself, as may give the reader some notion of what has taken place. The upshot of the Local Government Act in a word, has been the overthrow of the oligarchical systems which previously existed, and the government of counties and districts by popularly chosen bodies acting under the supervision of the Local Government Board.

Board of "National" Education.

The old educational policy of keeping the Catholics ignorant, unless they conformed to the State religion, was not wholly abandoned until 1831. The infamous Charter Schools, established in the eighteenth century for proselytising purposes, continued to receive grants from Parliament until 1832, and other such like institutions were helped by the State, up to about the same period ; while all this time not a shilling of the public money was given in support of Catholic Schools. The Ascendency said, in effect :—

> " The Catholics shall not be educated unless in the way we like ; "

and the Imperial Parliament supported the Ascendency for thirty-one years after the Union. In 1831, a new departure was made, and the National Schools were established on a principle of compromise acceptable to the Catholics, but not to the Protestants. These schools, supported by Parliamentary grants, were to be open alike to Protestants and Catholics. Four days in the week were to be devoted to moral and literary, and one or two days to separate religious instruction. A Board composed partly of Catholics and partly of Protestants, was to have the entire management and control of the system. Short of denominational education, which both Catholics and Protestants desired, no more workable scheme could be devised. In addition, it was yielded without force, and passed through Parliament without difficulty. But it was unfairly carried out. To begin with, the Board was composed of four Protestants and only two Catholics— in a country where the Catholics were to the Protestants as four to one.

Next, the control and management of the system was practically entrusted to a Scotch Presbyterian clergyman, without knowledge or experience of the country, or sympathy with its people. With one exception, all the books were prepared by Englishmen or Scotchmen, and pains were taken to exclude Irish history and to suppress all national or patriotic sentiments.

In one of the books we find this statement about Ireland :—

> " On the east of Ireland is England, where the Queen lives ; many people who live in Ireland were born in England, and we speak the same language, and are called the same nation."

Let us see how in another book, Scotland was dealt with :—

> " Edward the First annexed the Principality of Wales to his kingdom A.D. 1283. He afterwards attempted to do the same with Scotland, but was successfully resisted, particularly by Sir William Wallace. This celebrated patriot drove his troops out of the kingdom. He was ultimately taken and basely executed by Edward, and a new effort projected to subdue the Scots. But before the army of Edward entered Scotland he died, leaving his crown and enterprise to his son Edward II. This prince followed up the intention of his father, but was defeated at Bannockburn, and thus the independence of the Scots was established."

It was allowable to speak of Sir William Wallace as a " celebrated patriot," and to think with pride on the struggle of the Scots for independence ; but it would have been treason to mention the names of Art McMurrough or Hugh O'Neil, or to tell how Sarsfield fought or Emmet died.

Lines on the " Irish Harp " by Miss Balfour, Campbell's poem " The Harper," and Scott's " Breathes there a man," etc., were suppressed by Archbishop Whately.* But his Grace kindly allowed the use of the following hymn :—

> "I thank the goodness and the grace
> That on my birth have smiled,
> And made me in these Christian days
> A happy English child."

This boycotting of everything national or patriotic was accompanied by the gradual removal or amendment, in deference to Protestant opinion, of the rules originally framed to reconcile the Catholics to the scheme. The result was a popular agitation against the schools, which kept alive the memories of old wrongs, and ended by destroying the feeling of gratitude which Lord Stanley's plan had, at first, inspired. This state of things lasted until 1860, when, after thirty years of intermittent agitation, the system was reformed on more popular lines.

In 1861, the number of Commissioners was increased from seven (as originally fixed) to twenty—ten Catholics and ten Protestants ; in a country where the proportion of Catholics to Protestants is as four to one. According to the report of the Commissioners for the year 1905-6 the total number of schools in operation was 8,659. The total number of pupils attending those schools, 737,752.

Taking the religious denominations we find the following results:—

Catholics		549,234
Protestant Episcopalian	88,617	
Presbyterians	83,557	
Methodists	9,591	
Other denominations	6,753	
Protestants total ..	———	188,518

Some of the schools are exclusively under Catholic teachers, some exclusively under Protestant teachers, and some under Catholic and Protestant teachers

---

* These poems put in by the Scotch Presbyterian clergyman were struck out by the English Archbishop.

conjointly. I shall take these schools in detail, showing the number, and attendance by religious denominations.

Schools exclusively under Catholic teachers :—

Number of schools	1,907
Number of pupils	162,347
Catholics	153,788
Protestants	8,559

Schools exclusively under Protestant teachers :—

Number of schools	823
Number of pupils	62,806
Protestants	57,332
Catholics	5,174

Schools under Catholic and Protestant teachers conjointly :—

Number of schools	32
Number of pupils	4,878
Catholics	3,390
Protestants	1,488

The language used a short time since by Mr. Starkie, the Resident Commissioner, in speaking of the history of the National Schools, deserves to be recorded. Addressing the British Association in Belfast, in 1902, he said :—

> " We are told that national education is an expression of the social, religious, and political aims of the people which it serves."

Judging the character of the National Schools in the past, by this test, he continues :—

> " [Dr. Whately*] waged open war against the language and national feeling. The study of

* The original National Board consisted of the following members :—

Anglicans.—The Duke of Leinster, Dr. Whately (Protestant Archbishop of Dublin), Dr. Sadleir.

Presbyterians.—The Rev. James Carlisle (of the Synod of Ulster), and Mr. Robert Holmes (of the Synod of Munster).

Catholics.—Dr. Murray, Catholic Bishop of Dublin and the Right Hon. J. A. Blake.

The Board was dominated by Dr. Whately and Mr. Carlisle.

Irish was not permitted in the schools, even in Irish-speaking places, which were very numerous seventy years ago ; children were punished for using the language, and the extraordinary spectacle was presented of teachers who knew no Irish endeavouring to teach, through reading books, children who knew no English, and never heard a word of it in their own homes.

" Under these circumstances, it is not strange that [the italics are mine] '*the atmosphere of national sympathy,' which is now held to be essential to educational efficiency, was wanting. The thread of continuity with the past was not jealously guarded, as in Scotland, but was ruthlessly snapped. The familiar associations of cairn and ruin, and the heritage of legend, with its wealth of poetry and mysticism, were treated with disdain ; the Irish language was the badge of serfdom ; even Irish history was proscribed.* Although all experts in education had long taught that history and geography, ' like charity, should begin at home,' with the surroundings most familiar to the child,—the school-house, the village, the well-known scenes of every-day life—all alike were avoided as dangerous ground. Naturally, the national system, so alien from their race and traditions, could find no place in the sympathies and affections of an emotional people. Nature was expelled with a fork, but with complete success.

" Something might have been said in defence of this most petrified and soul-killing of all systems if it had succeeded in giving even a smattering of the three elementary subjects to an almost illiterate people ; but the report of the Powis Commission in 1870, removed the veil from the condition of education in the primary schools, and the Census Returns testified that illiteracy was almost universal and undiminished."

I am told that there is an improvement in the system now, and that Irish history is no longer boycotted in the Irish " National " schools. I gather that one of the rules provides that visits might be paid, under arrangements sanctioned by the Board, to places of educational value or interest.* This is certainly a step in the right direction, for the best way to teach history is to visit scenes of historic interest. I called the attention of one of the managers to this rule. He said that he had never heard of it, and that he thought that very few of the managers had heard of it. The ignorance of managers or teachers on this subject might be obviated if the rule were hung up in the schoolrooms. I would also have printed and hung by its side, the words of Mr. Starkie :—

> " The atmosphere of national sympathy is essential to educational efficiency."

The extraordinary spectacle of

> " teachers who knew no Irish endeavouring to teach through reading books children who knew no English, and never heard a word of it in their own homes,"

is, it must be confessed, very English.

Up to 1878, the Irish language was excluded from the Irish " National Schools " ; it was then admitted, the rate for teaching being fixed at ten shillings a pass per pupil for a three years' course.

In 1905, Mr. Long, the English minister to Ireland of the day, condemned the system, and in March of that year a Treasury Order was issued, declaring that the fees for teaching Irish should cease in June, 1906 ;

---

* The rule runs :
　　"The minimum time constituting an attendance may include　.　.　.
　　" (2) Any time occupied by visits paid during school hours under arrangements sanctioned by the Commissioners to places of educational value or interest.　.　."
(Rules and Regulations of the Commissioners of National Education in Ireland, 1907-1908, page 36 (e) (2).

which they did.* Thus the Irish language, which
had been originally excluded from the schools for
over forty years, which had then been admitted
for twenty-eight years, was once more excluded
by an English Minister, whose ignorance of Ireland
was profound and invincible. On the accession of
the Liberal Goverment to office (in 1905), the restoration of Irish to its rightful place in the national schools
was demanded ; and in 1906 Mr Bryce, the new English
minister to Ireland, in yielding to the popular wish,
substituted a new scheme for the one which had been
destroyed by Mr. Long ; granting 1s. per head in
second and third standards, and 2s. 6d. in higher
standards instead of the 10s. a head previously allowed.

Dissatisfaction having been expressed in Ireland
with this arrangement, Mr. Bryce promised to reconsider the subject if an alternative scheme were submitted
to him. The Gaelic League, accordingly, in consultation with educational experts throughout the
country, prepared and submitted a scheme of fees
ranging from 2s. in infants and first standards, to 8s.
in sixth standards, which would meet the necessities
of the language, and satisfy the Irish people. This
scheme, on being published, was supported by an
expression of opinion in its favour by the managers
and public boards of the country. While the subject
was still under consideration, Mr. Bryce retired from
his position in Ireland, and became English Minister
to Washington. He was succeeded by Mr. Birrell.

In March, 1907, an Irish member, Mr. O'Donnell,
asked a question relating to the matter, and Mr.
Birrell replied :—

"The Commissioners of National Education,
being of opinion that the scale of fees was insufficient for the remuneration of extern teachers,
made proposals for an increase in the scale in
connection with the estimates for 1906-7, and

* The fees then amounted to £14,000.

these proposals were supported by the Irish Government. The Treasury, however, felt unable to sanction these proposals."*

Since this statement was made the National Board of Education have adopted a new scheme, of which the following is the main provision ; that fees may be paid for Irish taught as an extra subject to pupils of the third and higher standards, according to the following scale :—for third standard, 3s. per unit of the average attendance at the Irish lessons ; for fourth, 6s. ; fifth, 9s. ; sixth and higher, 12s. But this " concession " is marred by three rules :—

1. *Extra* instruction must be given *before or after* the fixed day school hours.

2. The fees may be reduced or withheld at the discretion of the Commissioners.

3. The merit of the teaching is judged by the proficiency both in Irish and English, the former being the main factor in the case of the Junior Classes (where no fees are paid up to the third standard), and the latter in the case of the higher.†

I recall Mr. Starkie's words :—

" The atmosphere of national sympathy, is essential to educational efficiency."

A list of the present commissioners lies before me. I should like to ask Mr. Starkie (in a whisper) how far, in his opinion, do they constitute an " atmosphere of national sympathy."

* Memorandum of Gaelic League.—When the Queen's Colleges were established the scheme was placed before Prince Albert ; he asked how it was that there was no chair for Irish ; he was told that an Irish chair was not considered necessary in the new University. " What," he said, " Not a chair for Irish in an Irish University," and he insisted on the establishment of three chairs in the three colleges. I asked the well-informed and distinguished gentleman who gave me this information what was the upshot of Prince Albert's interference. " The chairs were established," he said, " but they were starved, and came to nothing."

† See Rules and Regulations of the Commissioners of National Education in Ireland, pp. 58, 59.

An incident has recently occurred which may enable us—which, shall I say, may even enable Mr. Starkie— to answer the question. A little book—an innocent looking little book—lies before me. It has a red cover—the orthodox English red.

On the cover are the words :

" The National Readers."
"Advanced Reader   -   8d."

I look at the title page and read :

" Brown and Nolan's National Readers.
"Adopted by the Commissioners of National Education.
" Dublin :
"Brown and Nolan, Ltd., 24 and 25, Nassau Street.
"Belfast : 79, Royal Avenue.
"Cork : 14, Winthrop Street."

I glance through the contents and venture to say that no one except a fool, a fanatic, or a commissioner of " National " Education in Ireland will find anything objectionable in it from a political or a religious point of view. Yet it has got into trouble. It has been condemned by the Imperial Protestant Federation and by the " National Board." I turn to the interesting correspondence which it has provoked. The first letter, dated April 21st (assuredly post-dated twenty days), is from the Secretary of the Imperial Protestant Federation to the " Commissioners of National Education " in Ireland. The writer calls attention to the rule of the Board which provides that :—

> " No book can be used for united secular instruction to which a reasonable objection might be entertained on religious or political grounds " Rule 124 (A).

and declares that the use of Brown and Nolan's Advanced Reader in the schools was an infraction of this rule. The Secretary of the National Board replied denying that the book had been adopted by the Commissioners. This denial brought the publishers to the front, and on June 13th, 1908, they addressed a letter to the Board asking the following pertinent questions :—

1. " Whether, on the contrary, it is not a fact that this book was accorded the necessary and fullest sanction now accorded to any book under your Commissioners' Rules, viz., the signified approval of your Inspectors after its submission for their examination, as provided in Rule 124 (B)."

2. " Whether it is not also a fact that in certain instances, before such approval was signified, the work was submitted for the consideration of the Commissioners themselves, in accordance with the terms of Section (C) of the same rule ? "

Up to the 1st of August no reply was received by the publishers to this letter.

On the 1st of August the Secretary of the National Board at length replied admitting that " official approval " had been given for the use of the book in four schools ; then " objection was raised to it by certain Commissioners," whereupon " the book was examined by the Resident Commissioner and disallowed on December the 9th, 1907, for use after July the 1st, 1908. The book was subsequently submitted for the consideration of the whole Board on July the 28th, 1908, and rejected."*

---

* The procedure in reference to the adoption of books is :—
" The Managers may [subject to the rule already quoted [124 A] select the books used in their schools for the purpose of secular instruction, but they are required to submit annually for the examination of the inspector the list of proposed books not later than three months prior to the commencement of the school year, and they must furnish a copy of any book which does not appear on the list authorised by the Commissioner ; or of any new edition of a book already sanctioned. No new book can be used until the official approval has been notified to the manager.
" The Inspector should, in all cases of doubt, forward copies of the book or books in question for the consideration of the Commissioners, to whom an appeal lies in all cases." Rule 124 (B).

Let us now see what are the admitted facts :—

1. The use of the book in four schools received " official approval."*

2. It was not until December, 1907, that certain Commissioners complained to the Resident Commissioner that the use of the book was a violation of rule 124 ; whereupon the Resident Commissioner read the book and condemned it.

3. In April, 1908, the Imperial Protestant Federation wrote to the Commissioners complaining that the use of the book in the schools was a breach of rule 124.

4. The Secretary to the Board replied on April 24th, 1908, that the book was not adopted by the Commissioners.

5. On June 13th the publishers wrote to the Board asking, in effect, if the use of the book had not been sanctioned in the usual way.

6. The Secretary to the Board replied, admitting that the use of the book, in four schools, had received " official approval."

7. On the 1st July, the book was disallowed even in the four schools where its use had previously received " official approval."

8. On the 28th July the book was submitted to the Board and condemned by that body. These are the admitted facts, and they make a strange story.

But why was the book condemned ? The publishers asked this question ; but the Board refused to answer

---

* On the subject of the use of the book having been limited to only four schools the publishers write :—

" As regards their assertion of the limited sanction accorded to the *Reader*, we maintain that while the book may have come before the Board itself for sanction in only four instances it nevertheless received their official approval for use in some 2,000 National Schools by the acquiesence of their Inspectors, after examination of its contents, this being the ordinary and regular mode in which the Commissioners' sanction is conferred."

" The 'Advanced National Reader,' during its three years service in the hands of nearly 23,000 children, was as fully sanctioned as any book can be under existing regulations."

it. The publishers with excessive amiability even said :—

> " In order to afford us the opportunity of having the *Advanced National Reader* revised to meet the wishes of the Commissioners we trust that they will be good enough to specify the passages in the book to which they have taken exception on religious or political grounds."

I need scarcely say that no self-respecting Irishman can have the least sympathy with this obsequious offer. If the publishers were prepared to *Bowdlerise* their book in order to make it English enough to suit the palate of the National School Commissioners then I say, in the language of Wolfe Tone, " May their own gods damn them." But why was the book placed upon the Index? In the face of the silence of the *National* Board, we have no resource but to turn to the reasons set forth by the Imperial Protestant Federation. Unless we hear something to the contrary we may fairly assume that the passages in the book which shocked the English organisation were the passages which shocked the *National* Board. I shall set out these passages without note or comment giving the name of the author in each case.

P. 35 "Some Irish Graves in Rome."

1. "So they sleep side by side in death, far away from green Tyrconnell, those noble princes of the North, so closely allied in blood, in virtue, and in deeds of valour on many a well-fought field, the names of which are among the most glorious recorded in the chequered annals of our sad island's story" (His Grace, Dr. Healy, Archbishop of Tuam).

2. " The ten years war maintained by O'Neill and O'Donnell from 1592 to 1602, was the most bloody and glorious of this prolonged struggle, and they have left us memories of Irish victories won over the generals of Elizabeth which will never fade from the minds of the people. 'The dauntless Red Hugh' was not the greatest general, but he was the noblest figure which looms across that page of Irish history—the boldest, the bravest, the most chivalrous of all our island warriors ; and hence it is that he holds so high a place in popular affection, higher perhaps than any other of our

national heroes.   He hated the Saxon with undying hatred, and not without good cause " (*Ibid*).

3. " Is it any wonder that the gallant boy hated the deputy who planned this crime, hated the queen who approved it, and hated all the oppressors of his country, who bore the Saxon name ?   And for ten years he gave it to them hot and heavy—sometimes in alliance with O'Neill, sometimes fighting on his own resources " (*Ibid*).

4. " They go down to the grave, but their example abides for ever—a living force to incite men to imitate their deeds, and, if needs be, to follow them to a noble death " (*Ibid*).

" Lament of Tyrone and Tyrconnell."

5.   " Embrace the faithful Crucifix " (Clarence Mangan).

[This one line, singled out for proscription, is taken from a well-known poem entitled " Lament of Tyrone and Tyrconnell."   Of this poem, we find the following criticism in the "Treasury of Irish Poetry "— a work edited by the Rev. Stopford Brooke, one of the most brilliant and cultured of living writers.

" Mangan transmutes the mourning Irish music of Owen Ward into English verse of monumental magnificence and monotony in woe, as he chants the lament for the Lords of Tyrone and Tyrconnell, The O'Neill and The O'Donnell, dead exiles sleeping together in holy Rome.   Each of the eighteen stanzas, with its elaborate structure, is like a funeral march, full of deep repeated chords, and a wailing cry that pierces up through the heavier tones of sorrow."

I shall quote the whole of the stanza from which the line is taken :—]

" Look not nor sigh, for earthly throne,
    Nor place thy trust in arm of clay,
        But on thy knees
Uplift thy soul to God alone.
    For all things go their destined way
        As He decrees.
Embrace the faithful Crucifix,
    And seek the path of pain and prayer
        Thy Saviour trod ;
Nor let thy spirit intermix
    With earthly hope and worldly care
        Its groans to God ! "

" O'Donnell's Address to his Soldiers."

6. "God be thanked, these robber Saxons come to meet us here to-day " (Dr. Healy).

[I shall give the whole of the stanza from which the line is taken :—

> "Brother chiefs, and clansmen loyal, tried in many a
> bloody fray ;
> God be thanked, these robber Saxons come to meet us
> here to-day.
> Boasting Clifford, Essex' minion, swears he'll make the
> rebels flee—
> We will give him hearty greeting, like to that at
> Ashanee."]

7. " Strike ! and drive the Swinish Saxon, herding in their sacred shade " (*Ibid*).

[I shall also quote the whole of the stanza from which this line is taken :—

> "Forward ! forward ! brave M'Dermott, strike for fair
> Moylurg's domain,
> For yon lake in beauty sleeping, for the holy island's
> fame,
> Strike ! and drive the swinish Saxon, herding in their
> sacred shade,
> Far from Boyle's old Abbey cloisters, where your fathers'
> bones are laid.]

8. " Holy Virgin ! we implore thee, by that Abbey's rifled
> shrine,
> Columcille of Daire Calgach, patron of O'Donnell's line,
> Good St. Francis ! for the glory of thy name in Donegal,
> Speed ye now Tyrconnell's onset, till we rout them one
> and all " (*Ibid*).

9. " Deathless fame in song and story will enshroud the men
> who died,
> Fighting God's and freedom's battle bravely by
> O'Donnell's side " (*Ibid*).

" The Pillar Towers of Ireland."

10. " Here was placed the holy chalice that held the sacred
> wine,
> And the gold cross from the altar, and the relics from
> the shrine,
> And the mitre shining brighter with its diamonds than
> the east.
> And the crosier of the pontiff, and the vestments of the
> priest ! " (D. F. MacCarthy).

"The Holy Wells of Ireland."

11. "But it is also certain that a lawful and becoming reverence of a religious character may be paid to those sacred fountains whose waters have been instrumental in performing miracles or have been especially sanctified by religious use, or by the blessing of some great saint. There is no other country in the world where there are so many of these truly holy wells as in Ireland, or where they are still so much reverenced by the people. We propose to explain the origin and the motives of the religious reverence which is still justly due to the holy wells of Ireland " (Dr. Healy).

[The whole of R. D. Joyce's poem "Sarsfield's Ride " (see Macaulay's " History of England, Vol. III., p. 670) has been apparently proscribed chiefly on account of a " contemptuous reference " to " Dutch Bill," The stanza in which the words occur runs :—

SARSFIELD'S RIDE ; OR THE AMBUSH OF BALLINEETY.—I.

(*A Ballad.*)

"Come up to the hill, Johnnie Moran, and ne'er such a
    sight did you see ;
The men of Dutch Bill in the lowlands are marching o'er
    valley and lea ;
Brave cannon they bring for their warfare, good powder
    and bullets *go léor*,
To batter the gray walls of Limerick adown by the deep
    Shannon shore ! "]

I have already suggested that certain words of Mr. Starkie quoted on page 244, should be hung up in every National School in Ireland. I shall go a step further now. I suggest that they be hung up in the Board Room at Marlborough Street. Then Mr. Starkie would be able, whenever the Commissioners were suffering more than usual from a fit of Anglophobia to point, I will not say a finger of scorn, but a finger of admonition to the minatory tablet. " The atmosphere of natural sympathy is essential to educational efficiency."*

* The following statement should be read side by side with the story of the suppressed Reader :—
    " As to the condition of affairs in Primary Schools, the spirit of Whately still lives, having undergone strange transmigration. As an instance, the following pictures were found in Rathmines National Schools :—

The Intermediate Education Board.

Between 1830 and 1854, little attention was paid, in the English Parliament, to the question of Irish Intermediate Education. In the latter year, however, a royal commission was issued to inquire, *inter-alia*, into the subject, and a mass of evidence was collected which proved the collapse of the existing systems ; yet Parliament did nothing at the time to create a better order of things.

In 1871, the Irish Census Commissioners published an interesting and able paper, showing that unless prompt steps were taken by the State to encourage secondary instruction, the youths of Ireland would

---

"No. 1. 'Familiar Folks. The Cavalryman.' An English hussar.

"No. 2. 'In the Nick of Time.' An English Cavalier about to be shot by English Roundheads.

"No. 3. 'The British Lion.' Pears' Annual, 1900.

"No. 4. 'The British Lion.'

"These were two copies of the same picture, hanging a few feet from each other, in the same room. The Lion was an ordinary sort of lion, with nothing British about him but the label.

"No. 5. 'The House that Jack Built.' An English sailor, with the name 'H.M.S. Dreadnought' in large letters on his cap, building a card house for a happy English child.

"No. 6. 'The Coming Nelsons.' An English lady, with two happy English children and a toy boat.

"No. 7. 'Little Bobs.' An Enghsh soldier teaching a happy English child to fire a revolver.

"No. 8. 'Farewell.' English soldier in khaki entraining.

"No. 9. 'Charge of Lancers at Omdurman.' Ferocious English soldiers.

"No. 10. 'Saving the Guns at Colenso,' Ghastly English soldiers.

"No. 11. 'The Last Grip.' A ghastly English soldier, bandaged and bleeding, with one hand holding that of a dying comrade, and the other pointing a revolver at some imaginary foe.

"No. 12. 'The Hero of Trafalgar.' Nelson : a print about four feet by three.

"No. 13. A Highland soldier dying in a snow scene.

"No. 14. 'Missed.' A Bengal Lancer tent pegging.

"No. 15. 'The Thin Red Line' of Scotchmen."

(Mr. Henry Mangan (Author of "Derry and Limerick" in *Studies of Irish History*), *Sinn Féin*, October 17th, 1908.)

lapse into a condition of deplorable ignorance ; would be rendered unfit to fight their way successfully through life, and to compete in its struggles with the youth of other countries. But Parliament still did nothing to terminate so lamentable a condition of affairs. At length, in 1878, Lord Cairns took the subject in hand, and carried into law an important and useful measure of Irish Educational Reform, the main provisions of which may briefly be described thus :—

(1) A sum of £1,000,000 was taken from the Disestablished Church Surplus Fund and devoted to the purposes of Secondary Education in Ireland.

(2) A Board was formed called " The Intermediate Education Board of Ireland," seven members of which were to be appointed by the Lord Lieutenant.

(3) Provision was made for the establishment of a system of exhibitions and prizes for students, and the payment of results fees to their teachers.

(4) Examinations were to be held by examiners appointed by the Board, at convenient centres throughout the country, in the months of June and July in every year: the subjects in which candidates were required to pass being :—

(a) The ancient languages, literature and history of Greece and Rome.

(b) English language, history and literature ; French, German and Italian languages, history and literature.

(c) Mathematics, including arithmetic and bookkeeping.

(d) Natural sciences.

(e) Such other subjects of secular instruction as the Board might prescribe.

The maximum ages at which students were allowed to compete were fixed at sixteen, seventeen and eighteen years respectively.

The Board was not to take upon itself any responsibility with respect to the management and control of any of the schools, but the three following rules were in all cases to be observed :—

(1) Students were bound to belong to some intermediate school from 15th of October of the year prior to the examination, and to have made at least 100 attendances.

(2) Students prepared by private tutors only, were not to be eligible.

(3) No results-fees were to be paid to the managers of schools where religious instruction was imposed, contrary to the sanction of parents, or where the hours for such instruction were so arranged as to trench upon the time allotted to secular study. These in the main are the provisions of the Intermediate Education Act of 1878.

I may, perhaps, add the opinion given of the system by the Principal of the French College, Blackrock, as stated by Professor Mahaffy in the Endowed Schools Commission Report, 1880-81.

" He objects altogether," says Professor Mahaffy, referring to the opinion of this gentleman, " to the Intermediate Examinations, and says, that his profession is ruined by the complete subjugation of all school work to the fixed programme, which is quite insufficient to occupy the better boys for a year, and which thus seriously impairs their progress. He fully agrees with me that it is the duty of that examination, not to test the coaching in particular books, but the various methods of teaching at various schools, and that if no course were prescribed, very different and sounder results would be attained. He thus differs fundamentally from the theory of the Jesuit Fathers of St. Stanislaus' College. He also protests against the variety of unimportant subjects which produces results fees, and thinks that a minimum of at least 33 per cent. should be struck off the answering if these subjects are retained."

" It is," concludes Mr. Mahaffy, " very satisfactory for me to find my own conclusions backed by the [practical knowledge] of this enlightened and experienced Roman Catholic school-master."*

These words were written a quarter of a century ago. The question is, are they applicable to the condition of things to-day ? I submit that what is wanting is efficient schools, not crammed pupils.†

General Prisons Board.

In 1827, the management of gaols and bridewells (places for the detention of those awaiting trial, or sentenced to short terms of imprisonment) were entrusted to Boards of Superintendence, appointed by the Grand Juries, and subject to the inspection of the Inspectors-General (two in number) of prisons appointed by the Lord Lieutenant. The expenses of these institutions were defrayed by presentments levied by the Grand Juries and Town Councils.‡

The second class of prisons (convict prisons for prisoners sentenced to transportation) consisted of hulks and depôts established by the Lord Lieutenant, and subject to the inspection of the Inspectors-General of Prisons.§

* Taken from " Fifty years' Concession to Ireland." In reference to the subject of religion the Act contains the following provision :—" The Board shall not make any payment to the managers of any school unless it be shown to the satisfaction of the Board that no pupil attending such school is permitted to remain in attendance during the time of any religious instruction which the parents or guardians of such pupil shall not have sanctioned, and that the time for giving such religious instruction is so fixed that no pupil not remaining in attendance is excluded directly or indirectly from the advantages of the secular education given in the school."

† See *Ante*, p. 147.

‡ 7 George IV., chap. 74. Under the 12 and 13 Vic., cap. 97, the Board was appointed in Dublin by the Town Council.

§ 7 George IV., chapter 74.

In 1854 these hulks and depôts were abolished, and convict prisons for prisoners under sentence of transportation or penal servitude were established instead.* These prisons were administered by three directors, appointed by the Lord Lieutenant, and subject to the directions of the Chief Secretary, to whom they reported annually. In 1873, the number of directors was reduced to one.

In 1877, the offices of Inspector-General and Director of Convict Prisons were abolished, Grand Juries were relieved of their duties as prison authorities, and a General Prisons Board to consist of a Chairman, and a Vice-Chairman, and not more than two other members was established for the management and control of all prisons.†

Originally the Board consisted of a Chairman, a Vice-Chairman, one paid member and one honorary member. In 1855, a Medical Officer was appointed. In 1886, the honorary member retired, whereupon the Medical Officer was appointed a member of the Board.

The Board now consists of a Chairman, a Vice-Chairman, and a medical member. The rules made by the Board are subject to the sanction of the Lord Lieutenant and Privy Council, and must lie on the table of each House of Parliament for forty days before being enforced. The Board also must report annually to Parliament.

Under the Act a visiting committee of justices is appointed by the Grand Juries, and it is also provided that any justice who has jurisdiction where a prison is situated, or where the offence was committed by any prisoner detained in the prison, may visit the prison, and may enter any complaint in the visitors' book ; and it is the duty of the Governors to call the attention of the committee of visiting justices to such entry.

* 17th and 18th Victoria, chapter 76.

† 40 and 41 Victoria, chapter 49.

The power given to any single Justice to visit a prison, in the manner prescribed by Section 26 of the Act (40 and 41 Vic., cap. 49), does not apply to convict prisons.

Prior to 1884 the Counties and Boroughs were liable for the safe conduct and removal of prisoners, until the prisoner was received into prison either when committed for trial, or summarily convicted. But by the Prisons Act of 1884 Parliament now defrays the expenses of maintenance, custody, safe conduct and removal from the time of committal to the time of death or discharge.

In 1898, an Act was passed (61 and 62 Vic., c. 60) which provided for the establishment of State Reformatories for Inebriates, the expenses for the maintenance of such establishments to be defrayed by Parliament. One Reformatory of this kind is now in existence.

An Act passed in 1901 (1 Edward 7 ch. 17) enacts that all expenses in connection with Criminal Lunatics shall also be paid by Parliament, such expenses to be included in the vote for Prisons. It may be added that a Royal Commission was appointed in 1882 to inquire into the state of prisons in Ireland. This Commission reported in 1884. They recommended that the number of Prisons should be reduced. They also proposed that certain prisons might be reconstructed, and that Lock-ups or Police Cells should be established. They were likewise in favour of the abolition of Bridewells and for the creation of a Public Works Prison for Male Convicts.

Reformatory and Industrial Schools Office.

The Reformatory and Industrial Schools established under 31 and 32 Vic., cap. 59 (1868), are private enterprises under State inspection and receiving State aid in addition to voluntary contributions. The Inspector, who is appointed by the Lord Lieutenant, has his office in the Castle. There are five Reformatory and sixty-nine Industrial Schools.

Ulster King at Arms.

In 1552, Edward VI. created a King of Arms for Ireland by the Title of Ulster.* Thus the office—merely a herald's office—sprang up. " The Ulster King " besides his duties as a herald, is custodian of the Regalia of the Order of St. Patrick. The Order of St. Patrick, says Sir Bernard Burke,

> " was instituted by King George III. in 1783, and derived its name from the tutelar Saint, and its decorations from the national emblems. The gold links of a collar of a knight, are ' roses and harps interlaced ' ; his badge is wreathed with shamrocks, and his motto is ' Quis Separabit,' —all suggestive of the cordial union of the kingdoms."

This is amusing. The motto " Quis Separabit " has been constantly flourished by " Unionists " in our own day as expressive of the necessity of a legislative Union between England and Ireland in order to prevent the " separation " of the two countries ; yet the motto was adopted at a time when Ireland had a separate Parliament ; in fact, in the very year, 1783, when the English Parliament passed an act declaring that the independence of the Irish Parliament should not be " questioned or questionable." The motto adopted in these circumstances, Sir Bernard Burke describes as " suggestive of the cordial union of the Kingdoms."

Board of Charitable Donations and Bequests.

Fifteen years after Catholic Emancipation, charitable trusts in Ireland (nearly three-fourths of which were

* Woodward Heraldry.

Catholic Endowments) were administered by an almost exclusively Protestant Board, instituted in 1800.* Lord Stanley described the Board in the English House of Commons in 1800. He said : †

> " It consists of the Lord Chancellor, the [Protest-tant] Bishops, the Judges of the three Superior Courts of Common Law, the Judge of the Pre-rogative Court, the Provost of Trinity College, the Dean of St. Patrick's, and the incumbents of the several parishes within the city of Dublin. Of this Board, five were to be a quorum, provided an Archbishop or Bishop formed one of the five. That constitution made the Board exclusively a Church of England Board."‡

He added :—" The powers given to that Board authorised them to search out for bequests, and authorised them, with five for a quorum, one being a [Protestant] Bishop, to apply the funds so acquired, not only in such manner as might be lawful, but in such manner as might appear to them to be expedient. That was what had excited the suspicions of the Roman Catholics."

At the same time Sir Robert Peel, quoting Mr. Scully's book on the subject, pointed out that the effect of the law relating to charities was :—

> " that no person could give or grant any land, or sum of money, to or for the support of any

* The Board was originally formed before 1800, and the pro-visions of the Act creating it were re-enacted after Mr. Pitt's Union (40 George III., c. 70). The Act of Union (40 George III., c. 38) received the Royal assent on the 1st August, 1800. The measure dealing with Charitable Bequests, in the same year, would seem then to have been passed in the absence of Irish members, who appeared for the first time in the English Parliament which met in January, 1801.

† See Sir James Graham's speech July 29th, 1844 ; Hansard 1511.

‡ Of course, in 1800, Catholics were excluded from the Judicial Bench.

Catholic establishment. The law was now (1843) changed, and a new Board was created."

The new Board was to consist of three *ex officio* members, viz. : the Master of the Rolls, the Chief Baron of the Exchequer, and the Judge of the Pre-rogative Court. There were, in addition, to be ten Commissioners appointed by the Crown, of whom five were to be Catholics and five Protestants. The change in law, *inter alia*, came to this : *First* (to use the words of Sir James Graham in introducing the Bill) :—

> " The Act limited the power of the Commis-sioners to apply donations and bequests according to the intention—and the intention strictly—of the donor or donors."
>
> *Second :*—" The Act enabled real or personal property, without limitation as to amount, to be held in perpetuity, for building and maintaining chapels, for building and maintaining residences for the Roman Catholic clergy, or for the use of the priests, for the time being, for the purpose of any particular charge."

The measure became law without any important alteration, and it now provides for the administration of charitable donations and bequests in Ireland.*

In 1867, the Judge of the Prerogative Court ceased to be a member of the Commission, and the Crown was empowered to appoint another Commissioner in his stead. The Commission now consists of the Master of the Rolls, the Chief Baron of the Exchequer, and eleven ordinary members.†

* 7th and 8th Victoria, cap. 87. Irish members criti-cised the Bill in an adverse spirit on the grounds that none of the Catholic clergy had been consulted about it. They also objected to the presence of the Judge of the Prerogative Court on the Commission, and thought that as three-fourths of the donations were by Catholics, the Catholics ought to have a stronger representation on the Board.

† 24 and 25 Victoria, cap. 111., clause 1.

I give the following summary of the powers of the Board :

Commissioners may sue for recovery of charitable donations, etc., withheld or concealed or misapplied.

Persons or bodies may by deed vest lands, etc., in the Commissioners, in trust for Catholic Priests in Ireland.

The Commissioners may entertain applications for their opinion or advice from trustees or charities.

Persons acting on advice of the Board are to be indemnified.

Commissioners may sanction compromise of claims on behalf of a charity.

Notices of legal proceedings as to any charity by any person, except the Attorney-General, are to be given to the Board.

In any case in which it shall appear to the Commissioners that the institution of legal proceedings is requisite or desirable with respect to any charity, or the estates, funds, property, or affairs thereof, the Commissioners may authorise or direct such proceedings to be instituted, and give such directions in relation thereto, as they may think proper ; and if it shall appear desirable that any such proceedings should be instituted by the Attorney-General, it shall be lawful for the Commissioners, if they think fit, to certify such case, in writing under the hand of the Secretaries of the Commissioners to Her Majesty's Attorney-General.

In case of certain bequests, etc., the Commissioners may apply or sanction *Cypres* Doctrine to funds vested in them or in trustees respectively.

The Commissioners may apply to the Court to frame a scheme *Cypres* for any charity.

Any Person or Trustee may transfer fund to Commissioners with their consent, to be held by them in trust.

Deeds, etc., may be deposited by trustees for charities in a repository provided by the Commissioners.

The consent of the Commissioners necessary to any change of investment by Trustees of Funds held for charitable or pious purposes.

The Commissioners may sanction building leases, working mines, doing repairs and making improvements, etc., and may authorise the application of the charity funds or the raising of money on mortgages for these purposes.

The Commissioners, under special circumstances, may authorise a sale or exchange of charity lands.

They may also authorise the redemption of rent charges.

Trustees of charities, with the sanction of the Commissioners, are enabled to purchase sites for buildings from owners under disability.

Property of any description, vested in a trustee for charitable purposes may, with the consent of the Commissioners, be vested in them.

The Commissioners are authorised, where difficulty arises from absence of trustees, etc., to give effectual receipts for payments for charitable etc., purposes.

They may apply to any court in which any fund for charitable purposes remains unapplied, to have such fund transferred to them.

Where a suit for the administration of assets instituted by the personal representative, the Commissioners may apply for the conduct of the suit on the ground of delay.

The Commissioners may compel trustees of a charity to complete the number of trustees.

The Commissioners may amend any of the schemes framed by the Educational Endowment Commissioners for Ireland.

The Land Commission.

During the whole period of the " Union," the land war has distracted the country and convulsed society. The landlords evicted without pity, and the tenants

retaliated without remorse. The landlord thought of
little but the rent. He recognised no duties; he
enforced only rights. The tenant "scrambling for the
potato" and left without any resource but the land,
offered an exorbitant rent, which the landlord accepted,
and exacted to the uttermost farthing. Freedom of
contract between landlord and tenant there was none.
The tenant came into the market under circumstances
which left him entirely at the mercy of the landlord.
The "bit of land" meant life to him; the want of
it death; for, in the absence of commercial industries,
the people were thrown upon the land mainly for
existence.

> "The treaty between landlord and tenant
> [in Ireland]," says Mr. Nassau Senior, "is not a
> calm bargain in which the tenant, having offered
> what he thinks the land worth, cares little whether
> his offer be accepted or not; it is a struggle like
> the struggle to buy bread in a besieged town,
> or to buy water in an African caravan."

In truth, the landlord had a monopoly of the means
of existence, and he used it for his own aggrandisement,
regardless of the tenant's fate and the public weal.

> "The landlords in Ireland," said Lord Donough-
> more in the House of Lords, on February 28th,
> 1854, "have been in the habit of letting land,
> not farms."

Never has a happier description of the Irish land
system been given than this. The landlord let "land"
—a strip of bog, barren, wild, dreary. The tenant
reclaimed it; drained, fenced, built; reduced the waste
to a cultivated state; and made the "land" a "farm."
Then the landlord pounced upon him for an increased
rent. The tenant could not pay; his resources had
been exhausted in bringing the bog into a state of
cultivation; he had not yet recouped himself for his

outlay and labour. He was evicted ; flung on the roadside to starve without receiving one shilling compensation for his outlay on the land ; and the " farm," which he had made, was given to another at an enhanced rental. What did the evicted tenant do ? He entered a Ribbon Lodge, told the story of his wrong, and demanded vengeance on the man whom he called a tyrant and oppressor. Only too often his story was listened to ; and vengeance was wreaked on the landlord, or new tenant ; and sometimes upon both. This, in brief, is the dismal history of the land trouble in Ireland.

It is one of the scandals of the English administration of the country that no effective measure, dealing with this condition of things, was carried through Parliament before 1881. Of course the first important Land Act was passed (in the throes of a revolution) in 1870 ; but it was not effective.* At that time Mr. Gladstone believed in the settlement of the Land Question on the basis of tenure ; and Mr. Bright advocated the purchase of their holdings by the peasantry. The Act was a compromise between both these schemes.

1. Mr. Gladstone tried to give the tenants fixity of tenure by compelling the landlords in cases of eviction, to give compensation for improvements, and under certain circumstances, for disturbance.†

2. The Bright Clauses (as they were called) of the Act, authorised the State to advance two-thirds of the

* I have dealt fully with this subject in the " Parliamentary History of the Land Question," and in " Fifty Years of Concessions to Ireland."

† The Act also legalised the Ulster Custom, which Mr. Hancock, the agent of Lord Lurgan defines as follows :—

" Tenant right," he says, " I consider to be the claim of the tenant and his heirs to continue in undisputed possession of the farm so long as the rent is paid ; and in case of an ejectment, or in the event of a change of occupancy, at the wish of either landlord or tenant, it is the sum of money which the new occupier pays to the old one for the peaceable enjoyment of his holding."

See also " The Parliamentary History of the Irish Land Question," p. 167.

purchase money to tenants desirous of buying their holdings from landlords willing to sell, the advance to be repaid in thirty-five years by an annuity at the rate of five per cent. on the loan.*

The Land Act of 1870 was practically a failure. The Bright Clauses did not work effectually, because facilities were not afforded for their operation. Rack renting continued, evictions increased, and the general discontent remained the same as ever.

In 1881, another Land Act was passed, under the pressure of famine and revolution and the magnificent leadership of Charles Stewart Parnell.

" The pivot of this measure," to use the language of Mr. Forster, was " the Land Court," established to stand between landlords and tenants, to fix " fair " or judicial rents. Previously, the landlord was master of the situation. The competition for land placed the tenant at his mercy, and he accordingly fixed the rent at his own pleasure. But, henceforth, rent was to be fixed by legal tribunals ; and while the tenant paid the rent so fixed, he could not be disturbed in his holding for a period of fifteen years. Roughly speaking, the Act changed Irish tenancies from tenancies at will to leaseholds, renewable every fifteen years, subject to revision of rent by the Land Commission at the option of either landlord or tenant or both.

So much for the Tenure Clauses of the Act. It also contained purchase clauses. These empowered the Land Commission to make advances to tenants for buying their holdings, and to purchase estates for re-sale to the tenants. The limit of advance

---

* It may be noted that, under the Act of 1869 disestablishing the English Church in Ireland, the Church Temporalities Commissioners were empowered to sell to tenants of Church Lands their holdings at prices to be fixed by the Commissioners themselves. If the tenants refused to buy on the terms offered to them, the Commissioners could sell to the public. (See paper by Mr. Commissioner Bailey, in Appendix to Third Report of the Royal Commission on Congestion in Ireland, presided over by Lord Dudley.)

was extended from two-thirds of the purchase-money (as in the Act of 1870) to three-quarters. The terms of repayment were the same—an annuity of five per cent. for thirty-five years.

Under the Act the Land Commission consisted of three Commissioners; namely, a Judicial Commissioner, who was obliged to be a practising barrister of at least ten years' standing, and who on his appointment became a Judge of the Supreme Court of Judicature* and two other Commissioners.

The Land Act of 1881 brought the landlords to their knees. Many of them felt that their occupation was gone.† They condemned the system of dual owner-

---

* The first Land Commissioners were Mr. Justice O'Hagan, Mr. Litton and Mr. Vernon. On the death of Mr. Vernon he was succeeded by Mr. Wrench. Upon the death of Mr. Justice O'Hagan, Mr. Litton became Judicial Commissioner, and Mr. Gerald Fitzgerald took Mr. Litton's place. Mr. Bewley succeeded Mr. Litton and Mr. Meredith succeeded Mr. Bewley. In 1906, Mr. Justice Meredith became Master of the Rolls, and Mr. (now Mr. Justice) Wylie became Judicial Commissioner.

Mr. Commissioner Wrench's career is illustrative. He is the son of on English clergyman. He was educated in England. He came to Ireland, and took up work in the office of an influential land agent, and eventually became agent to some extensive landowners in the North of Ireland. When a vacancy arose in the Land Commission, on the death of Mr. Commissioner Vernon, in 1889, Mr. Wrench, favoured by the landlords, was appointed at a salary of £3,000 a year. The Commission was then only temporary;—but it was made permanent in 1891. The salary of £3,000 was fixed on the basis of a temporary post. It was, however, continued with the new tenure. Mr. Wrench was made Privy Councillor in 1902. When the Act of 1903 was passed, he was nominated as one of the Estates Commissioners. As such, he could be brought under Parliamentary criticism, from which he was supposed to be exempt as a Land Commissioner. In these now altered circumstances his salary was raised to £3,500 a year; the highest salary paid to any member of the Civil Service in these Islands. Thus it will be seen that though Ireland is the poorest country in the world, the possibilities (for the official class) are tremendous.

† " A few years experience of this Act convinced the land-lords that, if the system of fixing rents by a State tribunal were allowed full play, economic principles would have to be applied that would gradually reduce rents to a very low point " (Mr. Commissioner Bailey).

ship (as it was called) which was created by the Act and declared that in purchase alone (provided they were paid enough) could the land difficulty find its true solution. Land Purchase then became the order of the day with Tory statesmen.* In 1885, a Purchase Act, pure and simple, was passed by a Tory Ministry. It was called the Ashbourne Act, after the Tory Lord Chancellor of Ireland, Lord Ashbourne, who introduced it.†

By this measure the Land Commission was empowered to advance the whole of the purchase-money (subject to the retention of one-fifth, by way of guarantee deposit), to tenants who had agreed with their landlords to purchase their holdings ; the repayment of the purchase-money, at the rate of four per cent. per annum, was spread over a period of forty-nine years. £5,000,000 taken from the Disestablished Church Surplus Fund were placed at the disposal of the Land Commission for the purpose of the Act ; the Commission being authorised to purchase estates in the

* " When Parliament consented to pass the Act of 1881, it gave its sanction to an agrarian revolution and a complete transformation of the system of land tenure. This was a thing which could not be accomplished at a single stroke ; that statute did not exhaust all the aspects of the land question in Ireland, for side by side with joint or dual ownership there had been from the first a desire for the establishment of a peasant proprietary. This desire found expression in some of the earlier Land Acts, and since 1881 it had been the keystone of the Unionist policy with regard to land in Ireland " (Mr. Gerald Balfour in the House of Commons, April 13th, 1896). (Annual Register, 1896, p. 88).

† In 1882, a temporary Act—the Arrears Act—was passed by which the tenants arrears of rent were cancelled on the following conditions :—

1. That the tenant should pay the rent due in 1881.
2. That of the antecedent arrears he should pay one year's rent ; the State another.
3. That the tenant should satisfy a legal tribunal of his inability to pay the whole of his arrears.

The Act only applied to tenancies under £30 a year, and the payments made by the State were taken from the Surplus Fund of the Dis-established Church. About two millions of arrears were wiped out under this Act.

Landed Estates Court,* with the view to re-selling them to the tenants.

Under this Act two Purchase Commissioners were appointed.†

In 1883, Mr. Parnell had said, that the rents " now being fixed are rack rents, and cannot be paid," and demanded a revision of them. In 1886, Lord Salisbury said, " We do not contemplate any revision of judicial rents. We do not think it would be honest in the first place, and we think it would be exceedingly inexpedient." Nevertheless, in 1887, Lord Salisbury passed an Act, authorising the revision of the judicial rents fixed during the years 1881, 1882, 1883, 1884 and 1885, in accordance with the difference in prices between those years and the years 1887, 1888 and 1889.

In 1888, another Tory Land Purchase Act was passed, making a further advance to the Land Commission of £5,000,000 (the £5,000,000 advanced under the Act of 1885 being exhausted) for the purposes of land purchase.

In 1891, another Tory Land Purchase Act was passed. £33,000,000 were set apart by the State for the purposes of Land Purchase in Ireland, on the basis of agreement between landlord and tenant. The tenant was not to pay the purchase money to the landlord. The State paid the landlord in specially created Land Stock, yielding $2\frac{3}{4}$ per cent. and redeemable at the end of thirty years. The Land Commission then advanced the whole of the purchase money to the tenant ; the

---

* In 1849, an Act was passed that a Court of Commissioners should be established in Dublin with power at discretion to sell any encumbered estate on the petition of the owners, or of any creditor of that estate, and to give to the purchaser an indefeasible parliamentary title.

Another Act—the Landed Estates Act—was subsequently passed, enabling the Court to deal with unencumbered, as well as encumbered estates.

† These Commissioners were Mr. Lynch, and Mr. John George McCarthy. Upon the death of Mr. McCarthy, in 1892, Mr. Murrough O'Brien took his place. Mr. O'Brien retired in 1904, and his place (under the Purchase Act of 1900) was not filled up.

tenant repaying the loan (into a land purchase account established by the Land Commission) in annual instalments, at the rate of 4 per cent. per annum (including interest and sinking fund), the repayments being spread over a period of forty-nine years.

In a word, the State paid the landlord in stock, and the tenant repaid the loan by means of his annuity to the Land Commission. In view of the possible failure of the tenant to pay the instalments into the Land Commission Account, in order to meet the interest on the Land Stock, a special guarantee fund* was created.

"This Fund consists of a cash portion, and a contingent portion. The cash portion is mainly made up of the Irish Probate Duty (now Estate Duty) grant, and an Exchequer contribution, and the contingent portion consists of the Irish share of the local taxation duties (customs and excise), and certain local grants." (Sec. 5, Act of 1891).

Any deficiency in the Land Purchase account is to be paid out of the guarantee fund. This financial expedient, of course, throws the securing of the repayment of the advances for land purchase on the ratepayers of the county, as any default will be recouped by deductions from the various payments and contributions in aid of rates that make up the guarantee fund.†

In 1896, another Land Act was passed. Under it:

1. The Land Commission was permitted to dispense with part or the whole of the guarantee deposit, required by the Act of 1885, if the security for the repayment of the advance was considered to be sufficient without it.

* See *post*.

† Mr. Bailey, Congested Districts Report, p. 330.
Mr. Gerald Balfour said in the House of Commons on April 13th, 1896:
"Under the Act of 1891, the real security to the State is the guarantee fund " (Hansard, Fourth Series, Vol. xxxix).

2. The amount of the instalments was reduced under a system which I shall explain in the words of Mr. Gerald Balfour :—

" First of all it provides for the reduction of the amount at the end of the first three decennial periods, by the amount of the accumulations of the sinking fund during those periods, making the tenant to pay his annuity of 4 per cent. on the outstanding amount. Thus, supposing the advance to have been £100, and the accumulations of the sinking fund to have amounted in the first ten years to £14, during the second ten years to £12, and during the third to £10, the effect would be that the purchaser would during the first ten years have to pay 4 per cent. on £86 instead of £100 ; at the end of the second ten years, 4 per cent. on £74 instead of £100 ; and at the end of the third ten years, 4 per cent on £64. It will be seen that this is a material reduction, and, if prices have fallen in the meantime, will be very welcome to the tenant."*

3. Where an estate had come into the Landed Estates Court, and a receiver had been appointed, or the estate was so circumstanced that it would be sold without the consent of the owner as to price, the compulsory sale of such estate, or any part of it, to the occupying tenants, was provided for under the Act.†

But the end was not yet (and, indeed, is not yet). It was found that the financial arrangements of Mr. Gerald Balfour's Acts were not sufficiently attractive to induce the Irish landlords generally to dispose of their estates under the measure. Accordingly, a new scheme was devised, and in 1903, the most important of the Land Purchase Acts became law.

* House of Commons, April 13th, 1896.

† 59-60, Victoria, c. 47, section 40.

Its chief provisions were :—

1. Financial arrangements were made under which £100,000,000 were to be provided for land purchase on the old basis of agreement between landlord and tenant.

2. The landlord was to be paid in cash instead of in stock.

3. A special guaranteed stock, yielding 2¾ per cent., and not redeemable for thirty years, was created to provide for the cash payment to the landlord.

4. The Land Commission advanced the purchase money to the tenants.

5. The tenant repaid the purchase money at the rate of 3¼ per cent., which included interest at the rate of 2¾ per cent. and ½ per cent. for sinking fund, the repayments being spread over a period of sixty-eight and a half years.

6. Losses which might be incident to the flotation of the stock in London were provided for out of the Development Grant which consisted of £185,000, due to Ireland as an equivalent for the £1,400,000 voted in 1902 for education in England.*

* Mr. Wyndham, in the House of Commons, 25th March, 1903. Annual Register, 1903, p. 88. (See Section 29 (2) of the Act, and *post.*

The following additional note may be useful.

The financial arrangements of the Land Purchase Act of 1903, were on the following basis :

The Government undertook to advance to judicial tenants the entire of the money necessary to enable them to purchase the landlords' interest in their holdings, provided the price agreed upon did not exceed the zone limits specified in the Acts ; and, in the case of holdings not held at judicial rents, the advance to be made in respect of each holding would be subject to inspection as to the security on behalf of the Land Purchase Department of the Land Commission.

The Act provided that for the money advanced to a purchasing tenant, he would *be charged £2 15s. per cent per annum interest,* and ten shillings per cent. for repayment of capital, extending over a period of about sixty-eight and a half years. These two items, making up the three and a quarter per cent. annuity on the purchase price of the holding, were understood by the tenant-purchasers to cover the entire liability which their holdings would be subject to for a period of sixty-eight and a half years in lieu of

How does the State recoup itself for the loss ? By the guarantee fund. That is to say, when the development grant is exhausted, the grants for local purposes are drawn upon until the deficit is made good by the locality.† The ratepayers will, therefore, be compelled to levy rates for these purposes, and accordingly they are really bound to make good the deficit varying from £8 to £15 on every £100 of stock, sustained by the State, from causes for which they are not responsible and in respect to matters by which they gain nothing.‡

7. The system of zones created by the Act is not, perhaps, easy of explanation. Briefly it comes to this : the legislature apparently desired to keep up prices— or, at all events, not to let them fall below a certain

---

rent, and when arranging terms with their landlords, they estimate the purchase price and their liability on this basis.

The British Treasury, however, acting as the Government financiers for these land purchase transactions, find themselves unable to borrow money at the rate of two and three quarter per cent. at which they undertook to lend it to the tenant purchasers to buy out the landlord. Their first issue of five millions of land stock was taken up, not at par value, but at a discount of about thirteen per cent. ; and subsequent issues of land stock were made at a discount ranging from eight to fifteen and a quarter per cent. The table on page 275 will illustrate the point.

The landlords have to be paid their price in cash, and the result of this depreciation is, that every £100 raised to be advanced to the tenant purchaser to buy out the landlord would cost £118 at the present price of stock ; and, in addition, a further twelve per cent., in the shape of a bonus, with the same loss on flotation, would have to be raised and paid in cash to the landlord ; so that in reality every £100 worth of land purchased from the landlord by the tenant would cost, at the present price of stock, £130.

† Sec. 29(2) of the Act, and *post.*

‡ In addition to the loss on flotation the State loses at the commencement of the annuity by a month's interest on the stock. Thus : the interest on land stock is payable, say in June, but the first gale day for the purchaser's instalment is in May. The interval is necessary to allow the Land Commission time to collect the instalments, but it is said to involve the loss of a month's interest. The instalments if punctually paid in May apparently lie dormant earning nothing for a month, while at the end of June the State has to pay seven months' interest when it has only received six months' interest. See Appendix B.

IRISH LAND STOCK ISSUES.

Return was issued in September, 1908, giving the issues of Guaranteed 2¾ per cent. Stock under the Irish Land Act, 1903.

Date of Issue.	Amount.			Price.	Cash Product Net.			Deficit.			Annual Charge on Ireland Development Grant for Excess Stock.		
	£	s.	d.		£	s.	d.	£	s.	d.	£	s.	d.
1904 Mar. 19	5,000,000	0	0	87	4,337,121	6	8	662,878	13	4	19,820	1	5
1905 Jan. 3	6,000,000,	0	0	89.88	5,354,332	15	0	645,667	5	0	18,885	15	4
1906 Jan. 2	1,103,448	5	7	90⅝	1,000,000	0	0	103,448	5	7	3,046	17	6
1906 Feb. 26	1,097,996	3	2	£91 1 6 × d	1,000,000	0	0	97,996	3	2	2,900	12	6
1906 Apl. 6	1,000,000	0	0	£92 0 7 × d	920,291	13	4	79,708	6	8	2,590	10	5
1906 June 12	7,000,000	0	0	89	6,212,093	5	7	787,906	14	5	23,046	5	5
1907 July 2	2,000,000	0	0	84¾	1,695,000	0	0	305,000	0	0	8,425	12	6
1907 Oct. 7	3,000,000	0	0	£84 17 11 × d	2,546,875	0	0	453,125	0	0	13,499	7	0
1908 Apl. 7	2,000,000	0	0	£89 16 7 × d	1,796,583	6	8	203,416	13	4	5,949	18	9
1908 July 4	5,000,000	0	0	89½	Est. 4,462,000	0	0	Est. 538,000	0	0	Est. 15,800	0	0
	£33,201,444	8	9		£29,324,297	7	3	£3,877,147	1	6	£113,965	0	10

figure. Accordingly, a clause was inserted, the tendency of which was to bring sales within the limits of from twenty-three to twenty-seven years purchase of the rents. This result was secured by peremptorily requiring the Land Commisson to make advances to purchasing tenants subject to judicial rents, without inquiry as to security or equity of price, where the annuity payable under the Act is not less than ten, nor more than forty per cent. below the existing rent.*

The table on page 277 may help to elucidate the point.

8. Another feature in the Act was the bonus, which I shall allow Mr. Commissioner Bailey to explain :—

> " To encourage sales of estates, and to enable owners to get such a sum as would give them their net income out of the purchase money, when re-invested in suitable securities, a bonus of 12 per cent. on the purchase money is paid to the owner on the completion of the sale."

> " For example, a landlord with a rental of £100 a year sells at twenty-three years purchase and gets £2,300. This sum, if invested at 3½ per cent. brings in only £81 a year. The payment of the 12 per cent. bonus gives an additional capital sum of £276, which will yield another £9 a year.

* (a) " In the case of the purchase of a holding subject to a judicial rent fixed or agreed to since the passing of the Act of 1896, if the purchase annuity, created under this Act payable in respect of the advance, will be not less than ten, nor more than thirty per cent. below the existing rent ; and

(b) " In the case of the purchase of a holding subject to a judicial rent fixed or agreed to before that date, if the said purchase annuity will be not less than twenty, nor more than forty per cent. below the rent." See Section I., s.s. I. of The Irish Land Act, 1903.

The Commissioners must be satisfied that at the time of the sale the tenants were in occupation.

" The Commissioners must be satisfied that each statutory tenant was in occupation of his holding at the date of his application."

Extracts from Messrs. Quill, Hamilton, Longworth on the Irish Land Acts of 1903-1904

Table showing the working of the Land Purchase System under the zones, and giving sums landlords may receive for every £100 of gross rental when the purchase money is invested at 3¼, 3½, 3¾ or 4 per cent. (from Mr. Commissioner Bailey's Table in Third Report of Royal Commission on Congestion, page 350).

| Rental. | Reduction per cent. | Annuity to be paid by tenant at 3¼ per cent. | Number of Years' Purchase of the Rent. | | Purchase Money with Bonus. | Annual sum Landlord will receive for every £100 of former gross rental if the purchase money, including bonus, is invested at | | | |
			Without Bonus.	With Bonus.		3 per cent.	3¼ per cent.	3½ per cent.	4 per cent.
		£			£	£ s. d.	£ s. d.	£ s. d.	£ s. d.
£ 100	10	90	27.7	31.0	3101	100 15 11	108 11 0	116 6 1	124 12 0
100	20	80	24.6	27.6	2756	89 11 4	96 9 2	103 7 0	110 4 9
100	30	70	21.5	24.1	2412	78 7 9	84 8 5	90 9 0	96 9 7
100	40	60	18.5	20.7	2067	67 3 6	72 6 10	77 10 3	82 13 7*

* The minimum reduction allowable in case of second term rents is two shillings in the £ or 10 per cent. The maximum 6s. or 30 per cent. In case of first term rents the minimum is 4s. in the £, and the maximum is 8s. in the £.

N.B.—Well secured ground rents in the heart of busy London are selling for twenty-four years purchase.

An insecure rental, issuing, it may be, out of an Irish bog or stony hillside, may realise $25\frac{7}{10} + 3$ (bonus)$= 28\frac{7}{10}$ years purchase, and this calculated on the gross. After making the usual allowances for collection, etc., an Irish vendor gets about thirty years at least.

Thus the purchase money and bonus will bring in a total income of over £90 a year, in place of the gross income of £100, which he previously received in way of rent.

" The land conference held that a landlord would be amply remunerated by getting £90 of his gross second term rental, as at least £10 per cent. should be deducted from the rental as a set off against costs of collection, bad debts and so forth."

9. I shall quote Mr. Bailey again. " Sales under previous Purchase Acts were carried out by holdings. A landlord could agree with one or more of his tenants to sell to them their farms, and if the Land Commission, after examination, found that the particular holding was security for the advance asked for by the tenant to buy out the landlord, such advance was made, irrespective of any other sales on the estate. The act of 1903 introduced the system of sales by ' Estates.' A landlord, to obtain the benefit of the Act, is obliged to sell his entire estate, or such portion of it as the Land Commission considers fit to be regarded as a separate estate for the purposes of the Act. The Commissioners, before defining any lands to be an estate, have to consider all the circumstances of the district and of the property. Once the estate is ' declared ' the holdings comprised in it are dealt with in accordance with the provisions of the Act."*

10. Three Estates Commissioners were appointed to administer the Act—two new Commissioners, who were to rank as members of the Land Commission, and one

* Mr. Bailey. Section 98 of the Act declares that an estate means any lands which the Estates Commissioners may declare fit to be regarded as a separate " estate " for the purposes of the Act.

Commissioner who was already a member of the Land Commission.*

11. The Estates Commissioners cannot interfere in the case of agreements for sale within the zones, the Act presuming that a holding subject to a judicial rent which is sold at a price, the annuity on which is from 10 to 40 per cent. less than the judicial rent, is good security.†

12. Holdings not subject to the zone provisions are liable to inspection as to security, and as to equity of price.‡

13. The Estates Commissioners can purchase estates (with a view to re-selling them to the tenants) where three-fourths of the tenants agree to buy.§

* The new Commissioners were Mr. W. F. Bailey and Mr. Finucane. The third Commissioner was Mr. Wrench, already a member of the Land Commissioners.

Under the Act of 1903, Mr. Fitzgerald was raised to the rank of a Judicial Commissioner to assist the Chief Judicial Commissioner in hearing of judicial rent appeals, etc. In 1907, Sergeant Dodd was elevated to a judgeship of the King's Bench Division, and immediately appointed by the Lord Chancellor, under the Judicature Act, to act as an Additional Judicial Commissioner under the Land Acts to clear off arrears.

† Though the Estates Commissioners were in one sense excluded from interfering within the zones by Section I., ss. (a.), they were by another section—the section authorising them to declare the property an " Estate "—allowed to have a look in. (See judgment of Mr. Justice Meredith in the Kinvarra case which however seems to have been modified by the Court of Appeal in *Weir's Estate.*)

‡ The Land Commission fully equipped consists then of a Judicial Commissioner (Mr. Justice Wylie), an Assistant Judicial Commissioner (Mr. Commissioner Fitzgerald), a Special Judicial Commissioner (Mr. Justice Dodd) ; and four ordinary Commissioners (Mr. Lynch, Mr. Bailey, Mr. Finucane and Mr. Wrench); besides being Land Commissioners, Mr. Bailey, Mr. Finucane, and Mr. Wrench are Estates Commissioners, under the Act of 1903. The Secretary to the Land Commissioners is Sir John Franks, the Secretary to the Estates Commissioners, Mr. J. T. Drennan.

§ Though the Act has now been five years in operation the meaning to be attached to " equity of price " is still in doubt. In the case of *King Harman's Estate ; Hayes tenant,* it was held by Mr. Justice Meredith that the word " equity " is here used in the

14. The decennial system, established by the Act of 1896, was abolished.

15. The Act contained provisions for the acquisition of land for the enlargement and improvement of uneconomic holdings. It was intended, to use Mr. Wyndham's picturesque expression, to get rid of the " ridged and rotten communities " of the west of Ireland. An " uneconomic holding " was first defined by Mr. Commissioner Bailey in his famous Report on the Condition of Tenant Purchasers under the Land Purchase Acts, which contained the evidence and authority for many of the provisions in the Act of 1903.

> " We may," said Mr. Bailey, " define an ' *uneconomic holding* ' as one which is of a size and character insufficient to enable it to be worked profitably by an occupier, without other aids to subsistence. The sale of holdings of this character presents many features of risk to the State which advances the money, as well as to the community."

Let me illustrate by a story the operation and effect of a sale under the Irish Land Purchase Act. A tenant holds a small holding at a rent of, say, £4 a year. His landlord makes up his mind to sell his estate of which this holding is a part. He gets the tenant to agree to buy at, say, twenty-five years' purchase of the rent, which comes to £100. This sum is to be borrowed from the State, through the Estates Commissioners. The agreement is accordingly lodged with that body, and an application for an advance is made. If the property is declared to be an " Estate " and if the rent is a judicial one, and the price

---

strictly legal sense and should be read in the light in which Courts of equity regard transactions between persons entering into contracts. This means that the purchase agreement, under which a tenant purchaser is buying his own improvements, is not inequitable under the Act.

Page 16.

is within the zones, the advance is sanctioned without question as to security and the amount is paid to the credit of the vendor. Now where does the money come from, and how is it to be repaid ? The landlord is now eliminated from the transaction. He has got his cash, but someone has to find it. The tenant, as a condition for the advance, agrees to pay the State an annuity of £3 5s. on the £100 he has borrowed. This sum is made up of £2 15s. for interest on the loan, and 10s. to form a Sinking Fund. This contribution for a sinking fund, at the end of sixty-eight and a half years will, at compound interest, produce the £100, and then all further payments cease. The State gets the money by the issue of Land Stock bearing interest at $2\frac{3}{4}$ per cent. This stock is put on the money market like any other financial issue, and sold for whatever can be got for it. Hitherto it has had to be issued at a heavy discount, averaging about 12 per cent. The result is that the stock does not produce the cash required. Consequently, when the State advances the £100 to buy out the landlord's interest, it has to get the money by an issue of stock for, say, £112. But the tenant only pays interest and Sinking Fund on £100, and the interest and Sinking Fund on the other £12 has to be found some other way. It will have, eventually, to be found by the ratepayers of the county in which the land is situated. Up to the present, and for some time to come, the loss must be met out of the Development Grant—a sum allocated to Ireland in 1902 for educational and other local purposes. When this fund is exhausted the loss will come out of the Guarantee Fund, that is, out of the contribution to local rates made by the Imperial Exchequer. Each county is entitled to certain annual contributions in aid of rates, as has been described. The losses on flotation of Land Stock will, after the Development Grant is exhausted, be a first charge on the share of the county in these State contributions to the rates. The contributions will be debited by an amount that otherwise would have been paid to the county treasury, and an additional sum will have to be raised in consequence from the ratepayers. The State is secured because it has the funds in hand, and will first help itself, paying over only the balance to the county. Under this system the ratepayers at large, for every £100 that is paid to a landlord for the purchase of his interest, will have to contribute from £10 to £12 to the price, while the Imperial Exchequer contributes another £12 per cent. by way of bonus.

The following table supplied by Mr. Bailey to the Commission on Congestion gives a summary of the numbers of tenant purchasers, and the amount of loans issued under the various Acts from 1869 to the 31st May, 1907 :—

Act.	No. of Purchasers.	Amount of Advances.
		£
I. Irish Church Act 1869	6,057	1,674,841
II. Landlord and Tenant Act, 1870 ..	877	514,436
III. Land Law (Ireland) Act, 1881 ..	731	240,801
IV. Land Purchase Act, 1885, 1887, 1888 and 1889	25,367	9,992,536
V. Land Purchase Acts, 1891, 1896 ..	46,806	13,633,190
VI. Irish Land Act, 1903	46,573	17,657,279
Total	126,411	43,713,183*

* The number of purchasers under the Act of 1903 and the amounts advanced have greatly increased since May, 31st, 1907. Probably the advances under the Act of 1903 now amount to over £25,000,000 and the number of purchasers to over 75,000.

The Act of 1887 was (in its purchase clauses) an amendment of the Act of 1885. The Amendment related to such matters as the investment of guarantee deposits, the application of trust funds, the apportionment and redemption of annuities and charges, the priority of charges for the advance, the reduction of interest on mortgages under previous Acts, and so forth. The Act of 1889 also an amendment of the Act of 1885,

I shall give the following summary of the situation from one who writes with authority on the subject.

"Before the passing of the Act of 1903 landlords were paid the price of their Estates in Land Stock bearing interest at $2\frac{3}{4}$ per cent. The interest on this Stock and the capital sum were recovered by annuities payable for about forty-three years at 4 per cent. on the price of the holdings sold. This 4 per cent. was made up of $2\frac{3}{4}$ per cent. for interest, and $1\frac{1}{4}$ per cent. for Sinking Fund. Under the Act of 1903 the financial arrangements were entirely changed, and the purchase money of Estates became payable in cash which was raised by floating stock bearing interest at $2\frac{3}{4}$ per cent. This stock has hitherto been issued at a heavy discount averaging over 12 per cent. The interest on the stock remained at $2\frac{3}{4}$ per cent, but the payment for sinking fund was reduced to $\frac{1}{2}$ per cent., making in all an annuity payment by the tenant of $3\frac{1}{4}$ per cent. for sixty-eight and a half years. It was intended that the loss on discount and interest thereon should be met in the first place, out of the *Development Grant*,† as long as it lasted, and afterwards out of the *Guarantee Fund* : that is, out of the Rates.

"It was provided by Section 38 of the Act of 1903 that the loss from the flotation of Irish

---

was a short Act to enable the Land Commission to advance money to tenants to purchase lands to increase the size of their holdings. (Mr. Bailey).

Mr. Wyndham, in introducing the Land Act of 1903, said in reference to the advances made under previous Acts :

"Of the advances made under these Acts, the State had not lost one penny, one reason for this being that the purchasing tenants did their best for the land, and another being that public opinion encouraged the punctual repayment of the money owed to the Exchequer " (Annual Register, 1903, p. 86).

† See *Post.*

Land Stock at a discount should be a first charge on the Development Grant, and when that was exhausted the loss would fall on the Guarantee Fund.*

"It is manifest that if these grants and contributions are used for meeting the losses on the flotation of Land Stock at a discount instead of for the purposes for which they are intended, that a corresponding extra rate must be raised for the purpose of enabling the local government of Ireland to be carried on."†

I shall supplement this summary by the following statement made by Mr. Runciman (the Secretary to the Treasury), in the House of Commons on the 22nd April, 1907, in reply to a question asked by Mr. Redmond.

Mr. Redmond said :—

" I beg to ask the Secretary to the Treasury if his attention has been called to the stoppages which have been made out of certain grants payable to County Councils in Ireland to meet alleged financial deficiencies in the working of the Irish Land Act of 1903 ; can he state how these deficiencies have arisen ; if he is aware that, if the Treasury persists in their present action, it will have the effect of dislocating local government all over Ireland, and also have a most injurious effect on the progress of land purchase in Ireland ; and will he publish

---

* See *Post.*

† The financial system here described dealt with the provision of Funds for Land Purchase, but a further Fund known as the *Reserve Fund* was made available for the benefit and improvement of Estates purchased or proposed to be purchased under the Act. The Reserve Fund was established under Section 5 of the Act of 1891, and was formed out of the Exchequer contribution of £40,000 a year to Irish Local Taxation and amounted in all to a capital sum of about £250,000. Of this about £100,000 has been already expended, mainly on the restoration of evicted tenants, leaving a sum of about £150,000, which will probably be insufficient for the purpose of completing the work under the Evicted Tenants' Act.

the rules under which the Treasury have acted in this matter ? "

Mr. Runciman replied :—

" *Under Section* 29 (2) of the Irish Land Act, 1903, the *Guarantee Fund* is liable to make good any deficiency on the Income Account of the Irish Land Purchase Fund. So far as these deficiencies are *caused by the issue of Guaranteed Stock at a discount*, the Ireland Development Grant, as one of the constituent parts of the Guarantee Fund, is the first to be charged under Section 38 ; so that no charge for deficiencies arising from that cause can fall on the Local Taxation Grants so long as the Ireland Development Grant is able to meet them. But there are other deficiencies on the income account with which the Local Taxation Grants, as constitutents of the Guarantee Fund, are directly chargeable, *and I fear that there is no possibility of avoiding the occurrence of such deficiencies when advances at 2¾ per cent. interest are provided for by the public issue of stock bearing the same rate of interest, and no margin is allowed between the rate of interest payable and the rate of interest receivable to cover incidental losses.* These losses arise from the following causes :—(1) *Arrears of payment of the purchase of annuities* (2) *The system of issuing stock entitled to a half year's dividend on the first following dividend day, although the subscribers to the stock are allowed to pay up their subscription by instalments, which may extend up to, or even beyond, that dividend day. It is clear that, when the National Debt Commissioners have to pay a half year's dividend on a certain day, and have not had the use of the money for a full six months before that day, a deficiency must result.* (3) The gale day, on which the purchase annuities are payable, is in each case one month earlier than the dividend day. This

interval is necessary to enable the annuities to
be collected and paid over to the National Debt
Commissioners before the dividend day. But
the result is that the payment received from a
tenant on his first gale day includes interest
for one month less than the period in respect
of which dividend is payable on the stock. (4)
The capital of the Land Purchase Fund, so far as
not required for advances, is temporarily invested
by the National Debt Commissioners in securities.
The interest on these securities is received on
varying dates, and at the date when the balance
of the income account must be struck, there is
always a temporary deficiency, due to the fact
that a certain amount of interest which has
accrued has not yet been received into the
account. (5) On large transactions, such as those
of the Land Purchase Fund, it is impossible to have
the whole of the capital moneys invested and
earning interest on every day of the year. There
must always, therefore, be a loss of income from
unproductive balances. A careful analysis of the
charge of £70,996, which has been made upon
the Local Taxation Grants, shows it to be attribut-
able to these five causes in the following propor-
tions :—(1) Arrears of annuities, £9,119 ; (2)
Unearned dividend on issues of stock, £23,750 ;
(3) Advances dividend, £13,650 ; (4) Interests
due but not received, £15,500 ; (5) Unproductive
balances, £8,977 ; total, £70,996. The arrears
of purchase annuities are, for the most part,
temporary. I understand that, since the account
was made up on 31st January last, a sum of £4,046
has been *recovered* on account of the £9,119 then
in arrear. The chief item of charge is the unearned
dividend of £23,750, arising out of the mode of
issue of the stock which is required by custom
and the convenience of the city. It is open to
question whether this charge could not properly

be treated as a capital charge to be paid for by annuity out of the Development Grant. But an amendment of the Act would be necessary to enable this to be done, as the Act, at present, requires (Section 29. 1.) that the dividends on the stock shall be paid out of the income of the fund. The advance dividend charge will not be made good until the purchase annuities are completed, many years hence. A further charge of the same kind must arise on every issue of the stock. The deficiency of income, which arises from unproductive balances is an inevitable and a permanent loss. The only charges which are of a temporary nature are those relating to *arrears*, and to interest accrued but not received. After analysing and reviewing all the charges, I have come to the conclusion that it should be possible to avoid charging the Local Taxation Grants in full, for those items, by making use of the working balance, which was rendered available by the Labourers' Act of last Session; and I propose to have the Treasury Rules amended to enable this to be done. I may add that the Treasury Rules were published in House of Commons Paper No. 151 of 1905."

I shall set out a conversation which I had with a person in authority with reference to the operation of the Act :—

Question.—" What do you think of the financial situation created by the Act of 1903 ? "

Answer.—" What do you specifically mean ? "

Q.—" For example the landlord receives £100 in cash from the Treasury. Stock is sold at £85 to meet this outlay. Here is a deficit of 15 per cent., and the payment of that deficit practically falls on the ratepayers. I would like to ask if you do not think that that is a serious condition of things ? "

A.—" Yes."

Q.—" What is going to happen ? "

A.—" The purchase of land must go on.   The purchase system has been a great thing for Ireland. It is making the people contented and prosperous. The Irish peasants are the most honest people in the world and anything that would interfere with the purchase of land by them would be a great misfortune."

Q.—" Then you are in favour of the legislation which has been going on since 1881 ? "

A.—" I am in favour of the legislation which has been going on since 1885.   I do not approve of the Land Act of 1881."

Q.—" Then you are in favour of the settlement of the land question on the basis of purchase ? "

A.—" Yes."

Q.—" The landlords, as a class, have not been in favour of the settlement of the question either by tenure or purchase ? "

A.—" Yes, that is so."

Q.—" As a class they have not been wise ? "

A.—" Yes, and I have lost friends among them because of my views as to the necessity of a settlement on the basis of purchase."

Q.—" In reference to this question of the deficit on the flotation of stock, you say that the work of purchase must go on and that the money must be found.   Where is it to be found ? "

A.—" Oh ! it can be found."

Q.—" You mean that it can be found without throwing the burden on the rate-payers, of which you disapprove."

A.—" Yes. I say no more."

Q.—" Is not the bonus applied to purposes not contemplated by the Act of 1903 ? "

A.—" I do not think so."

Q.—" Let me put this case.   The object of the Act was, to induce the landlords to sell. But the tenants were not, we will say, able to pay a price which would tempt the landlords. Then the bonus of 12 per cent. was given to the landlords to eke out the insufficiency of the best price which the tenants could pay. Say the tenant could only pay eighteen years purchase, but the landlord would not sell at that rate. Then the bonus was given of three years which, let us say, had the effect of bringing the number of years purchase up to twenty-one years. But a condition of things in reference to the number of years purchase has arisen which was not contemplated by the Act. That is to say the landlords are getting a greater number of years purchase than was expected.* Instead, so to say, of getting only eighteen years purchase they get twenty-four years purchase. Therefore, there is no insufficiency to eke out but still the landlords get their bonus at 12 per cent ?

A.—" I don't see that there is anything unfair in that."

Q.—" Let me put this case. In the case of the eighteen years purchase the landlord gets a bonus of 12 per cent. and in the case of twenty-four years purchase he gets the same. The man who sells at the eighteen years purchase, who may be a poorer man, gets a less amount on the purchase money than the man who gets twenty-four years purchase, who may be richer ; for, of course, the larger the capital on which the interest is paid, the larger the income ?

A.—" I do not see how you can help it if a bonus is to be paid at all."

* Thus, for example, a large portion of the Duke of Leinster's estate has been sold within the zones at twenty-five years purchase of the statutory equivalent of second term rents reduced by about 19 per cent. The purchase money is estimated at about £670,000, so that the bonus to be paid to the trustees of the Duke, who was a minor, will total £80,400 (Extract from Messrs. Quill, Hamilton, and Longworth on the Irish Land Acts of 1903 and 1904).

Q.—" You could have a graduated bonus ; give 12 per cent. to the man who sells at eighteen, and 8 or 9 per cent. to the man who sells at twenty-four ? "

A.—" I do not think that that would be fair. I don't see why the man who sells good land in the County Down at twenty-four years purchase should get a less percentage than the man who sells indifferent land in the West at eighteen years purchase. The object of the authors of the Act was to secure to the vendor an amount of money which would give him as large an income out of the purchase money as he had out of the rents as a landlord."

Q.—" You mean that the 12 per cent. given to the landlord in the County Down, who sells at twenty-four years purchase, only brings up his income to what it had been prior to the sale, and that it does exactly the same thing to the landlord in the West. But, as a matter of fact, is this system of bringing the landlord's income up to what it was from the rents quite right ? He gets a particular income from rents which are precarious, and he gets the same rents from Consols, which are a gilt-edged security. The safer the security the smaller the income from it. Is not that sound finance ; and are Irish rents as good a security as Consols ? "

A.—" I think so. Land in Ulster is certainly as good a security as Consols, though land in certain parts of the South and West may not. Look at the fall in Consols."

Q.—" Yes, the fall in Consols is considerable ; one's property in Consols is, of course, depreciated, but you don't suffer if you don't realise ? "

A.—" Yes, that is so, nevertheless I think that Irish land is a good security."

Q.—" Is not Ireland a very disturbed and unsettled country ? Above all, has not land been in a very unsettled state in the country ? "

A.—" But are the landlords to suffer because the government cannot maintain law and order."

Q.—" If law and order are not maintained the whole property of the country must suffer."

A.—" Oh ! but if one government cannot maintain law and order, it will be put out, and another will be put in."

Q.—" Can you depend that the government which comes in will be any better than the government that goes out. Look at the position of the Land Commission. What is it doing ? Administering a revolution ? I sat in Mr. Justice Wylie's Court the other day ; I was struck with what I saw. There was a revolution going on quietly, and the Judge at the head of it transferring the property of the country from one set of people to another."

A.—" Yes, the Land Commission administers a revolution under the constitution."

Q.—" A revolution really brought about by violence. There has been a land war in Ireland during all my time and long before. How can you speak of the security of landed property, in a country which is constantly in the throes of a revolution with governments which are always ready to yield to lawlessness and violence. Even now no one can be sure what will happen next. Will the annuities be paid if there are bad times ? "

A.—" The annuities will certainly be paid, because the tenants have got a good thing."

Q.—" Haven't they paid too much for the land ? "

A.—" No, I don't think so. No pressure was put upon them. They came in willingly."

Q.—" Yet the inducements to buy might have tempted them to give too much ? "

A.—" No, the inducement to purchase was not, after all, so great compared with their position as rent-payers under the Act of 1881, with a prospect of having these rents reduced in succeeding terms. No doubt, as purchasers paying annuities, they are secured in the possession of their land, and they are not bothered with bailiffs and people of that kind ; but the actual difference in the payment of the annuity as compared with the payment of rent is not so great as to tempt them to make an unreasonable offer for the purchase of their holdings. The possession of the land by the tenants is a great guarantee for the peace of the country. These men cannot be forced into agitation now."

Q.—" Yet, if there are hard times, and if the ratepayers have to pay deficit on Consols, there may be a stoppage in the payment of the annuities and a general blaze. May I ask if the tenants do not really regard the annuities as a sort of reduced rent ? "

A.—" Not at all. They know very well the difference. They know that they have to pay the annuities regularly to the government, that the amount cannot be raised, and that the property is theirs and their children's."

Q.—" Well, that is just the fact that might have induced them to pay too much for the land at the start ? "

A.—" No ; for there is a counter-balancing consideration. They know that they have to pay the government punctually, and that there can be no abatements ? "

Q.—" The circumstances which would prevent them from paying rents to the landlords would prevent them from paying annuities to the government ? "

A.—" I think Ireland is prosperous ; I think this purchase system is making her prosperous. I take a hopeful view of the future."

Q.—" How many agreements, estimated in money, have actually been lodged ? "

A.—" Agreements have been lodged to the extent of £50,000,000 ; but only £17,000,000 have been paid ; the remainder is wanted to go on."

Q.—" May I ask one more question ? On what basis are fair rents fixed under the Act of 1881 ? "

A.—" I would rather not answer that question."

I shall conclude with a financial catechism, which will be useful for the uninitiated. I am often asked what is the Equivalent Grant ; what is the Guarantee Fund ; what is the Ireland Development Grant and so forth. I have submitted these questions and germane questions, to a friend who had had occasion to give particular attention to the financial relations between England and Ireland, and he has been so good as to put his answers in writing. I append the result :—

Financial Questions.

Question 1.—" What is the Irish Equivalent Grant ? "

Answer—" There are several ' Irish Equivalent Grants,' the Irish Equivalent Grant or Irish Development Grant being the latest.

" The system of equivalent grants was initiated by the Conservative policy of subventions from the Imperial Exchequer to the Local Authorities. The following is a list of Acts under which various ' equivalent grants ' are paid :—

" 1888.   Probate Duties Act.
" 1890.   Customs and Inland Revenue Act.
              Local Taxation.   (Customs and Excise).
" 1891.   Exchequer Contribution Act.
" 1894.   Finance Act.   (Estate Duties Grant).
" 1896.   Estate Duty Act.
" 1898.   Local Government Act.   (Agricultural Grant).   Licence Duties (Annual sum).
" 1903.   Irish Development Grant

" The following are the sums paid under all the various Acts in 1905-6 :—

" Customs, Excise and Inland Revenue
    (1890) £132,911
" Estate and Probate Duties (1888-94-96) 238,178
" Local Government Act, 1898 :—
    " Agricultural Grant   727,655
    " Licence Duties   212,174
    " Annual Sum   79,000
" Exchequer Contribution (Act, 1891) 60,279

" Total   1,450,197
" Irish Development Grant, 1903   ..   185,000

" (See Local Taxation (Ireland) Account ; and Irish Development Grant Account, among Parliamentary Papers of Session.)"

Q. No. 2.—" When was the Equivalent Grant started ? "

A.—" See answer No. 1."

Q. No. 3.—" What is the Development Grant ? "

A.—" The Development Grant is the Grant voted to Ireland as an ' equivalent ' for the special votes to the English schools under the Education Act of 1902. The sum is fixed at £185,000 *per annum.* The Scotch ' Equivalent Grant ' for the same population was over £200,000 *per annum. The English provision is variable with the development of the school vote, and is increasing.*"

Q. No. 4.—" When was it started ? "

A. :—" The Act regulating it was passed in 1903."

Q. No. 5.—"How and why did this Development Grant come to be captured for the Flotation of Land Stock ? "

A.—" The Land Act of 1903 provided that the following charges should be met out of the Grant :

    " (1) £20,000 a year to the Congested Districts Board.

" (2) £5,000 a year to the Public Trustee to meet any deficit in the revenues of Trinity College, arising from the sale of its estates, or the redemption of its Head Rents by vendors under the Act.

" (3) £50,000 a year for four years to the Land Purchase Fund, to provide a ' floating balance,' and to *meet deficiencies of income arising from differences between interest paid by purchasers and interest paid on Land Stock in the first year of its flotation.*

" (4) Interest and Sinking Fund on all Stock issued to make up the difference between the proceeds of stock charged to the tenant-purchasers and the full purchase-money; that is, an amount of money equal to the nominal amount of Stock charged to the tenant-purchasers. *Under the Acts* 1891-6 *the landlord was paid in Stock.* When Stock went to a discount, as a result of the South African War, *Mr. Wyndham proposed that a cash payment should be substituted*, and that the discount should be paid for out of the Development Grant. The charge for discount in 1906 was £57,790, making the total Statutory charges £132,790, leaving a balance of £52,210 for other purposes. The Land Act also provides that, in the event of Land Stock reaching a premium, which is now a remote contingency, the premium remaining after the cash payment to the landlord should be paid into the Development Grant."

Q. No. 6.—" To what extent are these two grants related, and have the terms under which they were originally allocated to Ireland been observed ? "

A.—" See answer to questions 1 and 3.

" The terms have not been observed. The

Development Grant as explained by Mr. Wyndham, was to be applied to purposes of an exceptional kind, such as had not been formerly met out of the ordinary votes ; and its allocation was to be subject to the opinion of the Irish representatives. *Neither condition has been kept.* Despite the protest of the Irish representatives, the Grant has been applied to purposes that would have to be provided for out of the ordinary votes if it did not exist ; *and is thus used to relieve the Exchequer.* For example, the following grants, which formerly fell on the ordinary votes, were provided out of the Grant in 1906.

" Technical Education, £7,000, *paid formerly by Treasury order, Technical Education Act of* 1899.

" King's Scholars, *i.e.,* teachers in training, £5,000. *All scholars in English Training Colleges are provided for out of votes.*

" Marlborough Training College Building Fund, £18,000. A Government Institution hitherto maintained and provided for wholly out of Parliamentary votes."

Q. No. 7.—" What is the Guarantee Fund ? "

A.—" The Guarantee Fund is the Fund made up of moneys voted annually, by Parliament, for Irish public services, as specified in section 5 of the Land Purchase Act of 1891, and all the ' equivalent grants ' described in Answer 1, together with the balance of the Development Grant remaining after the discount charge has been met. This Guarantee Fund is liable for all the deficiencies in the Income Account of the Land Purchase Fund."

Q. No. 8.—" When was it started ? "

A.—" By the Land Purchase Act, 1891."

Q. No. 9.—" How has it worked out ? "

A.—" The first serious charge on the Guarantee Fund devolved upon it in consequence of the expense of flotation of Land Stock in 1904-5, 1906.

These charges amounted to about £70,000, of which only about £8,000 was for arrears of purchaser's annuities. The expenses were of the following character :—

" (1) Loss of interest, by reason of Land Stock being issued as a matured stock.

" (2) Loss of interest, by reason of purchaser's interest being payable a month before interest to stockholders is payable, this involving deficiency of a month's interest between the amount paid by the tenant-purchaser, and the amount payable to the stock-holder.

" (3) Loss of interest, through money lying idle in Bank pending its advance to vendors.

" (4) Interest due to the Land Purchase Income Account by Treasury, for Bills issued but not yet payable.

" (5) Arrears.

" Losses (1) and (3) are permanent. Loss (2) will be made good, but not until completion of redemption period, say about seventy years. Interest under heading (4) will be payable to current year's account. Arrears (5) are partially recoverable.

" But the serious risk to the Guarantee Fund will arise only when transactions have been completed, without any examination by a public official of the equity of the price or the security of the holding for the amount of the loan. All these losses, then falling on the Guarantee Fund, would entail deductions of equal amounts from the payments to the Irish local authorities, and the rates would have to make good the resulting deficiencies."

Q. No. 10.—" Take the County Kildare deficit as an illustration ? "

A.—" The deficiency of £70,000 was apportioned on the county's share of the Imperial

Subvention, forming the Guarantee Fund, in proportion to the amount of money advanced for Land Purchase within the respective counties. Kildare had the largest Land Purchase transactions to its debit, and had received the largest advances out of the proceeds of Land Stock issued. Accordingly its share of the expense came to over £5,000, which was withheld from the Grants-in-Aid due to County Kildare, under the various Acts mentioned in Answer 1. The sum will have to be provided by an increased rate to balance the Kildare County expenditure already arranged for."

Q. No. 11—" What is the Agricultural Grant ? "

A.—" The Agricultural Grant is the Grant 'equivalent' to the grant in aid of Agricultural rates under the English Agricultural Rating Act of 1896.

" It is the largest and most fairly proportioned of the Grants-in-Aid, because it was apportioned on a new principle.

" *Previous 'equivalent grants' were apportioned on the ratio of* 80 : 11 : 9 *for England, Scotland, Ireland, which Mr. Goschen estimated was the ratio of contribution from the three countries to Imperial Taxation. Mr. Sexton protested against the principle, as inconsistent with the theory of a Fiscal Union, and claimed that the subventions should be proportioned to the needs and necessities of the three countries.*

" When the English Agricultural Rating Act was passed, relieving English land of half the rates, and providing for their payment out of the Exchequer, it was first proposed that the 80 : 11 : 9 principle should be adhered to under which Ireland's share would have been only some £150,000.

" The Report of the Financial Relations Commission appeared at the time, and the reform agitation sprang up. The point was put by the Irish landlords to the Exchequer : if the provision is to be proportionate to taxation, the taxation ought to be proportionate to capacity ; if there is, as you contend, to be indiscriminate taxation, there ought to be indiscriminate expenditure based upon the same principles throughout the Union ; and Ireland is entitled to half her agricultural rates as well as England.

" Mr. Balfour reluctantly yielded, but seized the occasion to relieve the landlords of their liability for poor rate of which they paid half, and this induced them to accept the Local Government Act of 1898. The Grant amounts to £727,000.

Q. No. 12.—" Do these several Grants or Funds over-lap, and if so, to what extent ? "

A.—" See previous answers."*

The Congested Districts Board.

" There has always been trouble in the Congested Districts, owing to the poverty of the people. No statesman-like effort was made to deal with the subject until 1891, when the Congested Districts Board was established."†

So said one of the English officials in Ireland to me some time ago. In the first place what is a Congested District ? We have definitions from Mr. Bailey and Sir Horace Plunkett. The former says :—

" The term ' congestion ' has become generic in Ireland. It has acquired a special meaning as applying to *quasi* agricultural population living on holdings insufficient to support a family."‡

---

* In reference to appointments in connection with the Estates Commissioners Department, it may be said that Inspectors, Assistant Inspectors and Surveyors are appointed by the Lord Lieutenant after Treasury sanction has been obtained to the increase in number.

† 54 and 55 Victoria, ss. 34, 41.

‡ Royal Commission on Congestion (3rd Report, p. 337, 331).

The latter describes it as :—

" A condition of poverty, due to deficiency of land or other means of earning what is necessary to the maintenance of a decent standard of living."

Mr. Micks, one of the Commissioners of the Local Government Board has given the following description of the condition of the people in the Congested Districts:—

" There are two classes in the Congested Districts, mainly—namely the poor and the destitute ; there are no wealthy people except traders. There are some shopkeepers and officials such as schoolmasters, clergy, and Government officials, such as police and coastguards ; those people are, of course, comfortable, but their numbers are very small, and there are hardly any resident gentry in most of the congested districts. Nearly all the inhabitants are on one dead level of poverty. Their dietary is almost altogether vegetable. They have, at one meal a day, a little salt fish, or a very small piece of some coarse American bacon as a sort of relish with their food, that is, those who can afford it, but the majority of the people have nothing but vegetable diet, such as Indian meal, or oaten porridge, potatoes, and bread baked by themselves or sometimes by the bakers from flour. They also drink tea to a large extent ; as a rule eggs or butter from the farm are sold or bartered."*

Next, where are the Congested Districts situated ? The Congested Districts are in the following counties :— Donegal, Leitrim, Sligo, Roscommon, Mayo, Galway, Kerry, Cork.

What is the Congested Districts Board ? In a word the Congested Districts Board was created in

* Evidence Royal Commission on Local Taxation, Vol. v., p. 126), Mr. Micks adds,—" the poor mainly support the destitute " (*Ibid* p. 128).

1891 (for a period of twenty years) to improve the condition of the Congested Districts.

The Board consisted, originally, of ten members ; two *ex officio*, the Chief Secretary* and a member of the Land Commission [However, under the Land Act of 1903 the member of the Land Commission was replaced by the Under-Secretary] ; five permanent members ; three temporary members.

The Board now consists of eleven members ; the Vice-President of the Department of Agriculture having been made an *ex officio* member under the Agricultural and Technical Instruction Act of 1899.†

What are the powers of the Board ?

The Board are empowered to take such steps as they think proper, either directly or indirectly, for improving Congested Districts, in connection with the following subjects, namely :—

1. Agricultural Development.

2. Forestry.

3. Breeding of Live Stock and Poultry.

4. Sale of Seed Potatoes and Seed Oats.

5. Migration, enlargement and amalgamation of Small Holdings and improvements of Estates.

6. Emigration.

7. Fishing, including the construction of piers and harbours, and industries connected with fishing.

8. Weaving and spinning, and any other suitable industries.

Added to these functions is the power (practically) to purchase tenanted land in the Congested Districts, and untenanted land anywhere. Under Section 39 of the Act of 1891 the Land Commission were authorised to acquire and hold land for the purposes of the Act dealing with Congested Districts, and to place such land under the control of the Congested Districts Board,

---

* Under the Act of 1891, it was provided that in the absence of the Chief Secretary the Under-Secretary should take his place.

† It may be noted that the Chief Inspector of Fisheries (from the Department of Agriculture) is one of the temporary members.

on such terms and conditions as they deemed expedient, and under Section 40 (5), any property given to the Board, and any investments made by the Board, were held in trust for the Board by the Land Commission.

What, then, is the procedure in reference to the purchase of estates by the Board taken in connection with its association with the Land Commission in this particular business ?

When the Board agrees with the landlord for the purchase of his estate, they request the Land Commission to advance the purchase money. The Land Commission vest the estate in the Board, after investigating the title, and then pay over the purchase money to the parties entitled, on behalf of the Board.

Pending the distribution of the purchase money, the Board pay the vendor interest upon it, usually at the rate of 3½ per cent. ; and when the estate has been resold to the tenants, the Board pay off the debt to the Land Commission.

How is the Board financed ? A sum of £1,500,000 taken from the Church Surplus fund has been placed at the Board's disposal, and the Board receives besides a Parliamentary grant (included in the vote for the Department of Agriculture), and a contribution from the Development Grant. The income from these various sums is :—

Interest on £1,500,000	£41,250
Parliamentary Grant	25,000
Contribution from the Development Grant	20,000
Total	£86,250*

* The Board have also the residue of a Charitable Fund, which was placed at their disposal by the Act of 1891. The total capital of the fund amounts to about £35,000, and is used as a reproductive Loan Fund for Fishery purposes.

The Board has a fluctuating income from other sources such as interest on stocks, loans, rents, and so forth. I understand that the total receipts, including repayment of advanced capital, of the Board from all sources in 1906-7 amounted to £256,000.

In addition to the *fixed* income of the Board, they also receive Rents and Profits from Estates purchased by them for resale to the tenants, and held by them for some years. Out of these rents they have to pay interest at 2¾ per cent. to the Land Commission on advances made by that body to the Board for the purchase of the estates. Any surplus rents, after paying this and other outgoings, is applied by the Board to the improvement of estates, but I am told that the net result of these transactions (after making necessary improvements to purchased estates) is a loss not a profit.

The Board have also considerable receipts (but to a large extent in the nature of circulating capital) from various reproductive or partly reproductive schemes, *e.g.*, the Board supply boats and nets to fishermen on the Share System. Under the Scheme the *earnings* of the fishermen by sale of fish are passed through the Board's Accounts, and the proportion of the earnings payable to the crew, are shown as payments in the accounts.

The Board also borrow money from the Board of Works, for the purpose of improving the estate while on hand, and repay the amount on resale of the estate out of what is called the enhanced value, *i.e.*, the difference between the purchase price as advanced by the Land Commission and the selling price of the estate in its *improved* condition.

The revenue side of the Board's Accounts also includes stock transactions, the Board being empowered to purchase Land Stock in certain cases in the open market, and lodge it with the Land Commission in redemption of their debt under the Land Act 1896. While the stock is at a discount, the Board benefit to that extent, as the debt is written off at the par value of the stock. The purchase of the stock appears as a payment at the other side of the account.

The Board also makes loans for Agriculture, Industrial and Fishery purposes, which are repayable in half-yearly instalments, and these instalments form part of the receipts for the year.*

In July 1896, a Royal Commission was appointed to inquire into the working of the Congested Districts Board , and to consider its relations to the Department of Agriculture and Technical Instruction, and to the Estates Commissioners.

The intelligent foreigner surveying the English administration of Ireland, might perhaps say " does not the work of these three bodies in some respects overlap ? " and he might ask, " Why is there a Congested Districts Board ? " Well, in the first place, when the Congested Districts Board was created (1891) there was no Department of Agriculture and Technical Instruction (created in 1899), and there were no Estates Commissioners (appointed in 1903). " But," the foreigner might say, " there is a Department of Agriculture and Technical Instruction now, and there are Estates Commissioners ; and why should not the duties of the Congested Districts Board be distributed between these Departments ; why should not the Estates Commissioners deal with land within the Congested Districts, why should not ' the Department ' deal with Fisheries and Technical Instruction."

The Royal Commissioners were brought face to face with this question in the course of their investigations, and there is nothing more significant in their report than the manner in which they deal with it.

They state the reasons which have been given against the continuance of the Board with fairness and force. They say :—

* See pages 5 and 38 (Appendix) of the Board's Sixteenth Report which gives the total receipts and payments for the year ended 31st March, 1907.

" The question has been raised during our deliberations whether the Board should continue to carry out the work, which it is generally recognised must be done by some public body, of improving the condition of the people in the poor districts in the West of Ireland. It was pointed out that the Board is not, from an administrative point of view, an ideal body for carrying out this work. They meet generally but once a month, and sit then for three days at the most. Such a procedure is inconsistent with continuous day to day administration. It was suggested that the continuance of the Board would perpetuate dual administration and make for administrative waste."

The easiest way to deal with this condition of things would certainly be to merge the work of the Board in the work of the Department of Agriculture and the work of the Estates Commissioners respectively. Nevertheless the Royal Commissioners are in favour of the continuance of the Board. Why ? (And this is the most significant part of the paragraph). Because (so they say) the Board enjoys the popular confidence to a degree which no Government Department could possess. I must set out the exact words :—

" It has been urged, and we think with great force, that much of the success of the Congested Districts Board, who were given a very difficult task, has been due to the fact that they did not form an ordinary Government department but were an independent body of Irishmen, who, as regards their work on the Board, were generally regarded as being as free from officialism as from party politics. Rightly or wrongly it seems to be felt by many that a Government department in Ireland, not being responsible to some Irish body but only to the Imperial Parliament, is not readily responsive to Irish public opinion, and does not command the confidence which seems to be accorded to the Board. Whatever may be the truth of this argument, and whatever it was in the Board, whether their independence of Government or their *personnel*, that commanded confidence, it is obvious that functions such as those which have been discharged by the Board, functions which depend for their success on the consent and active co-operation of the people, might, under existing conditions, suffer from the substitution, for the Board, of a department, no matter how efficient. If no Board had been in existence, and the question merely was what would be the most efficient body for carrying out the work to be done in the West of Ireland, it might be considered desirable to entrust it to existing departments of Government. With things as they are in Ireland, we are strongly of opinion that it would gravely imperil the carrying out of the work that has to be done, to transfer to any department of Government, the functions of the Congested Districts Board, so long as the Constitution of Irish Government remains as it is."

I repeat this is a most significant statement. A Royal Commission declares that a particular public Body should be kept in existence because (as these Commissioners suppose) it enjoys some measure of independence of the government of the country, and therefore is likely to do efficient work. In the opinion of the Commissioners efficiency depends upon popular confidence, and popular confidence consists practically in distrust of the Government. I have not of recent years come across a more powerful argument in favour of Home Rule.*

* I have already dealt with the question as to how far the Congested Districts Board is really independent of the Castle (Ante p. 147). The Royal Commissioners propose the re-constitution of the Board to some extent; but I am surprised to see (having regard to the fact that they are apparently in favour of

Department of Agriculture and Technical Instruction.

When Mr. (now Sir) Horace Plunkett was striving to induce the English Cabinet to create a Department of Agriculture and Technical Instruction in Ireland, he said, one night in the House of Commons (referring to the difficulties which blocked his way, and quoting the words of an Irish Nationalist) :—

" There is no use in approaching an English minister unless you go to him with the head of a landlord in one hand, and the tail of a cow in the other."

However, Sir Horace got his Department without going to these extremes. There are exceptions to every rule. Nevertheless the " head " and the " tail " argument has been productive of useful legislation for Ireland.

What is the Department ? The Department consists of a President—the Chief Secretary for the time being—and a Vice-President appointed by one of the principal Secretaries of State.

The President, *i.e.*, the Chief Secretary (still in his *rôle* of Pooh-Bah), and the Vice-President are, so to say, the " Executive." The Executive is tempered by a Council of Agriculture, and two Boards—the Agricultural Board and the Board of Technical Instruction. An income of £166,000 (called the Department's Endowment), together with a capital sum of £200,000, is placed at the disposal of the Department, for the development of the resources of the country on the lines specially laid down for its work. Besides this endowment, moneys are voted annually by Parliament for the Administrative functions transferred to it.

---

cutting the Board adrift from the Government) that they should still suggest the retention of the Chief Secretary, the Under-Secretary and the Vice-President of the Department of Agriculture (links with the Government) on it. It may be added that two members of the Commission, Sir Anthony MacDonnell and Mr. Conor O'Kelly, were in favour of the discontinuance of the Board.

The Council of Agriculture consists of 104 members : 68 appointed by the County Councils,* 34 nominated by the Executive, 2 *ex-officio*, President and Vice-President.

The Council is elected every three years, and must meet at least once a year. As a matter of practice, I believe it meets twice a year. It is merely a consultative body, and has no administrative power whatever. But it can discuss " matters of public interest in connection with any of the purposes of the Act."

The Agricultural Board, which advises in subjects relating to agriculture and other rural industries, and sea and inland fisheries, consists of twelve members; eight elected by the Council, four appointed by the Executive.

The Board of Technical Instruction, which advises on subjects relating to Technical Instruction, consists of twenty-three members :—

4 members	appointed by	the Department.
3 ,,	,,	Borough of Belfast.
3 ,,	,,	Borough of Dublin.
1 member	,,	a Joint Committee of Councils of the Urban Districts, County of Dublin.
1 ,,	,,	Commissioners of National Education.
1 ,,	,,	Intermediate Board of Education.
4 members	,,	County Boroughs other than Belfast and Dublin.†
4 ,,	,,	Provincial Committee of each province.
1		President.
1		Vice-President } *ex-officio*.

23
—

* Two persons are appointed by each County Council ; Cork being regarded as two counties.

† The other county boroughs besides Dublin and Belfast are : (1) Waterford, (2) Limerick, (3) Londonderry, (4) Cork.

Unlike the Council of Agriculture, these Boards have real powers to a limited extent. The " Executive " can spend no money out of the Department's endowment in schemes relating to agriculture, rural industries or sea or inland fisheries without the sanction of the Agricultural Board.

With reference to the financial control of the Board of Technical Instruction this is the case ; under the Act creating the Department a sum of £55,000 is set aside for Technical Instruction. The amount is divided triennially into two sums, one for County Boroughs, and the other for Technical Instruction outside County Boroughs. The Triennial Allocation is subject to the Concurrence of the Board of Technical Instruction, as is also the application of grants in aid of schemes of Technical Instruction outside County Boroughs.

These Boards are elected for three years, and meet when summoned by the " Executive." The Executive summons each Board when money is needed out of the Endowment Fund, in reference to the subjects over which the Board exercises advisory functions. As a matter of fact, I believe the Agricultural Board meets seven or eight times a year. It may be noted that the Executive may go to Parliament or the Treasury for money without the intervention of the Boards, whose jurisdiction is confined exclusively to the Endowment Fund. In a word the Boards possess no administrative functions ; they simply have a veto on the expenditure of the Departments endowment. The Executive alone exercises administrative authority.*

I now pass to the work of the Department.

1. It includes the exercise of certain powers and duties in connection with the administration of various bodies which previously stood apart, thus :—

* The Act provides that an "annual sum of ten thousand pounds shall be applied for the purposes of Sea Fisheries." This money, accordingly, could be spent irrespective of the wishes of the Board.

Inspectors of Fisheries.
Veterinary Department.
National Museum.
Science, with an Agricultural Faculty.
Royal College of Science.
Geological Survey.
School of Art.
Botanical Gardens.
National Library.

These bodies, once separate, are now, so to say, departments of *the* Department. It is responsible for them, and they are maintained from its Parliamentary vote.*

In connection with Fisheries, it may be noted that the work of this branch :—

> " Includes the construction of piers and harbours, the supply of fishing boats and gear, investigation into the habits of fish and methods of fishing, instruction in fishing, the encouragement of any industries immediately connected with, and sub-servient to fishing, the supervision and protection of fishing grounds, and the enforcement of bye-laws relating to fishing."†

2. There is a Committee in every county, formed by the County Council in connection with the department, for the purpose of initiating and carrying out schemes for the agricultural and industrial improvement of the locality. The money for carrying out these schemes is found partly by rate levied by the County Council, and partly by a grant given by the department. These schemes relate *inter alia* to the

> " Aiding, improving and developing of agriculture, horticulture, forestry, dairying, the breeding of horses, cattle and other live stock and poultry, home and cottage industries, the cultivation and

* " Organisation of the Department," p. 13.
† " Organisation," p. 14.

preparation of flax, inland fisheries, and any industries immediately connected with and sub-servient to any of the said matters, and any instruction relating thereto, together with the aiding or facilitating of the carriage and distribution of produce."

Instructors are appointed by the County Council from a list of competent persons sent down by the Department, to deal with these subjects—such persons having been trained in Colleges, partly under the direction of the Department.

3. There is a Consultative Educational Committee which consists of five persons :—

1. The Vice-President (Chairman).
2. One appointed by National Education Board.
3. One by the Intermediate Education Board.
4. One by the Agricultural Board, and,
5. One by the Board of Technical Instruction.

The functions of this Committee are to co-ordinate Educational Administration ; and, so far as agricul-tural development and urban industries are concerned, to bring institutions devoted to Primary, Secondary and Higher Education into line.

4. The Albert Institution (residential school, Glasnevin, Dublin, in connection with the College of Science) ; and the Munster Institution (another residential school near Cork) are under the direction of the Department.

5. The collection of agricultural, banking and railway statistics, previously included among the functions of the Registrar-General, and the powers and duties relating to the Markets and Fairs Acts (hitherto within the jurisdiction of the Land Commission) are now embraced in the work of the Department.

6. The Lord Lieutenant may, with the consent of the Treasury, transfer to the Department the work of any Department exercising analogous powers and duties.

7. Full provisions are made for the training of experts in all branches of agriculture (including horticulture and dairying) at the Royal College of Science, and at the Albert College, Glasnevin, and at the Munster Institute.*

8. Grants are given to schools for teaching domestic economy and cookery, lace-making, laundry and dress-making.

Grants are given to assist in the organisation of agricultural banks in suitable localities.

9. Residential " Stations " (as they are called) are established at Athenry, Ballyhaise and Clonakilty where the sons of farmers, besides receiving a general elementary education, are taught the theory of agriculture in the " Station" (or school as it really is), and the practice of agriculture in the fields by which the Station is surrounded.

10. There are residential schools for the training of domestic servants at Moate and Stradbally in Leinster, and at Dunmanway, and Carrick-on-Suir in Munster.

11. The Branches into which the Department proper (that is excluding the former separate departments of government, which it has absorbed) is divided, are :—

    1. Agricultural Branch.
    2. Technical Instruction Branch.
    3. Fisheries Branch.
    4. Statistics and Intelligence Branch.
    5. Veterinary Branch.
    6. Accounts Branch.

The staff of the Department consists of a secretary, two assistant secretaries (one for agriculture and one for technical instruction), inspectors, instructors, and officers.

12. Finally, the duty of the Department is to devote itself to the scientific and practical teaching of farming

* Sir Horace Plunkett, " Addresses," p. 51.

and domestic economy, and the promotion of schemes for the development of the mineral, textile, and fishing resources of the country, with the view of adding to its wealth, and by educational and experimental methods increasing the commercial efficiency of the inhabitants.*

Registrar-General.

The office of Registrar-General was created in 1845, (7 and 8 Vic., cap. 81), and its duties were extended by an Act passed in 1863. These duties now include :—

1. The registration of births, deaths, marriages and successful vaccinations.

2. The compilation of Emigration Statistics, and the preparation of an Annual Report on the Criminal and Judicial Statistics.

3. The Superintendence of the Decennial Census for the carrying out of which a special Commission is appointed, of which the Registrar-General is Chairman.

* I had a short conversation with an official of the Department in reference to possible industrial developments (apart from agriculture) in Ireland. His statement came to this. Glass is a possible industry, but the difficulty is to get the proper kind of sand ; that is, sand without iron in it. This sand can be best got in France ; there is only one place in Ireland where there is sand free from iron, and that is in Muckish Mountain, Co. Donegal. Then the expense of bringing it from Donegal to Dublin is greater than bringing it from France. It would cost 10s. from France, and 16s. from Donegal. The sand free from iron is necessary for making delicate glass. Rough sand may be used for making bottles, etc. The other industries are coal, brick, roofing tiles, cement. The best coal fields are, perhaps, at Coal Island. Considerable deposits exist there. Then there is coal at Bally Castle, coal in Kilkenny; coalfields are worked at Castlecomer, but there is difficulty in transit. There is a train to Ballyragget : there is no train from Ballyragget to Castlecomer. There ought to be a train, the distance is six miles. The Castlecomer coal is anthracite. It is used in Kilkenny, and about the neighbourhood, and is rapidly developing. The Bally Castle fields are also being worked, and coal is being used about there.

In connection with the work of registration—which is the main work of the office—it may be stated that Ireland is divided into 159 *Superintendent Registrars' Districts*, conterminous with the Poor Law Unions, and 827 Registrars' Districts conterminous with the Dispensary Districts. The Clerk of the Union is, in almost every case, Superintendent Registrar, and the Registrars are, for the most part, *Dispensary Medical Officers*. The Registrars are paid out of the rates, for each birth and death registered by them 1s., and for each Catholic marriage 6d.

In addition to these there are 158 Registrars of Marriages under the 7 and 8 Vic., cap. 81, who are empowered to " solemnise " marriages. They are paid by fees, and are allowed £10 each for rent of office.

In the case of Catholic marriages the law requires that the certificate is to be furnished to the Registrar by the husband in each case ; but, in practice, for the convenience of their flocks, the Catholic clergy furnish certificates of the marriages solemnised by them, to the Registrars.

The Protestant clergy furnish Quarterly Returns of the marriages solemnised by them to the Registrar-General, through the local Registrar of Marriages, under 7 and 8 Vic., cap. 81.

In addition to the above-named officers, there are 190 Licensers of Marriages of the English Church in Ireland, and 173 Licensing Ministers of the Presbyterian Church, who are paid by fees, and all of whom are bound by bond to the Registrar-General for the due performance of their duties.

The copies of the local Registers of Births, Deaths, and Marriages, when received in the Central Office at the close of each quarter, are examined for errors, corrected, completed, and bound, and indexes to them prepared for public reference.

The statistics published in connection with the Decennial Census of Ireland, embrace a great variety of subjects, including area, houses (and out offices), tenements of less than five rooms with the number of occupants, population, valuation, conjugal condition, ages, occupations, social condition, birthplaces, foreigners, religious profession, education, schools, agricultural statistics, agricultural holdings in reference to population, emigration, the blind, the deaf and dumb, the lunatic and idiotic, the sick and infirm, the Irish-speaking population.

During the intercensal periods the Registrar-General prepares any returns or information which may be required by Parliament, or the Government, having reference to the work of the Decennial Census.

I had a conversation with a gentleman about the three scourges which afflict Ireland, Emigration, Tuberculosis and Lunacy. He said :—

"The number of people leaving the country is deplorable ; it is for the Imperial Government to take steps to stop it. The emigration is quite abnormal. There is no need for people to go away. The great flow of emigration was caused no doubt in the past by the land system, but that is now being changed. It is a pity that some such system is not adopted in Ireland as exists in Italy, with a view of finding out any special causes of emigration, and of learning what was going on in the district from which the people emigrated. In Italy, the Commune make a report, so that the authorities know what is going on in the district from which the people emigrate. In Ireland, the source of information about emigrants was chiefly from the manifests of the ships. The reports were sent from the ports. There was no statute governing this matter, so that the people might refuse to give any information if they choose. I think that the police in each town and district ought to be instructed to give an account of the quarter from which the emigrants go, and then it might be ascertained whether anything could be done in the nature of establishing industries to keep the people at home.

" At present the Registrar-General had only to report on the fact of emigration, and not on the causes. He ought to be authorised to report on the causes ; if he was so authorised it would be useful. Most of the money that came for the persons emigrating, came from America. Great inducements were held out by relatives in America for their friends at home to go out, then sometimes those relatives came home in a very prosperous state ; they were seen by their friends with nice dresses and rings and other fineries, which compared very favourably with the poor dresses of the people at home, and this tempted them to go away. There was a very slight falling off in the returns recently, but I do not attach any importance to that. The causes ought to be examined, and some means thought out for stopping the drain. There was another awful thing affecting the life of the country. That was Tuberculosis. This disease compared with the same in England and Scotland, showed a frightful difference to the detriment of Ireland. Measures were being taken of a sanitary character to check the disease, but with no results so far.

" The next fatal feature was the increase of lunacy. I shall tell you a curious story in connection with the matter. An Irish doctor, on coming from America met an attractive woman on board ship, with whom he got into conversation. She turned out to be a Polish lady, an official at a lunatic asylum in one of the states. She was coming to Ireland with two lunatics, one a melancholy patient, the other a raving lunatic. The Doctor managed to get into conversation with the melancholy patient. She said that she had gone into service in New York some years ago, and that her health had broken down, and she was taken away and put into an asylum. While in the asylum her money and clothes were taken away, and, ultimately, she was told that she was to be sent to Europe for a trip for the good of her health. They landed at Queenstown and the doctor learned that the melancholy patient came from a Townland in Waterford, and that the other patient came from the Co. Limerick. Inquiries were instituted and the parties traced to an hotel in Queenstown. The Polish official allowed the melancholy patient to find her way home to Waterford, and she arrived one day greatly to the surprise of her parents who thought that she was doing well in New York.

" With reference to the raving lunatic patient, the Polish lady, the keeper and the lunatic drove in a car to the house of the lunatic's father. The patient was dropped, so to say, on the doorstep, and then the car drove off with the Polish lady and the keeper. It was ascertained that there were several cases of this nature, so that the returns of lunacy in Ireland may not mean that the lunatics in every case have been stricken in Ireland."

This gentleman told me another story, which seems to point to the necessity of an alteration in the law.

"A lunatic came to the office of the Registrar-General, and wanted to be married. The Registrar-General had heard that the man had been detained in an asylum, and he mentioned the fact. The man said that it was a conspiracy against him. The Registrar-General asked if he would have any objection to be examined by two doctors, and he said no. He was so examined, and the doctors certified that he was insane ; he was then placed in an asylum. After a time he got better, and he was then certified sane

(temporarily).   Within a month after his release,
he met the woman again and they got married.
Of course the marriage could not be prevented
then, because the man had a certificate showing
that he was then sane.

"I think the law needs amendment to the
effect, that anyone detained in a lunatic asylum,
should not on being certified sane, be allowed
to get married until at least a probationary
period had elapsed."

I commend this suggestion to the wisdom of our
legislators.*

Treasury Remembrancer.

The first great Treasury Officer in Ireland was as
I have said the Lord High Treasurer.

> " The offices of the Treasury and Exchequer in
> Ireland," we are told, " appear to have been
> modelled upon those in England as early as the
> twelfth year of King John "

and by an Act of Henry VII. it was declared

> " that the Treasurer of Ireland should have
> as ample power in all things belonging to his office,
> as the Treasurer of England hath in his office."

Gradually the office of Lord High Treasurer became
a sinecure, and the Vice-Treasurer became the efficient
officer.

---

* I should like to call attention to the following useful publica-
tions issued by the present Registrar-General, Sir Robert
Mathison :—
  " Surnames in Ireland."
  "Varieties and Synonyms of Surnames and Christian
Names in Ireland."
  "Principal Results of the Census " (in Great Britain and
Ireland).
  "Housing of the People of Ireland during the period
1841-1901."

" He had the charge of all the King's Treasure, the receiving and issuing of it, and to account for it ; he, or his deputy, had to sign all receipts for money paid into the Treasury and received by the teller or cashier, as well as all orders."

The office of Vice-Treasurer seems to have been occasionally multiplied, for we learn that sometimes there were two Vice-Presidents and sometimes even three. Generally, however, there seems to have been only one. As the office of Lord High Treasurer gradually became a sinecure, so the office of Vice-Treasurer became a sinecure too. Nevertheless, the Vice-Treasurer enjoyed great emoluments ; but the Deputy Vice-Treasurer, and Teller did the work. It is they who were accountable to Parliament for all moneys received and paid by them.

" Payments were made from time to time, in accordance with the Civil and Military Lists, or by King's Letters, Concordatum Warrant, etc ; and accounts, with the necessary vouchers, were rendered quarterly to the Auditor-General."*

In 1793, Commissioners, eligible to sit in Parliament, were appointed, and the office of Treasurer was suppressed.† In 1795, a new arrangement was made. It was then decided that the receipt, custody, and issue of the public money should be entrusted to the Teller and Auditor-General of the Exchequer and Clerk of the Pells under the direction of the Lord High Treasurer or Commissioners of the Treasury, as in England. No change was made in this system at the time of Mr. Pitt's Union.

* The Deputy Vice-Treasurer received £500 a year from the Vice-Treasurer or Treasurers ; and the Teller £250 a year.

† This point is not very clear as to whether it means the office of Lord High Treasurer or Vice-Treasurer. (See account of Public Income and Expenditure, presented to Parliament in 1869, No. 366 of that year ; app. No. 13, p. 389.)

I have already said that between 1801 and 1817 there was a separate Irish Exchequer and a separate Irish Chancellor of the Exchequer. In 1817, the two Exchequers were consolidated, and the Chancellor of the Exchequer for England became the Chancellor of the Exchequer for Ireland too. Then there were new financial arrangements. The duties, hitherto performed by the Auditor and Teller, and the Clerk of the Pells in Ireland, were henceforth to be done in person under Treasury regulations ; that is to say, Irish financial business was henceforth to be done by clerks in Downing Street or agents appointed by Downing Street to act under its instructions in Ireland.*

The rest of the story may be told in the words of a Treasury minute, dated 4th January, 1871.

" Up to 1837 the Vice-Treasurer and Teller of the Exchequer in Ireland was a high officer, possessing large financial powers.† In that year Parliament empowered the Treasury to make regulations consolidating and simplifying the accounts of the Receipt and Issue of Public Money. The Office of Vice Treasurer and Teller of the Exchequer was, in consequence, reduced, and in lieu thereof a Paymaster of Civil Services in Dublin was created, an officer subject to the Treasury, who, in addition to the functions which his name implies, was to undertake any other

---

* This account is mainly based on Parliamentary Papers, No. 366 of the year 1869, App. No. 13, pp. 386, 387.   Haydn, in the " Dictionary of Dates " has the following note in reference to the Irish Treasury :

" The first [Lord High Treasurer of Ireland] was John de St. John, Henry III. 1217 ; the last, William, Duke of Devonshire, 1776 ; Vice-Treasurers were appointed till 1789 ; then Commissioners till 1817, when the revenues of Great Britain and Ireland were united."

† On the consolidation of the Exchequers, the office of Lord High Treasurer of Ireland was merged in the Commission for executing the office of Lord High Treasurer for the United Kingdom.   But the ancient office of Vice-Treasurer for Ireland was continued.

business which the Treasury might call upon him to perform.

"In 1860, on the death of Mr. Grey, the then Paymaster, this office was abolished, and the Pay Office at Dublin became merely a branch of the General Pay Office under charge of a clerk detached from the office in London.

"The Treasury, therefore, has now been for a period of ten years without a special and confidential adviser in Dublin."

The Treasury came to the conclusion that this arrangement was not satisfactory, and determined to appoint a special agent or adviser, who should reside in Dublin, to represent their interests.

"It is obvious," says the Treasury minute, "that the consultative officer, to be of any service, must in that capacity be independent of all authority save the Treasury, in fact that he should, as far as possible, represent the Treasury in Ireland."

The minute continues :—

"It is also desirable that he should be attached to some existing office both for the sake of economy and because his consultative functions will not engross his whole time.

"But there are only two departments in Dublin to which such an officer could be attached, the Board of Works, and the Pay Office, and of these two departments, it is clearly the Pay Office only whose duties have any affinity to the local Treasury functions, for which it is advisable that provision should now be made."

In 1872, the new officer was appointed under the title "Treasury Remembrancer and Deputy Paymaster."

The Treasury Remembrancer then is the agent of the English Treasury in Ireland. He advises the Treasury on matters relating to " Imperial " expenditure in the country. He is also the Deputy Paymaster General ; and all officials are paid by him.

Valuation and Boundary Survey.

In 1824, a Committee of the English House of Commons reported in favour of the valuation of Ireland. In 1830, the valuation was commenced (for purposes of county assessment) by Sir Richard Griffith.

To ensure uniformity an Act was passed in 1836 (6 and 7 William IV., c. 87), which provided for a relative valuation of townlands, based on a fixed scale of agricultural produce contained in the Act. Taking this valuation as a whole, it proved to be 25 per cent. under the gross rental of the country.

The valuation did not give general satisfaction, and, in 1844, another Committee of the English House of Commons recommended that the basis of taxation should be changed. Accordingly, in 1846, an Act was passed (9 and 10 Vic., c. 110), by which the principle of valuation was changed from being a relative valuation, of town-lands, based upon a fixed scale of agricultural produce, to a tenement valuation based on the probable letting of the land. The principle upon which this valuation was based, came also to be discredited, and in 1852 another Act (15 and 16 Vic., c. 63, Sec. 2) was passed, which, returning to the principle of the Act of 1836, provided :

> " That in every valuation hereafter to be made, or to be carried on, or completed under the provisions of this Act, the Commissioner of Valuation shall cause every tenement or rateable hereditament hereinafter specified to be separately valued, and such valuation in regard to land shall be made upon an estimate of the net annual value thereof,

with reference to the average prices of the several articles of agricultural produce hereinafter specified ; all peculiar local circumstances, in each case, being taken into consideration, etc."

A code of instructions was next issued by Sir Richard Griffith for the guidance of the valuators. These instructions open and close with a direction to the valuators to value the land according to the rent which a liberal landlord would obtain from a solvent tenant. Thus, apparently, recognising the force of the principle laid down by Mr. George Cornwallis-Lewis (though it seems contrary to the words of the Act of Parliament) that,

" there is no other standard which can be taken for the value of the land, but the rent."

Under the Act of 1852 the valuation of Ireland went on and was completed in 1866. There has been no general re-valuation of the country since, but Griffith's valuation, as it is called, is revised every year, and the Valuation and Boundary Survey Office exists for that purpose.

" This annual revision," says a recent writer, " has been limited, in the case of town property, to hereditaments where structural changes have taken place, or where there has been a fall in value, and in the case of land it is provided by the Act of 1854 (17 Vic., cap. 8) that in any alterations to be made consequent on changes in areas the aggregate valuation of the town-land shall not be varied. The Act 37 and 38 Vic., cap. 70, authorises the payment by the several counties and cities of the sum of £8000 a year as their proportion of the cost of annual revision. By the Local Government Act, 1898, provision was made for a re-valuation, on the application of the local authority, of the six County Boroughs

(Belfast, Dublin, Cork, Waterford, Limerick, and Londonderry), the expense to be borne in equal moities by the Imperial Exchequer and local rates."

* * * *

" All taxation in Ireland, whether Imperial or local, is based on the valuation, as carried out in accordance with the Irish Valuation Acts [and the regulations issued for that purpose by the Treasury]." *

The Commissioner of Valuation is also Boundary Surveyor " for the purpose of revising the boundaries of counties and other areas under the Act 17 Vic., cap. 17." As Commissioner of Valuation he is appointed by the Treasury ; as Boundary Surveyor he is appointed by the Castle.

Law.

(a) Lord Chancellor's Court and the Court of Appeal.
(b) Master of the Rolls.
(c) Second Chancery Division.
(d) King's Bench Division, which embraces *Nisi Prius*, and the several common law courts including, under recent legislation, the Admiralty and Bankruptcy Courts.
(e) Land Judge.
(f) Lunacy Department.
(g) Crown and Hanaper Office.
(h) Local Registration of Title Office.
(i) Record and Writ Offices.
(k) Consolidated Taxing Office.
(l) Accountant General's Department.
(m) Chancery Registrar's Office.
(n) Principal Registry Office of Probate.

William the Conqueror of England laid the foundation of the Judicial System which now exists in

* " The Irish Executive."

England and Ireland. He established the first court, introduced from Normandy, called the *Curia Regis*, where he sometimes presided himself, assisted by some of his principal officers of State, and by Bishops and Lords. In his absence an officer, styled the Chief Justiciary, presided. Gradually the Chief Justiciary came to be assisted by skilled lawyers called Justiciaries. The King ceased to preside regularly. The Bishops and Lords gradually disappeared, and the *Curia Regis* (King's Bench) became a tribunal of legal experts, hearing causes in Westminster, and going on circuit. The multiplicity of business led to the creation of other courts, and by the reign of Edward I., three Courts were established in Westminster Hall—the King's Bench (originally the Court for hearing criminal causes or other matters in which the Sovereign was specially interested), the Court of Common Pleas (the Court for the decision of suits between subjects), and the Court of Exchequer (originally having jurisdiction in matters relating to the revenues of the Crown).

These Courts—with enlarged jurisdiction—remained distinct in character until they were absorbed by the " Supreme Court " founded by the Judicature Act of 1875.

The Court of Chancery sprang from a branch of the *Curia Regis* called the Cancellaria where writs, charters, and other documents were prepared for the great Seal. The chief of this department was the Chancellor or Keeper of the Great Seal. At first, inferior to the Chief Justiciary, he ultimately became the head of the law, and often the head of the State, under the various titles of The Chancellor of the King, Chancellor of England, Lord Chancellor, and finally Lord High Chancellor. From these beginnings, the Judicial system of England, as we now find it, grew.

The legal institutions of the Normans in Ireland developed on the same lines as the legal institutions of the Normans in England. Some writers say that these institutions were first introduced in the reign of King

John, 1210 ; others ascribe their introduction to the time of Henry II. However that may be, we find the definite statement in authoritative books that the first Irish Lord Chancellor was Stephen Ridel, 1189 (Richard I.) ; the first Chief Justice of the King's Bench, Walter L'Enfant, 1300 (Edward I.) ; the first Chief Justice of the Common Pleas, Richard de Exon ; the first Chief Baron of the Exchequer, Hugh de Burgh, 1346 (Edward III.).

From that time forward the judicial system continued to develop until the Courts (Chancery, Kings' Bench, Exchequer, Common Pleas) and the legal offices grew into what we have been familiar with in our own day.

By the Judicature Act of 1877 (and other Acts) the Irish Courts were re-constituted, under the title the "Supreme Court of Judicature." And the Supreme Court was divided into two main branches—the Court of Appeal and the High Court of Justice.*

1. The Court of Appeal consists of the following Judges :—

The Lord Chancellor.
The Lord Chief Justice (*ex-officio*).
The Master of the Rolls (*ex-officio*).
The Lord Chief Baron (*ex-officio*).
and two other Lords Justices.

2. High Court of Justice :—
(*a*) Chancery Division.
The Lord Chancellor.
The Master of the Rolls.
The Judge of the Chancery Division.
The Land Judge.

---

* The Courts seem to have been originally housed in the Castle. Subsequently about the time of James I. perhaps they were removed to the vicinity of Christ Church and called the "Four Courts." In 1695, they were rebuilt, still remaining in the vicinity of Christ Church. In 1755, their removal from Christ Church to the present site was suggested ; and in 1796 the present building (begun by Cooley, and finished by Gandon) was completed. (Gilbert, "Dublin," Vol. III., p. 133, 136. See also Gerard "Picturesque Dublin.")

(*b*) King's Bench Division.

> The Lord Chief Justice.
>
> The Lord Chief Baron.
>
> Eight Puisine Judges (of whom one is assigned for probate and matrimonial causes, and a second for Admiralty causes, a third for bankruptcy, and a fourth assistant Judicial Commissioner under the Land Act).
>
> Two Judicial Commissioners of the Land Commission.

State Paper Department.

State papers were first deposited in the Bermingham Tower, Dublin Castle, in the time of the Lord Lieutenant Sydney, and they are deposited there still ; subject to the provision (30 and 31 Vic., cap. 70) that after fifty years' detention in the Tower, they shall be transferred to the Record Office at the Four Courts.

Public Record Office.

The Public Record Office was established in 1868 (30 and 31 Vic., cap. 70). It is under the authority of the Master of the Rolls. It is the depository of records and documents specified in the Act.

The official head is called the Deputy Keeper of the Records, who makes an annual report to Parliament.

By the permission of the Chief Secretary or the Master of the Rolls, Calendars, of State papers or other records, may be printed and published with the consent of the Treasury.

Public Trustee.

The office of public Trustee was created by the Land Act of 1903. The holder of it is appointed by the Lord Lieutenant. Rules for regulating the exercise of his powers and duties are made by the Land Commission subject to the approval of the Lord Lieutenant : Among other things it is provided that under these rules the Trustee may be directed, on the request of any person proposing to sell an estate, to give an estimate of the probable financial effect of such sale. Rules in accordance with the Act were made in December, 1904.

Registrar of Petty Sessions Clerks.

The Registrar of Petty Sessions Clerks is appointed by the Lord Lieutenant. The income of the office (which is self-supporting) is made up principally as follows :—

(1) Fees (stamps) ..	.. ..	£24,000
(2) Fines ..	.. ..	15,000
(3) Dog Licences ..	.. ..	41,000
(4) From investments	.. ..	6,000
		£86,000

The duty of the Registrar is practically to administer this sum out of which all salaries and expenses pertaining to the office are paid. The Petty Sessions Clerks throughout the country pay the various sums from time to time into the Bank of Ireland, the Registrar (*inter alia*) having to see that this is done.

There is a co ps of Inspectors attached to the office. The regulations for the appointment of the Petty Sessions Clerks are made by the Lord Lieutenant. The following is the process adopted in filling up vacancies. The Clerk of the Peace puts a notice into the newspapers. Then the magistrates appoint the approved candidate. The candidate then comes to the Registrar for examination on general subjects. After six months he comes up again for examination in legal subjects. The Lord Lieutenant can dismiss the Petty Sessions Clerks. This office was originally attached to the Chief Secretary's department.*

*See 21 and 22 Vic., cap 100., 41 and 42 Vic. cap 67 and 44 and 45, cap 18.

Public Loan Fund Board.

The Board inspects the affairs of a number of local voluntary loan societies who report their proceedings periodically to it. The Board itself makes an annual report to Parliament. It is appointed by the Lord Lieutenant, and the members are unpaid.*

The following offices as I have already pointed out belong to what is called general " Imperial " organisation, and are dissociated from the Castle :—

The Board of Trade.
Customs.
Inland Revenue
(*a*) Stamps.
(*b*) Excise.
(*c*) Estate.
(*d*) Income Tax.
Stationery Office.
Post Office.
Ordnance Survey.
Inspectors of Factories.
War Office.
Royal Naval Reserve.
Woods and Forests.
Joint Stock Companies.
Registry of Friendly Societies.
Civil Service Commission.
General Valuation and Boundary Survey.

Post Office.

The first establishment of a letter post in England, by the Government, was in the reign of James I., who, as is stated in a proclamation by Charles I., set on foot a post office for letters to foreign countries, " for the benefit of the English merchants."†

* See Mr. Bryce's statement in the House of Commons June 12th, 1906.

† House of Commons Paper. No. 366 for 1869, Appendix No. 13, p. 428.

In the reign of Charles I. the first post office for inland letters was organised.

In 1631, the King commanded his " Postmaster of England for Foreign Parts " to open a regular communication by running posts between the Metropolis and Edinburgh, West Chester, Holyhead, and Ireland.*

In 1635, we learn that letters were carried on foot in Ireland, and that the service between that country and England was naturally (and I am tempted to add, satisfactorily) bad. It took " full two months " to receive a reply sent from the one country to the other.†
In Cromwell's time we hear that the service was improved.

> " It was ordered in 1654 that packets should ply weekly between Dublin and Chester, and between Milford and Waterford. These latter, as well as the Dublin packets, did ply at first, but they were soon withdrawn and were not re-established for 150 years."

It was not, however, according to one authority, at least, until the reign of Charles II. that the post office, as at present constituted, was really established.‡

> " In 1662 the line of the packets between Portpatrick and Donaghadee was established, and direct communication between Scotland and the north of Ireland has been maintained without intermission since that date."

In or about, 1690, " the post office in Ireland," says Mr. Joyce,

> " was managed by a deputy postmaster, who was directly responsible to the Postmaster-General

---

* Haydn's "Dictionary of Dates."

† Joyce, " History of the Post Office," p. 16.
Post communications between London and most towns of England, Scotland and Ireland, existed in 1635 (Strype).
Haydn's " Dictionary of Dates."

‡ Haydn.

in London ; and the method of business was the same as in England."*

He adds :—

> " The Dublin establishment, clerks and letter carriers included, consisted of twelve persons, of whom five received £20 a year, and no one, the deputy-postmaster excepted, more than £80. The deputy-postmaster himself received £400."

The war 1690-91, of course, threw everything into confusion ; but afterwards the normal condition of things revived and the Irish post office remained subordinate to the English as before. Dublin grew quickly in prosperity after the war. Writing in 1709, Mr. Manley, the postmaster-general's deputy in Dublin (since 1703), says :—

> " There are not less than a thousand more houses now than there were at my first coming here. Besides, there are many new streets now laid out, and buildings erecting every day."†

In 1703, the Countess of Thanet proposed the establishment of a penny post office in Dublin. The Lord Lieutenant, the Duke of Ormonde, approved of the scheme. All arrangements were made, by the post office, for carrying it into effect,‡ when, at the last moment, the English Treasury refused its assent and the scheme had to be abandoned.§

* Joyce, p. 53.

† Quoted in Joyce, p. 69. In 1710, a General Post Office was established for the three Kingdoms and for the Colonies under one head and under the name of Her Majesty's Postmaster-General. House of Commons Paper *Ante*.

‡ Joyce, p. 70. The new post was to extend for ten or twelve miles in and around Dublin ; no receiving office was to be within two miles of the first stage of the general post ; the lease was to be for fourteen years ; and one-tenth part of the clear profits was to go to the Crown.

§ About this time and previously the English packets were due in Dublin on Sundays, Tuesdays and Thursdays, and provincial mails were despatched, some thrice and twice a week. (Watson's Almanac, 1756).

Seventy years afterwards the English legislature permitted the establishment of penny post offices throughout the two islands ; and Dublin—where a penny post was opened on the 10th October, 1773, was the only place which immediately took advantage of the innovation.

In 1784, under the political influences of the period, the English and Irish post offices were separated. In 1790 mail coaches were introduced in Ireland.

At the beginning of the nineteenth century the " British Mail Office " was established in Dublin, " for the management of the mails passing between England and Ireland."* The story of the relations of the English and Irish post offices, in reference to the Cross Channel Mail Service in the early part of the nineteenth century, is interesting and characteristic. It illustrates the English policy of thwarting Irish enterprise and initiative. By the arrangement of 1784 it was agreed that until the Irish post office had packets of its own, the English post office should command the mail service between Holyhead and Dublin, the Irish post office receiving a grant of £4,000 a year by way of compensation for the monopoly, thus provisionally given to England. This arrangement seems to have worked smoothly until after " the Union." Then the Irish post office came to the conclusion that the arrangement of 1784 was a bad bargain for Ireland, and that with the increase of the passenger traffic after " the Union " the English post office was reaping a rich harvest to the disadvantage of the Irish establishment. Accordingly the Irish post office proposed to give up the grant of £4,000 a year, and to carry the mails from Dublin to Holyhead in its own packets. These views were placed

* At the present day the term " office " as applied to the public service conveys the notion, possibly, of a palace and certainly of a building or part of a building, consisting of several rooms. The British Mail Office, though destined to play a not unimportant part in the history of the Irish post office, at the beginning of the present century, consisted of one room only, and this room was exactly six feet square (Joyce, p. 367-8).

before the Government, but the Government declined to alter the arrangement of 1784. The officials in Ireland argued that the arrangement of 1784 was provisional, and that by its terms the Irish post office was entitled to carry the mails across Channel as soon as they could run their own packets. That they were now able to do.

The answer of the Government was an uncompromising *non possumus*, but said the Dublin officials, in effect, if you do not allow us to carry the mails, assuredly it is only right in the altered circumstances to reconsider the arrangement of 1784. But the Government still said *non possumus*. So spake the English ministers, Pitt, and Portland and Percival.

In 1813, there was at the Irish post office a man of energy and resource, Mr. Lees, who had for a long time filled the position of secretary. He renewed the demand for an alteration of the arrangement of 1784. " We shall give up the grant of £4,000 a year," he practically reiterated, " and let us carry the mails in our own packets." But as Pitt and Portland and Percival spoke, so spoke Lord Liverpool. *Non possumus* was the unchangeable answer of the English Government.*

Lees was not a man easily baffled. For some time after the Union certain boats called wherries had been used to carry Government messengers and dispatches between Dublin and Holyhead. The special occupation of those wherries was now gone, and Lees now resolved

---

* " The number of passengers carried to and fro by the Holyhead packets was between 14,000 and 15,000 a year ; and there can be no doubt that the advantage which the British Post Office derived from this traffic was considerable. It is true that the fares went to the captains ; but, of course, except for the fares, the Post Office would have had to pay more for its packets. These were supplied at an annual cost of £365 apiece, or £2,190 altogether ; and such being the terms on which boats could be hired, Lees was confirmed in his opinion that Ireland would do better if, instead of receiving from Great Britain a compensation allowance of £4,000 a year she were to provide her own packets and share the packet postage" (Joyce, p. 380).

to charter these vessels, and to send the mails by them from port to port. He kept his plans to himself till all was arranged. Then one morning in July, 1813, Mr. Freeling, the Secretary to the post office in London, received a letter from Lees, incidentally informing him that :

> " As the intended packet station at Howth had sufficient depth of water for the vessels belonging to the Irish post office, it was in contemplation, until such time as the regular packets should be stationed there, that the mails from Ireland should be despatched in its own vessels, and that, as soon as the arrangements now in progress should be completed, the measure would take effect."

This tremendous announcement made, apparently, in the most casual manner, must have taken Freeling's breath away. Nor did Lees give him time to recover it. On the 23rd July, the English Post Office had received Lees' letter ; on the 24th, Freeling learned that the Irish mails had been refused to the English packet, and given to the Irish wherry. Nor was he yet allowed to recover his composure. The next intelligence which reached him was that Lees was placarding the walls of Dublin with advertisements, pointing out the advantages of the Irish route from Howth to Holyhead, over the English route from the Pigeon House. Finally (and this was the worst of all), the mail coach from Holyhead to London arrived in Lombard Street without the Irish letters, which, as we have seen, were refused to the English packet. There was consternation in Lombard Street, and perplexity in Whitehall. Merchants complained of the dislocation of the postal service, and their anger was not appeased by the explanations of Freeling. At the end of a fortnight the Prime Minister intervened, and ordered the wherries to be withdrawn ; but the order had no effect on Lees, and the wherries went on for four weeks longer. Then a compromise was arrived at. The wherries were withdrawn and the grant to the Irish post office was increased from £4,000 to £6,000 a year.

In 1815, there were fresh developments. A boat propelled by steam appeared on the Thames.* About the same time a number of private gentlemen met in Dublin, and formed a company called the Dublin Steam Packet Company.† Another shock was administered to Freeling's nerves when he learned that Lees was one of the directors of the new company. The Company was full of enterprise and immediately ran two steam-boats, as the new invention came to be called, between Dublin and Holyhead. These boats took away the passengers from the mail packets. But Freeling was this time equal to the occasion. The English post office built better steamers [the *Royal Sovereign* and the *Meteor*] than the Dublin Company's, and soon recovered the lost passenger traffic. But the end was not yet. The Dublin Company now ran steamers between Dublin and Liverpool.‡ Curious results followed. Let it be understood that the mail coach carrying letters to Ireland left Liverpool every day at 3 p.m., arriving at Holyhead at 6 a.m. the following morning, and reaching Dublin that same evening ; but the steamers from Liverpool to Dublin left the former place in the evening of one day, reaching Dublin in the morning of the next. Thus passengers by this route could reach Dublin a whole day in advance of passengers travelling by the Holyhead route. The result was that the passenger traffic was diverted from the post office boats *via* Holyhead to the Dublin Company's boats *via* Liverpool. Freeling now determined that the post office should run its own packets between Liverpool and Dublin direct. The new service was opened on 29th August, 1826.

* Haydn. Dictionary of Dates.

† I cannot quite ascertain whether this company was the beginning of what we now know as the City of Dublin Steam Packet Company or not.

‡ What we now know as the City of Dublin Steam Packet Company first ran boats between Liverpool and Dublin in 1824.

One of the boats, and the finest of her class, was appropriately called the *Francis Freeling*. On her way cross Channel, early in September, she foundered with all hands. The extraordinary spectacle was now presented to the public of the English post office, not only competing with a private company, but it would seem competing with itself ; for the boats which ran from Liverpool to Dublin, apparently competed with the mail packets running from Holyhead to Dublin ; the result of the competition being that the passenger traffic was as a matter of fact diverted from the Holyhead to the Liverpool route.

While Irish enterprise was asserting itself on the sea, it was no less in evidence on the land. In the early part of the century the mail coaches from London, carrying Irish letters, ran through Chester by a cir- cuitous route to Holyhead. In 1805, Foster, the Irish Chancellor of the Exchequer, proposed a change of route, suggesting that the coaches should run by Coventry and Shrewsbury to Holyhead—a change by which two hours would be saved on the whole journey. Freeling, the great obstructive, objected. Foster pressed his point.

In 1808, there was a meeting at Lord Hawksbury's to discuss the point. Freeling was present ; Foster was absent, but had sent a paper explaining his views, and Arthur Wellesley, the Chief Secretary of the day, attended to represent the case of the Irish post office. Freeling opposed all change, but Wellesley put down his foot, and said that everything should be sacrificed to shorten the journey between Dublin and London. A compromise was arrived at ; and for the nine years following, the coaches ran through Shrewsbury to Holyhead. At the end of the nine years the Coventry route was adopted, and thus Foster's efforts were crowned with complete success.

In 1831, the English and Irish post offices were amalgamated ; and the Duke of Richmond became the first Postmaster-General for both countries.

Between 1831 and 1834 the Irish letters were still carried by mail coach from London to Holyhead, and from Holyhead to Dublin—Howth being the station—by the post office packets. In 1834, Howth was given up as the packet station, and Kingstown chosen in its stead. In December, 1834, the mails were carried for the first time by train from Kingstown to Dublin.

In 1837, the Admiralty took over the mail packets from the post office. In 1839, the Dublin Steam Packet Company, which had been running boats from Dublin to Liverpool since 1824, had grown in repute and prosperity, and now possessed a fleet of steamers equal in efficiency to the Admiralty packets themselves. The Admiralty and the Company entered into a contract by which it was agreed that the latter should carry the night mails, and the former the day mails to Kingstown. It would seem that, at that time, there was a mail route from Liverpool to Kingstown, as well as Holyhead to Kingstown.* Before the end of the year, train service was open between London and Liverpool. The result was that the bulk of the mails was carried from Liverpool via Holyhead to Kingstown,† though many passengers, who did not fear the long coach drive from Holyhead to London, but who did fear the long sea voyage from Liverpool to Kingstown preferred the old route. Nevertheless, we are told that between 1838 and 1848 the Holyhead harbour was in a state of " suspended animation."‡

In 1848, the engagement with the City of Dublin Steam Packet Company from Liverpool to Kingstown came to an end. In 1850, the Government came to the conclusion that it would be more economical to

* Baines " Forty Years at the Post Office."

† The Cross Channel arrangements seem to have been as follows. The Admiralty carried the Day Mails ⸱from Liverpool to Kingstown and the Company the Night Mails by the same route. The London Mails were sent by this route. The Welsh and Chester Mails were carried by the Admiralty packets from Kingstown to Holyhead and by coach from Chester to Holyhead.

‡ Baines, Vol. I., p. 68.

have the mails carried by private companies than by the State. In the same year the Admiralty gave up its mail packets, and a contract was entered into with the City of Dublin Company, to carry the mails twice a day between Holyhead and Kingstown. The Company placed four steamers on the route, the *Eblana* and *Prince Arthur* newly built, and the *St. Columba* and *Llewellyn* bought from the Admiralty. In March 1850, the first locomotive ran through the Tubular Bridge over the Menai Straits, and the complete railway service carrying the Irish mails from London to Holyhead was soon an accomplished fact. In 1860, what has been called " the new Irish Postal Service " was established by which the London and North-Western Railway Company, the Chester and Holyhead Railway Company, and the City of Dublin Steam Packet Company, pledged themselves jointly and separately to perform the whole journey between Euston and Kingstown in eleven hours.

In 1885, the service was further accelerated, and the letters were carried from post office to post office in eleven hours.* They are now carried from post office to post office in about nine and a half hours.

The City of Dublin Steam Company still commands the Cross Channel service, and the passage between Holyhead and Kingstown is performed in about two and three-quarter hours by the famous boats *Ulster*, *Munster*, *Leinster* and *Connaught*.

Such, in brief, is the story of the mail service between England and Ireland, and of the part—the distinguished and honourable part—played by the City of Dublin Steam Packet Company in it. The Company has always been in the van of progress. It has always met with fierce competition. It meets with fierce competition still ; for an English Company now runs rival boats, not only between Holyhead and the North Wall, Dublin, but between Holyhead and Kingstown. It may be that the very existence of the Irish Company

* Baines, Vol. I., p. 82.

which placed the first steamers on the Cross Channel Service is threatened.

What, then, is the moral of this story, as illustrated by the fortunes of the City of Dublin Steam Packet Company from the days of Lees and Freeling to our own. Simply this : that whether it inspires the policy of the Government, or the operations of the individual speculator, the English commercial spirit is the most rapacious thing known to the student of human history.*

Commissioners of Irish Lights.

These Commissioners constitute the lighthouse authority for Ireland. There are twenty-two of them : five (the Lord Mayor of Dublin, the High Sheriff of Dublin, and three Aldermen), selected by the Corporation of Dublin ; seventeen co-opted as vacancies occur, subject to the approval of the Lord Lieutenant.

The Commissioners do not receive remuneration. All the estimates and proposed expenditure are submitted to the Board of Trade and all payments are made by that Department out of the General Lighthouse Fund for the United Kingdom under the supervision of the Treasury. The Elder Brethren, who are the Lighthouse Authority for England are always consulted by the Irish Commissioners before a Light is altered.†

The National School Teachers, Superannuation Office.

The recent writer from whom I have already quoted, says :—

" The fund from which the pensions to teachers are paid is administered by the Treasury under the authority of an Act of 1879 (42 and 43 Vic., cap. 74). The Fund consisted originally of a

---

* On the subject of the Inland post in Ireland see the Life of Bianconi by Mrs. M. J. O'Connell.

† See Merchant Shipping Act, 1894, Part XI., Sections 6-34, *et seq.*

capital sum of £1,300,000 provided from Church funds, supplemented by deductions from teachers' salaries. In consequence, however, of the insufficiency of the latter, a deficiency in the fund was found to exist in 1891, as a result of which a large provision was made by Parliament to secure its solvency, and a grant-in-aid amounting to £18,000 is annually voted by Parliament towards the same object.* Regulations for the Administration of the Fund are made by the Treasury and the Lord Lieutenant conjointly."

Customs.

The Act 15 Henry VII., c. 1 (Irish) seems to be the first enactment levying customs duties (*i.e.* fixed and uncertain duties paid on importation of wool, leather, etc., and exportation, according to the values of the commodities)† in Ireland—their legislative origin in England dates from the reign of Edward I.—and the rate chargeable thereby was the same as was chargeable by the usual subsidy in England, viz., 1s. in the £ upon the value. Wine and oil were exempted from the duty.‡

* *Irish Executive.*

† Wine was liable to the ancient duty of prisage, *i.e.*, certain fixed duties payable to the king on wine imported, as in England, save that in Ireland, by prescription the importer of prisage wine paid custom of 15s. per tun on such wine in lieu of all other duties whatever.

‡ Whilst, however, prisage was levied in Ireland, the composition of 2s. per tun for the wines of aliens called butlerage in England, did not extend to Ireland. In 1177, Henry II. granted the butlership of Ireland to Theobald, son of Herveius Walter, and thus granted to him the duty of prisage, whereby he and his successors were to attend the Kings of England at their coronation and present them with the first cup of wine, for which they were to have certain pieces of the king's plate. This duty remained vested in the same family, afterwards earls marquises and dukes of Ormonde. In later times (50 George III., c. 101) the government of England paid to the Earl of Ormond the sum of £199,384 for the commutation of this privilege, thenceforth vested in the Crown.

Except in the case of the prohibition on the export of wool in the reign of Henry VIII., and duty on the importation of wine and the exportation of wool in the reign of Elizabeth, the customs of Ireland were governed by this Act till after the Restoration.

The first Dublin Custom House seems to have been built in the reign of James I. in 1619. It was placed just below where Grattan Bridge now is, on the Castle side of the river.* Previous to the Restoration, the Irish Customs were leased out, like the customs of England to certain farmers. Not much is known of these farmers in either country, but in 1669 the Irish Revenues were farmed to John Forth, Alderman of London and others for seven years at the yearly rent of £219,500 and in 1676 they were farmed to Sir James Shean and his partners, with ten others, for an annual rent of £240,000. It is not clear what was the position of the farmers in relation to the Exchequer, for both farmers and Commissioners of the Customs appear to have existed at the same time, and to have had distinct spheres of duty. Both are mentioned in the first Irish Customs Act after the Restoration (14 and 15 Charles II., c. 9), and it is certain that the farmers had the power to appoint officers of their own to receive the duties. In the reign of Charles II., it was provided by the Excise Act to establish two Boards, one for the Customs and one for the Excise. However, the Act does not seem to have been carried out, and for a long period both were managed by one Board.

In 1772, effect was given to the policy of Charles II., and the management of the Customs and of the Excise was definitely placed under separate and distinct Boards. All the branches of the public revenue in Ireland were managed by the Commissioners of Customs and Excise. All Officers were appointed by the respective Boards, subject to the approval of the Lord Lieutenant, whose

* Gilbert, Vol. II., p. 134, " History of Dublin." Gerard, " Picturesque Dublin," p. 131-132.

Chief Secretary signed the approval at the foot of each instrument of appointment.

The separate Boards of Customs and Excise in Ireland were abolished in 1823 by 4 George IV., c. 23, and one Board of Customs, as well as one Board of Excise was established for the "United Kingdom." The present handsome Custom House building, begun in 1781, was opened in 1791.

> "The passing of the Act of Union," says Miss Gerard, "struck a blow to all foreign trade in Ireland."
>
> "The Customs Department in Ireland," says a correspondent, "is as you know, entirely controlled from the head office in Lower Thames Street, London. The Customs work proper in Dublin, at present, is insignificant, and the Customs staff occupies only a few ' *shelves* ' in the Custom House."

Inland Revenue.

(*a*) Excise, (*b*) Stamp, (*c*) Estate, (*d*) Income Tax.

(*a*) Excise.—Excise duties—that is, an impost paid on the retail sale or by the first buyer, manufacturer, or consumer of certain commodities, *e.g.*, ale, beer, *aqua vitæ* (inland) and drugs, raw hemp, flax, tobacco, silks, etc. (import)—were first imposed in England by the Parliament during the civil war of the seventeenth century "as the only method then left for raising money."

King Charles followed the example of the Parliament, and Excise duties became an institution. Once introduced into England they were quickly established in Ireland. At the Restoration (as already mentioned) an Excise Act was passed regulating the impost. At first the Excise duties were farmed ; but in 1678 the revenue (of course including the Excise) was taken out of the hands of the farmers, and commissioners were appointed by the Crown to manage it ; on this footing it subsequently continued.

In the reign of Charles II., as we have seen, the Commissioners of Customs and Excise though separated by Act of Parliament, continued to Act as one Board.*

In 1772, another Act was passed, giving effect to the policy of Charles II., and effectually separating the Excise and Customs Boards. They remained separated (as has been said) until 1823, when the Irish and English Excise and Customs were amalgamated.

(b) Stamps.—In the reign of Charles II., 1670-1, Stamp duties were imposed on certain legal documents. In the reign of William III., 1694, a duty was imposed for four years on vellum and parchment. At the end of the four years the duty was extended for six years longer. In the reign of George I., it was made perpetual ; and every year added to the list of articles upon which Stamp duty was made payable. Stamp duties were introduced into Ireland in 1774.

(c) Estate Duty.—

A wit has said that the full force of Thomas Drummond's famous aphorism " Property has its duties as well as its rights " was not recognised until Sir William Harcourt established Estate Duties in 1894. Death Duties have been described as " a toll payable on the transmission of property by death." This toll was levied in the reign of William III. (1694) and called Probate Duty. In 1774, it was imposed in Ireland. In 1780, Legacy Duty was imposed in England, and in Ireland in 1786. Real Estate was free from Death Duty until 1806 (46 George III.).

In 1842, English and Irish duties were assimilated. An additional Death Duty called Succession Duty was imposed in 1853 as a supplement to the Legacy Duty Act, and brought into tax all successions to property, real and personal. Legacy Duty and Succession Duty

* Indemnity Acts had to be passed to legalise what they had done while acting as one Board.

are not however a cumulative tax, that is to say, where property is liable to the one it is not at the same time liable to the other. In 1889, a " Temporary Estate Duty " was established on larger estates (£10,000 and upwards). By Sir William Harcourt's Act, 1894, all property was taxed on an equitable basis. The Act repealed the old Probate Duty, and introduced instead Estate Duty, which is payable in respect of all property passing upon a death, whether under a will, intestacy, settlement, joint tenancy, gifts of certain kinds or other disposition. The head office for the collection of State Duty is in Somerset House.

(*d*) Income Tax.*—Income tax was extended to Ireland in 1853 "in face of the strong opposition of most of the Irish members, who maintained that their country already contributed more than a fair proportion of the revenue."†

Up to the year 1833, the revenues of Excise, of Stamps, and of Taxes, were under the management of three separate departments, each consisting of a Board of Commissioners, with the necessary staff of officers.

In 1834, the Board of Stamps was united with the Board of Taxes.

In 1849, there was a further amalgamation of duties. The Inland Revenue Board was formed for the collection and control of the whole of the duties of Excise, Stamps, and Taxes instead of the two previously existing separate Boards.‡

* Immediately preceding the revolution of 1688, the only direct tax levied on the community which formed a part of the ordinary yearly revenue was that of Hearth Money, *i.e.* a tax on every fireplace or hearth first introduced, both in England and Ireland, in the reign of Charles II. It was repealed in England in the reign of William III. In 1795 it was abolished in Ireland in houses where there was only one hearth. Some years later it was abolished altogether. (House of Commons Paper 366 for 1869, p. 413).

† See " Two Centuries of Irish History."

‡ Parliamentary Papers, No. 366, 1. for 1869. Part II. Appendix. The saving by the amalgamation was some £17,000.

A correspondent writes :—

" The Inland Revenue Department is entirely controlled from Somerset House and has four sub-divisions in Dublin.

" (1) Income Tax.
" (2) Estate Duty Office.
" (3) Excise.
" (4) Stamps.

" Each sub-department has its own head and staff, and the offices for Dublin are at the Custom House. I should say that the Inland Revenue have 'Collectors' at Dublin, Dundalk, Belfast, Derry, Galway, Cork and Kilkenny, with staffs in each 'collection,' and each entirely controlled in every detail from Somerset House—Dublin has no more control over, say, Dundalk, than it has over Derby."

Ordnance Survey.

In 1824, as I have already stated, a Select Committee was appointed to consider the best mode of apportioning more equally the local burthens collected in Ireland. The object was to obtain a survey, sufficiently accurate to enable the valuators, acting under the superintendence of a separate department of the Government, to follow the surveyors, and to apportion correctly the proper amount of the local burthens. These burthens had previously been apportioned by Grand Jury assessments. The assessments had, in some districts of Ireland, been made by the civil divisions of ploughlands, in others, by the divisions of townlands ; the divisions, in either case, contributing in proportion to their assumed areas, which bore no defined proportion to their actual contents. The result was much complained of, inequality of levying the assessment, which it was a primary object of the survey to remove by accurately defining the divisions of the country. The Committee reported that it was expedient to give much greater despatch to this work than had occurred in the Trigonometrical Survey of England.*

They recommended that every facility in the way of improved instruments should be given to the Ordnance Officers by whom the survey was to be conducted; and concluded with the hope that the great national work, which was projected, " will be carried on with energy, as well as with skill, and that it will, when completed, be creditable to the nation, and to the scientific acquirements of the age."

It was furthermore designed that the Survey should be a more general Survey than any that had yet been made; should embrace not only geodetical facts, but also facts meteorological and topographical.

The first step in the Irish Survey was a " general reconnaissance " of Ireland made by Colonel Colby and Drummond in the autumn of 1824. They traversed the country from north to south, fixed upon the mode of conducting the survey, and selected the stations for the great triangulation, as well as the most fitting place for measuring a base. In the autumn of 1825 the triangulation commenced in the

---

* The Ordnance Survey of Great Britain began in Scotland after 1745, with the view of obtaining accurate knowledge of the Highland Districts. In 1763, the subject of a general survey was broached, but nothing was done. Finally, in 1783,

> " a representation was made from France to our Government, of the advantages which the science of astronomy would derive, from the connection, through trigonometrical measurements of the observatories of Greenwich and Paris, and the exact determination of their latitudes and longitudes. The French had by this time carried a series of triangles from Paris to Calais, and what they proposed was that the English should carry a similar series from Greenwich to Dover, when the two might be connected by observation from both sides of the Channel. The scheme was approved of by George III., and the English survey began by measurement of an initial line at Hounslow Heath by General Roy—the foundation of the triangulation since effected of Great Britain (See " Thomas Drummond Life and Letters").

Divis Mountain near Belfast. The actual measurement of the Lough Foyle base commenced in September, 1827, and was completed in 1828; and so the
Survey has gone on from time to time since.

It would be out of place in a book of this nature
to give an account of the work of the ordnance survey.
I shall only say in a sentence that the work has resulted
in the collection of valuable material relating to the
history and antiquities of Ireland. It has not been
merely a technical survey of the country; it has been
a scientific and scholarly examination of subjects full
of interest for the student, eager to collect topographical
and archæological lore. I shall, however, set out a
letter written twenty years after the work was begun,
from Captain Larcom :—

" In order to ascertain the correct names
of places for the engravings, that they might
become a standard of orthography as well as
topography, numerous maps, records, and ancient
documents were examined, and copious extracts
made from them. In this manner a certain
amount of antiquarian information has been
collected relating to every place, parish, and
townland in Ireland,—more than 70,000—and
the various modes of spelling them at different
times has been recorded. When these investigations were complete, it was usual to send
a person thoroughly versed in the Irish language
to ascertain from the old people who still speak
the language, what was the original vernacular
name, and we then adopted that one among the
modern modes of spelling which was most consistent with the ancient orthography; not
venturing to restore the original and often obsolete
name, but approaching as near to correctness
as was practicable. Numerous drawings and
characteristic sketches have been made, and
legends collected; and in these journeys, any
antiquities which had been omitted were noted

and pointed out for insertion on the maps which have thus become antiquarian as well as modern and utilitarian documents."

The Ordnance Survey is still under the direction of the military authorities (Engineers),the Director-General having his station at Southampton ; the Irish Head Office is in the Phœnix Park, and there are branch offices in Ennis, Cork and Belfast. A survey is, I believe, being at present carried out in the County Meath, with the view of preparing an Ordnance Map.*

Woods and Forests.

In England, up to 1851, the office of Woods and Forests, established in 1810, was combined with the office of Works (established in 1832). Since then they have been separated. The office of Woods and Forests are now in charge of two commissioners who are permanent officers.†

The officials in the Irish Office are a Senior Clerk (Superintendent), a First Class Clerk, a Survey Clerk and an Abstractor.‡

Stationery Office.

In England the Stationery Office was established in 1782. The duties of the office include the supply of books and stationery to Government Departments, the superintendence and control of Government printing. The Comptroller, under Letters Patents, is the King's printer of the Acts of Parliament, and in him is vested the copyright in all Government publications.

The Irish branch does for the Government in Ireland, what the English office does for the Government in England.

* See M'Lennan's "Memoir of Thomas Drummond."
† Todd's "Parliamentary Government."
‡ Thom's Official Directory.

Inspectors of Factories.

The Inspectors of Factories are under the control of the Home Office.

The War Office.

In Ireland there is a "Command" as in other parts of the English Empire, the Central Authority of course being the War Office in London.

Civil Service Commission.

Civil Service Examinations in Ireland are conducted as follows: The Civil Service Commission in London send the Examination papers under seal to some trustworthy person, selected by them, in the district where the examination is to be held. This person takes a room, gives out the papers, sees that the examination is properly conducted, and returns the papers to London. He is paid by the "job."

I shall add a complete list of the Offices and Departments with which I have dealt, stating in each case by whom appointments are technically made.*

List of Boards, Offices and Departments connected with the Administration of Ireland.

1. Lord Lieutenant, appointed by the Crown.
2. Household of the Lord Lieutenant, appointed by the Lord Lieutenant.
3. Chief Secretary, appointed by the Lord Lieutenant.
4. Keeper of State Papers, appointed by the Lord Lieutenant (Clerkships by public competition).
5. Ulster King at Arms, Lord Lieutenant, by letters patent under Great Seal of Ireland.

* I omitted to state in footnote on page 111 that six senators of the Royal University are appointed by Convocation.

6. Under-Secretary, appointed by Lord Lieutenant.
7. Assistant Under-Secretary, appointed by Lord Lieutenant.
8. National School Teachers Superannuation Office, Treasury.
9. Registrar of Petty Sessions Clerks, Lord Lieutenant.
10. General Prisons Board, Lord Lieutenant.
11. Reformatory and Industrial Schools, Lord Lieutenant.
12. Inspectors of Lunatic Asylums, Lord Lieutenant.
13. Public Loan Fund Board, Lord Lieutenant.
14. Royal Irish Constabulary, Lord Lieutenant. (Cadets by limited competition on nomination of Chief Secretary).
15. Dublin Metropolitan Police, appointed by Lord Lieutenant.
16. Local Government Board, appointed by the Crown on recommendation of Lord Lieutenant.
17. Board of Trade, branch of the Department in England.
18. Customs, branch of Department in England.
19. Inland Revenue—(a) Stamp, (b) Excise, (c) Estate appointed by English Department.
20. Stationery Office, branch of Department in England.
21. Intermediate Board of Education, appointed by Lord Lieutenant.
22. General Valuation and Boundary Survey, Treasury and Lord Lieutenant.
23. Board of Public Works, Treasury.
24. Civil Service Commission, branch of Department in England.
25. Land Commission, Commissioners appointed by Crown on recommendation of Lord Lieutenant, Assistant Commissioners by Lord Lieutenant.
26. Estates Commissioners, appointed by Crown on recommendation of Lord Lieutenant.
27. Office of Public Trustee, Lord Lieutenant.

28. National Gallery, Governors partly *ex-officio*, partly appointed by Lord Lieutenant (17 and 18 Vic., cap. 99 ; 18 and 19 Vic., cap. 44.)
29. Department of Agriculture :
    (*a*) Irish Fisheries.
    (*b*) Veterinary Department.
    (*c*) College of Science.
    (*d*) School of Art.
    (*e*) Science and Art Museums.
    (*f*) National Library.
    (*g*) Geological Survey.
        1. President, Chief Secretary *ex-officio*.
        2. Vice-President appointed by one of the Principal Secretaries of State.
        3. Staff appointed by Department, with consent of Lord Lieutenant and Treasury.
30. Board of National Education, Lord Lieutenant.
31. General Registrar Office, Lord Lieutenant.
32. Congested Districts Board, appointed by Crown on recommendation of Lord Lieutenant.
33. Registry of Deeds, appointed by Treasury.
34. Post Office Department, branch of Department in England.
35. Charitable Donations and Bequests, appointed by Crown on recommendation of Lord Lieutenant.
36. Commissioners of Education, partly named by Statute, partly nominated by Lord Lieutenant under Statute.
37. Ordnance Survey, branch of Department in in England.
38. Inspectors of Factories, appointed by Home Office.
39. War Office, branch of Department in England.
40. Royal Navy Reserve Office, branch of Department in England.
41. Woods and Forests Office, branch of Department in England.
42. Public Record Office, Deputy Keeper of the Records appointed by Lord Lieutenant (Staff appointed by public competition).

43. Stock Companies Registry Office, appointed by Board of Trade.
44. Registry Friendly Societies, appointed by Treasury.
45. Royal University, by the Crown on recommendation of Lord Lieutenant.
46. Irish Lights, out of 22 Commissioners 17 co-opted subject to disallowance by Lord Lieutenant in Council.
47. Law.
    1. Judges of the Court of Appeal, appointed by Crown.
    2. Judges of the High Court of Justice, appointed by Crown.
       County Court Judges appointed by Lord Lieutenant.
    3. Offices of the Courts :
       (*a*) King's Bench Division, appointed by the Chief Justice.
       (*b*) Lord Chancellor's Court, appointed by the Lord Chancellor.
       (*c*) Master of the Rolls, appointed by the Master of the Rolls.
       (*d*) Chancery Division, appointed by the Lord Chancellor.
       (*e*) Land Judges, appointed by the Land Judge.
       (*f*) Bankruptcy, appointed by Judge of Court.
       (*g*) Admiralty, appointed by the Judge of Court.
       (*h*) Lunacy Department (Registrar), appointed by the Lord Chancellor.
       (*i*) Crown and Hanaper Office, appointed by the Crown.
       (*j*) Local Registration of Title Office, Registrar of Titles appointed by the Land Judge of the Chancery Division of the High Court. The Central Office is under the Land Judge's Control.

Clerks of the Crown and Peace, where these offices are united, are the Local Registering Authorities.

(*k*) Record and Writ Office, appointed by the Master of the Rolls.

(*l*) Consolidated Taxing Office, appointed by the Lord Chancellor.

(*m*) Consolidated Accounting Office, appointed by the Lord Chancellor.

(*n*) Chancery Registrar's Office, appointed by the Lord Chancellor.

(*o*) Principal Registry Office of Probate, appointed by the Judge of Court.*

I shall conclude by setting out an extract from the views given, so long ago as 1896, by a distinguished official, Sir David Harrel (who was Under-Secretary at Dublin Castle from 1892 to 1900), on the subject of Departmental administration in Ireland.

Departments connected with the Government of Ireland.

" While it cannot be contended that the Lord Lieutenant should exercise direct authority in the departmental administration of Admiralty, War Office, Post Office, Customs and Inland Revenue, at the same time, where questions of policy involving Irish interests arise, it would appear to be not only reasonable, but absolutely necessary, that the Irish Government should be semi-officially informed and consulted.

" As regards the Irish business looked after by the Home Office, Board of Trade, Public Works Loan Commissioners, Local Government Board, and Science and Art Department, while

* As to these appointments see the several provisions of 40 and 41 Vic., cap. 57 ; Sects. 72-73. Under these provisions the higher offices would appear to be appointed as above, and the junior staff by open competition.

admitting the advantages resulting from connection with the London Departments, it may be suggested that many of the duties at present discharged by them in Ireland, might very naturally devolve on Irish Departments which are, at present, discharging duties somewhat analogous.

" *Home Office.* The inspection of factories and workshops, explosives, mines and quarries, is at present carried out in Ireland under the direction of the Home Office, but might, with advantage, be transferred—that for factories and workshops, to the Local Government Board ; that for explosives, mines and quarries to the Board of Works.

" *Board of Trade.* The work of the Standards Department, and the inspection of railways and canals might be transferred to the Board of Works, while the work performed by the Commercial Labour and Statistical Department would, certainly, appear to fall within the scope of the duties of the Registrar-General.

" *Public Works Loan Commissioners.* Their operations would seem to come under the Board of Works.

" *Local Government Board.* The only branch of the English Local Government Board which operates in Ireland, is that for scientific inquiry into the causes of diseases. The Irish Local Government Board some time ago applied for the services of such an officer but without success.

" The inspection of alkali works might be combined with those of explosives, etc., under the Board of Works.

" *Science and Art Department.* The control of the Dublin Museum, College of Science, and Science and Art Schools throughout the country, might, with advantage, be transferred to a central authority on Education in Ireland.

" The most noticeable features presented by a consideration of the different departments controlled by the Lord Lieutenant are :—

" (1) That many of them are administered by 'Boards,' or by two or more official heads possessing equal powers ;

' (2) That the duties of many of these departments bear a strong relation to each other, and might be placed under a common head.

" The system of administration by Boards, no doubt possesses many advantages where there is an exercise of uncontrolled authority, but in the case of an official department, acting under and amenable to the orders of the Lord Lieutenant, it does not appear to have anything to recommend it. The Board system is cumbrous in its action, and prejudicial to departmental discipline and efficiency. There may be safety in much counsel, but one man should be responsible.

" The work of the Prisons, and the Industrial and Reformatory Schools Departments might easily be carried on under one head, while the care of Lunatics would strike one as bearing directly upon the responsibilities and duties of the Local Government Board.

" Three departments are more or less engaged in advancing Agriculture, namely, the National Education Office, the Land Commission, and the Congested Districts Board. They are each doing some good, but their efforts cannot possibly be attended with that success which might be expected to follow the action of one department entrusted with the development and care of every branch of Agriculture.

" It is, however, in an examination of the department administering affairs appertaining exclusively to Ireland, but completely under the control of the Treasury, that the most unsatisfactory state of things is disclosed.

" The Board of Public Works is the only Irish department through which loans are granted, and expenditure is carried out at discretion. By no other department is the question of Ireland's material advancement so deeply affected.

" Loans for improvements of agricultural holdings, for the 'erection of farm buildings, the undertaking of works of public utility such as piers, drainage, light railways, etc., all are within the scope of this board's authority.

" It might be imagined that the Board of Public Works ought to be more in sympathy with Irish interests than any other Board of Irish administration, but, as a matter of experience, this is not so.

" So far as the Irish public are concerned, there is no motive for economy in their demands upon the Board for free grants ; they believe that money is spent or withheld in proportion to the pressure that is put upon the Treasury by public or parliamentary agitation.

" Irish men do not regard it as their business to consider whether the money is well or ill spent. They think that the question of getting more money is little affected by the consideration of the amount already received.

" It may be said that this, the spending department of Ireland, must be closely watched by the Treasury, but it is difficult to see how this aspect of the matter would be prejudiced by the placing the administration under the Lord Lieutenant.

" One result would certainly follow, namely, that the money spent, be it more or less, would be spent more in accordance with Irish wishes and necessities, while it would be to the interest of the public at large to see that sufficient value was being received for the moneys expended.

" Again, the Valuation and Survey Office discharges duties which are wholly and solely connected with Ireland. No doubt its powers and duties are defined by Act of Parliament, but it is controlled by and from the Treasury. This department exists at present, almost for the sole object of supplying information in connection with public ratings, and might very naturally form a branch of the Local Government Board.

" The Supreme Courts of Judicature are not regarded as examples of perfect organisation, either in the matter of expenditure, or administration. They are entirely under the Treasury.

" The foregoing brief observations are intended to convey :—

" 1. That the departments controlled by the Lord Lieutenant are not at present constituted in a way which makes them readily responsive to the Head of the Irish Executive.

" 2. These departments might, with economy and advantage, be diminished in numbers and placed under fewer heads.

" 3. That the Board of Public Works, the Valuation and Survey Office, and the Staff of the Supreme Courts of Judicature should be under the control of the Irish Government."

PART IV

FINANCE

PART IV

FINANCE

WHAT does the English Administration of Ireland cost *in money?* What it costs in character—English character—we all know. The Administration of Ireland is the shame of England. But John Bull would " jump " the shame if he could only show a good profit and loss account. But can he ?

I take the figures for the year ending the 31st March, 1907 :—

Ireland's gross contribution to Imperial
    Expenditure £9,490,000*
Cost of Administration   7,678,500

Balance available for Imperial Expenditure 1,811,500

Now let us turn to Scotland and see what are the figures concerning that country's contribution to the " Imperial " Exchequer :—

Scotland's gross contribution to Imperial Ex-
    penditure £15,837,000
Cost of Administration   5,962,500

Balance available for Imperial Expenditure 9,874,500†

* Revenue and Expenditure (England, Scotland and Ireland) for year ending 31st March, 1907 :—
    " This table shows the balances of revenue contributed by England, Scotland and Ireland respectively, which are available for Imperial expenditure after the local expenditure of those Divisions of the United Kingdom has been met, according to the figures shown in Parts I. and II. of this Return."

† Revenue and Expenditure (England, Scotland and Ireland), asked for by Mr. John O'Connor. Issued by House of Commons, to be printed 8th July, 1907.

Does John Bull rub his eyes ?

Contented Scotland, with a population of 4,472,103 contributes £15,837,000 to the Exchequer.

Discontented Ireland, with a population of 4,458,775 contributes the gross sum of £9,490,000.

The Administration of Scotland in accordance with the wishes of the Scottish people, and consistently with the prosperity of the country, costs £5,962,500.

It costs £7,678,500 to keep Ireland poor and disaffected, and to make the name of England detested in the land.

Mr. Runciman gave the following figures in the House of Commons on the 29th April, 1907, representing the total amount of taxation raised in Ireland between the year 1841 and 1906 :—

Financial Year.			Tax Revenue contributed by Ireland.
1839-40	..	..	.. £5,077,000
1849-50	..	..	.. 4,564,000
1859-60	..	..	.. 7,341,000
1869-70	..	..	.. 6,868,000
1879-80	..	..	.. 6,437,000
1889-90	..	..	.. 6,691,000
1899-1900	..	..	.. 7,619,000
1905-6	..	..	.. 8,254,000

Is this good business (looking at the matter from an English point of view) ? Is it creditable to a nation of shop-keepers ? What would that all-absorbing business entity of the nineteenth century—the American Syndicate—say about it ? This is what Mr. Gladstone said about it in 1886 :—

> " The House would like to know what an amount has been going on—and which, at this moment, is going on—of what I must call not only a waste of public money, but a demoralising waste of public money, demoralising in its influence upon both countries. The civil charges *per capita* at this moment are in Great Britain 8s. 2d., and in Ireland 16s. They have increased in Ireland in the last

fifteen years by sixty-three per cent., and my belief is that if the present legislative and administrative systems be maintained you must make up your minds to a continued, never-ending and never-to-be-limited augmentation."*

This is what Mr. Birrell says about it to-day :—

" I am satisfied that no person—I don't care to what Party in politics he belongs—who has ever occupied this office (Chief Secretary for Ireland), even for so limited a period as two years or less, would ever arise in this House and maintain with any degree of warmth or passion, or, indeed, at all, the argument that the present method of Irish government is *good or sound.* No one will say it is efficient, no one will say it is economic, or that it gives any real satisfaction to any *portion of the Irish people.* I, at all events, don't know to what quarter of the House I should look were I to seek for support for Irish Administration as a whole. Nobody who looks at it has much confidence in it, and no one called upon to administer it can speak a word for it.

" A man might say ' It is better than Home Rule,' or that ' it is better than it would be if Irishmen had to do it themselves.' But it is a rather lamentable state of things that, after all these years since the Union, the most anybody has got to say for the Irish Administration is that it is not efficient, that it is extravagant, that it does not satisfy anybody, but that it is, at all events, better than were you to entrust the task of spending their own money to the Irish people themselves. I only mention that simply as showing that nobody—I don't care to what Party he belongs—filling the office that I fill now can stand at this table and pretend that

* House of Commons, April 8th, 1886.

the present mode of administration, and that mode which has lasted ever since the Union, is good or sound."*

Mr. Gladstone said, in 1886, that the civil government of Ireland was then 16s. per head, and he warned his audience :—

"That if the present legislative and administrative systems be maintained, you must make up your minds to a continued, never-ending and never-to-be-limited augmentation."

The civil government charges in Ireland now amount to £1 8s. per head.†

Mr. Gladstone said, in 1886 :—

"And, perhaps, here again I ought to mention as an instance of the demoralising waste which now attends Irish Administration, that which will, perhaps, surprise the House to know—namely, that while in England and Scotland we levy from the Post Office and Telegraph System a large surplus income, in Ireland the Post Office and the Telegraphs just pay their expenses, or leave a surplus so small as not to be worth mentioning. I call that a very demoralising way of spending money."‡

Once more I appeal to the American Syndicate. Is this good business ? Let me assume that the Syndicate is called into consultation by Downing Street, or proposes to take Ireland over from England and run the country itself. How would it deal with the business ? First, I take it that it would ask what is the income of Ireland. Perhaps, Downing Street could not tell it. I have seen various estimates ; but let us take the statement of Mr. Blake, M.P. :—

* House of Commons, March 26th, 1908.
† Mr. Kettle, House of Commons, March 26th, 1908.
‡ House of Commons, April 8th, 1886.

" The gross income or yearly resources of Ireland are estimated too highly at seventy millions."*

Syndicate.—" Ireland's gross contribution to the common purse is, we have seen, £9,490,000. How do you raise this sum ? "†

Downing Street.—" By taxation on the following commodities."

Customs—

Exchequer ..	..	..	£2,960,000
Local Taxation	..	..	15,000

Excise—

Exchequer ..	..		3,082,000
Local Taxation	..		124,000

Estate, etc., Duties—

Exchequer ..	..	..	560,000
Local Taxation	..	..	131,000
Stamps ..	..	..	300,000
Land Tax ..	..	..	
House Duty	..	..	
Income Tax	..	..	1,102,000
Post Office ..	..	..	868,000
Telegraphs ..	..	..	192,000
Crown Lands	..	..	30,000
Miscellaneous	..	..	126,000

£9,490,000‡

* Speech on the Over-Taxation of Ireland in the House of Commons, March 29th, 1897. (Revised Edition, p. 6.)
"According to the book published by the member for North Paddington, between £70,000,000 and £95,000,000 per annum represented the annual income of Ireland, while £1,700,000,000 to £1,800,000,000 represented the income for England." Mr. Kettle in the House of Commons, March 26th, 1908.

† Return of Revenue and Expenditure for the year ending March, 1907.

‡ The customs revenue was made up of import duties or taxes, levied on cocoa, chicory and coffee, dried fruits, foreign spirits, sugar, tea, tobacco, wine and a few minor articles. A tax of

Syndicate.—" That is what you take out of the country."

Downing Street.—" That is what we get."

Syndicate.—" Get ? Why the people would give you nothing but the price of a single ticket from Kingstown to Holyhead. What you take in taxation you take against the protests of the whole nation.*

" Let us see what has been the growth of taxation since the Union. By the arrangements at the Union Ireland had a separate exchequer ; and she was to contribute to the common purse according to her resources. Lord Castlereagh made the point clear ; He said :—' As to the future it is expected that the two countries should move forward and unite with regard to their expenses in the measure to their relative abilities.' " †

Downing Street.—" Yes, and Ireland's contribution was fixed at two seventeenths."

Syndicate.—" Which was in excess of her resources."

Downing Street.—" No, I don't say that. Castlereagh produced statistics giving the resources of the country, and Ireland's proportion to the common purse was based on these statistics."

Syndicate.—" Yes, but Grattan and other Irish members stated that Castlereagh's figures were

---

nearly £1,300,000 was levied on tobacco, of over £600,000 on sugar, of over £550,000 on tea, of £25,000 on cocoa, £13,000 on chicory and coffee, £47,000 on dried fruits, and £92,000 on wines. The excise contribution was made up of nearly £2,000,000 levied almost altogether on whiskey, and some £1,200,000 levied on porter (including licences) (" Irish Year Book," p. 159-160).

* During the French occupation of Corsica in the eighteenth century, it was found that the Corsicans were taxed less under the French Government than they had been under their own. A French official pointed this out to a Corsican. The Corsican said " Ah ! yes, but then we *gave*, now you take."

† Lord Dunraven, " The Irish Outlook," p. 93.

inaccurate, and they were justified by the event.*
Ireland's resources were overtaxed ; she had to
borrow to meet her liabilities, and fell heavily
into debt in consequence."

Downing Street.—" We were not responsible
for that."

Syndicate.—" Yes you were ; you forced on
Ireland a burden she could not bear, and she
succumbed under it. All Irish Unionists say that
the financial relations of the Union were unjust
to Ireland. Pitt and Castlereagh were in a hurry,
and would allow neither discussion nor inquiry.
' The best Irish financiers,' Mr. Lecky tells us,
' say that Ireland's portion was excessive, and
their predictions were verified.'†

" Let us see what the course of Irish debt has
been up to 1817, when the two exchequers were
consolidated. In 1791, the Irish debt was two and
a quarter millions. In 1800, it was over twenty-
five and a quarter millions." ‡

Downing Street.—" We were not responsible
for that increase."

* It was repeatedly urged by Grattan and others, in the debates
which preceded the Union, that no information had been laid
before the Irish Parliament, justifying the ability of Ireland to
pay two-seventeenths of the joint expenditure. Figures were
procured by Castlereagh justifying this proportion, derived from
a comparison of the value of exports and imports from Ireland
for the three years ending March 25th, 1798, with the corresponding values in Great Britain for the same period. It is obvious
if any valid conclusion was to be drawn from these figures that
they should have been submitted to the most searching scrutiny.
The time and the opportunity for such scrutiny was resolutely
denied. Had it taken place it would have been found that
Castlereagh's figures were utterly untrustworthy. They were
statements not of real, but of official values, and the official values
bore to the real no fixed relation whatever. (Dr. Bridges in
" Two Centuries of Irish History," p. 253).

† Another evil which resulted from carrying the Union in time
of war was that its financial arrangements completely broke
down. (Lecky, "History of Ireland in Eighteenth Century,"
Vol. V., p. 475.)

* Smyth " Ireland, Statistical and Historical," Vol. II., p. 262.

Syndicate.—" Yes you were ; for your management of the affairs of the country had ended in
rebellion, which was chiefly accountable for this
immense increase."

Downing Street.—" That's a disputable point."

Syndicate.—" The rebellion is not a disputable
point ; and if your occupation of the country has
been characterised by a series of disturbances
and rebellions ending in the movement of 1798 there
must be something rotten in your system.   At all
events one thing is perfectly clear, you are not able
to make Ireland either tranquil, contented or
prosperous ; and the question is whether some-
body else should not have a try.   Now what are
the figures since the Union.

"In 1801   ..   .. £27,000,000 (nearly)
     1806 58,000,000
     1811 70,000,000
     1817 ..   .. 113,000,000* (exceeded)

" So much for the debt. Let me take the taxation
in round figures. In 1800 the taxation of Ireland
was under £3,000,000 ; in 1817 it amounted to
£6,000,000.†

" These are the broad features of the case.   I
do not go into complications. I state the main
facts.   Between 1800 and 1817 the revenue of
Ireland decreased ;   the debt and taxation increased.   The financial settlement which you
forced on Ireland at the Union broke down utterly.‡

* Dr. Bridge's " Two Centuries of Irish History," p. 251.

† A Select Committee of 1817 found that Ireland had advanced
in permanent taxation faster than Britain ; for while Britain's
permanent taxation had been raised in the proportion of 16½ to 10,
and her whole revenue including war taxes, as 21¼ to 10, Irish
taxation had been raised as 23 to 10.   A Select Committe of 1811
had reported a decline in the Irish Revenue (Blake's Speech, p.22).

‡ In 1807, the revenue of Ireland amounted to £4,378,000.   In
1821 to £3,844,000 (Lecky, Vol. V. p. 478).   In 1801 the
Funded Debt of Ireland was £26,841,219.   In 1817 it was
£86,838,938.   The Unfunded Debt at the same period rose from
£1,699,938 to £5,304,615. *Ibid.* 476-7.

In 1801, the English Parliament took Ireland in hand. Failure was the result.

" In 1817, the English Parliament took Ireland still more closely in hand. In 1817, the Exchequers of the two countries were consolidated.*

" The basis of the settlement of 1800 was that Ireland should contribute to the Common Purse, according to her resources. The basis of the settlement of 1817 was that Ireland should be taxed indiscriminately with England."

Downing Street.—" Yes, and quite right too. The Irishman was treated in the same way as the Wiltshire man. Why not ? "

Syndicate.—" The Wiltshire man belongs to a rich nation, the Irishman to a poor nation. You think that both should be treated on equal terms in reference to taxation."

Downing Street.—" Certainly."

Syndicate.—" You think that a man with an income of £500 a year should be treated in reference to taxation on equal terms with the man who has an income of £500,000 a year."

Downing Street.—" Certainly, that has. been the basis of English taxation."

Syndicate.—" Very well, let us see what that basis has done for Ireland."

Downing Street.—" As a matter of fact there was not equality of taxation between England and Ireland for several years after the consolidation of the Exchequers."

Syndicate.—" No doubt on the principle that you cannot take ' breeks ' from a Highlander, Ireland was too poor to bear equal treatment ; as Mr. Lecky says : ' Irish taxation in the years that followed the Union was chiefly indirect, and

* The seventh Article of the Act of Union provided that when the Irish debt was more than two-fifteenths of the British, the Exchequer should be consolidated with the consent of Parliament. This was the case in 1817. (Bridges, p. 255. See Lecky, Vol. V., p. 477.)

the small produce of the duties that were imposed
clearly showed the real poverty of the country.'*
You soon mended your hand. In 1842, the
work of equalisation began. Sir Robert Peel
increased the spirit duties, and equalised the stamp
duties. This fooling, however, was not, apparently,
successful, ' the additional revenue derived from
the stamps was lost in the reduction of the stamp
duties both in Great Britain and Ireland.'*   The
increased spirit duties were not apparently successful either, and the additional 1s. was taken off
. in 1843.   But in 1853 the work of equalisation
was carried out with a vengeance.   Before Ireland
had recovered from the terrible famine which
had brought her to death's door the income tax was
imposed on the country. ' A little later Mr.
Gladstone began the raising of the spirit duties,
on the plea that it was no part of an Irishman's
rights to get drink cheaper than an Englishman ';†
and in 1858‡ the spirit duties were assimilated by
Mr. Disraeli.''

Downing Street.—'' Yes but you forget that
when the income tax was imposed in 1853 the
advance of £4,000,000 made at the time of the
famine was wholly remitted.''

Syndicate.—'' Damned kind.   But you forget
that the remission was infinitely more than made
up by increased taxation. ' We forgive you the
£4,000,000,' you said, ' but (*sotto voce*) we shall
more than recoup ourselves for this generosity by
what we are going to get out of you by increased
taxes.' ''§

* Lecky, ''History of Ireland,'' Vol. V. p. 478.

† Mr. Blake's Speech on Over-Taxation, p. 26.

‡ Mr. Blake says 1859, p. 26;   Lecky says, 1858, p. 478.

§ '' The total amount of money remitted to Ireland was
£4,000,000, whilst the total amount of money Ireland has since
paid to England for this remission of £4,000,000 is, up to the
present, £109,250,000, and we are still paying 4¼ millions each year

Downing Street.—" But you forget that Ireland is exempted from the payment of taxes in connection with matters which are taxed in Great Britain. For instance we get £4,000,000 a year in England by the following taxes which are not paid in Ireland ; House Duty, Railway Passengers Duty, and the tax on horses, carriages, patent medicines, and armorial bearings."

Syndicate.—" Well, it is impossible to say whether you English are conscious or unconscious hypocrites. Assuredly you know that the proceeds which would be derived from taxing these things in Ireland would not be worth the collection.*

" Now what has been the general course of taxation. Between 1852 and 1862 ' the taxation of Ireland was increased 52 per cent., while that of Great Britain was only increased 17 per cent. ; and the proportion of the Irish to the British revenue, which, in the first sixteen years of the century, was between one-thirteenth and one-fourteenth, rose in the ten years after 1852 to one-tenth or one-ninth.'†

" To put the matter in another way. Between 1817 and 1894 taxation in Ireland increased 170 per cent. per head of the population ; while in

---

for the generosity that remitted £4,000,000 fifty-three years ago. Up to the present we have been forced to pay £27 for £1 remitted ("Irish Year Book," 1908, p. 161). An admirable book, published by the National Council. *Sein Féin.*

* At the time of the Financial Relations Commission Report the English Press generally urged that Ireland had received " set-offs " that counter-balanced the millions she was annually paying in over-taxation. The late Mr. Maunsell of the *Daily Express*, therefore, totalled up all the " set-offs " and placed the total against the total of over-taxation. By a simple sum in addition, this Unionist Irishman, whose patriotism and public spirit have not been much emulated amongst his political colleagues, showed that for every £10 of a " set-off " England extracted £86 from this country ("Irish Year Book," p. 161).

† Lecky " History of Ireland," Vol. V., p. 479.)

England during the same period taxation decreased 11 per cent. per head of the population.* And what has been the incidence of this taxation? In Great Britain 52 per cent. of the taxation is direct, and something over 48 per cent. indirect. In Ireland on the other hand 28 per cent. is direct and 72 indirect.† To state another fact in connection with the matter, the Royal Commission appointed in 1893 to inquire into the financial relations between England and Ireland found that Ireland was then overtaxed to the amount of 2½ millions per annum in proportion to her fair contribution to the common purse in accordance with her resources.

" ' Since the issue of this report, Ireland's relative taxable capacity has decreased. She is paying £2,000,000 or £3,000,000 annually more than she ought to pay, according to the financial principles of the Act of Union, and the report of a Royal Commission.' "‡

Downing Street.—" But we do not accept the findings of that Commission in all matters."

---

* Royal Commission on Financial Relations between England and Ireland (Mr. Kettle, House of Commons, 26th March, 1908).

† Lord Dunraven's letter *Irish Independent*, May 4th, 1908.

‡ Lord Dunraven, *Irish Daily Independent*, May 4th, 1908.— I take the following extract from the findings of the Commission :—

" (1) That Great Britain and Ireland must, for the purposes of this inquiry, be considered as separate entities.

" (2) That the Act of Union, imposed upon Ireland a burden which, as events showed, she was unable to bear.

" (3) That the increase of taxation laid upon Ireland, between 1853 and 1860, was not justified by the then existing circumstances.

" (4) That identity of rates of taxation does not necessarily involve equality of burden.

" (5) That whilst the actual tax revenue of Ireland is about one-eleventh of that of Great Britain the relative taxable capacity of Ireland is very much smaller, and is not estimated by any of us as exceeding one-twentieth."

Syndicate.—" Mr. Balfour, I understand, suggested that a new Commission should be appointed to revise the findings of the Commission of 1894."

Downing Street.—" Yes."

Syndicate.—" Was that Commission ever appointed ? "

Downing Street.—" No."

Syndicate.—" Then the Commission of 1894 still holds the field."

Downing Street.—" Yes, that is so, so far as the appointment of any other Commission is concerned."

Syndicate.—" Then we must stand by the Commission of 1894 until its findings are authoritatively overthrown."

Downing Street.—" But an important fact is constantly lost sight of in connection with this question of taxation. Assuming that Ireland is fully taxed according to her resources, it is forgotten that more than three-fourths of the money taken from her in taxation is returned to her again."

Syndicate.—" How ? "

Downing Street.—" For purposes of administration."

" *Syndicate.*—" I see. You extract millions by taxes on the necessaries of life, and you think it is a good answer to say that you send back £1,500,000 for the police to say nothing of what you give to your officials in Dublin Castle, and in the Boards and everywhere else."

Downing Street.—" We spend a great deal of Irish money in Irish administration."

Syndicate.—" No you don't. You spend a great deal—a great deal too much—of Irish money in *English* administration in Ireland—quite a different thing. The Irish reply is very simple. They are as sick of your administration as they are of your taxation. They say that you tax too much, and that you pay your officials too much, and that you are plundering and blundering all the time. What does the first Lord of the Treasury at the present day say about your operations in Ireland ? ' Ireland,' says Mr. Asquith, ' is by far the most urgent, because she is to-day, as she has been for centuries—does anybody deny it ?—the one undeniable failure of British statesmanship.'* I shall come to the cost of Irish Administration—to the money which you say you return to Ireland—later on. But I want to finish taxation now. The taxation of Ireland is not only heavy, but it falls on the poorer classes of the people, and it falls on the necessaries of life. What does the English Minister responsible for Ireland to-day say on the subject ? ' We have only,' says Mr. Birrell, ' got to look at the revenue return from Ireland, to see that she is a poor country.' In 1906-7 the revenues collected† in Ireland amounted to £11,499,000. Well, of that amount £8,000,000 was derived from Customs and Excise—eight millions of money out of eleven millions, because the people have to eat and drink excisable and customs-bearing articles. We all know that people who drink large quantities of tea, and smoke many ounces of tobacco, do so because of the very inadequacy of their sustenance. We find that the income tax in England produces £28,000,000 ; in Ireland it produces £999,000 ; therefore you find a country whose

---

* May 2nd, 1908, made in the House of Commons on Mr. Redmond's Home Rule Resolution.

† Revenue is *collected* in Ireland on spirits and beer consumed in England, and the Inland Revenue (Excise) Return on pages 6 and 7 shows that £2,401,000 represents the Excess Duty, or difference when adjusted as explained in the column headed "Remarks." Against this amount, however, is "set off" on the debit side, the amounts (1) in respect of Stamp Duty paid in England principally on patent medicines used in Ireland ; (2) Income Tax on property of persons residing in England or abroad ; (3) Customs Duty collected in England on tea, tobacco,

taxation is practically almost wholly derived from indirect taxation, and, therefore, we have to deal with a poor country.' "*

---

wines, etc., consumed in Ireland. The figures work out as follows :—

Gross Revenue collected (see page 4)	£11,399,000
Net Revenue " as contributed " (see same page)	9,490,000

Difference (accounted for below) £1,909,000

Excess Revenue collected in Ireland

spirits, consumed in England	£2,085,000
Beer, consumed in England	£316,000

Total Excess £2,401,000

Deduct :—

Stamp Duty, paid in England on Patent Medicines used in Ireland	£24,000	
Income Tax, on property of persons residing abroad	£103,000	
Customs Duty, collected in England on tea, tobacco, wines, etc., consumed in Ireland	£365,000	
		£492,000

Difference between Revenue "collected" and "as contributed" (after adjustment) £1,909,000 (as above).

* No figures are available as to the number of persons paying income tax in each part of Great Britain and Ireland or, indeed, in Great Britain and Ireland as a whole, owing to the system of collection at the source. But the Chancellor of the Exchequer recently gave us an answer to a printed question (p. 1495 of the Votes for Session 1908) the figures as to the number of persons with incomes exceeding £160 and not exceeding £700, which can be checked by means of the system of abatement. They are as follows :—

In England and Wales	..	..		628,307
In Scotland	..	..	..	74,697
In Ireland	..	..	..	33,275

These figures enable us to see what proportion of the respective populations are in a middling station. They show that, in round figures, nineteen per thousand of the population in England (or nearly one in ten if one counts by families) belong to the middle class, eighteen per thousand in Scotland and only seven per thousand in Ireland. The proportion of rich in Ireland is certainly not larger, and the figures illustrate in a striking way the relative poverty of the Irish people. The total tax yield per head

Downing Street.—" But it is a great advantage for a poor country like Ireland to be associated with a rich country like England."

Syndicate.—" That is the question.   What does Mr. Birrell say on the subject :—

" ' We are bound, in our consideration of Ireland to bear in mind the fact that she was a poor country of the sort I have described, and is, unhappily for her economical peace of mind, damnified by being so closely associated with a country of such expensive tastes as our own. I know nothing more disadvantageous to a poor man than to have rich relatives.

" ' I am a poor man myself, but I am very glad to say I have no rich relatives, and conseqeuntly, I have all my life been able to live my own life and to fix my own habits.   The moment you have rich relatives, if you are at all of a sanguine disposition, you are bound to launch forth into a life of extravagance, wholly destructive of your peace of mind and well calculated to bring you into the Bankruptcy Court.   Some relative might give you a motor.   You will triumphantly indulge in runs down to Brighton, and luncheons at the Hotel Metropole ;   but a few such runs in a motor car, and a few such luncheons at the Metropole, together with incidental expenses of the chauffeur, petrol, to say nothing of things by the way, will be quite sufficient in the course of twelve months to upset your standard of life and destroy your peace of mind (laughter). I think hon. gentlemen opposite were perfectly justified in saying : ' We do not *perceive the*

---

from Ireland is only brought to so near an approximation to the yield from Great Britain by the raising of so large a portion of the revenue by taxes on a few articles of general consumption. Putting the figures in another way, Ireland, which in 1907-8 had only 4.5 per cent. of the income tax payers of Great Britain and Ireland, found, in 1906-7, 6.11 per cent. of the revenue.

*advantage of being called upon to contribute such
heavy taxation for purposes which do us no particular good.* It might do us good if we were as
rich as you are ; but if you are not prepared to
supplement us, we object very much to be taxed
on the same footing as yourselves. We are not
able to share in those expenses, and consequently
we have to deny ourselves those glories which
are so dear to the British heart.' That is a
perfectly clear and legitimate answer."

" Let us see how Mr. Redmond puts the case :—
' Allow me to give to the House what has been
quoted in several debates upon similar occasions.
There are some tables given by the Government
Department known as the Congested Districts
Board as an appendix to one of their Reports,
and they give twelve examples of the income and
expenditure of twelve families in the poorer parts,
scattered practically over the whole of Ireland.
I will take these at random. Here is one example
of the receipts and expenditure of a family in
ordinary circumstances—judged by the Irish
standpoint—the ordinary circumstances being
profits from agriculture and home industries.
The total receipts are £23 8s. 7d. The total
expenditure includes these items :—meal £7 14s.,
because that is their bread, as my hon. friend,
who interrupted me, rightly pointed out a moment
ago. These people cannot afford the luxuries
of ordinary bread. They live very largely upon
yellow Indian meal, the kind of meal you feed
your dogs on in this country. Now, in the family
where the budget is £23, meal costs £7 14s., tea
£5 17s., sugar £1 19s., tobacco £3 9s. 4d. ; total
£18 19s. 4d., out of a total income of £23. The
Secretary to the Treasury was right when he
stated that in considering this tax it is not fair
to consider it alone. It is right we should take a
survey of the other taxes, and I say it enormously

strengthens my case. There are these poor creatures living in straitened circumstances such as that ; and you, from motives and with objects I will not delay now to examine, enter upon a great imperial policy and a great war to extend the dominions of the Crown, and what is the first thing you do ? You come to a poor, wretched family, whose whole income is £23, and you put a war tax first upon tea, then upon tobacco, then upon sugar, and now you come down and put a war tax upon bread and the poor man's meal. That was the instance of a family " in ordinary circumstances," so described in the Report of the Congested Districts Board.*

" ' Let me now take a family in the worst possible circumstances. The receipts and expenditure of a family in the poorest possible circumstances are as follows :—Receipts :—Eggs £1 3s., sixty days' labour at 1s., herding cattle, £4, total receipts £8 3s. On the other side the total expenditure for meal is £5 17s. Now, is it not appalling that in the case of a family whose whole receipts amount to £8 3s., and whose whole food is manifestly this meal, you are going to impose upon that family an additional burden of about 6s. a year for your new war tax.' "†

" While taxation has been going up, what has been the state of the population ?"

Downing Street.—" The population has certainly been going down."

Syndicate.—" What are the figures ? "

---

* " There was no tax on meat in Ireland. They were told that never in England would there be a tax on meat. That did not matter to the inhabitant of the congested district, who did not eat meat, because he could not afford it. He found tea and sugar the prime necessity of his life, and Ireland paid about £605,000 on those articles towards the cost of Irish Administration." (Mr. Kettle, House of Commons, March 26th, 1908, p. 1632).

† House of Commons, 13th May, 1902.

Downing Street.—

Year.			Population.
" 1851	..	..	.. 6,574,278
" 1861	..	..	.. 5,798,967
" 1871	..	..	.. 5,412,377
" 1881	..	..	.. 5,174,836
" 1891	..	..	.. 4,704,750
" 1901	..	..	.. 4,458,775."

Syndicate.—" Then, as the taxation has been going up the population has been going down. The Royal Commission of 1894 reported that Ireland was overtaxed at the rate of 2½ million a year.* Things have grown worse since. What has been the state of Ireland's contribution to the Imperial Exchequer ? "

Downing Street.—" It has been going down too."

Syndicate.—" What are the figures ? "

Downing Street.—

" 1859 Ireland's contribution was (roughly)				5,000,000
" 1869	,,	,,	,,	4,000,000
" 1879	,,	,,	,,	3,000,000
" 1894	,,	,,	,,	2,000,000
" 1905-6	,,	,,	,,	1,811,500
" 1906-7	,,	,,	,,	1,811,500

Syndicate.—" Then it would seem, on your own statement, that Ireland contributes not more than 2 per cent. to the Imperial expenditure.

" A recent Irish writer has said a *Royal Commission* appointed in 1894 stated, and since no one has ever controverted its arguments, it may be said to have proved, that Ireland is overtaxed by a sum of between *two and three million pounds every year.* Since then the amount of this over-taxation has *increased.* Then we paid in taxes £1 18s. 2d. *per head.* Now we are paying £2 3s. 3d.

---

* Since then the cost of home government in Ireland has been increased by £2,000,000.—Mr. Kettle, House of Commons, 26th March, 1908.

It is in the strength of this report and these figures that I venture to say that we are being plundered.

" The Treasury does not levy taxes. It collects them and keeps accounts. Keeps accounts ! That is where the skill comes in. It appears, for instance, that Ireland contributes no more than 2 *per cent. to the Imperial expenditure.* That is the official representation of the case. England pays 88 per cent. Surely we ought to be satisfied. But the Financial Relations Commission discovered that Ireland was really paying 9 per cent., and the proportion has not altered since then.

" Of the money raised by the Excise duties on spirits, beer, etc., a certain amount is handed back every year for purposes of local government. Last year the English local authorities received back £21 10s. 2d. for every £100 raised by Excise in England. The Irish local authorities received back £1 19s. 7d. for every £100 raised by Excise in Ireland. No doubt there is an explanation of this fact. Would it not be well to get it ?*

" The whole case, then, comes to this. The population has been going down. Ireland's contribution to the Imperial Exchequer has been going down almost to vanishing point, and taxation has been going up almost all the time. Is that good business ? "

Downing Street.—" Ireland has been a great burden to England."

Syndicate.—" A good reason why you should let us have her on low terms. Your unfitness to run her, either for your own advantage or for hers, is the one demonstrated fact in the whole situation. John Stuart Mill was right. He said : ' there is probably no other nation of the civilised world which, if the task of governing Ireland had hap-

* Mr. Hannay (" George Birmingham ") in *Sinn Fein,* May 9th, 1908.

pened to devolve on it, would not have shown itself more capable of that work than England has hitherto done.' Now let us turn to the financial details of the English Administration of Ireland.

" *First*, Let us take the Viceroy. What is his salary ? "

Downing Street.—" The Viceroy is on the Consolidated Fund."

Syndicate.—" It doesn't matter. We are not in the House of Commons. I want to get the whole cost of the upkeep of Ireland whatever may be the name of the source out of which it comes.* What is the salary of the Lord Lieutenant ? "

Downing Street.—" £20,000 a year."

Syndicate.—" Has that always been the salary ?"

Downing Street.—" No, in the eighteenth century it was less, and in part of the nineteenth

---

* For the sake of the uninitiated, let me give the following extract from Todd's Parliamentary Government (in England).

"Concurrently, however, with parliamentary taxation other imposts used to be levied by royal prerogative, independently of the action of Parliament, but none of these survived the Revolution of 1688. It was guaranteed by the Bill of Rights that henceforth ' no man be compelled to make any gift, loan, or benevolence, or tax, without common consent by Act of Parliament. And it was finally established by the Act of Settlement, ' That levying money for or to the use of the Crown by pretence and prerogative, without grant of Parliament, for longer time or in other manner than the same is or shall be granted, is illegal.'

" Since that memorable period the Crown has been entirely dependent upon Parliament for its revenues, which are derived either from annual grants for specific public services, or from payments already secured and appropriated by Acts of Parliament, and which are commonly known as charges upon the Consolidated Fund" (Vol. I., pp. 453-454).

" Formerly, the proceeds of Parliamentary taxes constituted separate and distinct funds, but, by the Act 27, Geo.. III., c. 47, it was directed that the various duties and taxes should be carried to and constitute a fund, to be called ' The Consolidated Fund ' " (*Ibid.*, p. 468).

With an insignificant exception

" the whole public revenue of the country, together with moneys received from loans, is placed to the account of the Consolidated Fund, out of which all public payments are

century it was more. Lord Townshend got £16,000 only.† Subsequently the salary was raised to £30,000. In 1829, the Lord Lieutenant of the day, the Duke of Northumberland, returned £10,000 to the Treasury and the salary has remained £20,000 since."

Syndicate.—" What was done with the £10,000 so saved. Was it ear marked for the Administration of Ireland ? "

Downing Street.—" Oh, no, it was kept for the general purposes of the Imperial Government."

Syndicate.—" Was that fair ? Assuredly, what is saved in Irish Administration ought to be devoted to Irish purposes."

Downing Street.—" We don't think so."

Syndicate.—" Clearly. Now the head of the State in Ireland, which is the poorest country in the world, receives £20,000."

Downing Street.—" The Irish need not complain of that. They don't pay it. It is paid out of Imperial resources."

Syndicate.—" That's not the point. Is it a wise allocation of money, no matter who pays it. It is paid by Englishmen, Irishmen, Scotchmen and Welshmen. The question is have they any-

made. Such payments are twofold : (1) By authority of permanent grants, under Acts of Parliament ; (2) Pursuant to annual votes in Committee of Supply, payable out of the Consolidated Fund by ways and means annually provided" (*Ibid*, p. 471).

The Revenue, or annual income of the country derived from the taxes imposed by Parliament, etc., is collected into the Consolidated Fund. The charges upon this fund are :—
(1) The payment of interest upon the National Debt.
(2) The Civil List (*i.e.*, the sum apportioned for all purposes relating to the up-keep of the Sovereign).
(3) Salaries of Ministers of State, Judges, and others. The remainder of the Consolidated Fund is paid into the Exchequer, for the public service, to defray the expenses of the Army, Navy, Civil Service, etc. See Fonblanque " How we are governed," pp. 22, 23.

† Smyth, "Ireland, Historical and Statistical." Vol. II., p. 158.

thing better to do with the money than to squander it on a mere ornamental office. Were Ireland an independent state like Switzerland, would the head of the State get £20,000 a year. The President of the Swiss Republic gets £720 a year for real work."

Downing Street.—" I don't think you should put the matter that way. You must take Ireland, as she is, united to a Great Empire."

Syndicate.—" I see. I have got a friend with £50,000 a year, and he drives a motor car. I have £1,000 a year, and I must have a motor car also on account of the bond of friendship."

Downing Street.—" What does it matter if *he* pays for the motor car ? "

Syndicate.—" If *he* pays it matters to *him ;* for it is better that he should keep the money in his pocket than squander it to no purpose ; but suppose the case is in this wise—suppose (for the honour and glory of his friendship) he insists upon my devoting part of my income to keeping a motor, while he ekes out the balance, then he plays the fool all round. He throws away his own money and mine without gain to either of us. Better no friendship than friendship like that— a national government in Ireland would not squander £20,000 of the country's income on a pageant. The money would be spent in educating the people or in some other productive work. What else is spent on the vice-royalty besides the £20,000 a year on the Viceroy himself ? "

Downing Street.—" The household of the Lord Lieutenant costs £4,672, and there are miscellaneous* charges which amount to £10,402."

* The miscellaneous charges for the year 1906-7 are :—

Buildings, Furniture, Fuel and Light, etc.	£8,006
Rates	1,200
Stationery and Printing	200
Non-effective	29
Post Office, Revenue estimates	64
Post Office, Telegraphs, Revenue Estimates	903

(Estimates for 1906-7).

Syndicate.—" Then the total cost for the up-keep of the Lord Lieutenancy is £35,074."

Downing Street.—" Yes, for the year 1906-7."

Syndicate.—" The Irish people are not, of course, consulted on squandering £35,000 on an office in which they take no interest."

Downing Street.—" Dublin Society takes an interest in it, and Dublin tradesmen."

Syndicate.—" That is to say, your officials in Ireland take an interest in it and the flunkey tradesmen of the Castle take an interest in it. But they do not represent Ireland? If the Vice-royalty evoked national sentiment the case would be different. Money is often spent extrava-gantly by the State in gratifying national feeling, and it is well spent. But the Vice-royalty, in existing circumstances, instead of evoking national feeling, repels it. The office, I repeat, in existing circumstances, is no good to Ireland, is no good to you, and is no good to the Viceroy. To Ireland the office simply emphasises the dominion of a foreigner. The Viceroy comes as an English party man to carry out the behests of an English party leader. The £20,000 a year isn't enough for him to keep up the trappings of State. He probably leaves the country in debt, and spends the remainder of his life in recouping his shattered fortunes.* The office is no good to you. If it helped to reconcile the people to the English connection the money might, from your point of view, be well spent. But it doesn't. In fact, you often spend the £24,672

---

* " Upon his retirement, [Lord Townshend] the offices under his control were found to owe £250,000 ; and although the salary of the Lord Lieutenant had been augmented during his time to £16,000 a year, he had so encumbered his private property with debts, as to be obliged to sell some of his estates, after his return to England, in order to satisfy the demands of his personal creditors " (Smyth, " Ireland, Historical and Statistical," p. 158).

in sending a Viceroy who exasperates the whole nation. And yet we hear constantly of English common sense. The Viceroy who opened the Irish Parliament of 1782 was worth his salary, because he represented a constitutional union, based upon the free will of two separate nations. He stood for peace. But the Viceroy of to-day is not worth his salary.

" He cannot reconcile the people to the loss of the constitution of 1782, and he is unnecessary as a force to keep them down."

Downing Street.—" Well, we don't want him. We do not care if the Vice-royalty were abolished to-morrow. We would save the salaries."

Syndicate.—" What would you do with them when you had saved them ? Devote them to Irish purposes ? "

Downing Street.—" No, we should keep the money in the Treasury and devote it to general imperial purposes as occasion required."

Syndicate.—" Ay ! Earmark it for the next Boer War. It is only the barest act of justice that every penny saved in the administration of Ireland should be devoted to Irish purposes. I now turn to the Judges."

Downing Street.—" They are also on the Consolidated Fund."

Syndicate.—" No doubt, nevertheless I will have a shot at them. First, I take the Lord Chancellor. Up to last year he received a salary of £8,000 a year. The President of the United States, the richest country in the world, receives a salary of £10,000. The Lord Chancellor of Ireland, the poorest country in the world, received up to yesterday as it were a salary of £8,000. He now receives £6,000. Let me take the other Judges :—

" The Lord Chief Justice £5,000
" Chief Baron 4,600

" Master of the Rolls £4,000
" Lord Justice of Appeal (1) .. 4,000
" Lord Justice of Appeal (2) .. 4,000
" Each Puisne Judge (there are eight
      of them) 3,500

" I pass from the Judges of the Supreme Court to the County Court Judges. There are sixteen* of them, each with a salary of £1,400 a year. I add the Recorders :—

" The Recorder of Dublin .. £2,400
" The Recorder of Belfast 2,000
" The Recorder of Cork 2,000
" The Recorder of Derry 1,500
" The Recorder of Galway 1,500

" I give the Law Officers :—

" The Attorney-General 5,000
" The Solicitor-General 2,000

" Again I put the case, would an independent Ireland (under a European and an American guarantee—the thing is thinkable) pay these salaries to Judges and other legal functionaries ? Assuredly not. It is not a question of what these distinguished men deserve, but what the country can afford to pay. And an independent Ireland could not afford to squander her resources in this luxurious fashion. It is the motor car system run mad."

Downing Street.—" But the Irish people would not like to have the salaries of the Judges reduced ? "

Syndicate.—" How do you know ? "

Downing Street.—" They would not like to have the money taken out of the country."

Syndicate.—" Just so. That is the point. But the money should not be taken out of the country. Money saved by reducing the salaries of Judges (and in all other Irish Departments) should be applied to other Irish purposes. The Irish people, might perhaps rather see the money squandered

* See *Ante* p. 79.

even on English Judges in Ireland than swallowed up by the English Treasury. That is the vice of your system. You do either of two things. You either squander the money on extravagant administration, or you take it away altogether. You do not spend the money in the best way for the development of the intellectual, moral, and material well being of the people. As for the money you spend on legal establishments it is simply corruption. You try to bribe the bar into loyalty. You purchase the intellect and sap the integrity of a great profession. What is the result ? The people distrust the Judges, and have no faith in the Bar as a national institution.

" A current of demoralisation runs through your whole administration, you make it worth the barrister's while by extravagant expenditure to enlist under your colours. Did you not make it worth his while, you know that every man in the Four Courts with a wig on his head would stand by his own country."*

I shall now take leave of Downing Street and the Syndicate, and quote some extracts from the estimates 1906-7 on my own responsibility.

I find the total amount, under the heading " Supreme Court of Judicature and other legal departments of Ireland " for the year 1906-7, is £102,586.†

* If you take the barristers in actual practice, the average income would not be more than about £800 to £1,000 a year.

Therefore it pays a practising barrister well to become a Puisne Judge with a salary of £3,500 or even a County Court Judge with £1,400.

† Estimates, 1906-7, p. 308.

Provision is made as follows in other estimates for expenditure in connection with this service.

Building, Furniture, Fuel and Light, etc. ..	£5,333
Rates	2,500
Stationery and Printing	3,000
Non-Effective	12,543
Local Courts of Bankruptcy	3,000

The expenses of " County Court officers and magistrates, with charges for revision," I find set down at £111,088, with miscellaneous charges, which make a total of £44,719.‡

I next take "Law Charges and Criminal Prosecutions " :

The Crown Solicitor receives	.. ..	£2200
The Treasury Solicitor	.. ..	2,200
Assistant to Chief Crown Solicitor ..	..	600
Assistant to Treasury Solicitor ..	..	407
Clerk to Treasury Solicitor	.. ..	165
The total charge in the estimates for the year 1906-7 is	.. .. ..	£62,652§

Post Office Revenue Estimates	177
Post Office, Telegraphs, Revenue Estimates ..	34
Consolidated Fund—For Salaries to the Lord Chancellor and Judges, and for Circuit Expenses	64,613
For Pensions and Compensations Supreme Court	8,629
	£99,829

‡ The miscellaneous charges are as follows :—

Stationery and Printing	£300
Non-Effective	9,264
Post Office, Revenue Estimates	3
Post Office Telegraphs, Revenue Estimates ..	35
Consolidated Fund—Salaries of Chairman of Quarter Sessions and Recorders	31,800
Consolidated Fund—Pensions of Chairmen of Quarter Sessions and Recorders	3,317
	£44,719

§ Provision is also made as follows in other Estimates for Expenditure in connection with this service :—

Buildings, etc., Class I., 14	£140
Surveys, Class I., 10	
Rates, Class I., 13	20
Stationery and Printing, Class II., 23	350
Non-effective, Class II., 1	
Post Office Telegraphs, Revenue Estimates No.	
	£510

Looking at the Scotch estimates for the same years, I find under the heading "law charges and Courts of Law Scotland," that the amount is £80,828.*

Let us now take the total of the law charges in Ireland as set down in the House of Commons Estimates, and in other Estimates, and compare them with the total of the law charges in Scotland similarly provided for.

IRELAND.

Supreme Court of Judicature	£202,415
County Court and Magistrates	155,807
Law Charges and Criminal Prosecution ..	63,162
Grand Total	£421,384

SCOTLAND.

Grand Total of all Law Charges ..	£228,383

Thus it will be seen that the law charges in Ireland are nearly double those of Scotland.

Let me observe that the charges for the judges of the Supreme Court and for Circuit expenses are £64,613

* Provision is also made as follows in other estimates for expenditure in connection with this service :—

	1906-7.
Buildings, Furniture, Fuel and Light, etc. Class I., 9	£2,270
Buildings, Furniture, Fuel and Light, etc. Class I., 5	14,600
Rates	850
Stationery and Printing	2,000
Non-Effective	460
Post Office, Revenue Estimates	217
Telegraphs, Revenue Estimates	86

The following sums are charged upon the Consolidated Fund, viz. :—

For Salaries of the Lords Justices	49,400
For Salaries of Sheriffs of Counties	14,625
For Salaries of Sheriffs' Substitute	39,600
For Salary of Sheriff, Clerk of Chancery	250

Non-Effective Charge on Consolidated Fund, viz. :—

For Annuities of Judges	13,500
For Annuities of Sheriffs	3,418
For Annuities of Sheriffs' Substitute	5,452
For Annuities of Judges' Clerks and Keeper of Rolls	827
Total .. £147,555

in Ireland, while the charges for the Lords Justices in Scotland are £49,400.

I shall take just one illustrative item from the details of the Irish expenditure, and compare it with an item from the expenditure of a free continental state.

Private Secretary to the Lord Chancellor £500 a year. The salary of the President of the Swiss Republic is £720 a year.

I turn to the Chief Secretary. His salary is £4,425.* Why £4,425 ? In England the President of the Local Government Board gets £2,000. The President of the Board of Trade gets £2,000. The Minister of Education gets £2,000. The Secretary for Scotland gets £2,000. The first Lord of the Admiralty gets £4,500. The maximum salary which a Minister of State gets in England is £5,000. Thus the Chancellor of the Exchequer gets £5,000.

Does any one suppose that if the Irish people had the transaction of their own business in their own Parliament that they would squander £4,425 on a Prime Minister out of the slender resources of their country, while there were so many urgent demands for the money in the development of Industrial and Educational work ? The Under-Secretary at the Castle gets £2,000. The Assistant Under-Secretary gets £1,200. The total expenses of the Chief Secretary's Department for the year 1906-7 were £26,118, with miscellaneous charges making a grand total of £41,471.†

* " His salary was formerly £7000 a year, but was fixed in 1831, and again in 1851, at £5,500 per annum, in lieu of all fees and emoluments. It has since been reduced to £4,000, but he has an extra allowance of £425 ' for fuel.' " Todd, " Parliamentary Government in England," Vol. II., p. 721. In Colchester's diary the salary is, however, given at £4,500 in 1801, Vol. I., p. 255.

†Buildings, Furniture, Fuel and Light, etc. Class I., 9						£810
Buildings, Furniture, Fuel and Light, etc. Class I., 14						2,893
Surveys	..	..	..	..	..	..
Rates	..	..	..	..	..	700

" I take the Police ; first the Constabulary. The salary of the Inspector-General is £1,800 ; the salary of the Deputy Inspector-General is £1,200.

" Each Assistant Inspector-General (there are two of them) receives £700. The total cost of the force for the year 1906-7 was £1,310,038.*

" Next I take the Dublin Metropolitan Police. The Chief Commissioner receives £900 a year. The Assistant Commissioner £685 ; the Chief Police Court Magistrate £1,200 ; other Magistrates (three in number), £1,000 each ; the total cost of the Force for the year 1906-7 was £95,721.†

I find that Mr. T. W. Russell, speaking in the House of Commons on 26th March, 1908, said :—

" The Royal Irish Constabulary according to the estimate, costs £1,354,902,‡ and to that must be added £96,632,§ the cost of the Metropolitan

---

Stationery and Printing	..	..	..	1,500
Non-Effective	.. ..	.. ..	.. ..	4,353
Post Office, Revenue Estimates	..	..	..	1,945
Post Office, Telegraphs, Revenue Estimates	..	..		2,682
Consolidated Fund—Inspectors of Anatomy	..	..		470

(Estimates 1906-7). £15,353

---

* Provision is also made, as follows, in other Estimates for Expenditure in connection with this service :—

Building, Furniture, Fuel and Light, etc.	..			£10,921
Rates	..	..	..	3,000
Stationery and Printing	..	..	..	1,600
Non-Effective	.. ..	..	..	1,292
Post Office, Revenue Estimates	..	..		963
Telegraphs, Revenue Estimates	..	..		3,758

£21,534

---

† Miscellaneous expenses amount to £13,081. Adding to the £95,721 in the Estimates the appropriations in aid which come to £53,859, and the miscellaneous charges which come to £13,081, the grand total of the expenses of the Dublin Metropolitan Police is £162,661.

‡ Estimates for 1908-1909.

§ *Ibid.*

Police, making a total of £1,451,534 for the police in Ireland. Hon. gentlemen would not find in the Scottish estimates a charge for the Scottish police, for this reason, that it was a local charge, and was locally managed. But picking out the sums from the various accounts of the counties, it was a strange thing to find that 4,500,000 Scottish people were policed at a charge of £600,000, but that it took £1,500,000 to do the same work in Ireland. It was enough to state a fact like that to show that something was radically wrong."

An Irish member, Mr. Hayden, put the matter in another way. He said :—

"The cost of the police in Ireland was 6s. 8d. per head, whereas in England the cost of police was only 2s. 4d., and in Scotland 2s. 2½d. per head.

"With the same population as Scotland and less crime, Ireland spent in law and police £3 for every £1 spent in the case of Scotland."*

The plain truth about the extraordinary expenditure on police in Ireland is simply this ; the masses of the Irish people are disloyal to the English connection. Is the fact creditable to English statesmanship? Before the establishment of the constabulary and since, the police in Ireland have been used to put down popular movements. Throughout the whole of the nineteenth century the law has been on one side ; the people have been on the other. I repeat, is this creditable to English statesmanship ? If the end of government be the rule of a hostile people by the sword, then the English Government in Ireland must stand on the highest pinnacle of glory. But if the end of government be to win the affections of the people by the just

---

* Mr. Kettle, House of Commons, March 26th, 1908. p. 1636.
The figures given by Mr. Birrell are Scotland, 2s. 6d. per head ; England, 3s. 6d. per head ; Ireland, 6s. 7d. per head. House of Commons, March 26th, 1908. p. 1683.

administration of good laws, then the English Government in Ireland has a record of unbroken failure.

" Really," said the late Queen Victoria, " it
is quite immoral, with Ireland quivering in our
grasp and ready to throw off her allegiance at
any moment, for us to force Austria to give up
her lawful posesssions.*"

The English Queen summed up the situation in a
single sentence. " Ireland quivering in our grasp "—
that is the story of three hundred years.

From Police to Prisons is an easy transition.

The important functionaries of the General Prisons
Board are the Chairman, Vice-Chairman, the Medical
Member, the Secretary and two Inspectors. The
salaries are as follows :—

The Chairman	..	..	.. £1,200
Vice-Chairman	..	..	.. 1,000
Medical Member	..	..	.. 900
Secretary	..	..	.. 450
Inspectors (two) together		..	.. 1,124

The total vote for Prisons in Ireland for the year
1906-7 amounted to £114,556.†

I now turn to Scotland. The important functionaries
seem to be Commissioners (two), Secretary and
Inspector (one), Chief Clerk. The salaries are :—

One Commissioner	..	..	.. £1,200
One Commissioner	..	..	.. 1,000
Secretary and Inspector		..	.. 540
Chief Clerk	..	..	.. 430

The total vote for the Scottish Prisons for the year
1906-7 was £89,600.‡

I take the following general items in reference to
prisons from the estimates for 1906-7 :—

* " Letters of Queen Victoria," Vol. II., p. 237.

† Miscellaneous charges amounted to £19,223.

‡ The miscellaneous charges amounted to £12,601.

Ireland.		*Scotland.*	
(a) Salaries ..	£9,098	(a) Salaries ..	£5,880
(b) Travelling Exps.	1,000	(b) Travelling Exps.	£500
(c) Incidental Exps.	100	(c) Incidental Exps.	150

Public Education.

The salary of the Resident Commissioner of the " National " Board of Education is £1,500 a year. There are two Secretaries with a salary of £700 each. The total vote for Ireland for the year 1906-7 was £1,393,223. The total vote for Scotland for the same year was £1,972,128.

In reference to Ireland, provision is also made as follows in other estimates for expenditure in connection with the service :—

Building, Furniture, Fuel and Light ..	£32,690
Rates	2,200
Teachers' Pension Office	2,399
Stationery and Printing	2,700
Non-effective	12,315
Post Office, Revenue Estimates	1,505
Telegraphs	59
Ireland, Development Grant	59,035
	£112,903

With reference to Scotland, similar provision is made. Thus :—

Buildings, Furniture, Fuel and Light, etc.	£3,442
Buildings, Furniture, Fuel and Light, etc., Whitehall and Office in Edinburgh ..	2,070
Rates	1,000
Stationery and Printing	2,250
Non-effective	4,680
Post Office, Revenue Estimates	1,596
Telegraphs	134
Consolidated Fund, Salaries and Allowances ; Allowances to School Boards of certain parishes in the Highlands	899
* Estimates 1906-7.	*£16,071

According to Mr. Kettle the amount per head of the population for Primary Education,*

	s.	d.
In England is	7	10½
In Scotland is	8	8
In Ireland is	6	5

Let us put the cost of Primary Education and of Police in Scotland and Ireland together, and see how the figures work out :—

Ireland.

				s.	d.
Education, cost per head of population			..	6	5
Police	,,	,,	,,	. 6	7

Scotland.

				s.	d.
Education, cost per head of population			..	8	8
Police†	,,	,	,,	.. 2	6

Mr. Kettle says :—

> " For every £1 spent by the State in England on Education 17s. went to education, and 3s. to office expenses. In the case of Scotland 16s. 2d. went to education and 3s. 10d. to office expenses. For every £1 spent in Ireland, only 13s. 6d. went to education and 6s. 6d. was spent in office expenses" (House of Commons, 26th March, 1908).

Local Government Board.

The salary of the Vice-President ..	£1,800
One Commissioner	1,200
Medical Commissioner	1,200
Secretary	800
The total expenditure for the year 1906-7 was	63,566‡

* House of Commons, 26th March, 1908, p. 1633.

† In 1901, a Select Committee of the House of Commons, presided over by Sir Howard Vincent, reported that there was no criminal class in Ireland (Mr. Hayden, House of Commons).

‡ Provision is also made, as follows, in other Estimates for Expenditure in connection with this service :—

Office Accommodation (buildings, furniture, fuel and light, etc.)	£876
Rates	£480

I now turn to Scotland.

The salary of the Vice-President is ..	£1,200
One Legal Member	1,000
One Medical Member	1,000
Secretary	900
The total expenditure for 1906-7 was ..	15,470*

I take the following general items of comparison between Scotland and Ireland :—

Scotland.		*Ireland.*	
Salaries & Wages..	£12,995	Ditto ..	£43,002
Travelling Exs. ..	1,400	Ditto Inspectors	7,310
		Auditors	3,700
Incidental Exs. ..	205	Ditto ..	650

Department of Agriculture and Technical Instruction.

The salary of the Vice-President	£1,350
Secretary	1,300
Two Assistant Secretaries, together ..	1,934
Total Expenses of the Department for the year 1906-7 were	190,146†

It is only fair to quote what Mr. T. W. Russell has recently said about the cost of the Department :—

Stationery and Printing	1,000
Non-Effective	3,957
Post Office, Revenue Estimates	2,688
Post Office, Telegraphs, Revenue Estimates	288
	£9,289

* Provision is also made as follows in other Estimates for Expenditure in connection with this service :—

Office Accommodation (building, furniture, fuel and light, etc.)	£220
Rates	60
Stationery and Printing	450
Non-Effective	1,658
Post Office, Revenue Estimates	372
Post Office Telegraphs, Revenue Estimates	52
	£2,812

† Miscellaneous expenses amounted to £38,465.

" His department was responsible for an expenditure of £400,000 per annum ; £215,000 was in the estimates,* the remainder belonged to the Endowment Fund. But he should say that £149,000 of the Department vote simply passed through its hands to other departments. He would say that the charge for salaries and executive officers in connection with the department was not over £65,000, although the total vote on the estimate was £215,000. But he claimed that the £400,000 was almost entirely productive and beneficial to the country."†

Land Commission.

There are two Judicial Commissioners ; one receiving a salary of £3,500 and the other receiving a salary of £3,000. There is one Lay Commissioner receiving £2,500 a year ; there are three Estates Commissioners receiving (a) £3,500 ; (b) £2,000 ; (c) £2,000. There are four (Legal) Assistant Commissioners receiving each £1,200. There are fifty-six Assistant Commissioners (non-legal) including twenty-seven temporary Assistant Commissioners, each receiving £800. There are fourteen Examiners of title, two receiving £1,000 each, and twelve £800 each.

The Secretary to the Commission receives £1,500. There are two Assistant Secretaries receiving £700 each.

The total expenditure in the estimates for 1906-7 was £214,215.‡

* Estimates 1908-9, £215,788.

† House of Commons, March 26th, 1908.

‡ Provision is also made as follows, in other Estimates for Expenditure in connection with this Service :—

Office Accommodation (buildings, furniture, fuel and light, etc.)	£10,010
Rates	240
Stationery and Printing	3,000
Non-Effective	3,611

The case of the Land Commission is another illustration of the motor car system run mad. The salaries are, of course, in excess of what officials in a poor country like Ireland ought to receive. But the department is carrying out a bloodless revolution. It is engaged in the admirable work of transferring the landed property of Ireland from practically an English oligarchy to the Irish people. That is its defence, and if extravagant expenditure can ever be justified, then there ought to be no stint in spending money to enable the Commission to wind up its business with all speed, and by so doing to settle the peasants of Ireland on the soil of Ireland.

Registrar-General's Office.

The salary of the Registrar-General is (a year) £1,000
The salary of the Secretary   640
The expenditure for the year 1906-7 was .. £12,132*
    The salary of the Registrar-General for Scotland is £1,200 ; the salary of the Secretary £465. The total expenditure for the year 1906-7 was £4,741.

Post Office, Revenue Estimates	1,036
Post Office Telegraphs, Revenue Estimates	126
Consolidated Fund—Salaries of Commissioners ..	12,000
Consolidated Fund—Pensions	2,334
	£32,357

  * Provision is also made as follows in other votes for Expenditure in connection with this Service :—

Office Accommodation (buildings, furniture, fuel and light, etc.)	£649
Rates	160
Stationery and Printing	1,250
Non-Effective	1,628
Post Office, Revenue Estimates	534
Post Office, Telegraphs, Revenue Estimates	44
	£4,265

Provision is also made as follows in other Estimates for Expenditure in connection with this Service :—

		1906-7.
Registrar-General's Salary, Class III., 11.	..	£1,200
Office Accommodation (buildings, furniture, fuel and light, etc.), Class I., 9	..	210
Rates, Class I., 13	..	200
Stationery and Printing, Class II., 23	..	1,500
Non-effective, Class VI., 1 ..	..	848
Post Office, Revenue Estimates, No. 3	..	679
Post Office Telegraphs, Revenue Estimates, No. 3		4

£4,641

Valuation and Boundary Survey.

The salary of the Commissioner is	..	£1,200
Chief Valuer	..	548
Chief Clerk	..	500
The expenditure for the year 1906-7 was	..	£17,276*

Record Office.

The salary of the Deputy-Keeper and Keeper of the State Papers	..	£800
Assistant Deputy Keeper ..	..	600
The expenditure for the year 1906-7 was	..	£5,484†

* Provision is also made as follows in other Estimates for Expenditure in connection with this Service :—

	1906-7.
Surveys, Class I., 10 (Maps)	£550
Rates, Class I., 13	100
Office Accommodation (buildings, furniture, fuel and light, etc.), Class I., 14	679
Stationery and Printing, Class II., 23	450
Non-Effective, Class VI., 1	4,573
Post Office, Revenue Estimate, No. 3	371
Post Office Telegraphs, Revenue Estimates, No. 3 ..	25

£6,748

† Provision is also made as follows in other Estimates for Expenditure in connection with this Service :—

Office of Arms.

The total expenditure for this office for the year 1906-7 was apparently about £900.

The various functionaries must be named :—

Ulster King at Arms	£500
Allowance for Clerical Assistance	£200
Athlone Pursuivant of Arms (in lieu of Official Fees)	20
Pensioner Messenger at Record Tower ..	55
Office Cleaner	30
Allowance to an Official Reporter during the Castle Season 1905-6	30
Coal Porter (occasional)	5

"Ireland is no joke," says Mr. Birrell. Certainly. But assuredly the Office of Arms is a joke.

Charitable Donations and Bequests.

Commissioners are unpaid.

The Chief Officers are two Secretaries, each, ..   £700

The estimated expenditure for the year 1906-7 £2,049*

	1906-7.
Office Accommodation (buildings, furniture, fuel and light, etc.), Class I., 14	£661
Rates, Class I., 13	110
Stationery and Printing, Class II., 23	100
Non-Effective, Class VI., 1	106
Post Office, Revenue Estimates, No. 3	11
Post Office Telegraphs, Revenue Estimates, No.	9
	£997

* Provision is also made as follows in other Estimates for Expenditure in connection with this Serivce :—

Office Accommodation (buildings, etc., as before) ..	£131
Rates	50
Stationery and Printing	50
Non-Effective	
Post Office Telegraphs, Revenue Estimates	2
	£233

Treasury Remembrancer's Office.

The Treasury Remembrancer and Deputy Paymaster receives a salary of £1,200 a year.

The Chief Clerk's salary is £655 a year.

Total expenditure is for salaries £3,319, travelling expenses £40, for the year 1906-7.

Reformatory and Industrial Schools.

There is one Inspector who receives, a year ..	£800
There is an Assistant Inspector receiving ..	352
The Senior Clerk receives	400
The estimate of expense for the year 1906-7	£110,995

Board of Works.

Chairman of the Board receives a salary of ..	£1,500
There are two other Commissioners, each receiving a salary of	1,200
The Secretary gets	781
Assistant Secretary gets	600
The estimate of the expenditure for the year 1906-7 was	£39,938†

* Provision is also made as follows in other estimates for Expenditure in connection with this service :—

Office Accommodation (fuel, light, furniture) ..	£25
Rates	100
Stationery and Printing	60
Non-Effective	227
Post Office Telegraphs, Revenue Estimates	13
Total	£425

† Provision is also made as follows in other Votes for Expenditure in connection with this Service :—

Office Accommodation (buildings, furniture, fuel and light)	£617
Rates	840
Stationery and Printing	1,000
Law Charges	3,200
Non-Effective Class VI., 1.	2,469
Inland Revenue, Revenue Estimates	15
Post Office, Revenue Estimates	1,546
Post Office, Telegraphs, Revenue Estimates ..	141
Total	£9,828

I end these extracts from the Estimates with the Board of Works. Everybody attacks the Board of Works. Everybody indulges in pleasantries at the expense of the Board of Works. But I offer no criticism on the operations of that body. Mr. Gerald Balfour said that it was a good thing that the Board of Works were not tried by their Peers (Piers). There is a story told of another Chief Secretary. On one occasion he pulled a bell rope at the Chief Secretary's Lodge. The rope came down. " Damn the Board of Works," said the Chief Secretary in the presence of the company. There is no use in consigning the Board of Works to special damnation. The whole system of the Administration of Ireland must be thrown into the melting pot.

Reference has sometimes been made to the cost of Civil Government in some of the smaller States of Europe. But so far as I am aware no definite statement of detail has been made on the subject, and such information is not easy to get. Recently, however I have received from men in authority certain communications bearing on the point, and I shall, in conclusion, set out these communications which, in any event, are interesting.

SWEDEN (Pop. 5,294,885).*

Police.

" The police all over Sweden are regulated by local authority. For towns there are special police regulations, applied by the local police authorities, who are under the Governor of the Province, who is the executive representative of the Crown. It would be to the Governor that the Swedish Civil Ministry (Home Office) would apply for any report involving police measures.

" The Governor of the town of Stockholm has a special department for the management of police affairs,

* Statesman's Year Book.

administered by the Chief of Police, the representative of the Governor of the town.

"The salary of the Stockholm Chief of Police is £500 a year. There are about 660 police in Stockholm.

"The cost of Police in Sweden, according to the latest available statistics is about £143,000 per annum (Kroner 2,573,000).

Judges.

"The highest judicial tribunal in Sweden is the High Court of Justice, with eighteen Chief Justices, of whom, as a rule, at most seven are engaged in the hearing of any one case. Salary of each Chief Justice, Kroner 13,000—about £722.

"The general Tribunals of the Second Instance are three Courts of Appeal, the Svea Hofrätt, Göta Hofrätt and Skåne and Blekinge Hofrätt. Each of these Courts has a President and a number of Judges of Appeal and Deputy Judges. Each Court is subdivided into " divisions," from two to seven in number, in which five or four judges sit. These are full Courts of Appeal for both civil and criminal cases.

Salaries in all three Courts of Appeal :—

President .. .. Kroner 10,000 — about £555
Judge of Appeal .. „ 6,400 — „ £355
Deputy Judge .. „ 5,300 — „ £294

"In the country, District Judges preside over the ordinary lower Courts of First Instance. Their salaries vary according to the extent of their district.

The highest are .. Kroner 7,900 — about £437
The lowest are .. Kroner 4,700 — „ £261

"There are 59 Judges in the district under the Svia Hofrätt.

"There are 45 Judges in the district under the Gota Hofrätt.

"There are 17 Judges in the district under the Skåne and Blekinge Hofrätt.

"In towns, magistrates are salaried by the municipality, and are mostly professional lawyers.

"In the last available statistics the number of cases tried in Sweden in all courts annually was given at 40,842.

Primary Education.

"The actual system of compulsory education, as given in the 'Folkskolar,' or National Schools, was first introduced into Sweden by statute in 1842, and is now governed by the law of December 10th, 1897. The National Schools are directly connected with the parish, and each parish constitutes a school district. The Church Assembly in each parish elects the local school board, which is presided over by the Rector. The National Schools are assisted by the State, and are under the control of the Department of Public Worship and Education, which appoints National School Inspectors.

"The cost of the National Schools, as just stated, falls partly on the State and partly on the school district. The district provides the school buildings and their equipment and maintenance. It finds the salary and allowances of the master, and contributes towards his pension. The State, however, refunds some two-thirds of the outlay on salaries, and contributes to the pension fund. The age during which instruction is given at the National Schools is between seven and fourteen.

No. of National Schools	13,533
No. of Teachers	18,260
No. of Pupils	845,739

Cost of National Schools, Kroner 26,404,547 — £1,466,419.

Cost of each pupil, Kroner 34.81 — about £1 18s. 7d."

BELGIUM (Pop. 7,160,547).*

June 24th, 1908.

"I beg to inform you that the pay of the Belgian police is regulated by the municipality, and that it

* Ibid.

varies with each municipality. The State gives a very small subsidy to each municipality for the police.

"The cost of education for 1907 was £1,391,800, with £400,000 for local expenses.

"As regards the Salary of Judges :—

1. A ' Juge de paix ' receives from £100 to £200, according to the importance of the town.
2. A Juge de première instance from £160 to £260.
3. Cour D'appel from £260 to £340.
4. Cour de Cassation, from £340 to £400.

"The most capable lawyers in Belgium refuse Judgeships, as it pays them much better not to accept them. Here there are three Judges to try a case as against one in England."

THE NETHERLANDS (Pop. 5,591,701).*

Police.

"The police service is exercised by *State Police* and *Municipal Police*.

"The State Police is composed of two corps, the State Country Police and the Frontier Police.

"In pursuance of the Royal Decree of December 17th, 1851, the authority over the State Police, thus both over the State Country Police and the Frontier Police is vested in the Minister of Justice.

"The corps of the State Country Police is entirely under the administration of the Department of Justice, while the corps of Frontier Policemen belongs administratively to the Department of War.

"A sum of £67,727 10s. was voted in the State Budget for 1908 for costs of the State Police.

"The computation of the costs of the Frontier Police for the year 1908 amounted to £74,223 14s.

"The costs of the Municipal Police (articles 190 and 191 of the Municipal Law) were as follows, according to the Provincial Reports of 1906 :—

* Ibid.

North Brabant	..	..	..	£21,707
Gelderland ..	..	..	..	28,732
South Holland	..	..	..	161,970
North Holland	..	..	..	138,851
Zeeland ..	..	..	..	9,098
Utrecht ..	..	..	..	22,615
Friesland ..	..	..	..	13,625
Overyssel ..	..	..	..	14,231
Groningen ..	..	..	..	12,333
Drenthe ..	..	..	..	3,677
Limburg ..	..	..	..	10,220

Total (omitting decimals)   ..   £437,059

Education.

"The total expenditure of the State and Municipalities for the benefit of Primary Education amounted in the year 1906 to £1,941,808."

PART V

CONCLUSION

PART V

CONCLUSION

WHAT THE IRISH WANT

LOOKING at the subject purely from a Departmental point of view, there can be no doubt that there is plenty of room for reform in the administrative system of Ireland. There are too many Boards, too many officials, and there is too much expenditure. Every one will admit that there must be a centre of government somewhere; and honest and sagacious men will agree that the centre of Irish Government must be in Ireland. All the reforms and schemes which the wit of man can devise—Land Reform, Education Reform, Administrative Reform—all will fail, unless the Irish people have confidence in the central authority. How is this confidence to be secured? That is the problem for statemanship. The answer is certain. Only by the establishment of an Irish Parliament and an Irish Executive for the management of Irish affairs. Irishmen, possessing the confidence of the Irish people, must be allowed to work out the destinies of Ireland through institutions founded on national sanction.

But it may be asked what would be the Irish Administrative System under an Irish Parliament? In the first place the Chief Secretary would be the head of the whole Irish Administration in the same sense as the English Prime Minister is the head of the whole English Administration. Then there would be Ministers of Departments—the President of the Local

Government Board, the Chancellor of the Exchequer, the Minister of Education, the Minister of Police, the Minister of Agriculture and so forth, as the necessities of the country may require. These Ministers would live in Dublin ; they would visit their offices every day, and have opportunities of becoming masters of their business ; and the ridiculous system by which one man (living chiefly in London) is responsible for everything without knowing anything, would be swept away. But it may be further asked what would become of the Castle ? The Castle would remain where it is, but not as it is. Some Englishmen think that by the abolition of the Castle all that is wrong in the Administration would be set right. Not at all.

The objections are to the English character of the Castle. Make it Irish and the objections will disappear. It can be made Irish by becoming a centre of government based on the popular will. Such a Government means National Autonomy. " They will not kill me to make you King," said Charles II. to his brother. The Irish people do not want the abolition of Dublin Castle in order to put the Home Office or Downing Street, or both, in its place. The stream of Irish Administration is corrupt ; but the poison flows from the source and is not generated by any of the tributaries. The source is on the English side of the Channel. A Governor practically chosen by the people, though nominated by the Common Sovereign ; a Parliament representing the people ; and an Executive (Dublin Castle) under the influence of public opinion—these are the terms which the present generation of Irishmen are prepared to accept in settlement of the account ; though it is only the expression of political wisdom to add, in the words of Parnell, that "no man has a right to fix the boundary of the march of a nation."

But it may be said, What would the Irish Parliament do with the various Boards, Departments and Offices which at present exist ? Well, Sir David Harrel has to some extent suggested changes which might possibly be made. Doubtless, in the first instance, there would be a departmental inquiry for the consideration of the whole subject. Sir David Harrel is of opinion that the duties of the Board of Works might even now be transferred to the Central Authority. To the Irish people it does not make the slightest difference at the present moment whether the duties of the Board of Works be transferred to the Central Authority or no, because the Irish people have confidence neither in the Board of Works nor in the Central Authority. However, I must say that the officials and ex-officials to whom I have spoken on the matter are quite in agreement with Sir David Harrel ; and it is probable that an Irish Government would make the proposed change. Instead of the paraphernalia of a Board of Works, there would be a Department of Works in Dublin Castle ; and instead of Commissioners of Works there would be a Clerk of Works. Of course the Department would be represented by a Minister in Parliament. Several matters which are now attended to by the " Home Office " would probably be transferred to the Central Authority ; such as Explosives, Mines, Quarries, Factories, Workshops. Matters relating to railways and canals would also be placed under the direct control of the Central Authority, as would be Prisons, Police and Reformatories.

Sir David Harrel thinks that matters relating to lunacy should be placed under the Local Government Board ; but he would perhaps agree that the Dundrum Criminal Lunatic Asylum should remain under Central Control. The office of Boundary and Survey Valuation would, as Sir David Harrel suggests, be abolished and the duties transferred to the Local Government Board. As an instance of the passion of our Rulers for multiplying Boards and Offices, the Office of the Registrar of Petty Sessions Clerks may be mentioned. The duties of this office were once discharged by a Clerk in Dublin Castle, and under an Irish Parliament they would be discharged by a Clerk in Dublin Castle again. The office of Treasury Remembrancer would be abolished. In the old days the Irish Chancellor of the Exchequer occupied the room where the financial agent of the English Treasury now sits. Under an Irish Parliament the Irish Chancellor of the Exchequer would return to the quarters of his predecessors. What would become of the Land Commission and the Congested Districts Board ? The Land Commission was created for a special purpose of a temporary character ; and when the peasants of Ireland are placed in possession of the landed property of Ireland the occupation of the Commission will be gone ; and so with the Congested Districts Board, which was also created for special work of (let us hope) a temporary character. All questions relating to land might then be transferred to the Department of Agriculture. Of course the Local Government Board would be a permanent institution ; and there would be a single education office, which would attend to all matters relating to Education, Primary and Secondary. In Law Administration there would, I hope, be trenchant reforms. The scandal of paying an Irish Attorney-General £5,000 a year would not be tolerated by a free Irish Parliament. The number of County Court Judges would be reduced by at least one half. All official salaries should be reduced in order to make them proportionate to the resources of the country, though not to an extent which would be inconsistent with the employment of first-rate men to discharge first-rate duties.

But I shall dwell no longer on this subject of administrative reform. As I have suggested, the first duty of an Irish Parliament should be to appoint a Departmental Inquiry on the whole subject. The result of that inquiry, would, I believe, be the establishment of a strong central executive, the abolition of the Board System, and the creation of efficient Departments for the government of Ireland.

However, Administrative Reform under the " Union " will not settle the Irish question, because Administrative Reform alone cannot gratify the national aspirations of the Irish people. Let any English statesman who does not realise the fact read the words of Mr. Goldwin Smith :—

" The real root of Irish disaffection is the want of national institutions, of a national capital, of any objects of national reverence and attachment, and, consequently, of anything deserving to be called national life. The greatness of England is nothing to the Irish. Her history is nothing or worse. The success of Irishmen in London consoles the Irish no more than the success of Italian adventurers in foreign countries (which was very remarkable) consoled the Italian people. The drawing off of Irish talent, in fact, turns to an additional grievance in their mind. Dublin is a modern Tara ; a metropolis from which the glory has departed ; and the Viceroyalty, though it pleases some of the tradesmen, fails altogether to satisfy the people. ' In Ireland we can make no appeal to patriotism ; we can have no patriotic sentiments in our school books, no patriotic emblems in our schools, because in Ireland everything patriotic is rebellious.' These were the words uttered in my hearing, not by a complaining demagogue, but by a desponding statesman."

So wrote Mr. Goldwin Smith more than a quarter of a century ago ; and his words are equally applicable to the state of affairs to-day. English statesmen have no imagination. The fact accounts for the failure of English statesmanship in Ireland ; Englishmen are moved as much by the sentiment of nationality as any people in the world. Yet they cannot realise that the sentiment of nationality may be a motive power in Ireland too.

" Sentiment," says Mr. Chamberlain, " is, indeed, a great and potent factor in the history of the world ; and how splendid is the sentiment which unites men of kindred blood and kindred faith."

When Mr. Chamberlain uttered these words he was thinking of England. No thought of Ireland crossed his mind.

Lord Rosebery does not lack imagination. He is a Scotchman. He really understands the Irish question. His fault is that he does not stick to his guns. Speaking at Glasgow in 1887, he said :—

" In 1782, the Irish seized the opportunity of England's weakness, an opportunity which, under those circumstances, you could hardly expect them to deny themselves. They took the opportunity of England's weakness and took what they wanted, which was a substantive Parliament. Now, I know it is a fashion to run down that Parliament, which is popularly known as Grattan's Parliament—a Parliament that lasted for eighteen years in Ireland. It had indeed many defects. It was a purely Protestant Parliament, and therefore represented only a section of the population. It was largely controlled by Peers. It was to some extent corrupt. But it had two great merits. In the first place it was what the Irish people wanted. There is no principle, gentlemen, which seems so simple, but which seems somehow to need so much instilling into some of our greatest statesmen, as the fact that the potato that one knows and likes is better than the truffle that one neither knows nor likes. And, therefore, when you wish to give a benefit to a nation it is better to give something that it likes and understands, rather than something that it neither likes nor understands."

In writing of the efforts made by England to force Protestant Episcopalianism on Scotland, Mr. Gardiner says that the Scottish people were determined to have the religion of their choice. The Irish people are determined to have the government of their choice. Neither the policy of coercion, nor the policy of concession has killed the national idea.

" But what do the Irish want ? " Englishmen constantly ask this question. One might suppose that by this time they knew. They certainly have had plenty of opportunities for learning. Recently I had a conversation with Mr. Redmond in reference to this stereotyped question. He said :—

" I should like to know what Englishmen mean exactly when they ask : ' What do the Irish want ? ' We have told them again and again—an Irish Parliament and an Irish Executive for the management of Irish affairs. Englishmen ought to know what a Parliament means ; though from the questions which they ask us, one might suppose that the idea was quite new to them. They have their own Parliament ; and there are the Parliaments of their Colonies and Dependencies—the Australian Commonwealth, New Zealand, the Cape, Canada, the Transvaal and so forth. An English statesman has plenty of examples to study in framing a constitution for Ireland."

Question.—" I sometimes think that not merely the English man in the street, but the average Englishman in the House of Commons does not realise that there ever was a Parliament in Ireland ? "

Mr. Redmond.—" Very likely, nor that that Parliament was six hundred years old, and was destroyed only one hundred years ago under circumstances of peculiar infamy. Neither do Englishmen realise that we have never acquiesced in the so-called Union. We have never allowed the Statutes of Limitations to run against our claim ; though it would not matter if we had, for as O'Connell said : 'no Statute of Limitation can run against a nation.' "

Question.—" I fancy that very few members of the English House of Commons at the present moment know what O'Connell's repeal agitation was about ? "

Mr. Redmond.—" Possibly. But the fact is important, that forty years after the Union, Ireland rang with the demand for the restoration of her Parliament. A quarter of a century later Isaac Butt rallied the country once more on the same question. And sixteen years later still, under the pressure of a vigorous agitation led by Parnell, an English Prime Minister introduced a Bill in the House of Commons for the establishment of an Irish Parliament and carried the bulk of the Liberal Party with him. Yet Englishmen now ask us what we want ; and this, despite the further fact that between 1886 and 1895, Mr. Gladstone never ceased to explain throughout Great Britain what we wanted, and what we meant by Home Rule."

Question.—" Englishmen ask for a concrete case ? "

Mr. Redmond.—" If they mean by a concrete case, that we should put our demand into a Bill, and present it to the House of Commons, I do not think that there would be any use in that. The House of Commons will give no attention to a Home Rule Bill which is not introduced by the Prime Minister of the day, and made a Cabinet question. But if they mean by a concrete case an illustration of the kind of thing we want, let them look to their self-governing Colonies and Dependencies. If they want a concrete case, let them look at Canada—let them look at the relations between the Dominion Parliament and England.

Question.—" I think that there are a great many members of the House of Commons who do not know what are the relations between the Dominion Parliament and England, or what are the relations between the Provincial Parliaments in Canada itself, and the Dominion Parliament ? "

Mr. Redmond.—" Very likely. But what I want to emphasise is that apart from the question of Home Rule itself, there is the pretence that we have not stated our case explicitly, and that we have not made it clear what we want. Mr. Chamberlain said to you that in the various proposals he made during the discussions on the Home Rule Bill of 1886 his object all the time was to kill the Bill. And I sometimes think that when people come forward and ask us what we want, they are simply trying to get away from the question altogether."

Question.—" Of course Englishmen are always asking conundrums about Home Rule and one of the conundrums is : ' Do the Irish want to sit in the English Parliament, as well as in their own ? ' "

Mr. Redmond.—" Well that is another instance of the difficulties we have in making Englishmen understand the reasonableness of our position. Parnell was ready to accept a Bill either excluding or retaining the Irish members. In 1886, under his leadership, we accepted a Bill excluding the Irish members. In 1888, he wrote to Rhodes :—

" ' To return to the question of the retention of the Irish members at Westminster. My own views upon the points and probabilities of the future, and the bearing of this subject upon the question of imperial federation—my own feeling upon the measure is that if Mr. Gladstone includes in his next Home Rule measure the provisions of such retention we should cheerfully concur with

28

him, and accept them with goodwill and good faith.'

" What we want is to be allowed to attend to the business of our own country. If Englishmen wish us to remain in their Parliament as well as to attend to the affairs of our own country in an Irish Parliament, we are prepared to do so, or if they wish us to remain in our own country alone and not to come to their Parliament at all, we are willing to accept that. Nothing can be fairer than this attitude."

Question.—" Yes, the English position is rather peculiar and trying in this respect. If Irish members are retained at Westminster, Englishmen say : ' Oh, well, they want to manage our affairs as well as their own.' If on the other hand, it is proposed to exclude them from Westminster, Englishmen cry out : ' This is separation.' "

Mr. Redmond.—" Just so, but the extraordinary thing is, that they do not cry out separation because Australians or New Zealanders or Cape Colonists or Canadians or Transvaalers do not sit in the English Parliament."

Question.—" Well another conundrum is : ' What are Irish questions, how is it to be arranged what affairs the Irish Parliament is to manage, and what affairs must be controlled in Westminster ? ' "

Mr. Redmond.—" There, again, the position taken up by Parnell (which is the position we still hold) was most reasonable. He was willing that the Home Rule Bill should either specify directly the affairs which should be left to an Irish Parliament or upon the other hand to confer complete powers of legislation on the Irish Parliament, subject to the exclusion of certain subjects. The Bill of 1886 is forgotten, and I do not mention it now with a view of suggesting that it should be revived. But to state what it proposed to do

will give an idea generally of what we want. I
take the summary from the life of Parnell.

" ' He [Mr. Gladstone] proposed to establish
an Irish Parliament and an Irish Executive for
the management and control of Irish affairs,
reserving to the Imperial Parliament the following
subjects : the Crown, peace or war, the army,
navy, militia, volunteers, defence, etc., foreign
and colonial relations, dignities, titles of honour,
treason, trade, post office, coinage. Besides these
exceptions the Irish Parliament was forbidden
to make any laws respecting (*inter alia*) the
endowment of religion, or in restraint of educational freedom, or relating to the customs or
excise.

" ' The Dublin Metropolitan Police were to
remain under Imperial Control for two years, and
the Royal Irish Constabulary for an indefinite
period ; but eventually all the Irish police were
to be handed over to the Irish Parliament.
Ireland's contribution to the Imperial revenue
was to be in the proportion of one-fifteenth to
the whole. All constitutional questions relating
to the power of the Irish Parliament were to be
submitted to the Judicial Committee of the
English Privy Council. The Irish members were
to be excluded from the Imperial Parliament.'

" Now I do not say at this moment whether
that was a good or a bad Bill, but it was a Bill
which we accepted in principle. No doubt we
would have insisted on certain alterations if the
Bill had gone into Committee ; but it is not
necessary to go into that now. I will only say
that the Bill was discussed in every shape and
form in the House of Commons and in the country,
and in face of these facts it is absurd to come forward at this time of day to ask us what we want.
An extract from the peroration of Parnell's speech
on the second reading of the Bill is worth quoting :

" ' The provision in the Bill for excluding the
Irish members from the Imperial Parliament
has been very vehemently objected to, and [it
has been said] that there is no half-way house
between separation and the maintenance of law
and order in Ireland by Imperial Authority.   I
say, with just as much sincerity of belief and just
as much experience as the right hon. gentleman,
that in my judgment there is no half-way house
between the concession of legislative autonomy
to Ireland, and the disfranchisement of the country,
and her Government as a Crown colony.   But, sir,
I refuse to believe that these evil days must come.
I am convinced there are a sufficient number of
wise and just members in this House to cause it
to disregard appeals made to passion, and to
choose the better way of founding peace and goodwill among nations ; and when the numbers in the
division lobby come to be told, it will also be told
for the admiration of all future generations that
England and her Parliament, in this nineteenth
century, were wise enough, brave enough and
generous enough to close the strife of centuries,
and to give peace and prosperity to suffering
Ireland.'   Parnell's prophecy was not fulfilled.
The English were not brave enough, nor wise
enough to restore legislative autonomy to Ireland.

" Now remember that in 1893 another Home
Rule Bill was introduced by Mr. Gladstone (retaining Irish members) and that Bill was accepted
by us and carried through the House of Commons
and rejected by the Lords.   So that Englishmen
have had ample opportunity for learning what
we want, whether they are disposed to give it to
us or not.

" When Englishmen ask us what we want
we answer in a sentence, A measure of legislative
autonomy similar so that enjoyed by any of your
self governing Colonies or Dependencies.   If you

want an illustration look at Canada, look even to
the Transvaal. The Transvaal is a new country,
yet it enjoys legislative autonomy; Ireland, a
more ancient kingdom than England, does not."

Question.—" I fancy that Englishmen are
under the impression that they will wear us out,
and that finally we will accept the union and be
happy."

Mr. Redmond.—" That is only another illustration of the inattention which Englishmen give
to Irish affairs, and of their ignorance of Irish
political history. What demand have our people
ever given up. Take the history of the nineteenth
century. There was Catholic Emancipation.
Catholic Emancipation was opposed, as Home
Rule is opposed now. People do not read the
newspapers of those times, and therefore, of course,
they cannot realise the English attitude towards
Catholic Emancipation which was precisely the
same as is their attitude towards Home Rule.
There were the same attempts to avoid it, the same
makeshifts for dealing with it ; and all ended in a
humiliating surrender at the end of twenty-eight
years of incessant struggle. The very year after
Emancipation was granted O'Connell demanded
the restoration of the Irish Parliament, and in
1834 moved his famous resolution (which was of
course defeated in the House of Commons) on the
subject. Then there was the agitation for tithes.
There were more delays, more resistance, more
makeshifts, and final surrender. The disestablish-
ment of the Irish Church was an event of our own
day. People now have no idea of the opposition
which was offered to the movement for disestab-
lishment. Liberal Ministers shirked the question.
In 1865, when Mr. Dillwyn moved his resolution,
simply asking the Liberal Government of the day
to give their attention to the matter, Sir George
Grey, the Home Secretary, said that ' no practical

grievance existed,' and that ' in attempting to redress the theoretical grievance a great shock would be given to our laws and institutions.'

" He added, ' I have no hesitation on the part of the Government in opposing the motion.' In 1866, there was another resolution simply demanding ' the consideration of Parliament ' in reference to the subject. Mr. Chichester Fortescue, the Irish Chief Secretary, took precisely the line with which certain English Liberal Home Rulers have made us familiar in these latter days. He opposed the motion, but said that the opposition of the Government was not based ' on grounds of abstract justice.' But ' upon considerations of common sense, possibility, time and circumstance.' That is in some respects the position of the front Liberal Bench. They do not oppose Home Rule. On the contrary they are in favour of it ' on grounds of abstract justice,' but they will not on the instant make it a Cabinet question ' upon considerations of common sense, possibility, time and circumstance.' What was the upshot of the Liberal policy of shilly-shally on the Church question ? The Fenians came, and the Church went down in a storm of revolution. Take the Land question. Did ever any question seem more hopeless. Nearly all the coercion Acts of the century were passed to put down the Land Agitation, and yet what is happening to-day. Liberals and Tories are vieing with each other to carry out the wishes of the tenants and to create that peasant proprietary which even John Bright was denounced for demanding forty years ago.

" Lord Salisbury I think said that it would be safer to give Ireland Home Rule than Local Government. Yet in 1898 Lord Salisbury's nephew, the Irish Chief Secretary of the day, carried a Bill for the Establishment of Local Government in Ireland practically without opposition. English

Publicists never refer to the working of Local Government in Ireland. Yet the successful management of Irish Local Affairs by the County and District Councils is an overwhelming argument in favour of Home Rule. Take the University question. For how many years were our people told that the English Parliament would never establish a University for Catholics. It was to be Trinity College or nothing. Then there were the makeshifts of the Queen's Colleges, and the Royal University. And how have all these efforts, to prevent the establishment of a National University, ended ? In Mr. Birrell's Act, which was conceived and carried through in the right spirit. In the crisis of 1890-91 it was thought that Home Rule would perish. There were divisions in the Parliamentary Party, there were divisions in the country. But in spite of those divisions there was only one seat lost to Home Rule at the Elections. And now an United Parliamentary Party faces English statesmen in the House of Commons again."

Question.—" What will be your policy in the near future ? "

Mr. Redmond.—" We shall, of course (as heretofore), attend to those social and economic questions which are of so much importance. We want to keep our people in the land, and to see they they are well housed and well cared for, and that they get fair play to advance in material prosperity. But Home Rule shall, more than ever, hold the front place in our platform. It may be that it will be the only plank in our platform, at the next General Election ; and we shall spare no pains to make it a foremost plank in the Liberal platform too. We must have very specific statements on the point.

" ' Are you prepared to make Home Rule a Cabinet question ? ' is the demand which shall be put to the leaders on both sides of the House. We cannot have mere pious opinions. The Irish vote in Great Britain shall be cast for the man pledged to use every effort to push Home Rule to the front, and to keep it to the front. English statesmen fully realise the strength of the Irish vote in Great Britain. I do not think that there is the same opposition in England to Home Rule to-day that there was twenty, or even ten years ago. Englishmen who have seen that the Irish view has been accepted on such fiercely contested questions as the land, local government, and University education are no longer terrorised by the Home Rule bogey. Then the new forces—the forces of the future—which have arisen in English politics are not out of sympathy with us, and are not influenced by the selfish interests and selfish fears of the classes. These new forces wish to get the Irish question out of the way, in order to push forward their own urgent demands ; and they know that the Irish question cannot be got out of the way, until the claims of Irish nationality are recognised."

APPENDICES.

APPENDIX A

NOTE ON DUBLIN CASTLE

THE following is a description of the old fortress: "The entrance was, as it is now, from the north side, but there are no remains of the drawbridge that led to it by two strong towers, called the 'Gate Towers.' The gateway between them was furnished with a portcullis armed with iron, such as may be seen on the Somerset Shield—this was intended as a second defence in the event of an enemy surprising and 'rushing' the drawbridge. To these two was added in later times a platform surmounted with two pieces of heavy ordnance.

"From the Gate Tower on the west a strong and high curtain extended in a line parallel to Castle Street, till it connected it with Cork Tower, so named because it was mainly the work of Richard Boyle, first Earl of Cork. This tower replaced an old one that fell in May, 1624. From Cork Tower the Castle wall continued in one curtain of equal height with the former, till it joined the Bermingham Tower, said to have been built either by John Bermingham, Earl of Louth and Atherlie, Lord Justice in 1321, or else by Walter Bermingham, who filled the same office in 1548 ; while others trace its name to William Bermingham, who, with his son Walter, endured in 1331 a long imprisonment within its walls. (Some of the cells are still to be seen.)

"From the Bermingham Tower the curtain goes on to the Eastern Gateway Tower at the entrance into the Castle —a building oblong and quadrangular, which was strengthened by a broad, deep moat. . . .

"Beyond the Castle walls, towards the east, was a chapel,* the Provost Marshal's prison, an armoury, the workhouses of the armourers and smiths attached to the artillery train, and the stables of the Chief Governor. There also at one time were the quarters of the groom-porter or croupier— an office not now recognised—and the offices of the Ordnance

---

* Mentioned in 1225. Gilbert, Viceroys, p. 515.

Department, for that of War and the Treasury, and for the Registry of Deeds and Conveyances throughout the island. Formerly there were two sally ports or postern gates in the Castle walls—the one near the Bermingham Tower, the other affording a passage to the Castle Yard. The former was closed in 1663 by order of the Duke of Ormonde, then Lord Lieutenant, on discovering the plot of Jephson, Blood, and others, to surprise the Castle by its means. The other remained for years, till the North Tower and its curtain were pulled down. . . .

"We learn from the letterpress of J. Rocque's map—a most interesting illustrated chart—that Dublin Castle was not converted into a regular residence for the Viceroys till the reign of Queen Elizabeth. They sometimes lodged in Thomas Court, sometimes in the palace of the Archbishop of Dublin at St. Sepulchre's, sometimes at St. Mary's Abbey, and sometimes at the Castle of Kilmainham. Thus in 1488 the Earl of Kildare received Sir Richard Edgcumb in the King's great chamber in Thomas Court, and there did homage and took the oath of allegiance to Henry VII. in the person of Sir Richard. . . . When Kilmainham Castle had been dismantled by a violent storm, Queen Elizabeth directed the Castle to be repaired and enlarged for the reception of the Chief Governor. Sir Henry Sidney put the coping stone on the renovated edifice. . . . Dublin Castle continued to be the ordinary hall of convocation for the making as well as the administration of law till the rebellion of 1641 and thence to the Restoration.

"During the past century (eighteenth century) the Castle has been almost entirely rebuilt, and the Wardrobe Tower is almost the sole survival of what Harris saw and described. The Viceregal apartments appear to have been in a semi-ruinous state in 1631, and indeed for another century were in hardly a civilised condition. . . .

"In Charles the Second's reign the mansion which is now known far and wide as the Vice-regal Lodge, was bought, with its curtilages, from Clements, Earl of Leitrim."

(O'Connor Morris, "Dublin Castle.")

In the time of Lionel, Duke of Clarence, money was granted for "the making of a castle of wood, a paling of wood, two iron chains for the Castle, and for pulling down the house in the middle of the Castle, which was called the 'Ledden-huche'; the making of a roof, a new chamber, adjoining to the little chapel; a new house, adjoining to the bakery of the Castle; and providing one hundred hatchets and six iron bills" (Gilbert, p. 219).

About 1430, there were further repairs, Richard Talbot, Archbishop of Dublin, Justiciary, ordered the repairs of the great hall, towers, and buildings in Dublin Castle, which had been damaged by rain and storms (Gilbert, p. 578).

In 1462, during the administration of Fitz-Eustace, the Parliament voted an annual grant of one hundred and eighty shillings from the issues of the Courts and Hanaper, and twenty shillings from the profits of the Master of the Mint, to be expended for repairs in Dublin Castle, where the Courts were held, and which is described in the Act as " ruinous and like to fall, to the great dishonour of the King " (Gilbert, pp. 588 and 589).

" We learn later that these repairs had been deferred " (*Ibid*, p. 589).

The following is in the Stow MSS. [" In] " Dublin resids the Deputy and the Counsell, there she recogves intelligences, advertisem⁵, instructions. The buildings are of timber and of the English forme, and it is resembled to Bristoll, but falleth shorte. The circuit of the Castle is a huge and mighty wall foure square and of incredible thickness, built by King John. Within it are many fayre buildings and there the Deputy keeps his Court " (Stowe, Tempus 1620 180).

APPENDIX B.

FLOTATION.

In addition to the loss on flotation, the State have to pay a half years' dividend on a certain day, and have not had the use of the money for a full six months before that day. This is caused by the system of issuing Stock entitled to a half years' dividend on the first following dividend day, although the subscribers to the stock are allowed to pay up their subscriptions by instalments which may extend up to, or even beyond, that dividend day. (Hansard, Vol. clxxii., page 1426.) Thus :—a person subscribing to Stock created, say, in April, would not have fully paid up his subscriptions for such Stock until 1st July, on which date he receives a full six month's interest ; in other words, he subscribes for Stock in April and receives it *cum dividend* on July 1st. The amount of this item of charge, termed " the unearned dividend " was stated in April, 1907, to be £23,750. (Hansard, Vol. clxxii., page 1427. Session 1907.)

APPENDIX C.

DUBLIN METROPOLITAN POLICE.

Section IV. of the First Victoria, Chapter 25 provides:—

Provision for assessment and levying Police Rates in the Metropolitan District.

" And whereas it is expedient to provide for the more just and equal Assessment of all Houses, Lands and Tenements in the said Districts towards the Maintenance of the said Police and for the purposes of the said Acts and this Act ; be it therefore enacted, that it shall and may be lawful for the said Justices appointed under the said first-recited Act of the last Session of Parliament, to raise and levy from Time to Time, on all Houses, Lands, and Tenements situated and being within the said District, such Rates or Taxes as they shall from Time to time find necessary for the Maintenance of the said Police, and the several Purposes of the said Acts and this Act ; provided that the Sum or Sums to be raised and levied shall not exceed in the whole in any One Year Eightpence in the Pound on the Annual Value of such Houses, Lands, and Tenements ; and the said Justices shall from Time to Time as they find Occasion by Warrant under their Hands appoint one or more proper Person or Persons to rate and assess all such Houses, Lands, and Tenements, to such Rate as shall from Time to Time be fixed and determined by the said Justices, not exceeding the Amount of Eightpence in the Pound, according to the full and fair annual value thereof ; and every such Assessor or Assessors shall, within Forty Days after the Delivery to him or them of the Warrant of his or their Appointment, deliver to the said

Mode of making the
Assessment.
Justices an Assessment for each Place named in such Warrant, which Assessment shall specify the Names of the several Owners or Occupiers of the respective Houses, Lands, and Tenements comprised in such Assessment, the full and fair annual Value of the same, and the Amount of Police Tax chargeable thereon respectively;

Allowance to Assessors.
and every such Assessor shall be allowed for his Trouble and Expenses such Remuneration as the Chief or Under-Secretary of the said Lord Lieutenant or other Chief Governor or Governors shall direct, and the same shall be paid out of the Funds applicable to the Maintenance of the said Police.

INDEX

INDEX

HEADLEY BROTHERS, PRINTERS, LONDON ; AND ASHFORD, KENT.